A Post-Racial Change
Is Gonna Come

To the Stevens
Career Development Office —
Thanks for the always
awesome support throughout
the years!

always,
Jonathan L. White

A Post-Racial Change Is Gonna Come

Newark, Cory Booker, and the Transformation of Urban America

Jonathan L. Wharton

palgrave
macmillan

First published in 2013 by PALGRAVE MACMILLAN® in the United States— a division of St. Martin's Press LLC, 175 Fifth Avenue, New York, NY 10010.

Where this book is distributed in the UK, Europe and the rest of the world, this is by Palgrave Macmillan, a division of Macmillan Publishers Limited, registered in England, company number 785998, of Houndmills, Basingstoke, Hampshire RG21 6XS.

Palgrave Macmillan is the global academic imprint of the above companies and has companies and representatives throughout the world.

Palgrave® and Macmillan® are registered trademarks in the United States, the United Kingdom, Europe and other countries.

ISBN: 978-1-137-27771-8

Library of Congress Cataloging-in-Publication Data is available from the Library of Congress.

A catalogue record of the book is available from the British Library.

Design by SPi Global

First edition: November 2013

10 9 8 7 6 5 4 3 2 1

This book is dedicated to my late grandmother,
Myrtle A. McKenzie, a dutiful community leader and participant of urban politics.

Contents

Acknowledgments

I moved to New Jersey over a dozen years ago, and I lived in Newark for several years. I was inspired by the state's largest city because of its location, people, and great potential. Many outsiders often view the city as a relic of post-industrial urban America. But I was struck by Newark's proximity to New York City, vast downtown, and awesome transportation infrastructure (subway, light rail, commuter and national train lines, as well as international airport). I immediately became an advocate for Brick City, and I made it my mission to defend the city and become engaged in local politics. As a native New Englander and seven-year Washingtonian, I was reared to be involved in my community no matter where I resided. Hence, I intensely followed Newark's City Hall not only as a new resident but also as a graduate student at Rutgers University. I was fortunate to receive an Eagleton Institute of Politics fellowship, funded in part by the Annenberg Foundation, to monitor local politics for their Newark Student Voices project. The idea behind the civics education project was to motivate high school students to follow community concerns and foster voter participation in local elections, particularly the mayoral election in 2002. As a graduate student researcher helping the Eagleton staff and high school students, I updated website content and discussed local concerns with students at their respective high schools. The reality of the 2002 and the 2006 elections was that Newark became ground zero for urban, generational, Black, and coalition politics. In fact, many scholars were interested in the elections, and, after I graduated from Rutgers, my doctoral advisor at Howard University urged me to focus my dissertation on both elections.

The notion of a seasoned titan mayor (Sharpe James) running for a fourth term against an idealistic city councilman (Cory Booker) had a storybook quality to many followers of the campaign, particularly for those outside Newark. As much as this book offers an understanding of the mayoral candidates and the elections, this work purposely considers the reality of Newark's history and local politics with a particular focus on coalition building and community development. If Newark is to become the prototype of twenty-first century urban politics, then a special consideration of the city's past as well as it's demographic future is critical to understanding urban America. Newark demonstrates that a city can advance in many political, social, and economic areas, but still the city's past and image can limit its potential. Cory Booker highlighted Newark's unique advantages as well as problems as both a candidate and councilman. As an early supporter and donor, I became especially interested in Booker because he often discussed how Newark could be an exemplary city. He wanted residents to join together in solidarity to address the city's problems. But along the way I recognized that as much as Booker and the city had an awesome amount of potential, both had significant shortcomings. The city had a negative image, and the councilman proposed idealistic goals. While these concerns may have been minor to many, for someone like myself who lived and believed in Newark, I grew concerned over the years.

I have worked on this project for over a decade, and, as a believer in America's cities, I will continue to follow Newark's progress. Thankfully, I had help from many individuals who were instrumental in this study and were equally concerned with urban politics, beginning with my family and friends. My brother Joseph and our parents, Drs. Richard Wharton and Lou Bertha McKenzie-Wharton, and my grandmother (whom I dedicate this book to) are mesmerized by cities and how they operate. They were surprised by my move to New Jersey and Newark but respected my interest in urban politics. The same has to be said of the Wertheim family who, as friends and supporters, allowed me to write much of this work from their house over many summers. Dr. Ronald Williams II, a colleague and friend, frequently offered advice and support. Certainly the staff at the Eagleton Institute of Politics believed in my research as well as my academic endeavors from the very beginning. Dr. Ruth Mandel and John Weingart, as director and assistant director of the Institute, were always helpful with my graduate study pursuits as was the Institute's professor, the late Dr. Alan Rosenthal, as he mentored me on state and local comparative politics. And, as program coordinator for the Newark Student Voices project, which was part of Eagleton, Angela Garretson has been and still remains one of the most supportive friends any political scientist would ever want. Dr. Clement Price, the invaluable professor of Newark's history at Rutgers University–Newark, played a key role as a Newark Student Voices board member and also as an academic mentor as he read my dissertation and this book. Price and his Institute on Ethnicity, Culture, and the Modern Experience and its staff, particularly Marisa Pierson, have been so helpful that a couple of interviews for this work took place in their facility. Without question, Howard University played a vital role in this research because their political science department focuses on state and local politics as well as Black politics. Dr. Lorenzo Morris not only served as my dissertation advisor but also as chief advocate for this research since he recruited me to attend the department's graduate program. In addition, Drs. Donn G. Davis, Maurice Woodard, and Marilyn Lashley served as dissertation committee members, and Drs. Babalola Cole and Daryl Harris were very helpful with my dissertation as well.

Beyond Howard and Rutgers Universities, I have to make special mention of Stevens Institute of Technology in Hoboken, New Jersey. Many view the college where I teach as a small science and engineering institution, but in many ways Stevens respects projects that involve history and politics. In fact my mentors and colleagues—Drs. Edward Foster, James McClellan, Silvio Laccetti, Susan Schept, and Lisa Dolling—pushed me to return to graduate school to pursue a project such as this one. In addition, Juanita Castillo and Debra Pagan have been equally supportive of my academic career, and I am very grateful for their assistance over the years. Fortunately, I also had countless students who, from the very beginning, supported this project and helped conduct surveys; many of them even attended my dissertation defense in Washington, DC. K. Edward Aguilar, Ryan Bennick, David Byrne, William Daly, Matthew Gray, Raymond Kirchhoff, Danny Kwok, Edward Kastrat, Murat Kocak, Chris Lin, Emmanuel Marasigan, Jonathan Matos, Patrick Nolan, Vidya Rao, Emanuel Rios, Ami Shah, Ricardo Slatter, Gregory St. Louis, Ryan Telford, James Watkins, Devon Williams, William Young, and Xiaoxu Zhao all helped collect and enter data. William Daly in particular helped with both the dissertation and the book, while Christopher Lantz urged me not to give up on this project and pushed me to have Palgrave Macmillan as a publisher. In fact, many members of their fraternity, the New Jersey Alpha chapter of Sigma Phi Epsilon, aided me with research for this manuscript, including Bryan Baranyay, Andrew Bean (who provided the book's cover design), Christopher Bisceglie, Kyle Buzby, Christopher Dorman, Daniel Gregorio, DeVon Lineman, Ryan Miskanich, Russell Nadler (who provided pictures), Evan Nelson, and Michael VonGonten.

The sources in this work are numerous since I have followed Newark's politics over the last 12 years by collecting various accounts in newspapers, magazines, and other media sources. But conducting interviews was a critical aspect of this project, and I am very grateful to the administration, city council members and their staffs, as well as several community leaders. I interviewed Mayor Cory Booker and administration officials Modia Butler, Stephanie Greenwood, Michael Meyer, and Adam Zipkin, as well as Council members Ras Baraka, Mildred Crump, Luis Quintana, and Anibal Ramos. Beyond City Hall officials, I also had the opportunity to interview community leaders Richard Cammarieri, Harold Lucas, and Clement Price. The mix of city council members, mayoral aides, and community leaders made for an interesting and inspirational account of Newark's history and politics. I am a firm believer in oral history and these officials and leaders reminded me of my passion for urban politics and history.

Finally, I am very thankful to Palgrave Macmillan and their staff, Farideh Koohi-Kamali, Matthew Kopel, Scarlet Neath, Brian O'Connor, Karen Berry, Rachel Taenzler, and Sundar Devadoss Dharmendra. Chris Cecot was extraordinarily helpful for indexing the manuscript as well. As publishers, they not only respected my project but were also very supportive of the numerous revisions and changes I offered. They were highly professional and very helpful throughout the publishing process.

Introduction

Newark, New Jersey, has been the focal point of urban politics and redevelopment, particularly in the last twenty years. While New Jersey's largest city gained an unfortunate reputation for urban blight and middle-class flight, Newark's charismatic mayor, Cory Booker, has been the center of attention in the city's local politics. But this work goes beyond the mayor and examines Newark's recent political past as well as the city's future directions in community development and coalition building politics. Urban redevelopment and local politics are imperative as cities like Newark aim to revitalize their downtowns and neighborhoods since New Jersey, like other heavily suburbanized states, is attempting to rebuild its urban centers into sustainable communities. If post-industrial urban areas similar to Newark are to rebuild their communities, politics, and reputations, then they must resolve their remaining urban problems.

Newark's history is infamous for its racial politics, particularly in the 1960s when the city experienced residential segregation and riots. From Italian American Mayor Hugh Addonizio to Black Mayors Kenneth Gibson and Sharpe James, late-twentieth-century Newark experienced a tremendous shift in City Hall and its communities. Many neighborhoods were residentially segregated by race and ethnicity. Presenting these challenges is essential in understanding not only Newark's history but also its present and future. Various works describe the milieu of racial politics in Newark. Recently published local history monographs like Brad Tuttle's *How Newark Became Newark* and Kevin Mumford's *Newark: A History of Race, Rights, and Riots in America* offer great insight into Newark's modern history, but often require additional political analyses. So many books and articles on Newark's politics frequently couch the city's history in a Black–White paradigm, when in fact Newark is heavily Latino, Portuguese, and Brazilian American (over 40 percent and increasing annually). What makes Newark so unusual is its shifting populations within a very diverse northeastern state. New Jersey's largest city has undergone various demographic waves of English, Irish, Italian, and Black American populations from its founding to its present day. Just in the last thirty years, the increasing number of Latino, Portuguese, and Brazilian Americans has made Newark one of the most diverse cities in the region. What was a majority White and European ethnic city until the late 1950s has since been a majority Black hub and is now becoming a city that will no longer have a single majority group. Newark might be 54 percent Black, but with an expanding Latino population nearing 30 percent and a White population (largely Portuguese and Brazilian) of 15 percent, the city is on the cusp of being a multiracial urban place. Within this generation, Newark will no longer be a Black–White biracial city; it will be a multiracial urban community like so many other medium and large cities in America. In fact, coalition building approaches between various racial and ethnic communities, similar to what scholars like Rufus Browning, Dale Rogers Marshall, David Tabb, Raphael Sonsenshein, John Mollenkopf, Paula McClain, and Joseph Stewart offer in their works, are key to implementing viable urban politics in a city as diverse as Newark.[1]

Groundbreaking scholars like Georgia Persons, Robert Smith, and Dianne Pinderhughes provide essential investigations into urban politics, largely from a Black politics viewpoint. Recent scholars like J. Phillip Thompson, Marion Orr, and Andra Gillespie challenge and provide provocative perspectives particularly related to Black mayoral leadership in this supposed post-racial era when politicians bypass racial politics. The "new Black mayors," as some have dubbed newly elected post-civil rights generation leaders, often embrace idealistic politics.[2] Some political scientists point out differences and similarities between new Black mayors and "insurgent mayors," also known as first Black mayors or "legacy mayors." Georgia Persons argues that *deracialized mayors* are new Black mayors who do not embrace racial politics like their predecessor legacy or insurgent mayors. Sharpe James represented the insurgent mayor and Cory Booker the deracialized mayor, according to Persons.[3] Several legacy Black mayors continued machine politics by granting favors to voters who supported their politics.[4] This proved no different in Newark, where Sharpe James and his predecessor, Ken Gibson, operated City Hall under patronage politics. But this did not mean these Black mayors leveraged machines as powerfully as their White predecessors. Marguerite Ross Barrnett recognizes that Black mayors offered little patronage to constituents beyond a few city jobs, housing, and other services since much of the wealth remained within a White corporate structure.[5] However, Richard Keiser takes the discussion of machine politics a step further by arguing that Black mayors often exploited Black voters. He suggests that many Black leaders have "contributed to the underdeveloped" and even "retard[ed] Black empowerment" because "messianic leaders play a huge role in denying legitimacy to other leaders by condemning them as Uncle Toms."[6]

The first Black mayors and their policy records provide some basis for understanding their pragmatic politics—and several noted models have explained their approaches. Legacy mayors or first-time Black mayors largely represented urban Black politics for the civil rights generation and gained tremendous respectability among their largely Black constituents so that they could not only get elected but also remain in office for several terms. Marion Orr argues that Black legacy mayors faced challenging moments since they often had to contend with agitating forces like teachers' unions and parents over education concerns, especially in Baltimore.[7] Moreover, corporate interests influenced these mayors' political fortunes and policymaking in different ways. Nelson and Meranto suggest that, in hardscrabble cities like Detroit and Gary, these mayors were hardly able to negotiate with the private sector because so many corporations and industrial plants left for the suburbs.[8] For the few legacy mayors who negotiated with corporate America, Persons argues that many of them held onto racial politics *and* balanced the private sector to maintain (or increase) jobs and a revenue tax base. David Dinkins,[9] Thomas Bradley,[10] Willie Brown, and Harold Washington were often more concerned about competing politics with other groups and tried to cater more to their majority Black constituents.[11] Persons argues that legacy mayors "emerged from a common socio-political movement," namely the civil rights movement and the political insurgency of the 1970s. She states that many of these legacy mayors, like Newark Mayors Gibson and James, stayed in office through years of "institutionalization" by getting reelected and creating viable machines.[12] Newark is unique, she argues, in that "the mayorality remains stuck in the insurgency phase" because of James' and Gibson's longevity in office. This is the *insurgency* perspective, arguing that Black mayors, especially civil rights generation mayors, embraced racial politics through grassroots support from urban Black communities and often remained in office beyond two terms. But Persons acknowledges that political scientists need to explore Black mayoral power further because "what is needed is a broader, more comprehensive analytic framework."[13] Paul Thompson says that Black mayors tend to fall into the "urban regime" paradigm or the "coalition politics" model. Mayors like Cleveland's Carl Stokes,[14] New York's David Dinkins, Los Angeles' Tom Bradley, and Chicago's Harold Washington[15] were largely successful at incorporating this coalition building model into their respective City Halls. This is the *coalition building politics* perspective, where various racial and ethnic communities and their leaders collaborate to resolve local issues. Agreeing with Persons' assessment of many Black mayors, he argues that "those who stayed in office for a long period of time" hindered Black interests and participation because of their machine politics.[16]

Only recently have a number of post-racial or new Black mayors strategized to defeat Black legacy mayors, according to Andra Gillespie and her *Black political entrepreneurship model*.[17] Gillespie and others believe that legacy mayors often counter their younger opponents with negative campaigning strategies. Images and paradigms play a significant part in urban politics, and they certainly affect public opinion, attitudes, and voting behavior as the 2002 and 2006 Newark mayoral elections demonstrated. Coalition building requires communities to engage in transformative political and economic reforms. Effective coalition building goes further than campaign trail politics and instead demands problem solving in local government through key City Hall appointments and proactive proposals to advance progressive and community-oriented change. Several progressive cities have embodied coalition politics to bring Whites, Blacks, Latinos, Asians, and other ethnic, religious, and gay communities into their City Halls' politics and agenda-setting initiatives.[18] In fact, multiracial cities like San Francisco, Los Angeles, and, in some instances, New York City offer textbook examples of effective coalition building.

California's largest cities have had multiracial populations for several genera-tions since Mexican Americans were already present and an increasing number of Whites, Blacks, and Asians became a key part of the cities' demographics by mid-century. By the 1970s, a number of Black, Asian, and Latino officials had been elected to public office since coalition building became the norm in Los Angeles, San Francisco, and several East Bay cities. Many constituents expected achievable results, and they often remained in contact with their elected officials.[19] At the same time, many residents, especially Whites, left California's older cities to create imagined utopias in the suburbs.[20] Far too many Black and Latino Los Angelinos saw how White Los Angelinos forged a "white resistance"[21] by migrating to Orange County and "building white walls" in their housing developments.[22] Los Angeles also lost much of its tax base because businesses left for outlying suburbs. Minority Los Angelinos then grew concerned over dwindling resources and police brutality, and they wanted to be engaged in City Hall politics. As Paula McClain points out about Los Angeles, "minority exclusion provided … the basis for coalition politics between blacks, Latinos, and Asians."[23] A number of officials, including Mayor Thomas Bradley, embraced coalition politics and were elected and appointed to City Hall.[24] Bradley proved very successful during his tenure by seeking to balance the interests of the Black, Latino, and Asian communities as well as the business sector. But because of his balancing politics, Blacks saw his leadership as courting other interests, namely the business community,[25] especially with downtown development.[26] And Latino Los Angelinos tried to promote their own agenda, despite their "relatively weak levels of pan ethnic identity."[27] Latinos were espe-cially successful in electing many council members and ultimately Mayor Antonio Villaraigosa.[28] They even revitalized many Los Angeles neighborhoods.[29] But the evolution of Black and Latino coalition building was largely due to social and eco-nomic inequalities and competition in Los Angeles.[30] California's cities in the San Francisco bay area experienced unique coalition building as well. Not only was there a private and public sector alliance in San Francisco to bring about urban revitalization and preservation,[31] additional cities surrounding the bay forged coalitions between Black and Latino populations and liberal Whites, Jews, Asians, gays, and other groups. It was the dawn of *incorporation politics* when many activ-ists won political seats and appointments in many California locales.[32]

While California cities were able to institute coalition politics, New York City lagged behind. According to a number of urban politics experts, New York is "the great anomaly"[33] because it has exceptional institutionalized features that prevent minorities from actively participating in city politics.[34] Among these distinctive systemic limitations is the city's government itself. It has a multi-layered process featuring not only the mayor, council, and court system but also borough presi-dents and other borough figureheads who preside over various sections of the city. This diffusion of power has limited minority participation on a number of levels.

According to Thompson, few Blacks and Latinos are inclined to be part of a weak borough government or a predominately White-led mayoral machine with city council term limits.[35] Beyond systemic problems, New York's heterogeneous population proves to be a hindrance for Black and Latino politics let alone coalition politics between these two communities. For example, the term "Black" in New York introduces unique problems since many Black New Yorkers identify themselves with specific nationalities—from Jamaican to Senegalese to Black American. Many Hispanic New Yorkers see themselves as separate nationalities as well—Dominican, Puerto Rican, Mexican—and not a monolithic Latino group.[36] Ultimately, New York has "complicated racial politics," and the city has an arduous process that lacks cohesion largely because many individuals do not see themselves as a collective unit or wish to work in tandem with another group to address economic and social ills.[37] Modern coalition politics in New York flourished between Latinos and Blacks during the 1988 mayoral election between David Dinkins and Ed Koch.[38] Dinkins increasingly politicized the need for New Yorkers of every background to work together and celebrate the city's population as a "gorgeous mosaic"[39] (or in reality a "conflictual canvas"[40]) where they could address racial strife together. Although Dinkins won on this idealism, his coalition lost momentum between Blacks, Latinos, and White liberals.[41] Dinkins was accused by Latinos of appointing few of their community's members to city jobs as well as offering little patronage and political attention to Latino New Yorkers.[42]

Clearly the New York and California models offer unique results for coalition building, especially in multiracial cities. My book centers on the nuances and pragmatic approaches of effective coalition politics in an emerging multiracial but racially politicized Newark with a post-racial mayor. I contend that the mayor and many Newarkers have increasingly politicized coalition building. While Newark is becoming increasingly diverse in population, especially with a high percentage of Latinos, Portuguese and Brazilian Americans, Booker campaigned on coalition building. Relying on Browning, Marshall, and Tabb's paradigm then, coalition politics demands effective and sustainable community building *after* election day. My book argues that Booker and many Newarkers articulated *electoral coalition politics* but not effective coalition building or what I call *sustainable coalition politics*. Too many candidates, activists, and voters largely campaign, elect, and speak about having communities united behind candidates like Cory Booker, but rarely does the city experience sustainable coalition building by electing and appointing progressive officials and then implementing transformative public policy proposals. Finding ways to bring Newark's communities together has been paramount for the city's politics in the last generation. Since Booker has been mayor, there have been several attempts to address long-standing urban issues. While the mayor campaigned on uniting Newark's communities, his electoral coalition was mostly made up of anti-James, Latino, and White supporters while many Black voters were divided about Booker. Beyond the voting booth, Newark *and* Booker hardly embraced nor fully embodied sustainable coalition building politics among the city's various communities. In fact, the mayor and many of his allies missed critical moments for sustainable coalition building when there were demonstrations against crime, City Hall layoffs, and the Municipal Utilities Authority proposal. Instead, many of Booker's foes, Black civil rights generational leaders, and some former supporters responded to these mayoral reforms in what I call *backlash coalition politics* by politicizing and rallying against the administration. So many Newarkers were involved in demonstrations and protests during Booker's tenure that various community grassroots efforts flourished in response to his policies. While he appears to have been blind to this backlash coalition, in an interview for this book, Booker claimed that his opponents grab too much media attention and portray him as an ineffective politician. He countered that his popularity ratings of 70 percent and election results of 60 percent prove that statistically his detractors are few and irrelevant and that no backlash exists.[43]

An idealistic leader, Booker faced unique challenges in three elections. His electoral experiences, especially in unseating former mayor Sharpe James, have been the focus of numerous investigative journalism articles and documentaries. Many of these accounts portray Booker as an exemplary politician in an era of post-racial politics where race is no longer the sole focus surrounding elections or politics. While Newark appears to be on the rebound, many residents view Booker as an anomaly partly because of his youthful exuberance, suburban pedigree, and his post-racial politics idealism. Booker bypasses racial rhetoric and instead supports coalition building, but mainly during elections. Instead of embracing Black–White racialized politics, which has long been a part of the city's history and was largely popularized by the James campaign and administrative staff, Booker employs a more post-racial era version of electoral coalition politics but offers little for sustainable coalition politics. A very pressing concern among Newark residents and officials has been revitalizing the city's downtown and many of its neighborhoods. Newark remains largely undeveloped, even though recent projects have been geared toward downtown professional suburban office workers and tourists. Booker, along with many city leaders, challenged the James administration over the existence of two Newarks: one for the office professionals and the other for overwhelmingly poorer residents. For the purposes of this book, I examine several downtown and community projects in Newark and how they relate to coalition politics and how the city's leaders either embraced or missed moments of sustainable coalition building, often through politicizing coalition politics. Investigating community development is a critical aspect of city and coalition politics because vast urban areas are being transformed for mixed-use, sustainable, and new development and suburban sprawl has become a grave concern in nearby suburbs and exurbs. If Newark undergoes critical urban revitalization through the policies of the Booker administration with mixed-use development approaches, where does this leave current Newarkers and future residents? This is where sustainable coalition politics can be useful for a city like Newark that is undergoing transformational political, social, and economic changes. Sustainable coalition building can go beyond Newark's demographic shifts and resolve ways to address political reforms and community-involved coalition politics. This work provides a detailed narrative regarding Newark's recent history in racial and ethnic politics, but its larger objective is to analyze Cory Booker's mayoral elections and his tenure during the city's urban revitalization process as a preeminent example of transformational coalition politics and urban revitalization.

Considering the community development trends taking place in American cities, many politicians have to weigh revitalization policies with continuing urban problems. How local officials address community concerns, especially where patronage politics is paramount and urban development is necessary, can be a constant struggle. According to Paul Peterson, "Cities have these interests because cities consist of a set of social interactions structured by their location in a particular territorial space."[44] Racial disparities and social stratification in healthcare, housing, and education remain problematic for many inner-city residents.[45] Many cities are trying to attract a "new frontier" population to return to the city through gentrification and redevelopment incentives; the cities hope to attain property tax revenue to help resolve urban problems like crime, unemployment, and lack of education, housing, and health services—issues that previous city officials had difficulty addressing.[46] How city leaders and residents from both sides of the socioeconomic fence handle these urban issues will be the most significant concern facing many American cities.[47] Bringing in additional revenue to local government through sports and entertainment projects has popularized urban development policy as well.[48] This urban-suburban relationship has often resulted in divided neighborhoods, reinforced residential segregation, and inequality.[49] Moreover, economic segregation has becomes the norm, with potentially profound implications.[50] "Cities that are much poorer than their suburbs are vulnerable to disinvestment and fiscal stress," warn Drier, Mollenkopf, and Swanstrom.[51] This often leaves many inner cities increasingly poor, Manning Marable concludes.[52]

Newark is no exception to this economic segregation reality, especially with the tax revenue suburbanites provide.[53] The city's revitalization in the post-riot era and the direction in which leaders were going to take the city became significant concerns in the 2002 and 2006 elections. Complicating the need for revitalization and the possibility of a gentrified Newark, many voters, especially inner-city residents, grew concerned supporting Booker if he represented a new urban gentry.

Mayor Booker investigated the feasibility of Mayor James' plan to have the city invest $200 million into the New Jersey Devil's downtown arena.[54] In fact, along stretches of Springfield Avenue, a once vibrant merchant corridor, blocks remain desolate since the 1967 riots. These urban dynamics of housing, development, and poverty policies are significant concerns in Newark where more than 25 percent of residents are classified by the federal government as living below the poverty line; 60 percent of high school students do not graduate in this city that is overwhelmingly minority (54 percent Black and 30 percent Latino). Between poverty, unemployment, education, social services, and racial politics, Newark, like most cities, is experiencing a tug-of-war with newcomers' interests.[55] A failure to effectively address struggling residents' issues along with financially successful gentrifiers' interests can lead to more than an urban and social imbalance: conflict in various forms can ultimately emerge.

A key component of Newark's urban development is the financial and politically influential private sector. The politically connected and financially powerful are those patricians, business leaders, and other elites who seek to influence Newark's politics, which is consistent with Dahl's model of private sector interests and Clarence Stone's urban regime paradigm.[56] Newark is embarking on a significant trend of recreating and building new commercial and residential districts, and many elites are actively engaged in downtown and community development. Through financial investing, state and federal tax incentives, and grants, Newark will be significantly transformed. Understanding these community development dynamics is imperative because Newark is going through tremendous revitalization and sustainability efforts. Suburban overdevelopment has been a significant concern in the metropolitan New York and Newark region. Sprawling outer suburbs or exurbs and rural areas have experienced increasing traffic and housing concerns. As a result, New Jersey's state government has implemented construction moratoriums, smart growth initiatives, and tax credits to encourage builders to develop existing areas in many of its older cities like Newark. Since public transit access, mix-use development, and infrastructure are key to sustainable communities, many are looking to Newark as an example of effective urban development. Mayor Booker recognizes the potential that the downtown and areas near mass transit offer to investors, developers, and realtors. Yet what are the implications for this kind of urban growth, and what distinguishes this form of urban revitalization from previous urban renewal policies? To what degree do cities like Newark have to undergo gentrification and development under a new mayor while many of its residents face a variety of social problems? This is America's urban dilemma. Newark is certainly not the only city experiencing this quagmire, but it proves an interesting case study in post-racial politics, coalition building, and community development struggles.

In Chapter 1, I offer a detailed narrative of Newark's modern political past from the mid-1950s to the post-1967 riots era. This is a significant chapter since the mid-century proved to be a key part of Newark's identity and still remains a part of the city's politics. Modern mayoral administrations, their politics, and their policies are discussed in this section. Similar to many post-industrial American cities, Newark leaders attempted to transform its image, but city officials faced competing racial groups' politics.

Chapter 2 examines the mayoral elections between James and Booker in 2002 and 2006, which received nationwide attention. In 2002, Booker attempted to cobble together an early coalition and attacked James for being corrupt and selfish, but the councilman failed and ultimately lost the election. Newark faced a variety of urban problems and several key issues were raised in both elections, including housing, education, employment, and crime. During the 2006 election, however, the question of James running for a sixth term became a more significant issue. Booker and Newark voters discovered just six weeks before the election that James would not run for mayor. This raised several issues for the city, including whether James' deputy mayor, Ronald Rice, would run for mayor. Consequently, much of the election focused on James and not so much on Rice or Newark's local issues. Rice made racist attacks against Booker, but Booker was elected with 54 percent of the vote. In addition to providing details surrounding the election, I include survey data that suggests voters' opinions of the candidates.

Chapter 3 focuses on the candidates' backgrounds and their racial politics. Since James politicized Booker's background, this became a focal point between the two candidates. With the mayoral election behind him, James faced corruption charges. The federal government accused the former mayor of misusing city funds and credit cards for personal travel. Moreover, the federal government discovered that James conspired to sell city land parcels to favored individuals, including his 39-year-old girlfriend. The married James pled not guilty, but was convicted of the charges and sentenced to a year-and-a-half in prison. I examine James' racial politics; he embodies the civil rights generation of black politics by trying to racialize Booker. In contrast, Booker exhibited more post-racial politics and attempted to enlist disenfranchised voters and marginalized Newarkers to join his 2006 mayoral campaign.

Chapter 4 investigates Mayor Cory Booker's community development efforts in Newark. This includes proposals to revitalize downtown and attract area corporations and suburbanites to its city center because suburban sprawl and building sustainable communities are pressing concerns facing New Jersey. Discussion focuses on the construction of the Prudential Arena for the National Hockey League's New Jersey Devils professional hockey team and downtown community village proposals like Teachers, Artists, Eco, and Warren Street Villages. Booker advanced proposals for the revitalization of city parks, new public housing, and zoning law reforms. As in many cities, the transformation of Newark's downtown became a significant aspect of the city's image and the new mayor's attempts to rebuild its reputation.

In Chapter 5, I explore how many Newarkers, including James and Rice supporters, continued to question Booker's motives as the first-term mayor ran for office again in 2010. Clifford Minor, a former county prosecutor and municipal court judge, challenged Booker but only received 35 percent of the vote (a year after the election, Minor was charged with accepting a bribe). During Booker's second term, the city made some zoning law modifications for commercial and residential areas. Unemployment and education reform (through a $100 million Facebook donation), prisoner reentry initiatives, crime issues (especially with a major police layoff), and problematic racial coalition building efforts were further concerns. How Booker addressed these long-standing issues at the threshold of his second term is the focus of this chapter.

The final chapter examines how the city's communities and the mayor's office still have barriers to prevent sustainable coalition building from developing fully in Newark. As mayor, Booker receives media fanfare, but many Black residents have grown weary of his post-racial politics. Racial and class politics remain long-standing concerns in many Newark communities, which prevents Booker, post-racial politics, and sustainable coalition building from flourishing; instead, backlash coalition politics have developed among a small but growing cadre of Newarkers.

1

Newark's Sordid Past and Early Community Development Politics

An important aspect of Newark's modern politics and urban experience began around the mid-twentieth century. Like so many medium and large cities, Newark has gone through a number of contentious and transformational eras. From the Great Migration to residential or *de facto* segregation to urban riots, Newark experienced challenging times. Essentially, Newark is "the metaphor of America's urban crisis."[1] Yet Newarkers weathered unique benchmarks in advancing the city's local politics. And many of these milestones in turn shaped many residents' political and social experiences. Not surprisingly then, many Newarkers still remember the time of the 1967 riots, thus shaping their political and racial perspectives.[2]

During the 1950s, Newark witnessed tremendous growth both inside and around the city. This decade has been regarded as Newark's heyday when many large businesses prospered, the population was at its peak, and significant opportunities flourished for many Newarkers. However, like most northeastern cities, Newark was a tale of two cities: one that was prosperous with a teeming middle class that was largely white and made up of second-generation European immigrants, and a second city that was significantly poorer with an increasing Black migrant population. The 1950s was a decade associated with the second wave of the Great Migration when tens of thousands of Black southerners relocated to cities in the north, including Newark, to find jobs and the American Dream.[3] This period continued the process of ghetto development in the city; only a generation earlier, thousands of Blacks had relocated to Newark's Black ghetto.[4]

The vast majority of Black southern migrants were poor and undereducated and had little vocational training.[5] Not only did this population discover the political, social, and economic limitations of a northern city,[6] they also faced the harsh reality of *de facto* segregation, or reinforced residential patterns, as well as limited social mobility. Newark's White population "had not witnessed such an influx since the immigration of Southern and Eastern Europeans in the late nineteenth century," observes Newark historian Clement Price. But the key difference, he notes is that "since they came in much larger numbers the white response was more unified and hostile" by local residents, city government, and Newark's business sector. In short, Newark's response to the Great Migration was a backlash, and both the public and private sectors institutionalized the restrictive covenant approach of limiting Blacks in predominately White areas.[7] While the media gave much attention to the notorious problems of southern Jim Crow state laws or *de jure* legalized segregation that many Blacks were trying to escape in the South, Newark's (and other northern cities') *de facto* segregation was largely ignored.[8] From a shortage of low income housing to being politically marginalized, the majority of Black Newarkers had limited access to basic city services for generations.[9] Health problems in Newark's Black communities went largely unnoticed by medical professionals and government social workers.[10] Newark's "leaders ignored the crass discrimination and deepening poverty," states New Jersey historian John Cunningham.[11]

While local politics operated under a commission-led system with no formally elected mayor and council, these leaders largely ignored the growing *de facto* segregation, housing shortage, and underfunded community resources in expanding Black neighborhoods.[12] Price notes that "in Newark it seems that progressive government only helped to obscure the city's problems, particularly those which faced the black community."[13] Newark's Commissioners viewed population congestion as a major problem, but the city had insufficient housing for decades and there was no real solution to address the growing issue. From the very inception of the Commission form of government, Newark continued to promote commercial zoning in desired areas, preventing much needed housing construction.[14] All the while, because Blacks were not allowed to live in White communities, Black communities continued to expand in marginalized areas, such as in Jewish communities or the inner city.[15] Outlying neighborhoods were notorious for their violent reactions towards Blacks in largely Italian and Irish neighborhoods.[16] So Black Newarkers, especially those in poverty, were relegated to the central part of the city because of racism, housing shortages, and residential discrimination by the government and commercial sectors.[17]

In 1953, Newarkers, hoping to elect publicly accountable officials to address the city's social problems, voted for a study to consider changing the city charter and incorporate a mayor-council system. Only 40 years earlier, Newark had adopted a commission-led system in the name of reform to ideally end ward bosses and political machines. Machine politicians had gained control of Newark, with commissioners running their departments like bureaucratic and unresponsive empires. Moreover, ethnic politics replaced good intentions, and only a few politically connected European-Americans held power. Since Newark had exclusive urban enclaves, "community development in many areas was parochial, thus giving each community its own stores, taverns, churches,—its own pride and its own way of life." Newark thus was not one city, as Price observes, "but virtually several ethnic villages tied together in large part by a centralized municipal government and its industrial and commercial life."[18] For Black Newarkers, he argues, "this meant that problems such as housing, employment, and segregation were disregarded by the city fathers who focused on the larger city environment and not ... conditions of a small [but growing] minority."[19]

Worse yet, commissioners were elected at-large in nonpartisan races, and no Blacks ever served on any commission, limiting Newark's Black politics and reinforcing Black political isolation. This was disconcerting because Newark was undergoing a second wave of the Great Migration, while the city could barely handle the first migration adequately and Black poverty remained a significant problem.[20] Ideally, having ward council members would address problems in the city's various wards, including Newark's growing Black communities. "The reform effort of 1953 was supposed to mark heightened awareness of minority and social problems," notes Newark attorney Robert Curvin. However, the political response by elected leaders did not benefit many Black residents and caused more of a backlash as thousands more Black migrants arrived from southern states. Ward council members and the mayors under the new government employed "'Jim Crow' strategies, attempts to contain the Black population in their present neighborhoods and schools and continue or ignore the long-standing mistreatment of Blacks by the police, courts and other elements of government."[21]

A year after the reform measures took shape, Newarkers voted in one of the commissioners, Leo Carlin, as mayor. Councilman Irvine Turner was also elected to represent the Central Ward and served as Newark's first Black elected official.[22] He was widely known for giving City Hall jobs to his constituents and forging relations with White ethnic mayors and their machines. Some, especially the Black middle class, saw Turner as an erratic, unprincipled demagogue who appealed to newly arriving southern Blacks. Not surprisingly, the National Association for the Advancement of Colored People (NAACP) and the Urban League did not favor his politics.[23] But Turner's relations with Carlin were strong in the beginning as the mayor sought government reform, assuring more mayoral power for his office as he lobbied corporations to remain in the city as they considered moving to the suburbs.[24]

Carlin was equally beholden to Irish interests, and he helped establish a corrupt machine. The mayor appeared cold to many voters because he attended few community events and public gatherings.[25] As a result, in 1962, Carlin was defeated by Hugh Addonizio, who later established a political machine of his own, with graft and patronage politics.[26] His administration was well-known for crime, corruption, and ties to the mafia.[27] Even though Addonizio campaigned to end police brutality and discrimination and hired some Blacks for city jobs, he did little to address wider social issues in Newark's Black communities. Addonizio reserved political power for himself, his machine, and his faithful Italian-American supporters, similar to Carlin before him.[28]

Once again, despite the re-chartering of the city government and the new mayoral administrations, elected officials did not heed the concerns of Newark's growing Black communities. Under the city government of both the Carlin and Addonizio administrations, few Black Newarkers had a political voice. The mayoral machines were so successful in fostering power for their offices that they largely aided the Italian, Irish, and Polish communities, while increasingly alienating many Black Newarkers. Public school enrollment was almost two-thirds Black; teaching positions, construction, and City Hall jobs went to few Blacks; and social injustice was blatant. On the surface, this political marginalization was familiar in many northern cities during this era. However, for Newark, it was common practice for local leaders to ignore Black segments of the city and treat them as a sub-community.[29] So with the Irish and Italian political machines operating City Hall, Newark's Black communities and their issues were considered an afterthought, while the city's Black population was exploding. In 1950, Blacks made up 17 percent of Newark's population; in 1960, the black population was nearly 35 percent, and by 1970 it was over 54 percent[30] (or between 1940 and 1970, the Black population quadrupled). Therefore, the Central Ward included 90 percent of the Black population by 1950. Despite this surge in numbers, Blacks were not able to attain much political power or social mobility.

Instead of addressing racial concerns and population surges, the Carlin and Addonizio administrations focused on downtown redevelopment because they wanted large corporations to continue to maintain their businesses downtown instead of moving to the suburbs. There was a tremendous building surge at this time, but mainly for white-collar professional businesses. Noted journalist Ronald Porambo argues that downtown construction was "one of the most ambitious rebuilding programs in the nation."[31] Trying to retain major corporations like Westinghouse, General Electric, Mutual Benefit and Prudential was the focus of Mayors Carlin and Addonizio—*not* retaining manufacturing or industrial entities. The result was a massive deindustrialization of the city and unemployment for many Newarkers, particularly Black residents, while Whites and industries relocated outside the central city. Essentially, poor inner-city Newarkers were forced to find employment outside of Newark; however, many professional jobs stayed in the downtown area, which made Newark's daily population grow more than 100 percent.[32] Despite new downtown construction, 250 manufacturers left Newark during the 1950s,[33] and, between 1950 and 1967, the city lost over 20,000 manufacturing jobs (or nearly a quarter of the workfare).[34] This missed opportunity for community rebuilding left many Black Newarkers disillusioned; they were no longer employed in nearby factories, and, because few poor inner-city residents owned cars, it was difficult for many to travel to a new workplace when companies relocated to the suburbs. In short, after years of attracting cheap Black labor from the south, few job opportunities remained in the once industrial Newark.[35]

The housing crisis was a concern for many Newarkers, particularly those arriving from outside the city. Newark had the highest percentage of substandard housing in the nation during the 1950s. With this housing crunch and crisis, the Newark Housing Authority (NHA) became the lead agency to handle housing issues; all the while, the NHA attained more political power and maintained various forms of racial segregation by forcing Blacks to live in central Newark. NHA's executive director, Louis Danzig, made the Authority the city's official redevelopment agency. During the city's re-chartering period, the agency was allowed to act as an autonomous entity. "The civic leaders settled for a role in renewal politics that excluded a dominant influence over the making of slum clearance policy," argues historian Harold Kaplan.[36] Danzig was essentially an agent for himself and rarely for the mayor. With formalized power, he and the NHA moved swiftly to receive federal monies for redevelopment proposals. "Less than eighteen months intervened between the passage of the 1949 Housing Act and the announcement of Newark's first slum clearance project. ... By submitting a concrete clearance proposal earlier than most other cities in the United States, Newark was able to secure a prior claim to federal funds," Kaplan reveals.[37] In the short term, attaining more federal support for housing projects pleased many constituents: the poor who wanted to live in these housing projects, the supposed political reformers who applauded slum clearance, and the organized crime bosses who benefited from construction contracts.

So the NHA attempted to redevelop large swaths of the city, often razing neighborhoods for construction of new low-income housing and larger college campuses and public spaces. It was a strategy of slum clearance that was too often associated with race since many poor Black residents were forced to relocate. In the process, Danzig gained the trust of Central Ward Councilman Irvine Turner, who agreed to mediate with Black ministers, leaders of the Black communities.[38] Even though advocates supported low-rise public housing, Danzig and Turner pushed for high-rise apartments because it lessened fears of racial invasion in White neighborhoods. Like New York City's legendary Robert Moses, Danzig was a flexible and autonomous negotiator who worked with the various governments and developers; however, he was not directly involved with communities or activists.[39] Danzig ensured a "clean deal" for developers because they did not have to be concerned with bureaucratic red-tape and simply had to discuss plans with a few officials in the NHA.[40]

The social implications of the NHA's slum clearance projects were legendary in urban policymaking. Newark built more units of public housing per capita than any other city in the United States. The city and federal governments pushed thousands of low-income families into concentrated public housing within the inner city, and public housing attracted an even larger number of poor residents.[41] The NHA's decisions affected Blacks more directly and persistently than any other group in Newark. But these policy and community development decisions rarely included Black leaders and community residents. When there were plans for redeveloping the Central Ward, for instance, several Black middle-class leaders who mostly resided outside of Newark criticized NHA's staff for not consulting them.

The NHA was very clear about their responsibility; they did not see themselves as negotiators or as social policy experts. The NHA only wanted to clear land and relocate residents, not to plan an even dispersion of Blacks throughout the city.[42]

In the urban renewal process, the NHA displaced many long-time Newarkers, often forcing them to move to other sections of the city or nearby suburbs. This proved true for many Italian Newarkers in the lower North Ward, for instance. "Rather than stabilize the community, urban renewal hastened its deterioration," notes Michael Immerso. Despite its name, the Christopher Columbus Homes housing project proved to be a monumental failure because it housed so many homogeneous, low-income Black Newarkers.[43] Worse yet, many displaced residents resented construction of new housing in their neighborhoods, and Italian Americans formed a group opposing quotas in the new projects. "Talking out of both sides of his mouth, Danzig promised the inclusion of black residents in a future cohort, while at another time he publicly repeated his adamant refusal to 'commit himself to a strict open occupancy in Columbus Homes' in the face of growing Italian American protest," states Kevin Mumford.[44] And Danzig and the NHA further institutionalized de facto segregation housing by separating White and Black low-income families, something the New Jersey Advisory Committee on Civil Rights studied years later. The committee discovered that three housing projects were over 90 percent White and four others were 90 percent Black. They concluded that the pattern of racial segregation was the result of discrimination in the assignment of public housing with Danzig's blessing.[45]

Locally then, Newark was suffering in several respects during the 1950s and early 1960s. With a newly formalized municipal government focusing its attention on the private sector, ignoring the housing crisis and social services, and razing neighborhoods, the mayoral administrations failed to recognize what was taking place in so many wards, especially Black communities. Newark's new Central Planning Board and city planning office were outdated since "Newark in 1960 would be just emerging from the Dark Ages."[46] Moreover, during this government transition, many of Newark's White residents, especially the middle class, left for suburbia instead of confronting residential segregation. These suburbs encompassed 88 square miles of new residential development. And, unlike other cities, Newark chose not to annex nearby towns.[47]

With invisible and often racist tendencies in Newark and its environs, newly created suburbs surrounding the city shut out many Black Newarkers. Of course, throughout America in the 1950s, many Blacks and other minorities were not allowed to relocate to or could not afford these suburban utopias. Instead, for many Whites, it was a love affair with the suburbs that pushed them to leave cities and live in new housing, even if they were not running away from Black Newark, as some have argued. Newly suburbanized Whites and their families would not need to confront race in their backyard if they relocated to homogenized towns surrounding the increasingly large Black urban communities. Thus, the suburbs served as an asylum for those seeking a false illusion.[48]

Not surprisingly then, for thousands of inner-city Black Newarkers, acquiring property in Newark or its suburbs proved to be an arduous dream. Banks and government institutions prevented Blacks from acquiring a piece of the American Dream by redlining (denying loans to minorities or charging minorities more for loans) and blockbusting (manipulating White homeowners to sell at low prices by convincing them minorities are moving into the neighborhood and then selling the homes at inflated prices); these activities were blatant, and agencies like the Federal Housing Administration (FHA) reinforced *de facto* segregation with these and similar policies. With racially specific and ethnically classified zones, groups in American cities were monitored by the government through Residential Security Maps.[49] FHA guidelines forbade underwriters from approving mortgages in crowded neighborhoods with "inharmonious racial groups." In New Jersey's Essex and Hudson Counties, Blacks, Jews, and many White ethnics were limited to racially defined areas; Newark's Central Ward had the least-desirable rating on the Residential Security Map.[50]

For many landlords, there was no incentive to maintain their properties in these least-desirable locations. Many had purchased these properties during the Great Depression when property values decreased and bankers gave low-interest loans requiring little, if any, money for a down payment. But taxes were high by the 1950s—$7.75 per $100 of assessed value (or in 2007 terms, $27,000 for an average New Jersey home valued at $350,000)—and landlords were often fearful of making improvements because it would likely increase their tax bills; thus, they began neglecting their properties.[51]

In Newark's suburbs, the FHA categorized "desirable" and "hazardous" ratings from grades "A" to "D" for northern New Jersey. Between the FHA and the Home Owners Loan Corporation, residential segregation was rampant in the metropolitan area. Jackson's work, *Crabgrass Frontier*, details this practice in the Newark region, describing how it ultimately limited Black Newarkers from moving into suburbia as well as purchasing land in their inner-city communities. Unlike their White counterparts who took advantage of the GI Bill to move to the suburbs, few Black veterans even qualified for mortgages. "Even though one of every nine servicemen during World War II was black, only one in 670 mortgages incurred by the GI Bill went to black veterans ... ."[52] And with the federal government implementing the Interstate Highway Act of 1956 to construct new highways to these suburbs, there was no funding for mass transit from the inner city to the suburbs. As Jackson notes about Newark, its suburbs, and federal policies, "the lasting damage done by the national government was that it put its seal of approval on ethnic and racial discrimination and developed policies which had the result of the practical abandonment of large sections of older, industrial cities."[53] Newark's *Star-Ledger* observed that "all the forces responsible for throwing the neighborhood into such decline in the decades leading up to the riots—suburbanization, highway construction, the erosion of the tax base, the massive migration of poor black Southerners into the city, the loss of manufacturing jobs, the decline of public housing, and so on—joined together to create a seemingly endless cycle of despair."[54]

With federal, state, and especially local governments limiting Black economic, social, and political progress, Black Newarkers were confined to a *de facto* segregated existence. Integration was elusive. As urban historian Thomas Sugrue observes about the Garden State, "The fact is, it was basically a massive federal subsidy that made possible the development of the suburbs. And New Jersey, as a largely suburban state, is ground zero for that."[55] For Black inner cities like Newark, life was harsh, limited, and too often a nightmare. Therefore, the seeds for racial politics and discontent were planted by officials in various levels of government and business. The result: in the 1960s, at home, work, school, and even in social circles, many Blacks in Newark were uncertain about their future even as the vast majority of Americans were gaining more economic and political power. Blacks were thus largely marginalized in the inner city, even though many of them desired to relocate to the newly constructed suburbs.[56] Ironically, just ten days before the 1967 riots, the *Star-Ledger* revealed the dreams of inner-city Black residents: "A large number of those questioned, voice a fervent wish for a better job to permit them to buy a home in the suburbs."[57]

Newark's 1967 Disorders

Newark's residents faced an unfortunate crisis in the late 1960s, just as many cities were confronted with severe urban social issues. The nature of race and politics in Newark made the city's 1967 riots especially unique. Newark reached a new milestone by 1966, achieving a 50 percent Black population as 32,000 Blacks moved into Newark and nearly 107,000 Whites left the city during the 1960s.[58] But Mayor Hugh Addonizio chose not to address social, economic, or political issues facing Black Newarkers during his administration. Considering Addonizio's increasingly powerful political machine, his focus on the business community, his blatant disregard for racial and social problems, "Newark was waiting for an explosion," says Cunningham. Blacks "had to occupy the worst housing, endure the gouging of slum landlords, take the most menial jobs, face the prospect of being last hired and first fired ... ." Thus, Newark was a tinderbox during the 1960s with its social and political circumstances, but the ingredients and zeitgeist for change were there all along, according to observers.[59] Black journalists, Black business leaders, and the Black professional middle-class were already race spokesmen invested in community politics during the Great Depression and even into the postwar era.[60] Yet, the Black middle class and much of the Black clergy engaged little in confrontational tactics.[61]

With the politics of Newark's growing middle class also came student activists moving into the city, provoking political change. Mostly White middle-class students associated with the Congress of Racial Equality (CORE) and Students for a Democratic Society (SDS) relocated to Newark's inner city. They were perceived as interlopers, adding more fuel to Newark's racial problems, according to some public officials. For instance, Central Ward Councilman Turner (who largely represented the area where these organizations were located) was an outspoken critic of CORE and other student groups. "They fan flames by mentioning ... violence ... where are we going with these inflammatory remarks?" Turner asked.[62] But the organizations were determined to change the direction of urban politics in Newark. Yet they had internal problems of their own, before they could try to tackle Newark's City Hall. CORE remained divided about how to advocate for community involvement. SDS, on the other hand, "fanned out into the cities and declared their commitment to a new movement for the poor." Mumford states that, "like the vision of a beloved community illuminated by Martin Luther King, the young activists imagined they could transcend social injustice."[63] Activists like Junius Williams, a Black Yale law student, came to Newark to be on the cutting edge of the movement.[64] Tom Hayden also relocated to the city to head the Newark Community Union Program (NCUP) and urge residents to push for more demands from city government. Hayden claimed that his group of mostly White radical student activists "were outside agitators, but we had to be, because there were no agitators from within the community."[65]

But Robert Curvin, a Black student activist with CORE, challenges how much Hayden's political weight carried in the city. "In truth, the Hayden group carved out a 20-square-block area of the lower Clinton Hill section in the South Ward as their theater of operation." Others argue that a political movement was taking shape before Hayden came to Newark. But Hayden and others saw Newark as a city in desperate need of civic engagement since the inner city residents were viewed as powerless because of City Hall's racial politics.[66] Hayden equated Newark with Vietnam as being under "colonial domination" and because both places were burning. Although much of the literature on 1960s Newark and urban America minimizes the New Left community building, their politics helped forge certain local movements. While some argue that these activists increased the disquiet in the inner city, others believe that New Left activists were not prominent in Newark's communities, let alone the city's politics. Nevertheless, activists like Hayden, Williams, and Curvin loudly challenged the Addonizio administration in count-less nonviolent ways just before the riots.[67] But City Hall was more in touch with older, more established middle-class Black clergy leaders than young activists or inner-city residents. Radical students like Stokley Carmichael pushed Black Power idealisms and incorporated anti-colonial ideology from Fanon's *Wretched of the Earth*.[68] When Carmichael appeared in Newark the summer prior to the 1967 riots, flyers simply stated, "Stokley is here." Over 400 people attended his speech, during which Carmichael reminded the crowd of the recent majority Black popu-lation milestone in Newark and yet how "in all other towns, they're afraid of a rebellion. But in Newark, New Jersey, they're not even afraid of you.... Whether you know it or not, you are the majority in this town. You should have taken Newark, NJ, over because it belongs to you."[69]

While political and racial agitation festered in Newark that summer, there were two significant underpinnings for the Newark riots: a medical school project and a police brutality incident. City Hall's and NHA's plans to raze apartments in the Central Ward for the $35 million expansion of the University of Medicine and Dentistry of New Jersey (UMDNJ) caused conflict that became known as the *medical school crisis*. As Porambo observed, the proposed relocation was "a game between the city administration and the college's board of trustees."[70] Essentially, the administration and their construction agents were seeking lucrative federal funds and contracts, but they did not want to include local residents in the process. They did, however, highlight housing shortage problems in their Model Cities federal grant application so they could receive significant funding.[71] On top of this, Addonizio's Chief of Staff, Donald Malafonte, who brokered the deal to have the school relocate to Newark, acknowledged that the medical school's trustees did not want to expand into Newark's central city but they also did not want to appear racist. So they told Malafonte that City Hall had to provide a minimum of 150 acres, figuring that Newark was too crowded to find the space.[72] At the time, the largest medical school in the country, Baltimore's Johns Hopkins, encompassed less than an acre. Yet "Malafonte called the trustee's bluff, taking a city map and drawing a line around 150 acres of Central Ward slum. But this was never communicated to the area's residents, most of them poor and black," states the *Star-Ledger*.[73] As Malafonte later admitted,

> The mistake we made is that in the effort to win the medical school, we focused so much on winning—just winning—we lost sight of the impact that would have been on the community. We were never going to give the medical school that much land. We just wanted to unmask the falseness of the demand for 150 acres. [74]

The secretive and callous manner in which the UMDNJ plan was one thing, but the NHA's approach to urban renewal had a more significant impact for the riots since some 20,000 inner-city residents would have to leave their homes. Many Black residents thought the plan had racial implications. "The grim joke circulating through the black neighborhoods was that 'urban renewal' was really the white man's code for 'Negro removal.'"[75] To the agency, neighborhood associations and communities were a minor irritant, and they refused to communicate with these groups, leaving many residents powerless.[76] In short, Central Ward residents were marginalized, and there were very few policy entities or community organizations to voice their frustrations about the UMDNJ plan. While the Committee Against Negro and Puerto Rican Removal and the Newark Area Planning Association complained to the City Planning Board, state, and federal authorities, they were alienated in the policy process as well.[77] Activist Junius Williams helped organize various protests (especially following the riots) to scale back the campus to 60 acres. He also advocated that the medical school should launch a minority apprenticeship construction program and hire local minorities since 2,600 jobs were available.[78] The federal government later demanded that New Jersey officials negotiate with local activists for these reforms.[79]

Besides the UMDNJ deal, the flashpoint that ignited the riots was the reported beating of taxi driver John Smith by White police officers on July 13, 1967. Similar to most urban riots of the 1960s, routine police actions would touch off the underlying tensions and grievances of a community.[80] Police officers John DeSimone and Vito Pontrelli arrested Smith for improper passing on 15th Street in the Central Ward. Smith was injured by either resisting arrest or most likely physical attacks by the officers, but there are differing accounts about what happened.[81] "The cops beat up cabdrivers every night in this city. It was sport for them," remembers Gus Heningburg, president of the Greater Newark Urban Coalition.[82] The riots exemplified much of the Black inner-city frustration against a racist White government, in particular a racist police force.[83] As Sharpe James notes, "We were always fearful of how our lives could be snatched away in a second by the police. Newark was a place where the majority felt powerless, felt abused, felt like they didn't have a voice."[84] And the police targeting Smith for a traffic violation blossomed into rumors that he was beaten to death.[85] It usually takes an incident like a beating to spark a riot, according to Professors Charles V. Hamilton and Clement Price. Price points out there were two events or phases to the rioting: a *shopping spree* by looters and a *shooting spree* by law enforcement. "The first phase was a commercial riot, when you have people breaking into stores and taking whatever they can carry," he states. "The second phase was a police riot when you have police and National Guardsmen firing their weapons indiscriminately. Both phases involve a level of lawlessness by certain individuals."[86]

Keeping Price's model in mind, at first a group of young people gathered at the police precinct where Smith was jailed, and then they damaged nearby stores. Many of these rioters were younger, second-generation Great Migration children, according to Cunningham, who often compared their achievements to Whites and believed they were entitled to social and economic equality.[87] Others argue that the motivation behind the riots was not just personal rage that led to the initial riots; it was also the deindustrialization of the 1960s that led to unemployment, hopelessness, and a Black population in flux that was upset with the status quo. One looter simply admitted they wanted to grab free items. "It was just stealing, that's all."[88] There may have been several thousand Black looters, but they represented a small percentage of the 200,000 Black residents. The average looter, of the nearly 1,500 arrested, was a Black male (85 percent), who had a job (73 percent), lived in Newark or nearby (96 percent), and was born in the south (54 percent, with only 27 percent born in Newark).[89] Some arrests took place and the media covered most of this, thinking that it was the beginning of a long-awaited riot. But the police department's "logistics were poor, their riot training and preparation nil."[90] The next day Governor Richard Hughes thought of the troublemakers as young people in a holiday mood, despite their continuous looting in various parts of the city well into nightfall. The looting was described at first as festive with some residents stealing anything they could carry.[91]

Mayor Addonizio and Governor Hughes, however, underestimated these incidents, and the delinquent activities exploded across the city, moving from a mile-long section of the Springfield Avenue shopping district to downtown. The mayor was considering running for governor in two years and contacting state officials for back-up law enforcement would mean admitting that he had lost control of his city and would ruin his chance of being a serious candidate. So he refused to talk with community leaders that night and even into the next day since silence was the official response.[92] But once Curvin and other leaders urged nonviolent protest instead, it became apparent that the crowd at the precinct was demanding more than reforms or negotiation. Additionally, there were reports of looting at Sears department store where they sold rifles. Suddenly, the thought of an armed looter concerned Addonizio as well as Newark police. In response, Addonizio and Hughes called in the state police and the National Guard, resulting in thousands of forces arriving in the early morning of July 14. The state police and National Guard had no specific areas to patrol, no maps, and they had different radio frequencies and little field coordination. The result was chaos between city residents, 1,390 Newark police officers, 627 state troopers, and 5,900 National Guardsmen. Thousands of inner-city residents and the newly arrived forces misunderstood one another.[93]

Armed with guns, riding in tanks, inexperienced with riot control measures, uncertain of targets, and weary of inner-city communities, the young, overwhelmingly White, state police and National Guard intensified the unrest in Newark's communities. Newark was a foreign place to most rural South Jersey guardsmen, and many of them were scared of Blacks. Hosting this alien police force was an awkward situation for many Newarkers. The law enforcers created as much of the disorder as the rioters, as many of them shot at rooftops, doorways, and into shops where snipers were falsely reported to be located. The state police reported nearly 2,905 rounds fired; the National Guard fired 10,414; and the Newark police had an uncountable number.[94] But the supposed Black sniper was more myth than reality, and the rumors allowed police officers to shoot at practically anyone, especially in public housing; many innocent bystanders and looters were shot. The *Star-Ledger* confirmed that "the sniper fire, on which many of the 26 riot deaths were blamed, was mainly gunfire from authorities, not snipers, who unwittingly shot at each other as a result of a communication breakdown." The police did not find one sniper. As photographer Benedict Fernandez remembers, the Springfield Avenue area had "the military there and they had no crowd control and they came close to shooting me!"[95] There was even a report from the state police instructing all departments "to be on the lookout for a 36-car caravan en route from New York City to either Paterson or Newark areas led by Stokley Carmichael." But news reports revealed that he was, in fact, out of the country. Between the conflicting reports, the National Guard and state police enforcing riot zones as well as curfews in Black neighborhoods, many Black Newarkers were increasingly frustrated with the governments' actions. Finally, nearly a week after John Smith was arrested, negotiations took place and the disorder ended on July 17th.[96]

With Newark's racially divisive atmosphere, the 1967 riot was a watershed moment for the city as well as America. Many political scientists and historians have called these urban movements *insurrections, uprisings, revolutions,* or *rebellions.* Local historian John T. Cunningham calls the riots the "Newark Disorders." What many outside Newark saw were sudden disturbances affecting the city, when in fact it was more complex. "The conventional version of what happened in Newark and other American cities during the 1960s is that things were fine, and then the riots came, and then things went downhill," states historian Thomas Sugrue.[97] But Komozi Woodard sees the riots differently, arguing that "to view the urban uprisings of the 1960s merely as destructive to the civil rights organizations does not capture the fullness of that historical moment for the African American freedom struggle. Black Power organizations arose from the ashes of the urban struggle."[98] Others argue that it was not just an isolated incident that led to the riots; there were racial and policy imbalances festering in Newark, and Addonizio was "extremely complacent about rising community tensions before the riots."[99] Whichever way one views the Newark riots, the uprisings resulted in 1,500 wounded, 26 dead, over $10 million in damages, and countless Newarkers becoming distrustful of one another and their government. As Newark historian Clement Price noted, the riots "symbolized for many Americans the death of Newark."[100]

The state and federal governments issued reports on the Newark riot in 1968. The New Jersey Commission on Civil Disorders concluded that "the evidence presented to the Commission does not support the thesis of a conspiracy or plan to initiate the Newark riot," and they pointed to discrimination and deprivation in jobs, housing, education, and welfare, to police action, segregation, and the institutionalized racism that alienated inner-city Newarkers as causes for the riot.[101] But police brutality was the significant factor. Addonizio and his police director "helped turn Newark into a corrupt whorehouse," according to Porambo, because they protected few Newarkers and maintained power for themselves with the mafia and other underground activities such as gambling.[102] Meanwhile, the U.S. Riot Commission Report pushed for a national resolution to address the economic, political, and social inequalities in America's inner cities. "Our nation is moving toward two societies, one black, one white—separate and unequal. Reaction to last summer's disorders has quickened the movement and deepened the division. Discrimination and segregation have long permeated much of American life; they now threaten the future of every American."[103] The report further stated that "white Americans have never fully understood—but what the Negro can never forget—is that white society is deeply implicated in the ghetto. White institutions created it, white institutions maintained it, and white society condones it."[104] But Black Newarkers largely doubted the local governmental system and certainly the Addonizio City Hall and police department. The Kerner Commission acknowledged that there was "a low level of trust in local government among blacks, including those who did not participate in the [1967] riot."[105]

Black Newarkers demanded immediate change on various levels. Because the riot brought the city's politics and social problems to a head, its outcome revolutionized Newark's political landscape as well as the city's reputation. Suddenly, the civil rights movement took an abrupt turn; some organizations changed focus, and urban riots like Newark's took center stage. For nearly a decade, the civil rights movement had been underway, and the mid-sixties was the zenith of the nonviolent approach of boycotts, sit-ins, and peaceful demonstrations in southern America. Although there were federal legislative victories dismantling segregation laws, especially in southern states, the 1957, 1960, and 1964 Civil Rights Acts did little to improve the deplorable socioeconomic conditions that many Blacks faced in northern cities like Newark.[106] CORE director James Farmer observed that, "civil rights organizations have failed. No one had any roots in the ghetto."[107] Dr. Martin Luther King and the Southern Christian Leadership Coalition (SCLC) appeared to genuinely focus on inner-city Blacks' plight when King visited Newark a week before his assassination in 1968. He emphasized that Newark should have a Black mayor and that there should be a concerted political strategy to address social and political problems.[108] At the same time, the SCLC had to contend with apathy, skepticism, and hostility from inner-city Blacks who frequently resented their nonviolent tactics.[109]

Ultimately, it was too late for civil rights leaders' to focus on inner-city problems in Newark because the city was left in shambles following the riots. While the riots awakened Black political power, the rebellion did little to resolve economic inequality in Newark.[110] Many parts of the city remained physically devastated. Urban blight and post-riot destruction was blatant, while much of the Central Ward, where the riots began, faced staggering social problems. Similar to other American cities, Newark lost many White and Black middle-class families to the suburbs following the riots.[111] And like other cities, the majority of Newark's remaining residents were Black working-class families who wanted better housing, schools, and more Black elected officials.[112] For example, along Springfield Avenue—the commercial area of the Central Ward—83 percent of businesses did reopen following the riots, but "they shuttered in the coming months and years when owners realized their suburban customers were too scared to return."[113] Also, many customers who moved to the suburbs wanted free parking and air-conditioned stores, things they could not find in a cramped and aging Newark. Besides, suburban clientele rarely came into the city.[114]

During the post-riot years, many Newark residents were strongly divided on race relations and politics. Race was already a polarizing factor before the riots, but race became a central flashpoint in the city's politics after the riots. The riots signified an uprising of more race-conscious leaders, who would become fully cognizant of Black needs and aspirations.[115] City Hall did little to address tensions between communities, so separatist politics filled the political vacuum in Newark. As Mumford argues, "like a bombshell in the public sphere, the disorders closed off avenues of cooperation between black and white activists, divided neighbors, and mobilized extremists."[116] Local citizen groups employed racial, even violent, tactics against integration. For instance, some White Newarkers supported Councilman Tony Imperiale's North Ward Citizen's Committee, a vigilante group, as Paul Goldberger called it, "to ward off criminals and/or invaders from the adjacent Central Ward, the black ghetto."[117] Community leaders like Imperiale radicalized Newark's racial politics and challenged state and federal initiatives that were trying to address social problems in Black communities. Imperiale felt many neighborhoods—like his largely Italian North Ward enclave—were being shortchanged financially and politically by City Hall. Imperiale and others owned guns, took karate lessons, and patrolled their neighborhoods looking for Black outsiders.[118] At the same time, Amiri Baraka's Black nationalistic politics resonated with many Black inner-city residents attempting to acquire communal economic and political empowerment as well as racial consciousness. He was forced into a leading role in post-riot Newark.[119] As James Haskins notes, "Politically the riots had three results: (1) a decline in Mayor Addonizio's popularity, (2) an increased awareness on the part of black community leaders of the necessity of strong black political organization, and (3) heightened tensions between the Black community and the Italian-American community."[120] Ultimately Newark's racial divide worsened between White and Black officials in the 1970s.

Newark's Post-Riot Era: Baraka, Gibson, and James

Amiri Baraka (born LeRoi Jones), a native Newarker, grew concerned with the political structure of the city. Newark's existing political machines were Irish and Italian, and Black politics in Newark was practically nonexistent even though the city's Black population was increasing every year. At first, Baraka, a poet, was a darling of New York City's White literati.[121] But by the mid-1960s, Baraka's consciousness was transformed; he transferred his religious affiliation to an Islamic sect, and he decided that he wanted to do more for his hometown. He felt that meaningful change could come from the ballot box and civic engagement. To further involve himself in politics, Baraka visited California several months before the riots. He and his new wife, Amina, went to the Bay area to help develop the nation's first undergraduate Black Studies curriculum. Several Black Panther student leaders called for the program at San Francisco State College, and they looked to the Barakas for guidance. Amiri Baraka met Black Panthers Huey Newton and Bobby Seale and witnessed the start of their political party; he also watched Black arts programs blossom in northern California. As Komozi Woodard notes, "[W]hen Baraka returned from California in the spring of 1967, he was confident that he might follow his movement along the lines of the Black Panthers and [the Los Angeles US Organization]. Ironically, over time, it would be Baraka and others who would forge more stable groups."[122]

The Barakas' California trip influenced them a great deal just at the time of Newark's infamous riots when civil rights groups radicalized their politics. That's

not to say that the Barakas did not already have their own community organizations, for they were known for the Spirit House arts center, school, and collective
kitchen; as well as the Committee for a Unified Newark (CFUN); and, later, the
Congress of African People (CAP). As Curvin recognized, "Baraka's artistic talent,
his polemical genius, his boundless energy, and his visionary zeal are the lifeblood
of CFUN and his several other organizations."[123] Many Black Newarkers supported Amiri Baraka's cultural nationalism movement and the Barakas' collective
education model, to which Woodard and Pinkney devote several chapters in their
works.[124] "It is Baraka's view that the creation of a black value system, a new way of
viewing the world, is essential if black people in the United States expect to free
themselves from internal colonialism," Pinkney explains.[125] In accordance with
this belief, Baraka felt Newark had several issues to address in July 1967, especially
the following, which were the most pressing:

1. the lack of political representation for the city's Black majority,
2. the local government's plans to replace a Black community of 20,000 people
   with the campus of a medical college [UMDNJ],
3. the lack of Black representation at the Board of Education, and
4. the outrageous acts of White police brutality against Black people.[126]

Due largely to their California experience and the Newark riots, the Barakas were
emboldened to implement local Black activism. The riots essentially catapulted
Amiri Baraka into the political arena. In fact, Baraka was arrested during the riots,
and the police beat him and framed him for gun possession. This caused him to be
"scarred for life."[127]

Coincidentally, the first National Black Power Conference was held in Newark
the same month as the riots. National Black leaders, as well as local leaders like
Baraka, advocated more local control in their communities. The conference was
supposed to have 400 delegates, but more than 1,000 were present. The national
call for Black Power and a Black united front helped galvanize organizations in
Newark and beyond.[128] Certainly Stokley Carmichael and Charles Hamilton's call
for Black Power resonated with Baraka and many Black inner-city Newarkers.
Carmichael and Hamilton encouraged Newarkers to challenge established, middle-class Black public officials like Councilman Turner, who lost his seat in the
1970 election.[129]

Between the convention and the cultural nationalism movement, Baraka's politics played a significant role in Newark's local politics. Baraka and other community, even national, activists sparked Black Newarkers to act and take hold of their
own political, social, and cultural destiny. It was an awakening for Black Newark
and Black America, demonstrating that many Black Americans had become so
disillusioned by racism that they embraced Black nationalism by advocating for
Black economic empowerment and political separatism at least in the short
term.[130] Baraka and Black residents transformed the city into "the most cohesive

black nationalist community in the nation."[131] Baraka also helped to create the Community Choice platform for Newark local politics and to publicize it among Blacks and Latinos.[132] Through coalition building with Latinos, particularly Puerto Ricans since they made up 10 percent of the city's population, Baraka, CFUN, and Hispanic organizations like the Young Lords increased their political solidarity. In fact, Baraka pushed for a Black and Puerto Rican Political Convention; "there was more brotherhood then between African Americans and Puerto Ricans," offers Councilman Luis Quintana.[133] These organizations also established the Community Choice Party to foster Puerto Rican and Black political alliances.[134]

Many of the city's Black leaders embraced nationalistic politics as well because membership in this movement proved to be crucial for them to get elected to local office. Only a few years earlier, Newark's majority Black population had inspired many Black leaders to create more race-conscious policies, and the nationalist movement caused many Blacks to think about building a united Black Newark community.[135] This was essentially Newark's race-conscious era. "We want to set an example in Newark," declared Baraka. "We want to get control of the space where 300,000 black people live not only for us to live in, to work and play in, but for our ideas and the development of concepts that are of benefit to us as a people with a particular ethos."[136] Community activists and public officials Donald Tucker and Kenneth Gibson became the next generation of Black elected leaders.

Gibson, a civil engineer and community leader, with the support of the Black and Puerto Rican Convention, challenged the Addonizio administration in the late 1960s.[137] Gibson ran in the 1966 election against the mayor and lost, but then he ran again in 1970 and won with 95 percent Black support even though voters faced racial confrontations at the polls. Voter turnout reached an unprecedented 73 percent in 1970; it was the first visible evidence of Blacks gaining political power. The June run-off election between Gibson, Addonizio, and Imperiale was held immediately after Addonizio's federal corruption trial, which diminished the incumbent mayor's chances of winning (especially since Gibson, as the city's chief structural engineer, reported Addonizio's corruption practices to the state prosecutor). The time appeared ripe for Gibson.[138] Yet the election remained racially charged. After all, it had only been three years since the riots; thus, racial tensions fueled the campaigns. Baraka recorded his poetry, which vilified White groups and their politics. Gibson's campaign played these messages to voters over the phone, while Addonizio's campaign generated fliers with pictures of Black students and the heading "Can Gibson Control Them?" and mailed them to voters. Addonizio also had the police director campaign on the idea that the election was about Black versus White.[139] Interestingly, after Addonizio's indictment and a teacher's strike, the city's White population remained split, and many of the mayor's former supporters stayed home on election day.[140]

When Addonizio lost the 1970 mayoral election, Gibson became the first Black mayor of Newark, as well as the first Black mayor of a large northeastern city. Newarkers hoped that, with a Black mayor, many of the city's problems would be addressed. As Sharpe James noted years later, it "took many years thereafter to learn it was never a question of from white to black. You have to evaluate those who serve in elected positions, see if in fact they are about the community, they are about bringing about change that will benefit the entire city and not just themselves."[141] James was elected as well in 1970, to the city council. However, he harbored bitter feelings toward Gibson, claiming that the mayor-elect did not help James' candidacy.[142] The 1970 election demonstrated that Newark had reached a new political era[143] and this was also the city's most intense period for racial politics.[144]

While Black political power appeared to enter Newark triumphantly, Gibson was more cautious about this milestone. "I'm a civil engineer, an expert in building and rebuilding," Gibson stated frequently. Curvin presents Gibson as appealing to a broad range of voters largely because of his memberships and activism in a variety of organizations, including Baraka's organization and CORE, and his position as co-chairman of the Business and Industrial Coordinating Council, for which he worked closely with local White business leaders. His understated political nature was quiet and confident, and it brought him support in many areas of Newark. Gibson's image was of diligence and honesty, and he emphasized that he was not a politician, thus defining his role as mayor narrowly. Some saw Gibson's leadership style as too cautious, however, especially when it came to hiring City Hall officials—even his largely White, young staff. Gibson was also a private man with few friends. A moderate who pondered decisions cautiously, he had no administrative experience and often lacked initiative and organization. Gibson was criticized for not always being accessible, though he responded that running the city was like a business, especially because no corporation would allow every member of the public to see the president. However, Gibson often remarked he worked for the community and that his ambition was not in politics or higher office.[145] Gibson also faced a City Hall with significant financial problems. Newark's government had operated with a deficit under the previous administration.[146] So reform and reorganization appeared to be urgent but difficult tasks for Gibson, considering the corruption of the previous administration. And, beyond the problems of the previous administration, there were still pressing social issues in Newark's communities. Newarkers hoped that Gibson could repair the city's finances, politics, and image, and Gibson believed he could lead Newarkers toward change, but these were high expectations.[147]

Despite these expectations, Gibson faced an uphill battle trying to get all Newarkers to agree on policy and social issues. One of the most pressing dilemmas was setting the city's education initiatives and teachers' contracts. Education was Gibson's most passionate concern, and he was determined to address the problems within Newark's school system.[148] In 1970 and 1971, hundreds of Newark teachers staged protests and demonstrations against the Addonizio and Gibson administrations over contracts, teacher safety, and curriculum demands. The teachers' strike largely centered on the Board of Education's opposition to binding arbitration and the teachers' union provision freeing teachers from nonprofessional duties.[149] The 1970 strikes, occurring prior to Gibson's election, added political pressure to Addonizio and helped Gibson not only win the election but also gain additional support from the strikers. However, in 1971, an eleven-week teachers' strike closed nearly half the city's schools. According to Golin, Baraka and Gibson's relationship became strained during this period. Gibson tried to work with Baraka to address curriculum standards for the school system, especially since they were childhood friends, but they became adversaries during Gibson's first term.[150] Before the 1970 mayoral campaign, Baraka had suggested to his organization that electing Gibson would be a step toward building a Black nation, and, after Gibson was elected, Baraka expected Gibson to push for separatist politics, especially through the teacher strikes. However, Baraka soon became upset with Gibson and grew concerned that Newark's teachers were enforcing White values and curricula, especially since the majority of Newark's students (85 percent) were Black and Puerto Rican.[151] Many education experts argue that, by the early 1970s, the Newark school system had already been corrupted by patronage politics, with teachers who commuted from nearby suburbs and had few community ties to an overwhelmingly Black student body. School administrators and the teachers' union acted as a cartel by seeking more political power for themselves.[152] Financially, Newark's school system was on the decline, receiving little government investment. So by the time Gibson took office, he faced a school system that was bankrupt and dysfunctional with few qualified teachers, even fewer Black teachers, an unruly student body, a corrupt school board, and demands for new school curricula and employee contracts. During Gibson's first term, the Newark teachers' union took advantage of the combination of the dismantled Addonizio political machine and the calls for educational reform to increase their political power.[153]

Gibson asserted that Newark teachers were not properly trained to deal with social problems, and he wanted reform. Yet it was a highly complex set of circumstances, and community leaders were exacerbating several issues.[154] In the center of the school system's politics were Baraka and Imperiale. They had a contentious past, and they argued about curriculum standards, contracts, and school integration in their Black and Italian communities. Baraka and Imperiale constantly exchanged spectacular tactical maneuvers, argues Mumford, and the teachers' strike was just one of many disputes they politicized for their communities and themselves.[155] Between the racial politics of Baraka and Imperiale and the teachers' strikes—with teachers often taking positions on either side of the racial divide and even going to jail in some instances—Gibson had a Herculean task. The cause of Gibson's troubles ultimately boiled down to the city's continuing race relations problem.[156] After trying three times to get all parties to negotiate, Gibson finally made some headway. He created a popular movement for peace through A Call to Reason, which urged all sides to come to the negotiating table. Gibson was able to broker a deal to get the teachers' union a modest raise and a new contract and curriculum standards. Ideally, the new Mayor's Task Force on Education would give his office and citizens involvement in future school policy, though this involvement was limited.[157] Gibson encouraged the teachers' union to keep the disputed provisions of the old union contract but promised the Black community that he would appoint a task force on education and a Board of Education that would, in turn, create a curriculum committee to study school programs.[158] Gibson proved successful in orchestrating voting members to support this initiative, although many teachers and some parents disagreed. While the teachers' union was fined and some members faced jail time, Gibson proved to be an integrationist mayor who kept his trademark cool negotiating style throughout this crisis.[159]

In addition to educational reform, Gibson worked to develop employment policies, pushing for apprenticeship programs, especially in the construction industry. One initiative, for instance, required that any contractor with a construction project receiving a tax abatement from the city of Newark would make a good faith effort to have 50 percent of apprentices from a minority group. This was known as the Newark Plan. Gibson also pushed to establish the Newark Construction Trades Training Corporation (NCTTC), an agency that recruited potential construction workers. Although it had a minimal impact on unemployment statistics, the NCTTC did help train many Newarkers. But, during the 1970s, there were few job opportunities due to a lagging economy and the fact that many employers relocated their businesses outside of the city. Also, the administration had to work around various unions as well as the Port Authority of New York–New Jersey, which was a large employer for the area. Willa Johnson states that, in some of these public and private projects, minority workers were often added to the project only toward the end of the construction. Most importantly, the greatest number of these construction jobs were temporary rather than continuous. In one instance, the Port Authority did not hire any Newarkers for an airport expansion project. For many inner-city residents, an entry-level position was not long-lasting. In the public sector, few minorities were hired or appointed under the Gibson administration as well (though this might have been due to a lack of administrative experience among the applicants and civil service requirements, according to Willa Johnson). In total, unemployment citywide was between 9 and 14 percent during Gibson's tenure, or double the state's average (in some parts of the inner city, it was nearly two to three times higher).[160]

While the city's social problems in the early 1970s posed challenges for Gibson, his relationship with the city council proved to be contentious as well. Gibson could not unite council members on various proposals and financial matters. During his term, Gibson discovered that few city council members supported his proposals; indeed, they charged that the mayor went out of town too frequently and spent too little time working with other lawmakers.[161] Several White council members often retaliated against Gibson with inquiry threats of his administration's finances. But city council members could hardly agree with one another and bitter politics, if not personal attacks, became the norm in city government, especially because divisiveness had been part of Newark's political culture for generations. But several council members agreed that Gibson was not communicating effectively and that he maintained distant relations with other lawmakers. For example, when Gibson failed to articulate how a portion of grant money would be spent and in which communities, Councilman Sharpe James led the opposition, which disagreed that the mayor should have the sole authority to decide where and how the funds were spent. Gibson and the council eventually negotiated on this issue, but only after the council introduced legislation threatening to control all financial matters dealing with outside funding. Toward the end of his first term, Gibson had gained little ground with the council even though they had to make mutual decisions on grants, applications, and other matters. This conflict had serious policy implications considering that Newark desperately needed state and federal grant funding in the early 1970s.[162] At this time, City Hall's elected leadership remained fragmented because the mayor and the council did not work well together. Issues like schooling, housing, and even the nomination of John Redden, a White man, for police director divided Gibson and the council as well as most Black public officials and activists. As a result, Curvin notes that, "Gibson could not piece together a political coalition that was able to exercise dominance over the outcome of key issues. To the contrary, Gibson fought most of his battles alone. His articulation of Black demands meant little for most of the Black community. In most key issues Blacks as a group lost."[163] In addition to little agreement among civic leaders, a bureaucratic city government structure allowed for few reforms. Any changes Gibson tried to institute meant that he had to face roadblocks by the city council and racial organizations like Baraka's or Imperiale's groups; Gibson also had to deal with civil service workers who were more loyal to their respective agencies than any cause. Under Gibson then, few policy changes were established to assist Blacks in Newark's inner city.[164]

City Hall's and local agencies' internal politics were a major time drain for Gibson and racial politics remained a longstanding concern. Working around divided Black politics in Newark remained a challenge for Gibson, but he could not ignore the growing Latino population and their political power either. A larger number of Latinos, particularly Puerto Ricans, had relocated to Newark during the 1970s. In fact, they achieved several milestones ranging from the election of East Ward Councilman Henry Martinez in 1978 to organizing the so-called Labor Day riots in 1974. Gibson confronted rioters head on, meeting with them and offering ways to address their concerns regarding political inclusion and community.[165] Racial politics also became a significant factor when Gibson was challenged by Imperiale during the 1974 mayoral election campaign. Imperiale reintroduced racial politics into the campaign, especially because Newark's Italian-American population was becoming increasingly smaller and retaining fewer jobs. Imperiale's reaction was to start a consciousness movement counter to Black nationalism and to characterize Italian-American politics as hypermasculine.[166] But Gibson won reelection, and he reached an agreement with Imperiale for mutual cooperation.[167] Yet Baraka's and Gibson's relationship soured further during this election. Baraka was bitter about Gibson's moderate politics and claimed credit for Gibson being elected.[168] Baraka's and the Congress of African People's (CAP) experience with local Black politicians led many Blacks to increasingly question their leaders' Black nationalism politics by 1974.[169]

Even though there were pressing urban issues facing the city government, Gibson still had to deal with financial difficulties and separatists' politics, such as the city's $60 million deficit due to the relocation of businesses and the middle class to the suburbs. For example, Newark's property tax base decreased 21 percent over 11 years or $319 million dollars. In fact, the city's tax rate was twice as high as many nearby Essex County suburbs, and the city desperately needed more income.[170] Not surprisingly then, Gibson proposed a payroll tax to Republican Governor William Cahill and the state legislature. The mayor also took 36 state legislators on a guided tour of the city to emphasize the city's deplorable condition.[171] After several months, the state legislature allowed the city to collect a one percent payroll tax on Newark businesses and six new tax levies. The state also gave the city $15 million in aid, but the rest of the money would have to come from Newarkers. These tax proposals, however, also had to be approved by the city council. Considering the hurdles the mayor faced with the council, this proposal brought the city council and mayor into conflict once again. Council members argued that they were never consulted on these proposals, and they at first rejected the plan. Then, at the first public hearing, the council adjourned for a week because of disputes between members. Governor Cahill reminded city council members, however, that he would not allow the proposals to be altered. In the end, the council approved some measures, including the one percent payroll tax.[172]

Although Gibson fought with the city council due to the problematic city budget, he succeeded winning reelection in 1978. But following his reelection, to comply with fiscal demands, he made an unpopular decision. Gibson announced that 2,000 city workers, including 200 police officers, would be laid off to reduce government costs; during this same time, Gibson and the city council pushed for pay raises for themselves. There was a $35 million deficit, and Gibson proposed a $17 million cut in school spending. Considering his previous experience with the school board and teachers' union, Gibson worked with the parties involved to reduce the number of teachers by 12 percent or more than 1,100. By the early 1980s, Gibson faced charges that he gave a former councilmember a no-show job (someone is paid for work that they do not actually do). Although this matter ended in a mistrial, this charge reduced Gibson's support for reelection in 1982 to a low of 52 percent.[173] Also, between 1970 and 1985, the city lost 69,050 residents, a decline of 17.8 percent. Unemployment in Newark by 1986 was 11.2 percent overall, and triple that for some segments of the Black community.[174] As a result, during Gibson's last term, he worked to renew the downtown by encouraging corporations to either remain in Newark or to relocate to the city from Manhattan. Since the corporate sector controlled billions of dollars and jobs, Gibson knew the business community had power.[175] Gibson wanted to try a "trickle-out" approach by spurring downtown development, believing that neighborhoods would eventually be revitalized. "But it never happened, because there were no policies in place to make it happen. None of the things that were happening downtown were really benefiting the people who lived in the city," charges Willa Johnson.[176] In fact the majority of the corporate jobs went to educated outsiders.[177] Gibson's proposal to expand the University Heights campuses of Rutgers, the New Jersey Institute of Technology, and Essex County College also encountered opposition since the plan would impact private residences. Several community leaders—including Baraka—felt Black Newarkers had been double-crossed by Gibson and publicly called the mayor and City Hall officials "degenerate Negroes."[178]

Local issues became more complicated for Gibson in 1984 when voters supported a publicly elected school board in hopes of preventing a state takeover since graduation rates hardly improved. Councilman Sharpe James, representing Newark's mostly Black middle-class South Ward, wanted an elected school board. He also challenged that education no longer appeared to be the key concern of Gibson's administration (although, as mayor, James would shift his position, favoring an appointed board).[179] In the 1986 election, James campaigned for mayor with the ironic endorsement of Anthony Imperiale.[180] As a teacher who had taught in the Newark public school system and at Essex County College and as an insurgent candidate looking to challenge the existing administration, he argued that the city's public schools still had problems and unemployment and crime rates remained high, especially in Newark's inner city, while Gibson focused on downtown development.

Once James was elected mayor in 1986, he pushed for political reforms. Born in Florida and raised in Newark, as an activist and three-term council member, James saw how local government operated.[181] As mayor, James' accomplishments included bringing the city beyond the stigma of its riot-prone image. "We have been changing urban blight to urban bright," James reminded Newarkers.[182] While Gibson was more mild mannered, James appeared more forceful in his approach to politics. The new mayor insisted on "building time" with the help of banks and the federal government. The construction of thousands of new public housing units, particularly in the north and east wards of the city, was the signature of the administration, according to Housing Director Harold Lucas.[183] Beyond housing, James reinstated mounted police units and streamlined Newark's permit process and urban renewal incentives, such as government incentives for large businesses to return to the downtown. Several corporations then relocated to Newark, largely due to tax incentives, and the airport and ports expanded significantly during James' tenure.[184]

Despite this early growth, the city still had a tarnished image, and much of the revitalization occurred in specific parts of the city, leaving many sections untouched. James and the city's Business Administrator, Richard Monteilh, admitted that Newark was "a city beset with problems of despair, decay, neglect, poverty, unemployment and crime."[185] Thus, the mayor reached out to the business community and created the new position of Deputy Mayor for Economic

Development.[186] By gaining the attention of the private sector, James was able to persuade corporations such as IDT Telecommunications, MBNA National Bank, Blue Cross-Blue Shield, and Vorizon to settle in the central business district during the 1980s and 1990s.[187] In addition, nonprofit organizations such as the New Community Corporation (NCC) created private and public sector incentives for the city to rebuild itself after the 1960s riots.[188] James was convinced that the best policy incentives were ones associated with people coming to Newark to work, travel, stay, and be entertained. Since Port Newark and Newark International Airport are located in the city's southeast ward, there are many airport-related businesses, including hotels and travel-associated companies in that ward. So James and other public officials played a significant role in the successful operation of the Port Authority of New York and New Jersey in this area because the bi-state agency controls a fifth of Newark's land and pays the city an annual fee. Moreover, the city benefited from the tax revenue of businesses associated with the airport business district.[189]

During the 1990s, James pushed for additional downtown projects including a minor league baseball field (Riverfront Stadium) and the New Jersey Performing Arts Center (NJPAC). He felt the best way to highlight the city's progress was to have entertainment areas in downtown. Subsequently, when the owners of the New Jersey Nets and Devils were considering new locations, James further stressed the importance of revitalizing downtown Newark by having the city and even the state government help construct a new arena for the teams. In fact, during the 2002 mayoral election, Governor James McGreevey endorsed the construction plan by reminding Newarkers that "under the leadership of Sharpe James, we will build an arena for the Nets and Devils. Newark, you give me Sharpe James (you get the) Devils and Nets."[190] Of course, other cities created similar incentives for professional teams. However, James believed that the Newark Bears, NJPAC, and a new arena for local professional sports teams would complete his triple pronged initiative for the city. Triumphantly, James felt his urban incentives had brought the city a long way from its 1960s riot-prone image. He won reelection in 1990, 1994, and 1998 and established a significant political machine largely due to these urban policies. James even won a State Senate seat as it was legal to hold two elected offices in New Jersey. Many Newarkers recognized and more often revered the experience and political power James wielded in City Hall. Private sector interests and urban policy professionals also recognized the James machine and his policy approaches. "For many years, Newark symbolized for an entire nation the malaise which has plagued urban America," states Silvio Laccetti. And in the 1980s, there was "some hope for other troubled cities for Newark [was] finally making a comeback, one which has accelerated under the current administration."[191]

As these urban incentives and electoral victories continued, certain Newark residents grew increasingly concerned regarding the policy implications of James' City Hall.[192] Richard Cammarieri of the New Community Corporation stated that, too often, tax abatements and riverfront development benefited corporate and outside interests more than residents. "Most development trickled down and trickled out and it wasn't very balanced."[193] Because James focused much of his interest on downtown development, many residents thought his proposals favored large corporations and entertainment venues for suburban residents. And much of the urban renewal taking place in various Newark neighborhoods was related to razing 1950s and 1960s government high-rise apartments for low-income families. Nearly 40 of these apartment complexes were razed to make room for $200 million neo-colonial townhouse-style developments, and there was a further low-income housing shortage as a result.[194] But NHA Director Harold Lucas argues that the agency focused much of its attention on relocating families and addressing the problem of so many vacant and run-down units. Moreover, the city had become such a "reservoir" for many poor families who relocated from nearby Essex County towns that providing them with adequate housing was the NHA's chief concern and most pressing issue. The agency was never meant to "warehouse" poor families (or keep the poor confined to a small area) but instead help with housing resources and social services. And, according to Lucas, during the late 1990s, James supported mixed-income housing (through Hope 6 and Choice Neighborhood programs), particularly as a federal government initiative to address the warehousing effect.[195]

In addition to housing problems, the city's school system remained problematic. In an effort to address the financial and political concerns surrounding Newark's public schools, the state took over the system in 1995. Because of New Jersey's *Abbott v. Burke* decision, the state could take control of any failing district.[196] As a matter of fact, a state judge noted that even though "Newark's spending per pupil was the highest in the state...only one out of four students passed the High School Proficiency Test."[197] A significant reason for the school district's financial shortfall was due to economic segregation. Because the state of New Jersey is so divided in terms of rich suburbs and poor municipalities (or largely White suburban school districts and majority Black and Latino urban school districts), much of the wealth generated from property taxes supports local school districts in the suburbs. As a result, inner-city school districts like Newark, where residents have little taxable property, are short-changed financially.[198] Another problem with Newark's school system is that the Essex County and New Jersey State governments hold significant power over Newark's public school system and the city's policymaking process. As an unfortunate consequence, in many New Jersey school districts (including urban ones like Newark that have been taken over by the state Department of Education), these authorities do *not* require that a government or civics course be taught in high school. In fact, only a third of the schools in the entire state offer a curriculum related to civics, government, or politics.[199] In addition, every test ranked Newark students almost bottom at every grade level and in nearly every school.[200]

Newark's social statistics during James' tenure remained especially bleak. In the 1990s, the city's unemployment rate remained twice that of the state's average; Newark's school system was under state control for over six years, retaining its reputation as one of the most corrupt in the nation[201] while graduating only 40 percent of high school seniors. The city had some of the highest rates of infant mortality, tuberculosis, lead poisoning, and AIDS cases and the third-worst rate of child immunization in the nation. A third of Newarkers lived below the poverty line, and only 23 percent owned property. Many long-time residents and even more newcomers questioned James' 16-year term and Newark's wobbly rebirth.[202] One of the Black community's most outspoken leaders was a young charismatic council member, Cory Booker, who challenged James in the 2002 and 2006 mayoral elections.

2

The 2002 and 2006 Mayoral Elections

In May 2002, a contentious election was held with two Newark mayoral candidates who had two contrasting views of urban politics. Sharpe James, a local civil rights activist and shrewd incumbent mayor, faced a strong challenger, Cory Booker, a 32-year-old neophyte lawyer and city councilmember.[1] As the *New York Observer* pointed out, "Mr. Booker's candidacy has a storybook quality, pitting a young reformer against an aging, entrenched incumbent."[2] Interestingly, Booker's and James' campaign volunteers reflected their politics and demographics. James depended on a "largely African-American cadre of city employees, union operatives and opinionated retirees who consider the four-term mayor a reliable provider and something of an adopted son," while Booker's camp was composed of "a starry-eyed collection of grad students, homemakers and fiery tenant leaders." Even their campaign headquarters' locations stated something about their politics. James' was across the street from City Hall and boasted campaign signs, whereas Booker's team worked out of a ramshackle plastic-bag factory on the city's industrial fringe with no outdoor campaign signs.[3] Ultimately, Newark residents faced two significant challenges: (1) to restore the city's reputation, leaving its image of urban riots behind them, and (2) to incorporate urban revitalization into political policies. James and Booker differed radically in their approaches to these concerns. While James believed that the best policy incentives related to private sector incentives (mostly in downtown, airport, and port projects), Booker believed that the focus of community development should be on revitalizing areas beyond downtown, especially Newark's neighborhoods. James' claim that Newark was experiencing a renaissance appeared to be a mirage in certain areas of the city.[4] Booker felt that by having the city rebuild dilapidated parks, construct new housing and new schools, and provide school vouchers, Newark could get past the stigma of the 1967 riot and become a progressive northern New Jersey city similar to nearby Hoboken and Jersey City.[5] Yet many residents felt that Booker's plans implied gentrification and parts of the city would be controlled and owned by developers and young urban professionals would displace many long-time residents. As James pollster Ronald Lester saw it, "the land in Newark is so valuable because of where it sits, as the nexus of transportation routes and so close to Manhattan, it's not only valuable property, but it's pivotal in statewide politics."[6]

But something more intrinsic was at the center of the candidates' community development approaches. Sharpe James and Cory Booker's policymaking approaches were extremely different. James was a 66-year-old Black politician and four-term mayor as well as a two-term State Senator. James thought Newark was experiencing a "gradual renaissance."[7] He was part of the old guard with the city council, state government, and constituents.[8] James' candidacy received support from Governor James McGreevey as well as a number of old guard Newark politicians, including Booker's eight city council colleagues; Newark's US Representative, Donald Payne; and State Senator and 1998 mayoral candidate Ronald Rice, who said Booker was "lucky I'm not running against him."[9]

Booker was a freshman city council member, and he was widely regarded as idealistic in his policymaking approaches. He created the organization *Newark Now* to address community concerns by going around the traditional process in city politics. Booker wanted Newark to experience a community renewal revolution in its neighborhoods as soon as possible.[10] Due to his progressive politics, Booker received the endorsement of the *New York Times*[11] and the city's *Star-Ledger* newspaper, as well as the Newark Firefighters Union; James then refused to negotiate a new contract with the firefighters. Outside Newark, notable Booker supporters included Princeton University Professor Cornel West, former Senator Bill Bradley, and film director Spike Lee. Booker seemed to have gained widespread appeal outside the city, but within it—particularly among voters—his image and loyalty were questioned.[12]

How Newark voters viewed the mayoral candidates proved very important to the outcome of the 2002 election. James was seen as an antiquated political titan who appeared ineffective in pushing community development proposals. His policies included constructing high-end apartment units following the demolition of large, low-income public housing complexes. As historian John Cunningham states, "James often joked, more than half seriously, that he rightfully could be called 'the implosion mayor.'"[13] James' urged city employees and contractors to donate money to his mayoral campaign and hired outside campaign consultants for the first time.[14] But James was viewed by many of his constituents as an original Newarker who had resided in the city long enough to "earn his stripes" and as an experienced, but partisan, rainmaker in Newark, Essex County, and New Jersey politics.[15]

While James was seen as a political powerbroker, Booker was viewed as too progressive, naive, and not pragmatic enough for Newark's legendary strong-arm city politics. For some, Booker's idealism was difficult to understand.[16] Many voters and local political powerbrokers saw him as too young and inexperienced to run for mayor.[17] Booker was viewed as a media darling not indigenous to Newark.[18] Although Booker tried to establish some credibility by residing in Newark's inner-city Brick Towers apartment complex and staging fasting and camping-out campaigns against drug dealers, many Newarkers saw him as fake, opportunistic, and an overeducated carpetbagger with little political experience who wanted to run the largest city in New Jersey.[19] In fact, some people were offended that he chose to move into Brick Towers, one of Newark's most chaotic housing projects. Many members of the political establishment frowned on his reality TV–style initiatives and his inability to make many changes as a city council member, being outvoted 8–1 in many instances.[20] Booker could not seem to shake this image, and James characterized Booker's events as grandstanding and contrived media stunts.[21]

Basically, James successfully used the fact that Booker was not a native Newarker against Booker. "'[Booker's] all smoke and mirrors,' said Mr. James, who often uses words like 'fraud' and 'phony' to describe his rival. 'These wealthy businessmen are investing in an opportunity to take over Newark.'"[22] Since Booker received two-thirds of his campaign money from non-Newarkers who mostly resembled a Who's Who of American Business, James was reminding residents that, unlike Booker, he received the majority of his money from Newarkers, including over $400,000 from 384 city workers, police officers, and firefighters and $123,000 from local developers, contractors, and construction firms. James thus disparaged Booker's political ties and Booker's own claim of "love money" by outsiders, including financial contributions from 26 different states (with more than one-third from New York). Yet Booker received only $47,550 from Newarkers and no city workers donated to Booker's campaign.[23] "'They want Newark,' [James] said, his voice rising. 'They want our port. They want Newark Airport. They want our city! They want to cut down Sharpe!"[24] James and many residents branded Booker as a political Trojan horse candidate sponsored by other interests, particularly because Booker was raised in the suburbs and was a product of integration—for which, ironically, Civil Rights leaders had agitated.[25]

For some Newarkers, however, voting for Booker would mean a change in City Hall; this sentiment helped Booker capture many Newarkers' attention, and this interest showed in the polls.[26] One pre-election 2002 survey conducted by WABC-TV revealed that the race was practically tied between Booker and James. James received 46 percent and Booker 44 percent, which was a statistical dead heat, with a 4 percent margin of sampling error.[27] For many, "not only does Mr. Booker dare to say he is better suited to move Newark forward, but polls indicate that voters may agree."[28] In addition, the poll also revealed that Booker was a serious challenger. An WABC-TV follow-up poll showed Booker led 48 percent to James 42 percent.[29] Not surprisingly, the candidates' slogans reflected their political intentions. James' slogan was "The Real Deal," which suggested that Mr. Booker was fake and a symbol of the divisive racial and class dynamics of his campaign.[30] Booker's slogan was "A Renaissance for the Rest of Us," which challenged James' community development policies. Both candidates thus hinted at their rivals' negative qualities.[31] Certainly, April and May 2002 proved to be contentious months in Newark politics, as polls demonstrated. Because predictions by political scientists, pollsters, and newspapers determined the election was too close to call, dealings between the candidates' supporters and campaigns grew increasingly tense. There were charges of pre-election dirty tricks, including theft and destruction of property; campaign signs being destroyed; and intimidation by both camps. In fact, federal investigators were called in to monitor the May 2002 election so that there would be no election tampering, voting irregularities, or violence. These were the outward problems that the Booker and James campaigns faced, but, for many, this form of Newark politics was nothing new.[32] "Newark elections have historically been marred by mischief and various kinds of tomfoolery," says historian Clement Price. "I've gotten calls from the press suggesting that the city is on the verge of political implosion, and it's just not the case. We're just having a race."[33] But the political sniping between the 2002 mayoral candidates and their campaign staffs proved far worse just prior to the election, seeming to turn from political to personal attacks.

Booker's and James' Challenges and Charges

Booker and his campaign highlighted the strong-arm tactics of the James political machine to the media, while many James supporters, including State Senator Ronald Rice, said that the mayor believed journalists were against the mayor and that James was going door to door to tell his story to voters. Booker responded that city employees were forced to donate money to James' campaign and that nearly a third of James' campaign funds came from city employees. Booker ultimately charged that the James machine fostered favoritism.[34] Booker and his campaign also painted the mayor as making too much money off of Newark taxpayers. As the *New York Times* observed, "For his part, Mr. Booker uses adjectives like 'fanatic' and 'dictatorial' to describe his opponent." Booker stressed that "the mayor is trying to win an election by intimidation and bullying. He's trying to undermine the democratic process."[35] Booker further emphasized that James held two political offices as mayor and state senator and that he had the potential for double incumbency, earning nearly $250,000 from both positions.[36] Since James had properties in Newark and Florida and owned a Rolls-Royce and a yacht,[37] Booker and his campaign characterized James as an aging, greedy, confident and cocksure northern New Jersey political powerbroker who held too much power and was as out of touch with Newarkers.[38] Booker argued that James had "been in office as long as I've been alive."[39] Booker's campaign also brought charges to the State Election Law Enforcement Commission that James and his campaign used public money to pay for billboards that supposedly featured city nurses yet were actually thinly disguised campaign ads.[40]

James and his campaign questioned Booker's political intentions and racialized the election by arguing that Booker was not a native Newarker or authentically Black. Instead, according to James and his supporters, Booker was a White-educated, gay, and Jewish Republican poser.[41] The homophobic and anti-Semitic charge that Booker was a Jewish-supported "faggot white boy" was viewed by many outsiders as a way to undermine Booker's authenticity as a Newarker, Democrat, and Black man.[42] Georgia Persons notes that in cities like Newark, the Black insurgent mayor often tries to contrast himself to "an ogre" or a political opponent. Thus, "Cory Booker was turned into an ogre, 'a wolf in sheep's clothing' by James and national leaders and supporters Jesse Jackson and Al Sharpton." James was also backed by various New Jersey Democratic Party leaders, including the governor and both Democratic US senators, who owed extensive political favors to James for delivering Black voter support over the years.[43] So, in addition to having a reputation as an outsider and being attacked by the incumbent mayor, Booker failed to win over New Jersey's political establishment.

An analysis of the May election results in the city's Black communities shows that the majority of Black Newarkers were increasingly split. The majority of Blacks supported James over Booker, giving the mayor another term. Not one Black ward overwhelmingly supported Booker at the polls (the total was 59 percent for James and 40 percent for Booker), but the Hispanic and Portuguese communities backed Booker in the election.[44] Thus, James "played upon internal ethnic conflicts, as well as class and social differences among many blacks in the still troubled city."[45] James' and his campaign's questioning of Booker's racial identity brought about many public conflicts.[46] From a distance, it appeared that the Newark mayoral race was between two generations of Black leaders, and it was "like a generation stepping forward and figuring out how to lead," noted a Booker campaign worker.[47] But the race, according to the *New York Times*, was also "emblematic of a major shift in urban politics, in which candidates are beginning to frame issues to a multitude of ethnic and racial groups," or, as Professor Price states, "Newark is increasingly a city that cannot be explained simply by a black-white social calculus."[48]

Booker tried to brand himself as a progressive Clinton-centrist Democrat, not a figure of traditional Black politics. Yet certain Black journalists, like Glen Ford, who co–publishes the *Black Commentator* website, viewed Booker's alliances with conservatives as a way "to dismantle public education, destroy affirmative action and gain an urban foothold for their views."[49] Because Booker supported school vouchers, many civil rights leaders, including James, labeled him a Republican. "His willingness to think beyond traditional liberal political thought put him at odds with the civil rights establishment that colored him as a wolf in sheep's clothing," notes S. Craig Watkins. "James and members of the old guard who supported him, Jesse Jackson and Al Sharpton, argued that Booker's political agenda represented a threat to the half-century struggle for black civil and equal rights."[50] On his campaign website, James posted a cartoon portraying Booker working on an assembly line behind black Republicans like Supreme Court Justice Clarence Thomas and National Security Adviser Condoleezza Rice, with the headline "Neo-Black Politicos."[51] Publicly, James attacked Booker's integrated suburban upbringing. At one public forum James said to Booker, "You have to learn to be an African-American! And we don't have time to train you all night."[52] Booker admitted that "I don't want to be a great black politician; I want to be a great politician," and he tried to distance himself from the racial politics of the previous generation.[53] Both Booker's campaign headquarters and the restaurant where his post-election party was held were located in a predominately Portuguese section of Newark, the Ironbound—not in a Black neighborhood; this fact did not help to portray him as a Newark Black politician.[54] "Realizing the demographic shifts that were remapping the city," notes S. Craig Watkins, "Booker refined his Spanish-language skills as a way to communicate more effectively with a constituency that in 2002 represented nearly a third of the city's population."[55] More bluntly, Clement Price argues that Booker was "taking advantage of the new realities of Newark. There's less emphasis on race, greater reliance on government, less reliance on black political power, more reliance on cobbling together a coalition of the disgruntled."[56] While Booker lost the 2002 election, Booker did chip away at James' base. "A 16 year mayor started the election with 70 percent approval rating and got 54 percent of the vote," states Booker. "That's a huge decline for an incumbent against an insurgent."[57]

2006 Redux? Booker, James, ... and Rice

While the 2002 election proved to be contentious between James and Booker, 2006 would have remnants of similar themes, yet there were different outcomes for the candidates. Booker decided not to run again for his Central Ward council seat and instead returned to his community nonprofit organization on a full-time basis; James entered his fifth term resolved to address whatever policies he wanted to implement, including putting the final touches on redeveloping the edges of downtown, especially where the Devils' hockey arena would be located.[58] Yet by January 2006, James was hesitant to announce whether he would run again in May. James organized and filed petitions to appear on the ballot but remained unsure whether he would officially seek reelection.[59] Booker announced his intention to run on January 11, but his campaign did little to orchestrate campaign events until well into March. February proved to be a month with few public exchanges between James and Booker; the media centered much of its coverage on whether James would run again and not on the political agendas of the candidates. As one columnist called the upcoming election, "Round Two: Booker Jabs, but James Stays Low." James' intention to run remained a mystery, and there were good reasons to think Booker would gain ground in a rematch, especially since he only lost by seven percent in the previous election. In the 2002 race, James painted Booker as a carpetbagger and a fake, which stuck with many voters. Booker tried to label James as an entrenched but ineffectual politician who was letting the city remain in poverty, but this strategy backfired on Booker. According to the *Star-Ledger*, "Many Newark voters, it turns out, felt Booker was chastising them along with the mayor." James was uncertain if he would run, and one journalist wrote, "So buy yourself a seat. Booker versus James was one of the best political shows around four years ago. It should be even better this time, if, that is, the old lion comes out to fight."[60]

James hinted for months that he had his petitions ready, though the deadline was not until the end of March. During his State of the City speech in early February, James highlighted his fifth-term accomplishments, including getting 500 guns off the streets and increasing real estate values in parts of the city. Throughout his speech, audience members chanted "four more years," yet that evening James never said whether he would run again.[61] James' political theater continued into March 2006. He held a fundraiser and sent petitions to the city clerk, but he did not have the required number of signatures to certify his candidacy. Also, for weeks, James remained silent about whether he would run again, he had no campaign team or headquarters, and, sadly, there was little public debate about the issues. Booker remained committed to running for the mayoral position, however, and attacked the leadership inside City Hall. In addition, one of the city's largest employee unions, Service Employees International Union Local 617, came out in support of Booker. At the same time, Deputy Mayor and State Senator Ronald Rice had quietly filed petitions to run for mayor.[62] As the filing deadline approached, speculation as to whether James would be running again had the rumor mill churning. On March 16, just minutes before the City Clerk's office closed, James, wearing shorts and a straw hat and carrying petitions with nearly 10,000 signatures, rode a police bicycle inside City Hall. However, he refused to declare himself a candidate.[63] As the *Star-Ledger* correctly predicted in an editorial following this episode, "It's unlikely the bicycle stunt will be his last trick."[64] In fact, not until the end of the month did James admit he did not want his name to appear on the May ballot.

James Leaves the Race and Rice Continues Politics

The last two weeks of March proved to be just as unpredictable as the first two months. James' deputy mayor, Ronald Rice, admitted that he would stay on the ballot, unless James was going to run again. Rice also attacked Booker and not James. Rice refused to "say a negative word" against James. "He's not my opponent," Rice suggested. "There's a window of opportunity for candidates to no longer be a candidate. It means he may drop out, or I might drop out. I'd like to see Cory drop out."[65] For Newark residents and the media, figuring out who would be on the ballot was more prominent than discussions of local issues. Instead, much focus was on James and Rice and which of the two would actually run or if they would challenge each other as well as Booker. James' "skittishness" as the *New York*

Times called his stance "clearly affected the race…. There is little talk here in this still-struggling city of 280,000 about competing visions, or about which candidate's proposals are most likely to cure the city's festering ills of poverty and crime." As a result, Booker challenged both James and Rice since he called their delay tactics political so there would be a shorter race.[66] For his part, Rice was unsure of the mayor's standing. Rice even resigned from his deputy mayor post because he was required to take a leave of absence while campaigning but he remained State Senator.[67]

Not surprisingly, on the day of the ballot drawing to determine the order of the candidates' names, Newark's anomalous politics brought even more revelations. Several council members were visibly upset that Booker sued the city and distributed literature stating that the council apportioned $80 million to help nonprofit organizations that would benefit them, including James' organization for redeveloping Newark. Some council members even filed a defamation suit against Booker. Councilman Ras Baraka (Amiri Baraka's son) commented, "[I]t makes it look like the council and mayor have made a deal to take care of ourselves in case we don't make it to office." And Council President Donald Bradley decided to withdraw his name for reelection, blaming Booker. "It's terrible when someone tries to destroy your reputation after 69 years in the city," argued Bradley.[68] Only a couple of days later, just as the mayoral election ballots were going to the printers, James requested his name be removed from the ballot. He sent a letter to the City Clerk's office stating that he would "not be a candidate for re-election in the 2006 Newark Municipal election and hereby request that my name be removed from the ballot." He said that Newark is "healthy, well and primed to continue to be the leading city in New Jersey under the right leadership."[69] James also disclosed that he wanted to be a full-time State Senator and not be Newark's mayor at the same time as he suddenly opposed holding dual office (since New Jersey's laws allow for an official to hold multiple public offices).[70] Surprisingly, after writing the letter, James refused numerous interviews. His decision to drop out of the race confused many Newark residents and political watchers. As Professor Price said of these events,

> It's an anticlimactic closure to one of the more fascinating political careers in the history of urban politics. I must admit I'm confused. I thought he might do what political leaders tend to do and seize the moment of departure by articulating what he wants for Newark's future and what (he) contributed to Newark's past.[71]

However, James' decision also brought about serious complications. He was a formidable local leader with a vast amount of political power and clout.[72] The city suddenly did not have an incumbent mayor running for office, which is a rarity in Newark. This created a political vacuum for mayoral leadership in City Hall just six weeks before the election.[73] As a matter of fact, half of the James 2002 campaign team and several prominent labor unions had already defected to Booker, leaving Rice uncertain of victory. Few issues were discussed between the candidates, forcing voters to figure out how the candidates stood on local issues. Many residents were unsure whether to support Booker or Rice or other candidates on the ballot, such as businessman David Blount and Socialist Worker Party candidate Nancy Rosenstock.

James' late decision hurt Rice and equally helped Booker. Rice waited to see if James would drop out of the race, hoping to gain James' support. Rice did file petitions by the March deadline, though he filed them months after Booker filed petitions. In addition, Rice did not have a campaign office and raised little campaign money. This left the former deputy mayor and State Senator in a poor position to win the race. As the *New York Times* said of Rice, "He is entering the race at a tremendous disadvantage, having waited patiently for Mr. James to make up his mind about running before beginning his own campaign in earnest." On the day James dropped out of the race, Rice mentioned that his campaign was working on opening two campaign offices in the South Ward, where many James supporters lived.

Finally on March 28, Rice held a press conference to announce his official candidacy for mayor. He promised to protect city employees from firings or any reforms Booker was advocating. Rice also gained the support of the Newark Teachers' Union and three incumbent council members.[74] There were nearly 260 appointments to more than 30 boards and commissions, and many of these employees had been beholden to the James political machine for decades. Rice immediately tried to secure this base. Michael Preston argues that this is the nature of the political machine and "machine politicians use those things that are a their disposal—patronage jobs, personnel appointments inside the administration. It's a simple matter of paying your dues. If you are part of the organization, get out and help; then you have a job."[75] But, after James dropped out of the race, Rice did not promptly request an endorsement of his candidacy from James; at that time, Rice had only $42,000 in campaign funds while Booker had $4 million.

Without James at the helm, orchestrating this campaign, how were city employees to vote in the 2006 election? Considering the political leverage James possessed, many city employees had been hesitant to support other candidates. "If somebody like (James) has been powerful and leaves on good terms, what he does is turn the machine over to someone else. If not, he will release everybody," argues political scientist Ronald Walters. In Newark, many city employees not only give much of their time to support their mayor, they also donate significantly to their mayor's campaigns. For instance, the *Star-Ledger* revealed that from 1998 to 2005, 30 percent of the $2.4 million James raised for his campaigns was given by city employees.[76]

One campaign strategy Rice picked up from James was attacking Booker personally—a tactic that carried over from the 2002 election. Like James, Rice questioned Booker's political motives. "I think people should be asking questions about how someone who just finished college and popped into Newark can be become a savior."[77] Even days after announcing his candidacy, Rice said that Booker was not genuine and could not be trusted. "If Saddam Hussein came here and played on people's frustrations by giving away computers and apple pies, they're going to think he's a wonderful person," said Rice. "They're only going to find out who he really is later. So the real question people have to ask [the candidates] is: Who are we? Why are we here?" Booker responded to Rice's attack by stating that Rice was oversimplifying policy approaches. "It's a shame that Ron Rice would bring up a known terrorist who slaughtered thousands of innocent people. This city does not need that kind of campaigning. We had enough of that in the past." Attacks continued that week, however, and personal references to Booker gave many voters a feeling of déjà vu, according to the *Star-Ledger*:

> In likening Booker to the Redcoats, Rice fashions himself as a "field general" who will "protect our city" from "outsiders" just as George Washington's army once repelled the British he said. "I'm the most experienced candidate in the race to take Newark to the next level. I know where we've come from, where we are, where we're going. The people are looking for someone who has been a part of Newark and who is from Newark, not someone who just showed up here.[78]

While Rice sharpened his rhetoric, Booker's idealistic politics matured, and he seemed more hardened as a candidate than in the previous election. This time, Booker incorporated fewer statistics and less historical information into his speeches. He received more money from the city's contracting businesses that had once supported James, and he hired seasoned campaign officials like Oscar James (no relation) from Sharpe James' campaign. Oscar James was legendary for reelecting Mayor James by playing up Booker's outsider image and causing voters, especially those in the South Ward, to doubt him; now Oscar James was working for the other side. Booker also refrained from highlighting Newark's overwhelming problems of poverty and crime. It appeared Booker had become more seasoned. As the *New York Times* observed, only four years before "Cory Booker was a 32-year-old idealistic insurgent, a Don Quixote from the suburbs who assailed Mayor Sharpe James as the dictatorial leader of a political machine that suppressed Newark's true potential." He used fewer statistics, made few references to his education, and lessened his ties with the media. As Clement Price noted, "He is more mature and more hardened as a political personality than he was four years ago when he seemed to be running on the winds of idealism." In essence, Booker became a different kind of candidate for the 2006 mayoral race.[79]

In April, a poll revealed Booker's standing among the candidates, including his strongest opponent, Ronald Rice. If James had remained in the race, the Blum and Weprin Associate telephone survey revealed, it would have been a tight race. More than half of voters supported James and the job he was doing in City Hall. However, "[o]nly 30 percent of the respondents who said they voted for James in 2002 said they would vote for Rice this time. By comparison, 44 percent of James voters said they would now back Booker." Booker lead in every demographic group, according to the poll, whether by age, race, or education; this was largely because his campaign had started early, as opposed to Rice, who had gotten a late start and had achieved little citywide name recognition. Rice said that the survey results were an example of how Booker was taking over the city and that he was in the campaign to run against Booker. Admittedly, Rice mentioned that, "people don't know that we're running, and we're just starting to get out the word."[80] The poll also revealed that 36 percent felt that they did not know enough about Booker. Considering that 25 percent of those polled were unsure whom they would vote for and the election was a month away, Booker's campaign believed they had to do more to get his agenda out to Newarkers. However, a higher number of those polled said that they were unfamiliar with Rice's politics. And since many voters do not begin to follow the race until two weeks before the election, Rice barely had any time to deliver his message to many potential voters.[81]

Also, Rice lagged behind other candidates in setting up his campaign office; he finally opened it on April 8—only a month before the mayoral election. Rice still did not get the financial or political backing that Mayor James had gotten in the previous election. Instead, Rice focused on questioning Booker's politics and the money that Booker raised for his campaign. "I don't know what these political relationships are. Something's not right with this picture. Maybe I'm not a rocket scientist, but I can tell when something smells. And it stinks," Rice said of Booker's connections. In addition, Rice still cast Booker as an outsider. From his newly opened Bergen Avenue campaign office, Rice's new slogan said the deputy mayor is "from Newark. Dedication, time, commitment."[82] Rice told the press he wanted to have six debates with Booker, but only one, on May 3, was actually scheduled. Rice attempted to do what James succeeded in doing during the 2002 election: politicizing Booker's background. However, Rice had to work without James' endorsement and with little campaign money. Rice challenged Booker's stance on school vouchers, for instance, claiming that Booker's suburban, educated background meant that he was not "black enough" and, thus, that Booker was unaware of the true issues in Newark's public schools. Moreover, Rice charged that Booker was a proxy for "ultra-white, ultra-conservative outsiders" who were trying to privatize Newark's public schools. Booker responded that his "determination is to reform the public school, but I will never oppose programs that help children." Nevertheless, Rice lambasted Booker, calling him the "New Jersey point-person of the far-right wing of the Republican Party," especially with Booker's speech to a conservative Manhattan Institute think tank in 2000.[83]

Booker largely glossed over Rice's charge about his campaign finances, and, for the most part, he tried to ignore the school vouchers concern. In fact, by mid-April, Booker acted as though he was operating a political machine by not addressing specific issues and instead focusing on fundraising efforts. The *Star-Ledger* noted that Booker was advancing his politics by having a $200 per head April fundraiser for Newark police and firefighters, a tactic similar to one James used in the 2002 race.[84] The editorial questioned his boss-like politics, claiming that Booker was becoming like James:

> We hope Booker is not starting to look like James, The Sequel. Considering Booker's war chest now tops $4 million in a race in which his opponent, Sen. Ron Rice has

$131,000, it's hard to understand the need for this level of fundraising. Couple that with a secret meeting with James that Booker acknowledges took place but won't elaborate on, and his $1,000-a-person fundraiser in Manhattan Monday night—an event from which the press was barred—and voters have to wonder whether he'll deliver on the open government he has so earnestly promised. So far, the signs are not encouraging.[85]

Support from Newark's various public, nonprofit, and private sectors varied between the candidates in both elections. Traditionally, these endorsements are important not just in terms of fundraising but also in gaining volunteers to help elect public officials.[86] In Newark especially, these organizations are effective in getting voters out to the polls. Because the mayoral elections focused on racial and machine politics, these organizations' support spoke volumes about their racial and political interests. Since the 2002 election centered on James and Booker, endorsements from unions and government employees went solidly to James, though it could be argued that James might have coerced this political support. Whereas Booker had support only from the firefighters in the 2002 election, he received more union endorsement in the 2006 election after James bowed out of the race. In 2002, the Newark Firefighters Union endorsed Booker largely to spite James. The firefighters were unable to negotiate a new contract with the James administration, and, in an effort to counter City Hall, union officials decided to back Booker. The firefighters were further for not supporting James as negotiations did not take place for many months. As union president David Giordano commented, "This is the worst political retaliation I've ever seen."[87] The firefighters were the only public union to support Booker in the 2002 election. However, a Black firefighters group, the Vulcan Pioneers, endorsed James. John West, the president of the Vulcan Pioneers, argued that Booker "embraces fellas who don't live here." West's perspective reflected that of some officials who believed that James supported Newarkers—something James embraced and carried over in racial politics, reminding supporters that he might not have received the endorsement from all firefighters, but he had the Black organization's nod. In addition, the majority of Newark's unions supported James' candidacy because, under his political machine, he controlled the political levers.[88]

Was union support for James swayed by machine and racial politics? No doubt James put pressure on the unions as it was his City Hall. But there was also pressure from Booker, and Booker often argued that James was dictatorial with his political power. "The mayor is trying to win an election with intimidation and bullying," he told the *New York Times*. And the paper revealed that there were dozens of reports of intimidation and harassment tactics. "In numerous interviews, municipal workers and those who do business with City Hall said they strenuously avoided even the slightest hint of disloyalty." Marshall Curry's documentary, *Street Fight*, focuses on James' political clout and how he obtained support from unions and organizations to win the 2002 election. James' victory in 2002 may have been a result of his machine politics or his publicized image as "the real deal." He demanded loyalty across the board, even from city council candidates whom he supported. In addition, unions and businesses supported the incumbent mayor as they provided a third of his campaign budget. The last thing James and his officials wanted were outsiders coming in and taking over Newark's City Hall; this had a trickle-down effect in terms of local and racial politics. Any appearances of disloyalty translated into a questioning of commitment to not only the city and the mayor but also racial and class politics because Booker was the antithesis of many Newarkers, according to James.[89]

Not surprisingly, the Newark Teachers Union (with 5,000 members) supported James' 2002 campaign, as did the police union, local government, and construction unions (the Service Employees International Union with 4,000 members and the New Jersey Laborers Union with 1,900 members).[90] Therefore, in 2002, James received overwhelming support from unions and businesses having contracts with the city, while Booker's support came from the firefighters union. In the 2006 election, however, James opted not to run for reelection. Because James did not endorse Rice until two weeks prior to the election, many unions supported Booker instead. Most importantly, the only organization that remained firmly against Booker was the Newark Teachers Union. They supported James and Rice in both elections as Booker openly campaigned for education vouchers in Newark's public schools. Many considered the Newark Teachers Union lack of support for Booker to be detrimental to his campaign efforts in both elections. James, the teachers union, and countless others considered that Booker's stance on vouchers meant that he was "a tool of white conservatives—a suburbanite who was not black enough to lead what has long been considered one of the African-American capitals of the United States." Similar to Baltimore, Newark's public school teachers and administrators are overwhelmingly Black and middle class, while over 80 percent of the students are either Black or Latino. So the Newark Teachers Union was a powerful entity that helped garner momentum in Newark's Black communities, especially during mayoral elections. The Newark Teachers Union even placed ads against Booker around the city during the elections and during his first term in office. The Newark Teachers Union and the Vulcan Pioneers were especially poignant about racial politics. In fact, the teachers union latched onto James' and Rice's attacks on Booker for his support of private school vouchers. Union officials endorsed James' and Rice's rhetoric that Booker embraced White conservative politics. To have one of the largest unions in Newark support James and Rice in their attempts to racialize Booker's politics proved to be detrimental to Booker's campaigns and demonstrated the racial politics of the elections. While the teachers union backed James, Rice, and their politics against Booker, Booker did little to respond against their charges. Instead, Booker rarely discussed his intentions publicly and only pointed out that "public education is the use of public dollars to educate our children at the schools that are best equipped to do so" whether they are religious or independent schools.[91]

The *Star-Ledger* and *New York Times* examined Booker's reform agenda, even comparing James with Booker in a series of quotes about their policies. Interestingly, many journalists and City Hall watchers thought that voters could replace one political machine with another. Jessica Trounstine stated, "[I]t's interesting in machine cities that what you often find is a person who runs to reform the machine and then they realize it's just much easier to keep the machine going. Machines create structures that help government work. What often happens is someone comes in with good intentions and finds it much easier to insert themselves into the structure that has already been created." Trounstine's point about machine politics describes generations of Newark's government. Many Newarkers and New Jerseyans have come to rely on some political machine in their respective City Halls, and thousands of people have benefited from these machines. Whether Irish, Italian, old-guard Black machines, or the one Booker appeared to be establishing, Newark relied on some form of machine leadership. The problem, however, rests with the fact that many residents and county and state taxpayers do not have a direct connection to Newark's politics. A political machine can flourish in a city like Newark because there is a large political disconnect between the city and the residents of the suburbs and the state as a whole. However, New Jersey residents are connected to the city in more ways than they think: One out of eight state residents have lived or worked in the city; nearly a million people annually visit the New Jersey Performing Arts Center (NJPAC), the Newark Museum, or Bears Stadium; and, most importantly, the city receives a significant amount of money from outside the city (for every dollar spent by the city, 81 cents is not *from* the city).[92]

The city is hardly self-sufficient, and Newark residents' decision about who the next mayor would be affected many people beyond the city. Sadly, many Essex County and state residents fail to see their connection to the city. As North Ward Newark political consultant Steve Adubato reminds New Jerseyans, "If you don't care about Newark, you're brain-damaged. People sitting in their suburbs who think what happens in Newark doesn't affect them are idiots. Even if you're totally selfish, even if you're not socially conscious at all, even if you're just practical, you should still be concerned with what happens in Newark."[93]

Some suburbanites claim that Adubato's statement is harsh, and they see the city still mired in mediocrity. The leadership of the city should be questioned, say some Essex County residents, who mostly pay for the city's survival. As one suburbanite offered, "The city's leaders seem incapable of inspiring their constituents to reach their true potential."[94] Nevertheless, the mayor helps lure the private sector to the central city so there will be some semblance of a financial foundation for the city's budget. James did this as mayor for 20 years, but he only aided some sections of downtown Newark and some suburban residents who commuted to these areas. Therefore, by the end of the 2006 election, Booker and Rice tried to center their political agendas around community development.

Community Development Politics

One of the most important incentives to spur redevelopment, especially in downtown Newark, was the creation of the light rail line, which opened in summer 2006. Ideally, public transit would allow riders (particularly suburban visitors and tourists) to get to public venues like NJPAC, Bears Stadium, the Newark Museum, and the future Devils' hockey arena. According to Kenneth Jackson, Newark "ha[d] already been on a bit of a roll," and the new transit line would gain additional development projects for the city and add to property values.[95] Conventional wisdom suggests that if developers saw the potential of the light rail, they would invest in the city—something that the James administration and the Rice and Booker campaigns all tried to capitalize on. Yet the three politicians had different visions of the light rail and how the city would develop in the future. Rice embraced the James vision of a gradual revitalization of Newark. Having specific developers involved in the city's plan to renew parts of the city would ensure a common vision, according to Rice. Booker saw this select group as hindering Newark's redevelopment progress and preventing the city from hiring people outside of the city and county. "Developers from all over the country don't want to come to Newark to do the right kind of projects because they believe a very small circle of people who are connected to the elected get the things done," Booker stressed. Instead, Booker suggested that if he were elected, he would review various public and private projects to make sure that they were meeting cost expectations and that there were no political connections associated with the construction contracts. He especially wanted to this kind of review of the Devils' hockey arena construction, though he was not in favor of this project. The *Star-Ledger* discovered that much of the land for that arena was sold at an unusually low rate. "[E]ven with real estate values soaring, the city continues to discount land [for developers], translating into big profits for the dozen or so developers who won most of the no-bid contracts, and still indiscriminately awards the tax abatements."[96] The one thing Booker and Rice agreed on, however, was that construction companies needed to find innovative ways to build affordable housing and pass the costs onto buyers.

Understanding the two candidates' community development plans proved important for city residents, but many voters were more interested in the headlines that James made in April. Only weeks after declaring he would not seek a fifth term as mayor, James agreed to return to his previous post at Essex County College, from which he had been on a leave of absence for over 20 years. James would be the director at the college's new Urban Issues Institute, earning nearly $150,000, while still serving as the Newark's state senator in Trenton.[97] While many Black mayors leave office with few career options, James' situation was different, especially since urban problems and community development politics are persistent issues in cities like Newark.[98] A more problematic headline for James centered on the state's freeze of all finances related to the $80 million for development projects, including money going to James' nonprofit foundation. The state's Department of Community Affairs also questioned the city's contributions to the Newark Symphony Hall and the Newark Public Library. James fired back at state officials, declaring that the city should be ruled by city lawmakers. "I believe for the first time in the history of this state you have state government interfering with local government for political reasons. This is a dangerous precedent for all local governments." A spokesman for the Department of Community Affairs denied James' charges. Booker denied that he was involved with this financial scandal, even though James said that Booker knew about the money since Booker and James' meeting, which took place before James dropped out of the election. "James is a liar," responded Booker. "He is using the meeting as a politically convenient tool. The meeting was very cordial."[99]

The squabble was really between state and city governments. Yet James, who was not seeking reelection against his former challenger, was in the media spotlight. Booker also joined the fight, suing to prevent the city from dispersing city funds to questionable projects. Booker said that the mayor's response to the state put City Hall "in danger of further abusing public trust, public process and the law. This is the public's money, not theirs." The *New York Times* concluded that "the plans, as approved, lacked rules defining how grants would be awarded or how long trustees would serve, giving the mayor potential clout to influence events in Newark...."[100] The newspaper later said, "[T]he state acted correctly."[101] James appeared to be a political boss as he served on the board of one of the newly created development nonprofit groups. He denied the charge. "I'm not a boss. I'm not a machine. I'm here as a duly elected official...."[102] Ultimately, an unprecedented yet racially charged and very tense meeting occurred between Governor John Corzine, James, and the Municipal Council, and certain funds were released to the Newark government, while Newark agreed to rescind the creation of the nonprofit groups.[103]

A more potent April headline concerned an attack by James on Booker, where James called the fire and police unions' fundraisers for Booker an example of "the worst abuse that you can have." James mocked Booker's practices, even though James had used similar tactics as mayor, requiring city employees to donate to his past mayoral campaigns. James asked, if there's a Guns and Hoses fundraiser, why not a Pumps and Pipes gala for utility employees or a Calculators and Computers party for those in finance? At the same time, James criticized the police union because they decided to support Booker; Fraternity Order of Police (FOP) president Derrick Hatcher responded, saying his speech was "sad and distasteful."[104] The next day Booker attacked James for giving away the city's land to politically connected developers. It appeared *Street Fight II* was in the making or that James and Booker were back in the 2002 election, even though James had dropped out of the race three weeks earlier. The 2006 election was only ten days away when Booker held a news conference telling residents and the media that the James administration had sold property for $1 a square foot.[105] Booker stood by a parcel of land that City Hall sold for $87,000; at market rates, he charged, it would have sold for $3.7 million. "No one has taken a step back and said, 'Wait a second, is this what's best?' These decisions are being made by developers, based on greed," argued Booker.[106] Booker's accusation made development politics the focal point of the 2006 election. The press coverage centered on this issue, and many Newark residents became increasingly concerned that the city government was losing money while at the same time had sold city property at below-market prices to politically connected developers and donors. And these parcels were not just in outlying areas or neighborhoods; much of it was in downtown commercial areas.[107]

When Booker pointed out the development politics surrounding the sale of the city's land, he transformed the direction of the election. Instead of directly attacking Rice, Booker challenged James head-on, as though the mayor were running for reelection. Thus, James and allies like Rice appeared uninterested in the majority of the city and only helpful to their supporters, such as developers. Moreover, in the 2002 election, Booker had been accused of wanting to aid outside developers because he was not from Newark and he received much of his money from non-Newarkers; however, many of the developers receiving these city parcels from James' administration were not from Newark. Booker took James' previous charge and turned it on him, without James even being in the race this time. As political scientist Ross Baker observed about the land deals, it was an easy target to discuss during the campaign season. "I think anybody looking at that would say that $1 a square foot for downtown Newark is absurd."[108]

What followed that week were cries for reform. Many public officials grew concerned about this issue and called for a moratorium on city land sales. Even Booker's political enemies, like Councilman Ras Baraka, questioned the sales; Baraka said, "[W]e have to slow up that process a little bit and get a return on our investment."[109] However, Baraka also stressed that Booker's motives for highlighting the sales was political: "These kinds of statements are borderline accusing people of being unethical." Other council members argued that property costs had to be reduced for developers, otherwise investors would not be interested in the property. For example, Councilwoman Mamie Bridgeforth said that "whole neighborhoods were decimated," especially since the 1967 riots, including parts of her west ward community. "If we are at a point now where we have defeated the negative image of Newark, do we increase land costs? But at what cost?" Bridgeforth questioned.[110] While many of James' allies defended the property policy, Rice for the most part agreed with Booker. Rice also mentioned that he was unaware of all the particulars of the land sales, and he left the issue alone. Thus, Rice was not on the offensive and he did not separate himself from James. James publicly endorsed Rice, his loyal deputy mayor, that week but not until just days before the election. James also did not attend a planned stumping event for Rice.[111]

Days Before the Election

James waited three weeks before he endorsed Rice, and his endorsement came at an awkward time in the 2006 election, when James' community development policies were being debated. Most importantly, during this election, James and Booker made the headlines, and Rice was often in the shadows; indeed, many voters were unaware that Rice was even running. If anything, this fact demonstrates the difficult situation Rice faced. As one political watcher observed, Rice's time to be mayor was 15 or 20 years ago. "But politics is all about timing and his is terrible," argued Walter Fields, a former NAACP political director.[112] Clement Price adds that Rice "may have stood in the shadows too long."[113] Rice even admitted that he should have run in 1994 as he lost to James in 1998.[114] As James had once said about that election, he "fried Rice" in the upset.[115] Hence, James and Rice had an off-again and on-again political relationship. Or as the *Star-Ledger* put it, Rice's political "life has continued to be steered by James, his sometime-advocate, sometime-adversary and full-time foil."[116]

So Rice had the political credentials to run for mayor but had poor timing, even securing James' endorsement barely two weeks before the election.[117] Rice's son, Ronald C. Rice, Jr., who ran on Booker's ticket for city council, said that his father "was loyal to his detriment. [James] has such a sway over the electorate. Any realistic chance my dad has as mayor is based on getting support from Sharpe James' army. You are forced into this situation where you want to inherit his organization and it's unfair."[118] Rice also remained committed to James' approach of making personal attacks against Booker. Rice told the *New York Times*, for instance, that Booker was involved in "a conspiracy to take over the government, not for the interests of the people but merely to privatize the public education and alter other policies that affect people of color, like Affirmative Action." He further questioned Booker's commitment and even racial complexion:

> "Don't you know who Mr. Booker is? Coming out of nowhere with his academic spin? 'I went to college. I'm a Rhodes Scholar. I got a lot of money coming in'.... People vote. And we know that in Newark. And we know when we're being bought.... What's he running for?" he asked, without waiting for an answer. "Where's he running to? Or where's he running from? But nobody wants to know. The media says but don't talk about that. That's not important. Well you know what? To you it's not important but to the people that have to live here, it is very important because the biggest mistake we can make is to turn this city over to someone who is not worthy." He said voters were constantly telling him, "'You can't let him in here.'" He added that "some people" have told him that Mr. Booker, a light-complexioned African American running in a city more than 80 percent minority, looks strange. "You know in terms of his eyes," Mr. Rice said.

Booker responded that Rice's politics were personal and that there had not been an adequate discussion of the issues, even though they agreed on some policies. Rice, however, stressed that their differences went beyond policy approaches. "Well, No. 1, you don't have the C.E.O. of a major corporation just come out of college. O.K.? So it's a matter of experience, No. 1." The *New York Times* concluded that, "Mr. Rice has had a hard time articulating a clear policy rationale for his candidacy in the May 9 election. And listening to him can at times seem like being in a time warp as he returns to the rhetorical flourishes the mayor [Sharpe James] employed against Booker four years ago."[119]

Rice's focus on attacking Booker and lack of focus on political issues backfired on him and his campaign. The *New York Times* and the *Star-Ledger* endorsed Booker, largely because Rice employed James' tactics from the 2002 election. According to the *Star-Ledger*, voters should support Booker because he "exudes a reformer's zeal and promises an ethical government that residents can respect." The paper's editorial board further stated that "the next mayor also should expect to battle the favored few developers who have grown fat building high priced houses on land they got cheap from the city."[120] On the other hand, the *New York Times* admitted, "Mr. Booker himself remains something of a question mark. His political career, after all, consists of a single term on the Municipal Council."[121]

The most important local concern remained crime. For decades, the city had had high burglary, assault, and murder rates. With almost 7,000 former inmates coming back to Newark during the next mayor's term, making sure they did not get arrested again was also a general concern.[122] Both candidates stated that ex-offenders should get the help they needed and that funding for halfway houses and job training should be increased. However, Rice claimed that Booker "knows nothing about fighting crime," and that as a former Marine and Newark police officer, he himself had a solid plan. Even though both candidates wanted a larger police force, their programs differed in some respects. Rice did not specify the number of new police officers he wanted to hire, and Booker was unsure of costs.[123]

Education was also a divisive issue in Newark, yet there was little debate about education between the candidates until only a few days before the election. The Newark Teachers Union supported Rice because Booker was not opposed to a tuition voucher system for private school education. However, the city's schools had been under state control since 1995 so the mayor could make little actual reform. Booker argued that he would seek more mayoral control of the operation of schools if possible. In contrast, considering that Rice had supported the state takeover as a council member, he did not want to get in the way of the state government and the state-appointed superintendent.[124] Yet education policy experts Jean Anyon and Alan Sadovnik argued that reforming the problematic school system needed to be the most crucial task for the future mayor. If the new mayor failed to comprehend the importance of the community in this effort, then school reform would be the greatest challenge facing Newark. With the schools' low proficiently rates and low graduation rates, they argued, "Newark's new mayor, buoyed by mayoral control over schools in cities like New York and Chicago, may eventually seek legislative action to duplicate that feat. Before doing so, however, he should weigh carefully the evidence on the effectiveness of mayoral control, which to date is mixed. Nor is it a realistic option until Newark is returned to local control." Anyon and Sadovnik concluded that the new mayor needed to make his office a bully pulpit for education and "to develop a plan for urban educational improvement that recognizes that an entire community, not just the school system, is responsible for the education of its children."[125]

Housing finally became an important issue toward the end of the 2006 mayoral race. Because the Housing Authority had been corrupt for decades and, during the election, it was under federal review by the US Department of Housing and Urban Development for missing federal funds, tenants demanded reform. Rice and Booker, as politicians and community leaders, had a similar approach to address the public housing crisis. However, Rice wanted to bring back the citywide Tenants Council and let local tenant associations be more active, while Booker wanted more code enforcement.[126]

The candidates were finally discussing the issues of housing, education, crime, and unemployment in late April. A number of newspaper articles had highlighted these issues, especially the labor gap problems: Newark was the second poorest city of its size in the nation, and almost half of the city's working age population was unemployed. A series of debates was finally scheduled just before the election. Besides Booker and Rice, two lesser-known candidates attempted to enter the fray. Socialist Worker Party Nancy Rosenstock and businessman David Blount campaigned, but received little attention. Although Rosenstock tried to discuss employment and labor rights (especially at her campaign table at the Broad and Market Streets' bus exchange), her agenda was relatively unappealing to most voters. She spoke more about Marxism and Iraq than about specific local issues like education and crime in Newark. As for Blount, he stressed his neighborhood roots and promised that, as Executive Director of the University Heights Science Park Residents, Inc., he would make housing, crime, and education his policy focus as mayor.[127]

The first event where all four candidates debated was a Rutgers University–Newark forum on May 2. Because Booker did not attend the Greater Newark Chapter of the League of Women Voters debate a week earlier (and audience members questioned his politics), he came to the Rutgers debate, which featured high school students' questions. At first Rice, Blount, and Rosenstock asked why Booker had $6 million in campaign funds and why outside donors wanted to give money to a Newark mayoral candidate. Booker responded that he was proud to get broad-based support. But much of the debate was concentrated on Booker and Rice and their politics. At the end of the debate, however, Blount's stirring closing remarks interested the crowd the most. "You can go down one road and that can lead you to gentrification," he warned. "Or you can go down another road that will lead you to more of the same. Or you can follow me and I can lead you to the promised land!"[128]

The next day, during the only televised debate, the candidates continued to make similar exchanges. Once again Blount and Rosenstock were not the focus of attention, but Rice's and Booker's politics took center stage. Instead of addressing key issues, they attacked one another. Booker called Rice's deputy mayor post a "do nothing and say nothing position" and said that if he were elected mayor he would try to eliminate the job—which a former governor thought was a clever idea.[129] Booker asked how Rice could be effective as mayor, considering that Rice had remained silent about the city's development projects and the questionable $80 million given to selected nonprofits. Rice attacked Booker for staging an outdoor hunger strike as a councilman to get the media to focus on drug problems in his Central Ward. Rice asked if anything had changed in the area since then.[130] Booker mocked Rice's arguments, claiming that Rice was coming close to James' bullying style. In his opening remarks, Booker stressed his connection to Newark. As the *New York Times* noted, "[T]he comments seemed to offer a nod to how much civic loyalty means here in this struggling city, which is only now beginning to recuperate after decades of declining population and a shrinking economy. And it served as a reminder of the tactics successfully employed by Mr. James four years ago."[131]

Thus, instead of the issues, the 2002 election remained prominent in many voters' minds. Nevertheless, Booker was driven to remind voters that he could address crime, housing, and other urban problems. His promises appeared encouraging to some residents, but voters were aware that, if Booker were elected mayor, he would have a difficult time meeting his own very high expectations.[132] Or, as Richard Roper, former adviser to Ken Gibson, put it, when his boss "was elected (Newark) mayor, the expectations were so high they could not be met. Cory may fall victim to the same thing."[133] Booker's expectations and his overall image as an outsider who was not Black enough continued to resonate with voters. Unfortunately, the negative campaign literature only made it worse. For example, anonymous fliers were distributed around the city before the election, which stated "BOY BOOKER HATES BLACK PEOPLE" and "Warning: Do not vote for Booker—this Nazi Negro republican must Go."[134] As Clement Price responded to these fliers, "The intent of this kind of literature is to emotionalize the campaign. Sometimes it can get very crude. Rhetoric about authenticity and race and origins always works in Newark politics."[135] Even though the 2006 election did not include James this time, it seemed as though there were some remnants of the 2002 election in the 2006 race. As the *Star-Ledger* pointed out about the previous election,

> the contest was bitterly divisive, focusing more on personalities than issues. James called Booker a Republican and questioned if Booker was black enough to lead the city. The sting of some of those comments still lingers...in the end James' strategy worked.[136]

Four years later, in 2006, James' and his supporters' charges against Booker remained. James never truly left the media spotlight. If anything, he took much of the light away from Rice, as they both continued to poke at Booker's background. "People want to write the easy racial narrative in that election and there's so much going on than the issue of race even though the press got intoxicated by Sharpe's racial language," said Booker.[137] But the negative campaigning continued, and Booker was characterized as "a self-aggrandizing interloper ... despite Booker's best efforts, the same questions persist," stated the New York Times.[138] As for Booker's political record, James reminded the press that as a city councilman, Booker was not able to redevelop or revitalize his ward, which could be the case for the city if Booker were elected to City Hall. Rice further stated that Booker "ha[d] no record in the ward, even though he spent four years on the council."[139] With all of the media attention surrounding the race, Rice suggested that the US attorney and state officials monitor the May election because he was concerned that illegal voting activities could occur, which allegedly happened in 2002.[140]

At a Rice fundraiser on the eve of the election, James commented that Booker's candidacy demonstrated that "this is a hostile takeover" and that electing Rice would be the "one way we're going to tell the world we're not as dumb as they think."[141] For his part, Booker continued to slam the James administration by accusing the mayor of leaving Newark in a financial crisis. So while it seemed that Booker and Rice were running against each other, the reality was that the 2006 race was more frequently about Booker against James. The personal politics of the mayor and Booker's idealistic and often defensive politics were continually in the public eye. This made the May 9 election worth watching. Even though James was not running again, "much of the campaign ... amounted to a referendum on his five terms as mayor."[142] The election results were stunning: not only did Cory Booker win by a 72 percent landslide, but there were also significant differences among Black voters.

Election Analysis

In light of the influence the 2002 election had on the 2006 election, it is essential that an analysis of the results address the personal and political conflicts that existed between Cory Booker and Sharpe James. Despite James' decision not to seek reelection in 2006, his political presence was highly visible to the Newark electorate. Recognizing this revolutionary shift in Newark's politics, researchers collected empirical evidence to better understand the mayoral races. The differences between the candidates were extreme. Booker offered an idealistic cultural pluralism, and he emphasized that Newarkers should see beyond Black and White politics. For this, as well as the fact that Booker was raised in the suburbs, he was often cast as an outsider or a non-Newarker, which James politicized, not just in the 2002 race but also in the 2006 election. Even though James was not officially a candidate in the 2006 election, there were moments during that race when he chastised Booker. At the same time, Booker challenged James' community development policies—from selling land at cut rates to developers, mostly outsiders, to giving politically connected nonprofit groups city funding. Did these political challenges influence voters' opinions and their decisions? According to surveys conducted by this author, Booker's and James' politics played a significant role and ultimately did impact voter behavior.

The mayoral candidates introduced racial, generational, and class conflicts into the election; therefore, survey questions largely reflected how much of an impact Sharpe James' and Cory Booker's politics affected voters. The survey was conducted in several Newark locations on Thursday May 4, 2006—five days before the mayoral election. The survey focused on two important questions:

1. How much did the candidates' characteristic considerations (race, age, education) influence a Newark voter's decision?
2. Did a candidate's disparagement of his opponent's background impact a Newark voter's decision?

Surveys were conducted randomly and respondents were asked to fill out surveys on a clipboard provided by the surveyor, or the surveyor would ask the questions and record the responses. Seventeen surveyors (including this author)[143] conducted the surveys in five Newark locations:

1. Newark's Pennsylvania Train Station is a terminal teeming with Newarkers and nonresidents. It is a transportation hub for Black, White, and Latino residents and many suburbanites who take the New Jersey Transit commuter rail, PATH train, subway, Amtrak, Greyhound, and city buses.
2. The city's main bus transfer location at Broad and Market Streets is frequented by many Black and Latino residents. A large number of Black Newarkers take the bus, and one hundred or more people wait for several bus lines at the Four Corners area of downtown Newark every day.
3. The Gateway Center is a downtown business complex with internal shops, businesses, and corporate offices away from Newark's streets. Several buildings are connected by indoor walkways. The majority of the employees are affluent professionals (lawyers, bankers and architects).
4. Newark's Central Ward Pathmark shopping center is in the center of Newark's Black neighborhoods. This is primarily where the majority of this community's residents shop. This location was the starting point of the 1967 riots and since then remains an impoverished inner-city area with many low-income housing projects.
5. Newark's East Ward Pathmark shopping center is in the heart of the Ironbound neighborhood. This location has a variety of stores and restaurants and is constantly busy. It was once a predominantly Italian enclave, but, within the last forty years, Portuguese and Brazilians have relocated here. In addition, a number of Latinos have also moved to this working-class community.

Altogether, 333 Newark residents, from several communities, completed the survey. A clear majority felt that crime was the most pressing issue. Interestingly in July 2006 following the election, the *Star-Ledger* conducted their own survey, which revealed similar results.

Survey results revealed that Booker received solid support among White and Latino Newarkers. Yet among Blacks, respondents were split and did not readily support Booker. They were uneasy about supporting Booker completely, unlike White and Latino respondents. Instead, much of the Black support in the 2002 election went to James. And, in the 2006 election, Booker's "outsider" image remained in many Black Newarkers' minds. In other words, James proved successful in exploiting Booker's background not just in the 2002 election but also in the 2006 race, even though James was not running in that contest.

Ultimately, these survey results demonstrate the *Star-Ledger*'s assessment of the 2002 election: James "did best in districts identified by the census as having a black majority, while Cory Booker did best in neighborhoods with a Hispanic or white majority."[144] In the 2006 election, Booker received 72 percent of the vote. Just as in 2002, Booker remained strongest in the largely White and Latino North and East Wards, capturing over 65 percent of their votes. While Booker's percentages increased greatly in the Black wards in the 2006 election, only 65 percent of majority Black districts favored Booker. Even in his own home district in the Central Ward, he received less than 50 percent of the votes, possibly because Blount captured some votes as he was from the same ward. In addition, Booker might have won the 2006 election by a landslide, but there was doubt about Booker in many of Newark's Black communities because he was not the overwhelming favorite in these areas.[145] In other words, despite winning higher percentages of Black voters compared to the 2002 election, in the 2006 race, Booker did not receive a higher rate of Black residents' support compared to White and Latino votes. This phenomenon stood out clearly in the survey results. Booker was the heavy favorite among White and Latino respondents in the 2002 and 2006 elections. Yet among Black respondents, he received little support in the 2002 race but considerably more in the 2006 contest, especially after James bowed out. Once again, this demonstrates a racial discrepancy among respondents and points to how effective James' politics were with many Black Newarkers and how ineffective Booker's politics were with that same group.

Among Black voters, and especially among those surveyed, Booker received very little support, for a number of reasons. Booker often responded that he wanted to give back to Newarkers as an elected official, but many Blacks did not trust his intentions.[146] Yet the *Star-Ledger*, finding his politics credible, endorsed Booker in both elections, arguing that residents should put aside any hesitancies about voting for Booker. For Newarkers "to reject Booker because his parents overcame racial barriers and achieved success in the suburbs is beyond parochial," argued the editorial board. "To reject him because he was smart and industrious enough to win scholarships at the nation's best universities is self-defeating. To expect hordes of invading foreigners to flock here if Booker wins is idiotic."[147] Nonetheless, James challenged Booker's education and professional and personal background, and a large share of Black residents sided with their incumbent mayor in 2002 and were reluctant to fully support Booker in 2006. James was successful in casting Booker as an outsider, and the incumbent mayor created his *Real Deal* platform, insinuating that he was a real Newarker (unlike Booker).[148] Booker wanted to advance Newark beyond the city's "gradual" community development approach that James and Rice embraced. James and Rice further challenged Booker's agenda by describing his policies as catering to more outsiders like himself rather than to Newarkers.[149] James successfully raised doubts about Booker's intentions by stressing that Booker received a significant portion of his political financing from non-Newarkers. For his part, Booker argued that he was trying to appeal to a broader base beyond Newark; he called much of his campaign donations "love money."[150]

Booker's response to James' charges was that Newark could do better. From high unemployment and high crime to healthcare and education problems, Newark's residents had numerous concerns that James had failed to address. Not only was Booker pointing out dismal statistical information, many voters felt that he was attacking Newarkers, especially Black Newarkers, and their beloved mayor. As James saw it, Booker was acting as though "the sky was going to fall."[151] James countered Booker's statistical claims and stated that that was what was wrong with having opportunistic outsiders come to City Hall—they would find ways to paint a bleak picture of Newark and the existence of Newarkers.[152] According to James, Booker was saying that James had not done enough as mayor, that all Newarkers were facing dire circumstances, and that Booker would be a shining knight to save their city.[153] This further established a credibility gap for Booker. While Booker found James' attacks galling, "the reality was that when we went to people's door steps, people wanted a safer city, tired of corruption scandals, didn't believe that Sharpe and others needed to get out of here," said Booker. "So on the ground, none of us found race—it was only Sharpe's incredible rhetoric that distracted people of what the issues were in the city. My pollster had never seen anything like it."[154] Still, many thought Booker was not only idealistic, but also politically naive. How could an outsider point out all the flaws of Newark and its public officials, yet aid everyone in the city at the same time? Many Blacks grew even more skeptical when Booker promised that he would find ways to solve crime, unemployment, housing, healthcare, and education problems.[155] Some did believe in Booker's idealistic politics, though Booker tended to overpromise.[156]

Questions about Booker's background were a significant factor in both mayoral elections. For Booker's part, he argued that his internal polls indicated that the attacks against him were insignificant. "You still have people who use race in order to propel their politics. Even the racial rhetoric of Sharpe James during my election, we polled his attacks on me and it wasn't that close but a difference of 7% to 9% of African Americans bought into it."[157] But Black Newarkers were increasingly unsure about, if not skeptical of, Booker. As the surveys revealed, a significant number of Black respondents changed their views about Booker being an outsider between the 2002 election (44 percent not an outsider and 22 percent unsure) and the 2006 election (52 percent not an outsider and 18 percent unsure). Also, a majority of Black respondents disagreed with the statement that Booker was not authentically Black by 57 percent with 24 percent unsure. In other words, among Black respondents, a significant number of voters remained unsure about Booker. There certainly was hesitancy to cast Booker as one of Newark's own, which is important because Blacks make up a majority of the city's population and hold a lot of leverage in city politics.

Black residents' perception of Booker remained fragmented. While more Black residents voted for Booker in 2006 than in 2002, many of them still had reservations about him. This was especially evident when surveyors asked Black residents if Booker was still seen as an outsider. There was little change. "[E]ven with James out of the way," observed the *Star-Ledger*, "Booker's shift from outsider to insider has been slow, and some residents still view him suspiciously."[158] To overlook Black support would be detrimental to any candidate, but Booker had mixed results among Black Newarkers in both elections. And among Black respondents, barely half of them disagreed with the view that Booker was an outsider. A credibility gap still remains for Cory Booker among many Black Newarkers; this proved problematic for Booker in the elections and during his first term as mayor.

3

The Mayors' Identity Politics and Their Political Shortcomings

As illustrated by Newark's history and modern mayoral elections, racial politics has remained a significant aspect of Newarkers' political behavior. Race was an important concern for a good portion of Black Newark voters in 2002 and 2006. Yet how these voters and the candidates viewed one another varied greatly. As the previous chapter showed through the survey results, Cory Booker was not popular among Black voters. Not only did he have to fend off attacks from Sharpe James and James' supporters over his identity as a Black man, Booker also had to offer voters some proof that he was not just a Black candidate but a post-racial candidate. By emphasizing that he would not be a racial politics candidate, however, did he reinforce that race was not a paramount issue for him? Booker recognized race along historical and anecdotal lines, but he rarely disclosed personal accounts related to race—unless he was provoked by Sharpe James. James saw race as a significant concern in the mayoral elections as well as in local politics. He argued that Booker was politically unaware of race and not Black enough. In other words, these two candidates were at opposite ends of the racial politics spectrum; James capitalized on Black political insurgency from the past, and Booker sought to disassociate himself from racial politics.

While Booker was enigmatic to many Black Newarkers, Sharpe James evoked Newark's racial experience. James was well versed in Newark's history and regarded racial challenges as empowering experiences. During the elections, he frequently introduced the topic of the 1960s riots and the civil rights movement in Newark. James stressed his own involvement in these revolutionary moments, from being elected to the city council in 1970 to his election as mayor in 1986. James successfully reminded Newarkers that he was one of the first Black leaders in community and City Hall politics, and he enumerated his prior achievements. Many Black Newarkers could therefore easily identify with James and his politics. In other words, James was successfully positioned himself as a leader for Newarkers, particularly Black Newarkers, because he combined history, politics, and race, whereas Booker distanced himself politically and personally from Newark's history and racial politics.

James expressed his racial politics by attaching himself to local racial history and arguing that he embodied Newark's politics. He thought racial typecasting or racialism was an inherent part of urban politics in a city that represented racial political strife. By incorporating James' racial political outlook with the persona he was famous for, the titan mayor easily translated racial politics into Newark's politics. James, after all, was convincing and dynamic, and his ideas resonated with so many Newarkers that it's not surprising Booker lost the 2002 election. James' approach was significant because many Black Newarkers still remembered the city's transformational milestones: the 1960s riots, the 1970s teachers' strikes, and the 1980s redevelopment initiatives. And James was an active participant during these watershed moments in Newark's history. James reminded Black Newarkers where they came from and where they were ultimately headed under his leadership. He was buoyant about Newark's history, and—similar to Gibson—he exaggerated how Newark would lead the way in urban redevelopment. James often claimed that Newark was a city undergoing a renaissance.[1] James' constant cheerleading, as some viewed his politics, was something he reinforced as both a city council member and mayor. In fact, there were several moments when Newark received negative attention or joking commentary and he championed the city. "Time after time, James fiercely defended the city against any negative charge. Anyone who made a superficial judgment (or even a studied appraisal) that the city was dangerous, unmanageable, or worse, a joke, earned his instant attention."[2] James was always on the defensive, refusing to believe Newark was a downtrodden city. He believed that the city was headed toward greatness. James, as a Black mayor in a majority Black city, wanted to disprove naysayers and demonstrate that Newark's urban revival was exemplary.[3] Many Black Newarkers followed their mayor's lead in refuting negative comments about the city's image or history. Therefore, James' racial identity was evident throughout his time as mayor, and many Newarkers appreciated his viewpoint.

Beyond his defense of Newark, what registered most significantly for Black Newarkers was James' life experience. Race and politics were the center of his life—as race was for so many Black Newarkers. James epitomized the local Black civil rights struggle, speaking frequently about the local civil rights movement, and Black Newarkers were familiar with his achievements because many of them went through similar events. As a child, James relocated from the south (Florida) to Newark during the Great Migration. His family was poor, yet James remained determined to be financially and professionally successful. James graduated from nearby Montclair State University and went on to teach in the public school system and later at Newark's Essex County College.[4] As a community activist, James advocated ending police brutality and advanced issues important in his South Ward neighborhood. His life was the quintessence of the Newark *and* the American Dream—that a "poor boy from Howard Street" could be mayor. James embodied Black Newark's recent history, and his racial outlook was apparent in countless ways. James had a dramatic speaking style, and his demeanor was reminiscent of the Black urban experience. He was expressive, dynamic, and captivating in public forums. His speeches were often called stirring and evangelistic.[5] In addition, James was proud of his dancing abilities, as he organized community fairs and political fundraisers in Newark's Black neighborhoods. His line-dancing and electric slide moves were well known, and Black Newarkers were anxious to dance with their mayor at public forums. Even James' campaign song, "He's our mayor—Sharpe James—he's our mayor" had an infectious and certain soulful rhythm to it.[6] His showmanship, even in his legendary State of the City addresses, was dramatic and memorable, including in his final address (when he performed skits, brandished actual guns taken off the street, and showed a short film "From Riot to Renaissance").[7] In other words, if one were to measure racial identity by cultural attributes, James epitomized the urban Black experience, at least outwardly, through his style and charisma. Many Black Newarkers were not only proud of their mayor's expressive nature, but they also considered James one of their own. As S. Craig Watkins notes, "James was clearly the choice of Newark's old black vanguard and citizenry. Newark residents who remembered the struggles of the sixties and the seventies remained steadfast in their support of the man they believed stood by them when the city's race relations reached catastrophic dimensions. James, they believed, understood their hopes and their dreams. He was one of them."[8] James likely had as many supporters as well as enemies, considering his ego and politics. This was plainly apparent when, for instance, the judge presiding over James' corruption trial found that 135 potential jurors agreed that they might be swayed by race, religious, or ethnic bias or had personal sympathy or personal dislike for the mayor.[9]

James demonstrated racial politics in his policymaking by emphasizing that more Blacks and Latinos need to be elected to public office in Newark and Essex County. In addition, he supported a number of Latino candidates for public office, including Councilman Luis Quintana.[10] James also lobbied the city council to confirm a Black police chief, and he employed many Black Newarkers at City Hall. Before the state took over the school district, he wanted Newark's public school system to hire more Blacks. Following the school takeover in 1995, he pushed Black Newarkers to be a part of the education decision-making process. At the height of the 2006 election, the city council passed an $80 million financial package to largely support two nonprofit development foundations with which James was involved. Booker and others filed a lawsuit to have the state freeze these assets. James responded that the state was playing politics and should not interfere with local city government. This issue created a combative atmosphere between Governor Jon Corzine, James, and city council members since James interjected racial politics by arguing that the state government prevented home rule in a majority Black city.[11]

Municipal–state power politics was certainly the theme at the summit between the mayor, council, and governor to discuss what should be done with the $80 million, but race was also a significant factor because the city council and the majority of Newark citizens were Black. James and other officials charged that the state would not interfere in suburban governments' policymaking, so why did they interfere in Newark? According to journalist Joan Whitlow, "I was told the council played the race card at the meeting. As far as I could tell, it was flipping weak deuces…. Why, oh why is the state picking on Newark and not any other city, hamlet or town? Is any other place trying to treat $80 million like petty cash from the municipal piggy bank?"[12] The state's actions appeared racist to some officials, and the meeting was tense with threats of civil disobedience and lawsuits. Some observers, however, viewed James' and other public officials' charges of racism as a reflex. Reverend Reginald Jackson, head of the Black Ministers Council, said an "easy way out is to blame it on racism."[13] In the end, certain funds were released to the Newark government, while Newark's leaders agreed to rescind the creation of the nonprofit groups.[14] There were so many political dynamics at the meeting that it is difficult to decipher the cause of the problem. Were local officials seizing on a financial opportunity? Did Booker and others want to leverage more clout before the election? Did state officials want more political power? Was racism the intrinsic reason for the state's interference? It was a complicated ordeal, and James, along with his supporters, argued that Booker's politics and state officials' racist actions were the villains. Considering Newark's sordid history, it was especially easy for James to claim that state officials' actions were racist. However, James and the city council were the ones who largely politicized this city–state dispute; more than anything else, this episode demonstrates James' use of racial consciousness and his ability to exploit race for political power. This incident was hardly the first time that James highlighted, if not politicized, race. In the 2002 and 2006 mayoral races, James continually emphasized his race consciousness to appeal to Newark's Black voters. The most disconcerting aspect of the 2002 election (and to a certain degree in the 2006 race) was James' attacks on Cory Booker's race, class, and age. James' doubts about Booker became the focus of the mayoral campaigns, and the press concentrated much of their attention on James' demonstration of his racial consciousness and his intra-racial prejudice against Cory Booker. Because the focus of the mayoral races was James' charge that Booker was not Black enough, local issues were rarely discussed.[15]

The elections appeared to be a racial and generational contest between the candidates and little else. Orlando Patterson thought that James' racial consciousness politics helped him win the 2002 election, essentially, that the "black chauvinist card" worked. James frequently misrepresented Booker's background to Newarkers. He stated publicly that Booker was Jewish (when he is Christian), a Republican (when he has been a life-long Democrat), and gay (because he is single). Thus, James charged that Booker was not Black enough or not really Black, which caused the elections, particularly the 2002 race, to become "Blacker-than thou" confrontations.[16] Certainly James, a seasoned politician, sought Black votes, but he also capitalized on race by implying that Booker was a carpetbagger who would allow outsiders to come to Newark and change the economic and racial make-up of the city. James' charges against Booker spoke volumes about his racial identity. Not only was James astute to racial politics, he also accentuated his experiences as a Black leader and contrasted himself with his deracialized opponent. James rightly emphasized his civil rights and political background.[17] But James challenged the paradigm of traditional Black politics when he attacked Booker's Black identity. Of course, James' approach also spoke volumes about the electorate.

In addition to attacking Booker's race, James also added elements of class con-flict to the race by arguing that Booker's level of education was unusual: "[W]hy would someone like Booker come to Newark?" Booker had little in common with many Newarkers because he was from the suburbs, James argued. Even the media stressed that Booker could do better running in other areas or, better yet, could work on Wall Street or in other professions. Why did he want to be Newark's next mayor? What was his underlying motive? Would Booker leave Newark after one term and seek a higher office such as governor or senator? The uneasiness raised by these questions left many Newarkers concerned about Booker's motives and his future intentions. Booker was an opportunist, alleged James.[18]

And, in addition to challenging Booker's racial authenticity, class, sexual orien-tation, party affiliation, and education, the incumbent mayor also questioned Booker's lack of political experience. James boasted of his many years of experi-ence in public service as mayor and city councilman, and teacher, whereas Booker had served only one term on the city council. James argued that Booker had recently graduated from law school, so what leadership experience could he claim?[19] James contended that Booker was too young and naïve, emphasizing Booker's youthful appearance and his idealism. James' campaigned on the idea that he had "experienced leadership," in contrast to Booker.[20] At the same time, some Black Newarkers questioned Booker's lack of experience and wondered what they would get if Booker ran City Hall instead of the veteran politician, James, with whom they had dealt for decades.[21] In addition to his experience, James also emphasized his claim that he was more authentically Black than Booker. His cam-paign theme was "The Real Deal," and James stressed that he was more of a Newarker than Booker, that he was more Black than Booker, and that the city's leaders did not have time to teach Booker how to be Black.[22] Therefore, James influenced much of the 2002 election with his racialist attitudes and typecasting. However, his outlook and tactics were aligned with those of many Black Newarkers who feared Cory Booker's unknown post-racial politics. James accentuated his doubts about Booker in the 2006 race as well, even though he withdrew his name from the ballot weeks before the election.[23]

Many Black Newarkers faithfully believed their long-time mayor's claims that Booker wanted to redevelop the city for outsiders. Considering Newark's commu-nity development history, urban redevelopment has been tied closely with race and politics. From the problems in the 1960s with the University of Medical and Dentistry of New Jersey's expansion to 1980s downtown business development, much of Newark's renewal has centered on White professionals in the medical and corporate sectors. So James' charge that Booker would allow redevelopment of the city for outsiders resonated with many Black Newarkers. James stated that Booker's campaign money came from suburbanites and large corporate sponsors whereas James supposedly received funds only from Newarkers. In reality, James' donors were developers and contractors closely aligned with City Hall, some of whom were from outside Newark. Booker did receive a sizeable share of his money from outside Newark, but it was not the amount James asserted.[24] Nonetheless, James claimed that Booker would help these outsiders make Newark into a developer's paradise; this sparked fears of displacement among the city's residents.[25] Therefore, for some, James' allegations reminded them of what James stood for (at least ideally as James dealt with favored developers and faced federal investigation a year after the 2006 race).[26]

While some considered James' approach problematic, others thought his views were poignant and pertinent. For many Black Newarkers, Sharpe James' attempts to racialize Cory Booker's background and politics were a referendum on the long-time mayor's legacy. Whichever way Black, White, and Latino residents viewed the elections, many journalists and political experts agreed that Newark's urban politics was headed toward a confrontation along racial and class lines and between James and much of Newark's civil rights generation and younger community leaders. This confrontation was spearheaded by James, but it was also embraced by many old guard community and City Hall leaders. James fostered a contentious atmosphere in the mayoral elections, and he also ignited racial politics because of his own overinflated racial identity politics. Or, James' Black chauvinism and his actions demonstrated his racial identity, while Booker offered deracialized politics. In other words, Booker and James represented the extremes of racial politics. At the same time, their perspectives certainly carried over to Black Newarkers' perceptions and opinions of the candidates as reflected in surveys taken during the mayoral elections.[27]

James' Corruption

Unfortunately, James' politics involved him in several serious court cases. A Superior Court judge barred the city from selling city-owned land after his administration had approved at least 15 proposals to sell land at $4 a square foot, which the judge called a fire-sale of no-bid real estate transactions. Many of the developers were James' supporters and financial backers, and Booker brought suit against the administration to stop the sales, particularly as additional sales were completed during the last weeks of James' tenure.[28] As Booker saw it, "We saw this as a very crass, blatantly greedy way of hijacking the city's economic well-being for the benefit of a small number of private individuals. I felt I had the leverage of an imminent mayor, so I acted." James also engaged in a complicated web of community development projects, land deals, and financial corruption. The

Star-Ledger discovered that in his last months as mayor, the city closed on 21 separate deals that involved dozens of lots and at least 20 acres of vacant land; a city planner and a housing and economic development director were even able to purchase discounted property.[29] The FBI accused James of misusing city funds and credit cards for personal trips to Brazil and other destinations (accompanied by eight different young, female "travel companions"). Moreover, the federal government discovered that James conspired to sell city land parcels to favored individuals, including a 37-year-old publicist, Tamika Riley. She bought nine parcels from the city for a total of $46,000, and resold them (in some cases only a month later) for $700,000; she was also contracted to work for the city on various community and education-related programming and projects.[30] Newark also paid $6,500 for James and his bodyguards to go on a five-day trip to Rio de Janeiro where he stayed at a luxury hotel and dined at several upscale restaurants. While the mayor claimed that it was a business trip to discuss America's urban problems, he reportedly lectured for only one hour during the five days he was there.[31] Moreover, the *Star-Ledger* found that there were two publicly financed credit cards for the mayor's office that had charges of nearly $80,000; these charges included costs for 17 trips to several American and international cities. The US Attorney General's office issued a subpoena for items related to the trips and expenses,[32] and the *Star-Ledger* also discovered that James charged more than $200,000 to the two cards in almost four and a half years; more than $125,000 of that amount was attributed to travel, even though the mayor's office had a $25,000 travel account approved by the city council.[33] When federal officials searched for the hard drives from the James administration's computers, they could not find them because they had been removed.[34] James not only denied the allegations against him, he also blamed the city council. "I have nothing to hide," he said. "They have every right to investigate me, because when you are in political office you live in a fishbowl. But I will say that many of the things they are looking, such as the land sales and the travel, were the purview of the City Council and not the mayor."[35]

In July 2007, due to information uncovered by the FBI's investigation, which was code named "Operation Corner Lot," a federal grand jury indicted James for conspiracy and corruption. US Attorney (later New Jersey Governor) Chris Christie alleged that James used his mayoral and state senatorial offices "as a personal piggy bank," but James stated that he was innocent of all charges; James was arrested and then released on $250,000 bail.[36] In the 86-page indictment against James, the federal government also charged Tamika Riley with fraud because James improperly distributed city properties to Riley and helped her resell several of those properties for a significant profit. Allegedly, a large share of that money went to James' political campaign. In addition, the former mayor was charged with wire and mail fraud and illegally using government credit cards for personal items, dinners, entertainment, and trips.[37] However, for many Newarkers, the timing of the indictment was memorable, but hurtful. The date James was indicted, July 12, was the date that the riots started in 1967 as well as the date that the state took control of the city's public schools in 1995. In typical James' style, the former mayor made a bad day into a campaign for public support: he boarded a public bus hours after the indictment and traveled to downtown Newark, greeting riders and gaining their support, especially over the physical mistreatment he received during his arrest. A reporter spotted him on New Jersey Transit's no. 59 bus and noticed that he pointed out various downtown projects to other riders. James also went into City Hall the next day to visit council members and receive support from public officials.[38]

In the spring of 2008, James again captured many when the case went to court. Judge William Martini presided over the trial, and, as the *Star-Ledger* stated, he was "arguably the perfect judge for this complicated case, one that involves politics and real estate law, urban problems and land development, obscure rules of evidence and the power of prosecutors." Martini was a former Clifton city councilman, Passaic County freeholder, and a US Representative (even his father's uncle was mayor of Passaic).[39] The mayor's lawyers claimed that James never placed pressure on the city council, the housing department, or any city employees to complete the land deals, and they also said that there was no evidence that James had ever received any financial benefit from Riley's land sales. The government claimed the Riley and James were having an extramarital affair.[40] Riley's lawyers admitted that she had had a "personal and intimate" relationship with the mayor for six months in 2002, but they claimed that the affair had nothing to do with the land sales; federal prosecutors, however, argued that James' relationship with Riley was his motive for selling nine city-owned properties to her through an urban revitalization program. The government further argued that, in return, Riley carried on the relationship with James, gave him boxing tickets worth $5,000, and went with him on several trips to the Caribbean. But Riley's lawyers argued that the development program had provisions for buyers who were not developers and that the affair had nothing to do with corruption. At the same time, James also stood trial for using city-issued credit cards.[41] During more than three hours of opening arguments, Assistant US Attorney Phillip Kwon stated that, "[T]he case is about fraud, favoritism and concealment. And, ordinarily, what Sharpe James and Tamika Riley did in their personal lives is their business. But when Sharpe James used his office and city-owned properties to foster and maintain his romantic involvement with Tamika Riley, he gave up the privilege to keep that his business." However, James' attorney, Thomas Ashley, told the jury that Riley had received the same fair treatment that other aspiring developers would have received in a blighted city: "That was Sharpe James resurrecting the South Ward from scratch. And Sharpe James did not receive a dime. There are no kickbacks, there are no schemes, ladies and gentlemen, there are no hidden financial interests."[42]

Witnesses included James' personal secretary, Rose Marie Posella, and Riley's mentor, Diane Fuller-Coleman. Both offered their perspectives on the affair and the land deals. While Posella suggested that the mayor was obviously close to Riley, she stated that the affair occurred in 2000, before the land deals took place, not in

2002. Fuller-Coleman described Riley as an opportunist, especially in knowing how to attract influential people such as the mayor. Riley's "goal was to make a million. That was her goal ever since I met her," charged Fuller-Coleman.[43] Evidence also included a memorandum from James requiring the Department of Economic and Housing Development to blind carbon copy the mayor on communications with the city council, including the land deals. Among another dozen documents, there was one that instructed city officials on how to divide city land into 20 lots, not seven. James was questioned about meeting with developers, but he claimed that the city council, not the mayor, was required to meet with developers before making decisions to sell land. However, James' secretary suggested otherwise, stating that the mayor had met with developers about land deals.[44]

Another witness, a former Economic and Housing Development director, Basil Franklin, testified that, in the late 1990s, Newark started a special program to sell land in the South Ward to qualified builders for prices as low as one dollar per square foot in order to spur development in that area. Franklin reviewed and approved developers who wanted to take part in the initiative, but, by the early 2000s, this program had ended because land was selling for more money and land sales were based on political connections. "There was no professional or legal vetting of anybody," argued the former director. Recommendations had to come from city council members, high ranking mayoral aides, or the mayor himself (James' former chief of staff, Jackie Mattison, and his partners were able to buy 100 city lots). Therefore, when James suddenly sent a letter to Franklin instructing him to halt land sales to Riley, the housing director was surprised.[45] But federal prosecutors challenged Franklin's testimony, calling him a turncoat witness because he did not fully articulate that James helped Riley buy land.[46] Instead, Regina Bayley, a former secretary for the Department of Economic and Housing Development, said that the mayor was directly involved in the land sales to Riley and that the mayor was "the force" moving the deals forward. Bayley even suggested that Franklin had a romantic interest in Riley. James' attorney argued that special treatment was routine but not illegal and that there were three other female developers who were given land deals similar to Riley's because of their connections to the mayor or city council.[47]

The federal prosecutors also called Riley's former business associate, Wendee Bailey, who testified that in order to buy land in Newark, "you've got to know somebody." And, after an attorney introduced her to Riley, who had already bought city land at discount prices, Bailey purchased six properties from Riley and rehabilitated two others before Riley sold them. Bailey handled the financing, spearheaded the construction, and found buyers for the properties, but Riley did no development work; Riley's sole contribution, therefore, was her connection to City Hall.[48] Prentiss Thompson, a friend of the mayor and former investigator for the Essex County Prosecutor's Office, testified that James offered to help him purchase city land. Thompson's testimony suggested that the mayor was in charge of city land sales, but the former investigator never actually purchased city land in light of the federal investigation.[49] One of the key and ironic pieces of evidence prosecutors presented against the mayor was his own speech on the state senate floor, in which he called for reform of municipal land sales. The bill James sponsored would have prevented a mayor and council's involvement in selling city property to their "boyfriend, girlfriend, momma, poppa, brother, friend or organization. This law is needed to ensure that we protect the public trust. That we do not allow thievery with municipal property."[50]

After presenting 33 witnesses, hundreds of pages of property records, financial documents, and other evidence, the government rested its case on March 28. On April 1, defense attorneys called former Councilwoman Gayle Chaneyfield-Jenkins to testify that city lawyers were responsible for city land sales. She also confirmed that James never spoke with her about Riley or any city properties. In addition, another former councilwoman, Mamie Bridgeforth, stated that she had approved the sale of city properties and was aware of the relationship between James and Riley. Other city officials also testified that James did not have a direct role in land sales to Riley.[51] As expected, neither James nor Riley testified. On April 16, the jury found James guilty on all five charges, including fraud and conspiracy, while they found Riley guilty of the same charges and eight additional ones relating to tax violations. As US Attorney Chris Christie stated on the courthouse steps, "Today, [James] is taught the lesson: that for those who disgrace their public office, for those who betray the public trust, there is only one place for you, and that is federal prison." Booker responded, "I'm staying focused on the future. I hope the citizens of Newark stay focused on the important work we must do and the great things happening in the city."[52]

The former mayor was schedule to be sentenced in July, and in May the government announced that due to additional costs, they would not pursue fraud charges against James for his misuse of city-issued credit cards.[53] More than 100 people sent letters praising James to Judge Martini; the letters asked Martini to show leniency to James, crediting the former mayor for his vision of a revitalized city and claiming that James was a role model for Newark.[54] Ultimately, the former mayor was sentenced to 27 months, not the 10 to 15 years that many people, including the prosecutors, thought he deserved. The judge thought that if prosecutors were convinced that James had been corrupt for decades, they would have tried him for more than just this one set of land sales. The judge said that James did breach the public's trust by failing to disclose his affair with Riley on the city's land deals paperwork, but it was a far less serious offense than bribery or extortion. Meanwhile, Riley was convicted for tax evasion and lying about her income to collect housing subsidies, and she was sentenced to 15 months and ordered to repay $27,000 to the city. Although Christie and prosecutors wanted longer sentences, the US Attorney for New Jersey said at a news conference, "in seven weeks, he will be away from the house at the beach, the Rolls-Royce, the romantic strolls down Broad Street to catch the bus with regular people." Many Newarkers found the former mayor's trial and sentencing harsh and regarded James as a local hero,[55] while others thought that the sentence was discretionary since the land sales did financially hurt Newarkers.[56] James later filed a notice to appeal the corruption charges and stated that he would represent himself (but Alex Dexter Bowman, a Newark attorney, eventually notified the court that he would represent the former mayor and request the US Court of Appeals throw out James' conviction based on lack of evidence[57]). Riley also filed an appeal. Even US Attorney Christie filed an appeal, arguing that the judge was too lenient.[58] In April 2011, James also claimed that one of the jurors, who worked for the city, worked under the Booker administration during the trial and that his political ties should have come out during the jury selection process. James' motion described Booker's City Hall as "venomous" and "oppositional" to James and his administration. James requested a retrial, claiming that the juror had lied, but US Attorney for New Jersey Paul Fishman said that the juror did his public duty, justice was served, and "enough is enough"[59]; a federal judge agreed with Fishman and did not grant James a new trial.[60] Nevertheless, James still had legal issues to contend with, including the lawsuit filed against him by the state's Election Law Enforcement Commission (ELEC), which claimed that James had illegally used $94,000 in campaign money to pay for his criminal defense in the federal trial; the agency was seeking full repayment as well as a $6,000 penalty because using campaign funds for a criminal defense violates the ELEC rules. However, James claimed that the money was spent prior to his indictment and went toward necessary campaign expenses.[61]

Not surprisingly, James has remained in the shadows of Newark's politics since his release from jail. He had $725,000 left in his campaign fund, and he did not rule out running for public office again, especially because former Washington, DC, Mayor Marion Barry was able to win a city council seat after he was charged with cocaine possession. James gave $40,000 to local churches, $60,000 to the local charity he had founded, and additional money to local candidates.[62] Unquestionably, from a financial standpoint, James appeared to be engaged in local politics. James also attended city council meetings, and, in one meeting, he publicly challenged the property tax rate increase. He said that as a property owner, he found the proposed 16 percent hike a "confiscatory rate" that threatened the city's middle class. James also supported a newly created organization, Reconnect Newark, which monitored Booker's administration and questioned its policies. Newark's old political guard, including many James supporters, were heavily involved in that organization. One of the chief organizers, former councilwoman Gayle Chaneyfield Jenkins, said that the group had been meeting for months before its first public event in November 2010, which James and 200 others attended. This organization was established to challenge Booker's politics, and some members even talked about recalling Booker and provoking city council members at meetings.[63] Many Newarkers supported James after his release from prison because they considered the former mayor fundamentally one their own. According to Councilwoman Mildred Crump, "James believes in Newark and Newarkers believe in him even after the fact."[64]

Booker's Post-Racial Politics

The 2002 and 2006 mayoral elections taught Booker several lessons. Admittedly, he was a more seasoned candidate the second time around. After his 2002 defeat, Booker, who was already familiar with the Central Ward that he represented on the city council, made ties with more Black communities in Newark by attending more community events and spending more time in Newark's Black areas, including the South and West Wards. As a result, in 2006, Booker, who had lost significantly in Black wards across Newark in 2002, picked up more Black votes (closer to 50 percent). Booker also hired former campaign and political officials from the James campaign for the 2006 election. Even though he became a more veteran candidate, however, Booker's post-racial politics continued.[65] He rarely talked about his personal experiences or identity politics during the elections. While Booker's responses to Rice's or James' statements about his identity as a Black man were a part of the 2006 campaign, Booker spent more time on the offense than on the defense. For instance, speaking before the Newark Teachers Union, he avoided responding directly to Rice's attacks that he had received financial donations from White conservatives who supported school vouchers.[66] Booker also deflected concerns about racial politics and instead confronted the machine politics of the James administration and its community development policies and land deals.

Booker saw the potential for corruption in the land sales, but he did not attack James' revitalized Newark as he did in the 2002 election. To do this again in the 2006 election would point fingers not only at James but also at Rice, two homegrown public officials. When Booker challenged James' politics, it appeared as though he was attacking Black Newarkers and their identity. As Kevin Mumford recalls, "[W]hen Booker attempted to appeal to … poor black men in the worst neighborhoods, he did so by attacking the economic background of James."[67] Besides, Booker did not want to delve into racial politics, especially after the 2002 contest. In that election, he had invited Cornel West to discuss race and examine social progress in minority communities. This was one of the rare moments when Booker was able to get others to challenge James' doubts about Booker's racial experience, though a James campaign van drove past, declaring loudly, "You ain't Black. You suspect, boy!"[68] James had already publicly labeled Booker a carpetbagger, a Republican, a Jew, gay, and White.[69] Nevertheless, Booker wanted to get past racial identification. He admitted that "I don't want to be a great black politician; I want to be a great politician."[70] Yet, in a city like Newark, where there has been an extended, if not devastating, history of race *and* politics, to not address racial politics is problematic for any candidate. James knew this in 2002, which explains why James attacked and exploited Booker's background and his outsider status. "We didn't struggle for so many years just to have some rich kid and his friends ride into town and take over city hall," as James reminded Black Newarkers.[71]

Few Newarkers related to Booker's upbringing, let alone his racial outlook. He frequently tried to identify with Black Newarkers through anecdotes. For instance, hearing that the Booker family settled in Harrington Park and faced incidents of racial and class conflict left many Black Newarkers wondering what connections they had with Cory Booker. Booker often recounted stories of his family's struggle to integrate in his childhood town, saying that it were as though his family were the "only raisins in a sea of vanilla."[72] His middle-class family's experiences in the suburbs were something many poor inner-city Black Newarkers did not readily understand because they clashed with the experiences of the majority of Black Newarkers, who had remained in the city following the riots and the city's rebuilding era. Indeed, numerous Newarkers boasted about their lifelong roots in the city; longtime residence in the city is considered a badge of honor that many take seriously. Thus, this is often a requirement for Newark's public officials.[73] James embodied this principle. He was a reminder of Newark's past, and he proved to many Black Newarkers that local politicians support lifelong residents and vice versa.[74] Booker was not connected to their shared inner-city history. In addition, Booker was a Rhodes Scholar, and some resented his achievements and accomplishments.[75] He settled in Newark as a tenant rights lawyer and a one-term councilman, living in a low-income apartment for several years. Why, many residents asked, would someone of his caliber even want to settle, let alone run for mayor, in Newark, a city where almost half the residents did not finish high school? He could easily have become a highly paid lawyer. Besides his career choices, many found Booker's lifestyle odd; he's a vegetarian who does not drink or smoke, and he also frequently cites Jewish and Buddhist religious texts.[76] Therefore, James successfully characterized Booker as an outsider and not Black. "Booker was enigmatic to many black Newarkers not only because he was light skinned and visibly strained to speak the local black vernacular, but because his campaign proved difficult to interpret and locate on the political landscape," notes Mumford.[77]

Admittedly, Booker did inject some identity politics into his understanding of race and sexuality when he was in college. In 2013, his undergraduate alma mater, Stanford University, republished op-eds that appeared in a 1992 column for the *Stanford Daily*. In one op-ed about the Rodney King verdict, for example, Booker says that as a young college student, he feels the urge to repeat "not guilty" when police harass Booker or he is being racially profiled in retail stores. "But late one night, as I walked the streets of Palo Alto, as the police car slowed down while passing me, as his steely glare met me, I realized that to him and to so many others I am and always may be a Nigger: guilty till proven innocent." Booker goes on to compare himself with King only to discover that even though he has a stellar education and background, many still perceive him as a threat and that his race would always overshadow his achievements.[78] In another op-ed, Booker shows his disgust for gays and states that he "hated gays." But he also illustrates a transformative experience with a peer counselor that changed his homophobic views. "It was chilling to find that so much of the testimony he shared with me was almost identical to stories my grandparents told me about growing up black," Booker wrote. "People found it revolting to share a meal with them and often felt it to be their duty to beat them so that they would learn proper living." He later reveals that his hatred of gays "did not lie with gays but with myself" and that he chose to tolerate gays and embrace them. At the same time, Booker admits that he would react defensively if someone accused him of being gay or become silent when others were taunted for being gay. Years later, he wrote about his teenage struggle for integrity on Twitter.[79] Booker's early recognition of the similarities between gay and Black struggles demonstrates a poignant moment of personal growth and of his own identity politics.[80]

On the campaign trail, however, Booker rarely introduced racial and sexual identity politics but instead emphasized his quest to lift all Newarkers out of poverty and fix urban problems. Booker seemed to have empathy for the poor, but many inner-city residents grew concerned about his racial identity. His experiences of living in a van and later low-income housing evoked memories of the 1960s NCUP days in Newark when outsiders resided in inner-city Newark; many residents felt as though Booker was only in the city temporarily to provoke political change.[81] Booker truly believed in uplifting Newarkers, no matter their racial background. All things were possible, he argued, and Newarkers could achieve the American Dream; Booker claimed to be involved in a "righteous struggle, a righteous fight" to help residents.[82] Booker envisioned a unified struggle to improve Newarkers' lives, a struggle similar to others in the Black experience. He often expressed race as a part of inner-city or rural southern existence. Certainly, there were problems with education, healthcare, unemployment, and crime, but all Americans have these problems, said Booker, and they are not exclusive to a single Black American experience. In other words, all people, "Black people, White people, Brown people," can strive together toward a greater tomorrow.[83] During his campaigns, Booker regularly urged voters to join forces, combine dreams, and intertwine goals. "But he frequently failed to appreciate the extent to which the black community once needed massive efforts to gain representative inclusion into the democracy," argues Mumford.[84]

One of the greatest concerns about Booker's post-racial politics was that he saw race as important to the past, as it was during his parents' generation, and not the present, and he often grew weary of racial politics. His personal view toward racial politics was revealed four months after his mayoral inauguration, when he told business leaders, "I'm tired of racial politics ... leaders wrapping themselves in kente cloth."[85] Racial incidents affecting his father and his parents' difficulties in buying a home in the suburbs were his family's experiences of race and not his own.[86] As far as racial coalition politics, he mostly viewed that approach as belonging in the past as well, especially because "we're a city that's 80 percent Black and Latino and people who coalition build; we have had 3 black mayors spanning for so many years. So you have my entire lifetime of Black mayors. So it's different."[87] He further added, "Can a Black boy born to a single mom in the South Ward get better access to food, education, security, housing and economic opportunity? That's the kind of racial challenge we have in America right now."[88] Indeed, Booker exhibited racial identity politics only a few times, either in the historical sense or in anecdotes. "That's the thing about our generation, we don't really have the perspective," suggests Booker. "We were born after King's assassination. In many ways, these conversations have me a little less reactionary to tension."[89] So Booker constantly referred to Booker T. Washington, Malcolm X, and Martin Luther King Jr as historical examples.[90] Aside from Booker quoting influential people, he often used high-level vocabulary which demonstrated more his educational background than his connecting ability with many Newarkers. As one councilman suggests, "Walking around with him, you need an encyclopedia and a dictionary."[91]

While Booker framed race in the past and embraced post-racial politics, he had several political racial lapses. For example, at a party in suburban Summit, New Jersey, Booker "spoke of dodging bullets in Newark" like a character in the movie *The Matrix* and mimicked a maneuver by Keanu Reeves, twisting his body. In fact, one of the most emphasized incidents during Booker's first year as mayor was his speech about Judith Diggs. She was a housing advocate who, according to Booker, was portly, missing teeth, and cursed frequently. According to Booker, Diggs also accepted a $100 bribe from Sharpe James during the 2002 election. Booker told this story to his hometown crowd in Harrington Park, and he added that when Diggs died, she was reading a book to an elementary school class. (She actually died in her office of a heart attack.) It appears that Booker wanted to embellish the story for his suburban audience. The speech was uploaded to YouTube and gained statewide attention, highlighting Booker's storytelling abilities, as well as his negative racial stereotypes. This speech infuriated many Black Newarkers, including Amiri Baraka and other anti-Booker activists in addition to several members of the city council. Some said that for Booker to depict Diggs as a "foul-mouthed Aunt Jemima" was demeaning. Councilman Anibal Ramos said that it was unnecessary "to portray a demeaning image of the city because it sends a bad message." Councilwoman Dana Rone called Booker's story more than a negative incident. "It is racist," she argued. "Why deliver this story in a room full of white people?"[92]

Booker did apologize for his comments, but he simply issued a statement and failed to address the council's concerns. Moreover, the Diggs family initially refused any contact with Booker. This episode speaks volumes about Booker's approach and how he has come to handle sensitive, if not political, circumstances of race. The *Star-Ledger* remarked that Booker's "'stories,' in the view of some, can reinforce negative stereotypes." While Booker has shrugged off naysayers and activists who charge him with selling out the city to outsiders, especially in the suburbs, he continues to speak negatively about many Black Newarkers. From lectures at New York City's New School to fundraisers outside Newark, Booker tells tales of crack addicts "getting their morning fixes" and convicts threatening his life, portraying Newarkers as racial stereotypes to many White audiences. Booker has conflated the inner-city experience with anecdotal comments about city residents as negative racial stereotypes, which has further reinforced Booker's misunderstanding of the relationship between racial stereotyping and racial consciousness.

He has recounted stories of Black Newarkers as negative images and problem residents to suburban, business, and noncity residents. As the *Star-Ledger* states, "When Cory Booker speaks to groups outside of the city, he often relates stores about those he encounters in it."[93] Booker is proud to boast about how he helps Newarkers with their lives, but he also presents troubled Black Newarkers as having drug, crime, and family problems. Booker has shown a pattern of constant negative storytelling and the airing of Newark's dirty laundry, not offering positive images of Newarkers. For instance, Booker frequently speaks of an unsavory young Black male named "T-Bone" who threatened Booker when he arrived in Newark:

> "I said hello to this guy and I'll never forget he leaped off the steps where he was standing and looked at me and threatened my life. He said: 'I don't know who you are, I don't know where you come from but if you ever so much as eyeball me again I'm going to bust a cap in your'…let's call it my posterior region," Booker said to laughter during the New School speech.[94]

Some have even questioned whether T-Bone exists. "That's what white people think a drug dealer in Newark would be named," charges Newark's union leader Rahaman Muhammad. "T-Bone is non-existent. It's a figment of his imagination." Yet Booker continued telling the story and others similar to it to demonstrate that "we live in a society today (where) we are 40 years from the civil rights movement but we have a lot of work to do. There are young men who have genius inside of them … so much of this talent is getting wasted through violent crime," argues Booker.[95]

Some listeners truly believe Booker's stories about the city. For example, Elana Kay, a nonresident, conceded that Booker further established the view that Newark is crime-ridden and has a racial problem in her mind. "He reinforced that impression," she concluded.[96] Booker's mentor, Reverend William Howard, acknowledges that "I think the mayor is using stereotypes that register with the stereotypes of some of the people beyond Newark … I think he's beginning to understand he can't do these stereotypes without there being this kind of public uproar about what he says."[97] Booker did exhibit genuine interest in helping to address the recidivism rates of chronic ex-cons who re-enter Newark, especially as the city later received a $2 million federal grant to help with this problem.[98] Because the vast majority of ex-cons are young Black men, Booker was often outspoken and advocated marches, sit-ins, and civil disobedience in the state capital to force legislators to reform drug laws and place nonviolent drug offenders into treatment programs and halfway houses. "The drug war is causing crime," Booker claimed. "It is just chewing up young black men. And it's killing Newark."[99]

If these episodes demonstrated Booker's sensibility to race, then they also allowed his opponents to politicize his post-racial outlook. Since race and racism are facets of so many Black Americans' lives, politics is frequently tied to race. Booker's stories did little to help improve his standing among many Black

Newarkers, particularly among his opponents. Critics like James and many other Black leaders told the press that Booker's brand of post-racial politics was idealistic, whitewashed, and ultraconservative. Booker largely ignored these criticisms and instead tried to take Newark residents of color beyond traditional models and demonstrate that post-racial politics could operate within Newark's historically problematic political system. He often connected Newark's racial issues with the past; he even states, "[N]ow when people say racial politics, I sometimes wonder what they're talking about because there's no great coalition of people out there voting along racial lines."[100]

But race remains entrenched in politics for many Black Newarkers, and many of Booker's opponents used this fact against him. They often described race and politics as inseparable due to the city's sordid history and the political and economic alienation of so many inner-city Black residents. This history is a common Black Newark experience, and a part of inner-city residents' racial identity. "[Passage] through the fire of the riot has been the badge of authenticity for many of Newark's political and social leaders," says the *Star-Ledger*.[101] Though many of Newark's old guard leaders politicized the riots, Booker did not, and James capitalized on this in addition to reminding voters that he grew up in poverty, unlike Booker. While James lived through a childhood filled with poverty and racial prejudice, Booker studied books on the problems of Black urban poverty.[102] For officials like Councilwoman Mildred Crump, she argued that, "Booker has the ethnic perception of being Black."[103]

But Booker's failure to connect with many Black Newarkers during his first-year as mayor remained a point of contention between him and local activists who were more politically aligned with the previous administration. As the *New York Times* noted, "Mr. Booker, whose skin tone and privileged upbringing have long brought accusations that he is not authentically black, ... still enjoys broad support, especially among Hispanics, Portuguese-Americans and business leaders, but he is increasingly bumping up against a knot of opposition from African-Americans led by the old-guard political establishment who have long viewed him with suspicion."[104] One of these old-guard critics was Amiri Baraka. Baraka suggested that the new mayor was more concerned about "rich white folks" than Newark's poor Black and Latino residents. Baraka said this at several forums, including a film festival and city council meetings. "Mr. Booker does not love our people! He's on his way to paradise for himself." When Booker laid off city employees, "the core of the city's middle class," Baraka protested that Booker instead hired outsiders.[105] Furthermore, at a council meeting filled with dozens of his supporters, Baraka claimed, "Some people around the city are beginning to call this place 'occupied Newark.' Booker is what they call a comprador that is an agent of outside interests. And a comprador will sell us out." Baraka's charges resonated with many Black Newarkers, and there was even a movement to recall Booker, which required some 32,000 signatures. While it remained a small movement, it nonetheless demonstrated the doubts many Black Newarkers have about Booker.

A number of these individuals challenged Booker's idealistic vision of solving Newark's urban ills. These anti-Bookerites were overwhelmingly old-guard, long-time Black Newarkers who were mainly supporters of Sharpe James, but some were also individuals who had been laid off from City Hall and thereby excluded from the Booker administration. From Baraka to union representatives, their walks of life varied, but they had a common and determined goal to challenge, if not oust, Booker as mayor, and they forged the ultimate coalition. "He hasn't endeared himself to the black folks, and that is going to get him into trouble," warned Paradise Baptist Church's Pastor Jethro C. James.[106]

Yet Booker shied away from confronting his opponents and instead labeled them "dark angels," which introduced further negative racial imagery to the conflict. "Newarkers have this sense that their city was abandoned and that the only people who benefited lived outside the city. They have this belief that these people are going to come back from over the hills to take over."[107] While these "dark angels" continue to hold protests and attend many council meetings to oppose the administration, Booker states that they are small in number and they have been mainly a distraction for him and have received too much media attention.[108] However, the number of Booker's detractors is growing; the cadre of James supporters and many older Black residents have been increasingly speaking out against Booker the longer he remains in mayoral office. Booker argues that his election results and internal polls, however, find him increasingly popular even among Black residents and that his opponents are not numerous. "But the curious question is—and this may be a racially political issue—why in a city would a guy with a 70 percent approval rating, would his opposition get so much more attention than any other place in America?" says Booker. "But [why] is it that people are so enraptured by a small group of people? Many of these folks were spouting out the same kind of thing even against Sharpe James. [For] any leader in power there's this small group of people that hold onto the same rhetoric of the 60s and framing of the 60s." While many of Booker's opponents inject racial politics into his post-racial politics, it is interesting to note that Booker introduces the possibility that the media and his adversaries have subjected him to some scrutiny because of race.[109]

Booker's First-Year Coalition Challenges

During the election, Booker might have vowed to build coalitions, but, unfortunately, he had difficulty creating sustainable coalition politics after he took office. Like previous mayors, Booker campaigned on a promise to work with Newarkers of various political, racial, and cultural backgrounds. He even reiterated this ideal at his inauguration, saying that he wanted to see residents engage with his City Hall to revive and change Newark. He offered a bold agenda that included adding hundreds of police officers to work in the city's communities, finding ways to reduce violent crime and address recidivism rates (especially since 1,500 convicts are released from prison in Newark and two-thirds of chronic offenders are rearrested annually),[110] introducing campaign finance reforms, and expanding parks and recreation programs. His inaugural speech reflected many of the coalition building themes critical to coalition politics. But the key aspect of Booker's speech and his agenda was his demand for residents to participate in changing the city. "I warn you that I will be a mayor that asks for more from our citizens. If we are to achieve anything more than incremental change [then] we must all step up now," Booker told residents. Besides encouraging citizens to be directly engaged in the political process and to address problems, he also emphasized that Newark "can no longer stumble on those who wish to divide our spirit, [pit] us against each other ... It's either us or them, downtown or neighborhood, black or Latino or white, suburban or urban, Jewish or Muslim or Christian. We are a city liberated by the 'and.' It is all of us in it together." He added that, "Newark must now lead our nation in an urban transformation."[111]

During the transition period in summer 2006 when Booker first took office, he had a very broad base of Newarkers, supporters, and experts consider various proposals of reforming city government. He attracted a number of dignitaries, scholars, and the media to various meetings. "To me it was one of the most beautiful moments as my term as mayor," says Booker. "It was this democratic coming together where we had to break into teams and talk about what was important. It really did help frame and guide our administration. Every single team talked about re-entry, but interestingly environmental policy blew me away on how conscious our community was at the grassroots levels of environmental issues."[112] While the transition teams were large and addressed multiple issues, the groups were mainly controlled by a few individuals, and various ideas were shelved.[113] In an effort to advance reform-oriented and proactive policy proposals, Booker (like most mayors) supported a group of potential candidates for city council. Moreover, using his $6.6 million campaign war chest, he helped a number of candidates with financing. But was this the mayor attempting electoral coalition building or machine politics? All six city council candidates Booker supported won their election on June 13, 2006. On the city council's run-off election night, Booker and a large crowd symbolically held brooms, reflecting the clean sweep. Booker's city council candidates certainly reflected Black and Latino coalition politics: Luis Quintana, Mildred Crump, Carlos Gonzalez, Donald Payne Jr., Oscar James Jr., and Ronald Rice Jr.[114] Booker even hired more Latino employees, arguing that the city government hardly reflected their community, but many residents grew concerned that these new Latino hires were replacing Black workers.[115] Still, "it was a new era and another attempt to coalition build," states Booker's chief of staff, Modia Butler.[116]

The newly elected council members and the mayor practiced coalition politics by creating strict new ethics laws, re-evaluating the New Jersey Devils hockey arena at the Prudential Center, and promising to end the discounted sales of city-owned land and to hire urban policy experts against the party leaders' wishes.[117] Booker even outlined a bold 100-day plan to report within three months about the problems with and successes of his agenda, which some called lofty and idealistic.[118] But he appeared determined to follow his mission statement, even if there were still long-standing problems facing Newark, especially as the city "remain[ed] a stubborn synonym for urban dysfunction."[119] As the headmaster of St. Benedict's Preparatory School stated, "People's expectations are that this guy is going to fix everything that's wrong with urban America. I worry about that for him."[120]

During his first months on the job, Booker and many of his supporters appeared to recognize the various issues facing Newark. Because 59 directors and City Hall workers had been fired, a vast number of officials were new to Newark. One of the directors first hired was Keith Kinard from the Pittsburg Housing Authority, who served as the new director of Newark's Housing Authority (NHA). Since the NHA was ranked in the bottom five percent of all housing agencies in the nation, it was almost taken over by the federal government. Kinard was approached twice by the new administration, and he eventually joined Booker.[121] Kinard would later cut 425 jobs from the agency because the US Department of Housing and Urban Development cut its federal subsidies by 20 percent.[122] Bo Kemp, a former CEO, was selected as business administrator, and former campaign aide Pablo Fonseca was chosen as Booker's chief of staff. Aney Chandy, a state assistant attorney general, was named corporate counsel, but she and Kemp would resign 18 months later and serve as consultants.[123] Stefan Pryor, president of the Lower Manhattan Redevelopment Corporation, was selected as Deputy Mayor for Economic Development in August of 2006. Pryor and Booker had been law school classmates, but Pryor lived in Manhattan. Maria Vizcarrondo, selected as director of the Department of Child and Family Well-Being, was one of only a handful of directors who were from Newark.[124] Garry McCarthy, the New York Police Department's deputy commissioner, was chosen as the city's Police Director,[125] but there were concerns surrounding his nomination as he was not Black or Latino and he had been involved in a scuffle with highway patrolmen.[126] However, McCarthy would oversee the creation of a narcotics division in the Newark police department—something Newark had surprisingly never had before.[127] Anthony Campos, a Portuguese American and native Newarker, was later appointed as a police chief under McCarthy, although many Black activists wanted Booker to appoint a Black candidate, Niles Wilson[128] (Campos was later suspended for five days for arguing with McCarthy over personnel changes[129]). In any event, a significant number of these officials did not live in Newark and were hesitant to move to the city. In fact, Fonseca refused to move from nearby West Orange, New Jersey, even though he owned property in Newark. But Booker stated that he would require officials to live in Newark and would grant waivers of this requirement only if absolutely necessary (in contrast, the James administration reportedly only loosely enforced the residency requirement).[130]

Despite the optimism for change, some of these new officials received significant pay raises only a few months after their hiring, costing nearly $500,000; Booker had to sign 63 executive orders without council approval to account for this money. Booker claimed that he chose to give salary increases to new officials and employees because they now had additional responsibilities and Newark had to remain competitive with other cities.[131] Even though Booker claimed to respect coalition politics, it was not represented in city agencies or his office. Booker appeared duplicitous because he hired outside consultants and contractors at the same time the city faced a financial crisis and the administration laid off city employees. Instead of hiring additional legal staff, Booker gave ten law firms contracts for over $1 million; seven of these firms had donated funds to Booker's campaign, and many of these firms were not located in Newark.[132] Booker's administration hired a number of consultants, but the city council challenged the appointments of some officials who had also served as campaign consultants.[133] The city council also questioned some officials' connections and intentions and claimed that their consulting firms lacked diversity.[134] However, consultants whose projects were not approved by the city council often found ways around the approval process. For instance, Carolyn Coleman, a campaign volunteer turned unpaid director of the Department of Neighborhood and Recreational Services, was denied a $105,000 contract for B&D Consulting. But the council did approve her appointment as a federal lobbyist for the city through the National League of Cities for a fee of $168,000. The city council might have rejected some consulting opportunities, but its members found ways to give their supporters contracts and consulting fees that were paid by the city.[135] By failing to hire officials who reflected Newark's diverse communities and failing to support proposals addressing Newark's population, Booker once again missed an opportunity for pragmatic coalition building.

Instead of advancing coalition politics among Newark's communities, Booker preferred to participate in numerous media events. He was featured in several national magazines and newspaper interviews and on *The Oprah Winfrey Show*.[136] Various articles and editorials not only portrayed Booker in a positive light but also characterized him as the city's rescuer. The *New York Times,* throughout his first term, highlighted his victories and moments when he "saved" Newark. For example, in one editorial, the newspaper described a meeting between Booker and constituents in a neighborhood school, where residents discussed their fears, unemployment, and financial troubles, and Booker claimed to be willing to listen and help. The piece ended: "And so it goes until long after dark. There are no TV cameras, none of the usual trimmings of political office—just a big-city mayor in a fluorescent-lighted school-room."[137] Booker appeared obsessed with protecting and promoting his favorable image as a determined mayor watching over and safeguarding the city's residents. Booker demonstrated his mayoral leadership in the cable television series *Brick City*[138] and rebuffed Conan O'Brien's jokes about Newark,[139] seeming to be more concerned about the media's interest in his leadership skills and his attempts to "spin" Newark's image (often leaving out details about Newark's Black middle class to emphasize its working class)[140] than he was about issues. Booker even wrote a piece in *Esquire* magazine chronicling his first months in office. "Now I am mayor, and in my first two weeks in office, every shooting, every murder, came with a new level of gravity. I am responsible," stated Booker. "True leadership is not exhibited by how many people one can get to follow but by how many people join together in leading."[141] Fundraising became another significant focus for the new mayor, and some council members found it troubling that he received so many donations from notable public figures. Several newspapers, critics, and even former Booker supporters found Booker's fame disconcerting. While Booker claimed that the attention would help bring needed resources to Newark, the image of residents having to be saved by their mayor cast the city in a negative light, which did not help Newark. For example, on the October 30, 2006, Oprah show, Booker showed unflattering images of Newark's streets, rundown buildings, and uneducated residents. As one Booker supporter and neighbor said, "It was him being condescending to the poor people of the community."[142] By various accounts, Booker spent considerable time before cameras and journalists portraying Newark as a city desperately in need of help and promising that he would be there not only to protect residents but also to reveal what was wrong with the city.

Another example of Booker as the center of attention was his move from his low-income apartment complex, Brick Towers, after the complex was slated to be demolished.[143] "I'm moving to a building in a drug-infested neighborhood," Booker stated, even though his aides said he should buy a home.[144] The housing complex proposed to replace Brick Towers would be mixed-income, instead of just low-income, housing. Between 25 to 50 of the 250 units would be reserved for median income earners (making about $31,000), and many units would be rented at market rates while others would be subsidized.[145] In mid-November, the mayor announced that he would relocate to a troubled section of the city, on Hawthorne Avenue in the South Ward, paying $1,200 rent in what the *New York Times* called, "a browbeaten stretch of Newark's South Ward, where boarded-up homes outnumber inhabited ones and crack dealers hawk their product outside an elementary school." But many critics thought Booker's decision was a publicity stunt that featured the mayor saving another community but not purchasing property in the city. One of his most famous neighbors and ardent critics was poet Amiri Baraka. Baraka said that Booker's move was "… all a romantic fantasy. It's politician's hooey, part of the myth-making."[146] Some thought that Booker would better understand the impact of a proposed eight percent property tax increase if he owned property in the city.[147] The *Star-Ledger* even published an article called "Bachelor Pad Shopping for Newark's Renting Mayor" that suggested several available condominiums as potential homes for Booker because the mayor had lived in Newark for 11 years and was "a busy guy."[148] Booker did eventually buy (and later tried to sell) two empty "fixer-upper" houses on Court Street; however, for years he chose not to live in those houses, and so they remained empty while neighbors grew concerned about high weeds, squatters, and fire damage.[149] With Booker grabbing the headlines because of his move across town and the media still following his every decision, the mayor's attempts to create sustainable coalition building seemed to be more about politicizing coalition building and political grandstanding than actually building coalitions.

There were instances during Booker's first term that were key coalition-building moments, including the new mayor's attempts to address several crime- and community-related incidents. From 2007 to 2010, there were several times when Booker had opportunities to support and aim for coalition building among Newark's diverse communities and their leaders, but instead he chose to either politicize or grandstand. During the summer of his inauguration, for example, homicide rates increased significantly. While Booker worked with the governor to establish state support and he created a crime task force between various agencies, some activists charge that there was little community involvement.[150] Booker unveiled his "Safe Summer Initiative" by deploying more police in 30 "safe" zones and encouraging churches, city employees, and community groups to help with job training, entertainment, and other activities. Booker urged city residents to take back their streets and boasted that crime rates had already lowered in just the few days that he had been mayor (however, he confused the period he compared with the week prior).[151] Booker even decided to take up the cause himself, and he often said that he would not only be held accountable but also culpable for the city's problems. "I'm taking responsibility for everything from littering to changes in policy," Booker claimed.[152] While overall crime in July and August dropped to its lowest point since 1995, homicides were up 50 percent and shootings were up 13 percent. And this statistic did not include the violent Labor Day weekend where five people were shot, two fatally. Many community activists were increasingly concerned about Newark's violence;[153] meanwhile, Booker and members of his administration frequently referred to numerous confusing charts to explain how crime was down overall.[154] In September, Booker expanded the safe zone initiative into schools, calling for 14 safe zones around neighborhood schools. Cameras were placed around schools, and more truancy and police officers were added to monitor problematic areas; later, downtown sections received cameras as well.[155] In addition, churches and community organizations were asked to participate in the initiative with community programming. "The whole community is pulling together to protect our children," said Booker.[156]

Another challenging issue facing Newark and the new administration was the financial trouble facing the city. City Hall faced a significant deficit, estimated at $44 million, and not a $30 million surplus as the previous administration had touted. The Booker administration discovered unpaid invoices and water bills; also, a number of city employees had been compensated for unused vacation and sick time and millions of dollars in outside contracts had been awarded but only one auditor controlled these accounts. Booker and his officials easily placed the blame on the previous administration, especially after a $1.2 million audit revealed waste, disorganization, mismanagement, and failures of the city government to collect over $80 million in tax revenue and water bills.[157] But the new administration also realized that, in addition to the city's other financial difficulties, state and federal aid would be cut.[158] Matters only worsened when Booker announced days later that between 400 and 800 of the city's workers would be laid off, even though police and fire departments would be untouched. However, reorganization of the city's fire department and the closing of three firehouses brought concerns from residents.[159] Surprised city council members resisted laying off workers, and union officials charged that the mayor was playing politics by firing supposed political enemies.[160] Booker later announced that the city government he had inherited had been financially mismanaged by the previous administration and property taxes would have to increase; James claimed that Booker's charges were wrong.[161]

Booker and his administration successfully implemented several initiatives during his first 100 days (Table 3.1). From hiring new workers to reforming government and developing the city, his administration appeared to be on track by the end of his honeymoon period as mayor. Booker later admitted to deserving a "B or B-plus" for his performance in office during this period because he did not meet all of his goals. His administration did ban city employees from contributing to mayoral campaigns (even though city employees had donated $226,856 out of Booker's nearly $7 million in campaign funds during the 2006 mayoral election),[162] and Booker pushed for ethics legislation and pay-to-play proposals that would cap campaign contributions at $300 for individuals who do business with city government; his administration also banned all donations from with those engaged in redevelopment projects, required builders to reveal any past political contributions, and established an inspector general to oversee abuse and ethics concerns (even though Booker signed an executive order to table some of the ordinances for a few weeks due to some council members' concerns about possibly receiving less campaign money in the next election).[163] However, these reforms were mostly in response to the local media's focus on Booker's connections to donors, contracts, and consultants in City Hall. In fact, Booker politicized the opportunity for reform in his first State of the City Address,[164] but "his right hand [didn't] seem to care what his mouth [was] saying," said one critic. "... Booker ... handed out fat contracts to legal firms that donated to his campaign, to a company with ties to his campaign manager and ... to an insurance company whose principals gave $37,000 to his campaign."[165] Even after these reforms, eight law firms—six of which had donated campaign money to Booker in the 2006 election—were to receive $2.45 million in contract increases.[166] Moreover, ten law firms—five of which had donated to the Booker campaign—were working with the Newark's Housing Authority, and they received almost $2 million in legal contracts. Even Booker's former law firm received a contract to redevelop his old home, Brick Towers.[167] In addition, some city employees alleged that they were pressured to sell fundraising tickets for Booker campaign events.[168]

Table 3.1   Booker's 100-day checklist

Completed	Hire a new police director
Completed	Graduate a new class of officers from the police academy
In progress	Enroll a new class of officers into the police academy
In progress	Graduate a new class of firefighters
In progress	Update the facilities plan for the police department
Just beginning	Hire a homeland security director
Completed	Double the size of the police gang unit
Completed	Expand the use of computer technology and surveillance in the police department
Completed	Launch the "Safe Summer" and "Safe Schools" initiatives
Completed	Commence forensic audits of city contracts, financial records, and personnel records
Completed	Develop and implement a transparent open appointments process
In progress	Restrict political fundraising on public property
In progress	Promote a fair and open bidding process for local developers
In progress	Update the city's Ethics Code and offer ethics training for city employees
Completed	Continue community engagement forums for citizen input
Completed	Re-enact the "right to speak" at council meetings
Completed	Start the mayor's open office hours
Completed	Adopt a budget for the 2006 fiscal year
In progress	Hire a labor commissioner
In progress	Hire a prison re-entry coordinator to create a transitional employment plan for ex-offenders
In progress	Analyze the Newark arena (the Prudential Center) and determine the city's disposition and strategy on the project
Just beginning	Establish criteria for how city-owned land is transferred and developed
Completed	Hire a deputy mayor for economic development
Completed	Invest $2 million to create employment opportunities for Newark youth during the summer.
In progress	Create a transitional employment plan for former prisoners in Newark
In progress	Conduct an affordable housing reassessment and develop an affordable housing plan
Just beginning	Expand the Division of Planning
Completed	Create the Department of Child and Family Well-Being and hire a director
Completed	Create the Newark Council on Family Success, to foster a collaborative environment that will allow for shared resources and information

Thus, during Booker's first year, he repeatedly blamed James and his administration for the financial mismanagement, deficit problems, and property tax increases, but many in the Black community felt Booker had betrayed them by laying off city workers.[169] Several community groups even called for protests against the mayor. These were the early signs that Booker's electoral coalition was faltering.[170] Also, he seemed to be challenged by the numerous lofty goals he had set for himself, his administration, and the city. After several months, many critics, early supporters, and observers grew concerned that Booker remained more idealistic than realistic, particularly about his appointments to City Hall. Some even charged that his appointees were arrogant and that many of them were highly paid White New Yorkers and Booker would have done a better job by hiring native Newarkers.[171] Booker also hired several consulting firms, and the city council often approved their contracts. For example, Booker gave a $1.5 million contract to a consulting group that was connected to his campaign manager. The 6Sixty Group was assigned to change people's perception of Newark through branding, marketing, and creating newsletters and interactive websites, including the city's own Internet page[172] (although they failed to completely update the web page until years later[173]). Much of the media's focus on Booker, contracts, consultants, and campaign donations occurred in the spring of 2007, after the executive order to end these connections. One critic claimed that the mayor might have signed legislation to end the practice, but there were many examples of it in the past and some even in the present because the executive order banned future donations but had not prevented previous donations related to the mayoral election. Or as she said, "Booker's executive order means they can either give a donation or get a contract but not both—from now on. From now on? But the cat's out of the bag. The horse has left the barn. The check—well the check's in the mail. It's been cashed."[174] At the same time, information in some reports and about some consultant hires were not always available to the public. For instance, when the SafirRosetti consulting firm commissioned a study on Newark's police and department morale, the report was not made public, and Booker's administration refused to release it. In a scathing editorial, the *Star-Ledger* found City Hall's actions duplicitous; the editors wrote, "Good leadership and a commitment to change must accompany any analysis. The Booker team owes it to Newark to be open about every step it takes as it tries to move from what was to what the city needs its police force to be."[175] City Hall reacted by obtaining a court order to prevent the *Star-Ledger* from discussing and printing stories about the police report. But a county superior court judge refused to prohibit the newspaper from discussing or printing stories about this report, arguing that the newspaper's First Amendment right and the public's right to know about the report had priority. Ultimately, the city dropped its suit against the newspaper, but city officials still claimed that printing the report created security risks.[176]

At the end of 2006, Booker was once again tested when Newark Public Schools Superintendant Marion Bolden announced she would step down. Bolden had held the position for seven years, but for nearly a year, particularly after Booker was elected, there had been rumors that she would resign. Moreover, because her contract was not renewed by the state, it appeared that the state, and possibly the city, were also ready to part ways with Bolden.[177] Interestingly, the first event at Sharpe James' Urban Issues Institute at Essex County College discussed Newark's problems, including Bolden's contract and Reverend Al Sharpton's criticism of "laboratory-created Negroes" challenging post-racial Black leaders like Booker.[178]

But Booker had bigger worries because by December the homicide rate had reached over 100—the highest number in 16 years,[179] and the statistic seemed to diminish the mayor's achievements. Booker said, "It's frustrating because these murders are overshadowing all the progress we've made making Newark a safer city."[180] The Newark Teachers Union took the opportunity to criticize the mayor by orchestrating a public campaign against the shootings and creating fliers and billboards stating, "Help Wanted: Stop the killings in Newark now!" However, union leaders claimed the campaign was in response to concerns that they would be unable to find educators who wanted to teach in Newark due to the shootings and the city's reputation.[181] (And in their second campaign a year later, the union paid for billboards stating, "Pay to Play: Alive and Well at the Newark City Hall, Follow the Money Trail. It Hurts Newark's Children and Taxpayers," reflecting the union's concerns about contracts and agreements that the administration had made with charter schools and favored individuals.[182]) But the mayor and many business owners argued that the signs were negatively affecting the local economy as well as the city's overall image.[183] Regardless, Booker thought 2007 would bring reduced crime rates. "I still believe that by the end of the year we'll be one of the most exciting crime-reduction stories in the country," he said.[184]

Another issue Booker's campaign faced was that they had been fined nearly $80,000 for filing late and incomplete reports related to the 2002 election with the New Jersey Election Law Enforcement Commission. The commission found that some donor occupation and employment information had been filed late. In 2002, Booker had had a fundraising network with many prominent donors and two campaign committees, Booker Team for Newark and Friends of Cory Booker for Mayor, and the organizations had received millions of dollars in donations; however, this campaign hiccup was embarrassing for the Booker administration.[185]

The unfortunate reality of Booker's first year was that while he received glowing media attention, there were several significant problems. Homicides increased, and Booker took ownership for it; many residents felt insecure in their communities; the city council challenged his appointments, their pay raises, and his consultants. Most importantly, by the beginning of 2007, Booker's honeymoon period had ended, and the coalition he had envisioned had never cemented. As much as he urged residents to join him in curbing the increasing violence, it proved very difficult to resolve this issue. Or, as some critics claimed, the mayor promised but frequently did not deliver.[186] Because Booker was so busy with public speeches and his bimonthly open office hours and the numerous difficult challenges the he attempted to solve, few residents received follow-up phone calls from him, and Booker estimated that his office was only able to help 30 percent of those who came to City Hall. Slowly, his office scaled back his open office hours to once a week, and staff took fewer notes about residents' issues. In fact, the mayor claimed that there was value in just listening to people's troubles and offering them a word of encouragement.[187] Even some former Booker supporters challenged Booker's and his administration's intentions and joined forces with his political foes. This was apparent during the 2007 state legislature election when all six state legislators were up for reelection. Booker was willing to test his newfound political capital, but a growing number of others opposed it. For instance, while Booker supported Donald Payne Jr. for city council, the mayor did not support his uncle, William Payne, for the state Senate seat; instead, Booker urged William Payne to run for the other house, the General Assembly, along with Latina Teresa Ruiz, the vice chair of the Essex County Democratic Party. This was an important opportunity to continue a Black–Latino coalition at the county level. But the Paynes saw that Blacks made up the majority of the legislative district, while Booker appeared to avoid this fact. Booker was willing to flex his political influence especially because it was clear that Essex County was experiencing a political rift between the candidates and Black and Latino leadership.[188] In fact, the *Star-Ledger* reminded readers that many younger Blacks and Latinos seemed primed for coalition building, while many older Black civil rights generation leaders were resistant to change; that group included William Payne, who sent a letter warning of the ending of Black representation to the newspaper. "That shrill pitch based on race—one that has worked like a charm in Newark—may finally be starting to wear thin," warned the newspaper. Booker also said, "It worries me that there are people who will appeal to the lowest common denominator, to racial divisions."[189]

While Booker was willing to challenge the Payne family and county party, another political alliance emerged. Steve Adubato, a legendary North Ward machine leader, and Rahaman Muhammad, president of the Service Employees International Union Local 617, agreed to join forces to prevent Booker from taking over county politics. However, Booker had so much outside financial and political support that Adubato and Muhammad found this fight a challenge. In any event, later in the campaign season, Adubato supported Booker's candidates largely because he recognized the growth of the Latino community. One of the most intriguing dynamics was that Muhammad embraced some of the early concerns about Booker, especially those discussed in Newark's Black communities. While James challenged Booker's Blackness, some like Muhammad questioned his support of Newarkers, in particular Black low-income workers, versus outside professionals like lawyers and contractors. Muhammad thought that the mayor hired too many consultants and law firms and fired too many city employees, such as people who worked at the Newark Housing Authority, many of whom were Black. "You can pay lawyers $220 per hour but you can't pay a security guard $14 per hour? If you aren't politically connected in this city, you can't get a break," claimed Muhammad.[190] In addition to Booker seeming to favor outside campaign supporters, some thought he ran a politically connected City Hall for his own gain and not the city's benefit. Booker appeared to use consultants and nonprofits rather than existing agencies and officials. "You have to be associated with the organizations he's involved in and not a community or city entity and reaching out has been limited," stated Richard Cammarieri. "Patronage politics still persist but reaching out to the community regularly is often lacking with this administration."[191] Others offered a more damning assessment of Booker by claiming that his consultants and officials were seeking more power. "He wants to run everything and he's not running anything. He's not a politician. He's come to save Newark," Muhammad said of Booker. "I don't feel like Newarkers control their destiny with the way he's governing. We want to make sure Cory Booker doesn't put clones of his philosophy in power."[192]

What Muhammad suggested speaks volumes about Booker's image in many of Newark's Black circles. It was significant that Booker found ways to go around local government and political bosses as an outsider, but, after his election as mayor, he also began to open internal political divisions among many senior officials, and he replaced some officials with the six new candidates he supported for the state legislature. For example, in 2007, Booker sought to defeat State Senator Ronald Rice Sr., who had been his opponent in the 2006 mayoral race. The mayor claimed that Rice refused to cooperate on legislative issues related to Newark and that he was at times hostile to the administration. But Rice denied the charge and said that Booker was a liar and that, as Muhammad claimed, the mayor "want[ed] to take over other cities and governments" by being a political powerbroker.[193] Booker denied the insinuation and said that he was more than willing to meet with Rice and that he still remained on cordial terms with William Payne.[194] In the end, Rice returned to the state senate, even though the Booker slate won five out of six legislative seats in the 2007 race. Booker said of Rice, "We're hoping we can appeal to his better angels, not the bitter ones." But Rice responded, "I'm not going to be so nice anymore."[195]

In spring of 2007, the city council was considering a nearly $786 million budget with no tax hike. It was the first time the legislative body had introduced the budget by the state-mandated deadline, and City Hall placed the 400-page budget on the Internet. They also pieced together a three-year fiscal plan—something never before done by a New Jersey municipality. But Newark still faced an $80 million budget shortfall, even though City Hall used the New York-New Jersey Port Authority settlement over airport land expenses to plug the operating budget. The *Star-Ledger* grew concerned that the budget "[was] held together with one big wad of bubble gum, and some unanswered questions [were] mixed in with the good news. Newark [used] $115 million from a city settlement with the Port Authority of New York and New Jersey to balance the budget. The payment [dropped] to $40 million [the following] year, and there [was] nothing to indicate how Newark [would] make [up] the difference."[196] Booker argued that the Port Authority deal was one of the "biggest mistakes Sharpe made." Indeed, "everybody knew Sharpe settled and he had the Port Authority over the barrel. They couldn't issue bonds and their lease was running out. We could have taken back the whole operations of our ports."[197]

As a result of the financial crisis, Newark later planned to buy out up to 60 percent of city employees and then extended the buyouts to include police and firefighters; however, City Hall did not reveal exactly who would be impacted until late June.[198] Once again, Booker blamed the James administration for the city's financial problems and said that everything was on the table, including hundreds of layoffs (about ten percent of the workforce), but no police layoffs—yet.[199] "We inherited a city whose finances should have been declared a national disaster area," the mayor claimed.[200] And months later, he emphasized that his administration had saved $10 million by cutting overtime pay, by winning several lawsuits, and by collecting 85 to 92 percent of parking and property taxes.[201] The city ultimately proposed to cut 400 jobs to save $50 million as 190 employees had been approved for the buyout, which saved the city $13 million.[202] (Ultimately, the city eliminated 200 jobs and left 95 jobs unfilled; 203 city employees accepted a voluntary buy-out.[203]) Some thought that by criticizing the former administration early in his first year Booker would help his reelection chances, while others thought it was a scare tactic.[204] At the same time that Booker was casting blame on James, the former mayor decided not to run for another term in the state senate. This news did not surprise anyone, considering the ongoing federal probe of James' finances and land deals as well as Booker's slate for the state legislature. James denied that the investigation against him had anything to do with his decision, but he was in the headlines once again.[205] (James also resigned from his college post months later.[206]) Besides, according to the former mayor, "Thirty-seven years in politics is a mighty long time, especially when you have led New Jersey's largest city, Newark, from urban blight to urban bright."[207]

While James did not run again for state senator and Rice won another term in the state senate, the city council grew increasingly concerned about Booker signing contracts with selected law firms and consultants. Nearly a year after the 2006 election, several council members questioned the administration's connections, especially considering the numerous campaign supporters who had become contractors with the city. The council introduced an ordinance requiring five yes votes to pass any resolution because some members boycotted meetings or voted present. Council members often complained about voting on items, including contracts, about which they had little information or specific details. One member said that while the council criticized the administration regularly, they voted for Booker's measures anyway.[208] In any case, Booker was determined to continue his approach of hiring highly paid professionals, signing executive orders, granting salary adjustments, and hiring new workers despite the budgetary deficit, layoffs, and buyouts,[209] even in the following years.[210] Paying the teenagers who worked for the city's Newark Summer Youth Work Experience was also an issue by the end of July. Booker organized press conferences and apologized for not paying a third of the teenagers on time, offering them lunch and bus fare; however, this did little to help the teens and their families believe in their new mayor's assurances that he was addressing the problem.[211] Some weeks after the mayor said the teens would be paid, almost 100 teenagers had still not been paid; some were not paid even by the end of summer, and Booker finally said that he would use his election fund money to pay them.[212]

By far one of the most significant events in Newark in summer 2007 was the schoolyard shootings in August that grabbed national headlines and even inspired an episode of the television series *Law and Order*.[213] Iofemi Hightower, Dashon Harvey, Terrance Aeriel, and Natasha Aeriel—four college friends from Newark— were shot execution-style on Mount Vernon Elementary School's playground on August 4. Only one of the four survived the shooting: Natasha Aeriel lived to tell the gruesome story of how Latino MS-13 gang members assassinated her friends and brother as part of a gang initiation (one of the killers, a 24-year-old Nicaraguan national, persuaded three others to kill the students).[214] Because the killers were immigrants and Booker supported the city's sanctuary policy that did not require residents to reveal their immigration status in order to receive city services, many were concerned.[215] But New Jersey Attorney General Anne Milgram ordered local law enforcement to inquire about the immigration status of the people they arrest.[216] The immigration issue only moved the Latino and even the Portuguese and Brazilian communities further away from Newark's Black communities.[217] The aftermath of the schoolyard killings was a key moment for coalition politics, not just between the mayor and Newark's communities, but also between the Black and Latino communities because the college students were Black and the killers were Latinos. Instead, many Newark outsiders, including 2008 presidential candidates Rudolph Giuliani and Tom Tancredo, politicized the triple murder to advance their policies on immigration reform and their political agendas. Tancredo even went so far as to encourage the victims' families to sue the city.[218] Meanwhile, some of the city's leaders asked whether Booker's responses to the triple murder were intended to unite the communities or to make the crime a grandstanding moment for his administration. As much as Booker apologized for the triple murder at press conferences, his apologies offered little solace to critics and even his support- ers on the city council. "We need him to bring communities together, and I don't think he displayed the leadership qualities we know he has," stated Councilwoman Dana Rone. Moreover, community activist Donna Jackson suggested that the mayor "need[ed] to pack his bags and go back to where he came from." Some even politicized the moment and called for the mayor's resignation. However, Booker said that "[w]e have to use this as a pulling together, not a ripping apart" moment.[219] The shooting victims' families ultimately sat through five years of court proceed- ings as the six murderers were tried; the defendants received sentences totaling 1,000 years—the longest in Essex County history.[220] The families did eventually sue the state (because the city's schools are state controlled) and received a $5 million settlement[221] over Newark Public Schools failure to address gang graffiti, have ade- quate security, and add new gate locks in the playground, which, as Councilman Rice forewarned, allowed "illegal activity or a crime" to happen.[222]

As much as the Booker administration worked with the state and county governments to solve the murders and offer cash rewards for arrests, getting the communities to come together and addressing internal and community concerns through coalition building unfortunately proved to be elusive. While Booker spoke about finding ways to address crime, rarely was he able to motivate the dif- ferent communities to address issues between them. As the *New York Times* stated in an editorial, "When Mr. Booker took office 13 months ago there were high hopes—in Newark and nationally—that he would bring the city together and turn it around. The killings have dimmed those hopes and further divided the city."[223] The newspaper suggested, as coalition politics requires, that the mayor and the city's leaders should not only come together, but they should also get ministers, community leaders, parents, activists, and others to rally around ending the violence in Newark's communities. Interestingly, some Newark residents, such as Al Tarik Onque, cofounder and director of the Stop Shootin' community organization, attempted to do it themselves, getting residents to sign pledges to prevent violence.[224] And Rahaman Muhammad revived his support group for fathers, Fathers in the Hood, in the wake of the shootings.[225] Several antiviolence groups also came together, marched on Broad Street, and held a rally to protest the triple murder and prevent future murders (but some of these community organizations disagreed about the administration).[226] Finally, letters from school children at the Mount Vernon School poured into the *Star-Ledger* office; these letters suggested that the mayor should try to resolve the violence, gang presence, and community problems children like them faced in their neighborhoods.[227]

Although these organizations and residents organized the community against crime, some of the same activists supported the Committee to Recall Cory A. Booker and began collecting signatures. With 80 volunteers and a $1,000 budget, the group had to get signatures from 25 percent of registered voters (or 32,000 signatures) in 160 days.[228] After only one year in office, Booker had inspired his critics to organize and attempt to coalition build, which proved to be more of a determined backlash against the mayor than actual sustainable coalition building.[229] Many of Booker's critics attended public forums and city council meetings trying to gather signatures to hold a special election.[230]

While homicide rates increased significantly during Booker's first year, by the end of 2007 and into the next year, rates dropped significantly (for almost 43 days in the beginning of 2008, in fact, there were no murders in Newark). And overall crime rates dropped as well. people questioned whether this decrease in crime was due to the administration's efforts or police reforms,[231] but Booker promoted himself as the one who solved this problem. However, Booker rarely evoked sustainable coalition building at the local level to address community issues. Regardless, the media focused on Booker as the city's savior. For example, following the playground shootings, he appeared on ABC's "Good Morning America" and "Nightline," CNN's "Anderson and Cooper 360," and other television and radio programs.[232] "Mr. Booker, having sold himself as Newark's savior, finds himself saddled with the burden of being superman," claimed the *New York Times* after the schoolyard shooters were found. "But he can use this moment—the sorrow, fear and outrage—to shepherd Newark to another chapter. Many community leaders are hoping he can use his charisma, passion and the news media spotlight to spark a civic renaissance and inspire local residents to take responsibility for what happens in their neighborhoods."[233]

The triple murder was a reminder to Booker and Newark's residents that coalition building could offer community approaches to addressing public safety concerns. While Booker was receiving national attention from the media, his critics were organizing against him. Newark and its new mayor had ideal moments for sustainable coalition politics, but the first six months of Booker's administration proved to be a daunting period. The homicide rate surged in 2006, and Booker attempted to establish the safe zone concept in various communities and schools. But many of Booker's foes and even supporters challenged the new mayor's crime initiatives. Booker also lost support and gained critics due to city government lay-offs, buyouts, and resignations. "Those austerity measures of reducing so many city employees affects so many residents," stated Councilman Ras Baraka. "It's bad government policy especially for a city like Newark with such high unemployment."[234] Even worse, Booker hired many outside firms, contractors, and consultants, which only added to Booker's inability to build a pragmatic coalition. Unfortunately, it appeared that the new mayor was aiding his financial backers rather than Newark residents, and this caused many residents to challenge the new mayor rather than establish actual coalition building. In other words, coalition building was organized against Booker more than to resolve the city's problems; this coalition building was an early beginning to backlash against the administration.

4

Booker's Community Development Initiatives

For Newark and its new mayor, resolving the city's numerous problematic urban issues proved to be a difficult feat during his first term. The one significant policy area that Booker attempted to resolve was Newark's community development. Whether it was because the city's residents had increased concerns about urban redevelopment due to policies of the former mayor, Sharpe James, and his administration's controversial land sales or because Booker tried to proactively respond to revitalization in Newark, the new mayor centered many of his policies around community development.[1] Because James had designated all of Newark as needing rehabilitation, he and other officials were able to sell and transfer city properties directly to developers instead of putting land up for sale in public auctions. The city was initially able to sell land at $4 a square foot (and some land for $1 a square foot) when private lots were easily selling for ten times as much. Some of these sales included significant discounts, especially for politically connected buyers. After Booker filed suit against the James administration to suspend land sales in 2006, the Superior Court prohibited the city from selling publicly owned property, which was an unusual ban.[2] Even the 2006 newly elected city council (including several members who had initially supported the previous administration's development proposals) voted to rescind two $80 million redevelopment trusts for neighborhood projects in light of ongoing concerns about these land sales.[3] And once Booker entered office, he tried to have the city reclaim 250 lots sold by the previous administration to 32 builders, who had failed to build on the land within 18 months.[4] The city was even able to sell 16 parcels of land to Lilac Development Group for nearly a $1 million instead of the initial amount of $268,000 proposed by the James administration.[5] Parks, downtown development, and special-needs housing were signature initiatives for the Booker administration.[6] "People don't often think the poor urban communities are that sophisticated when it comes to their environmental health," suggests Booker. "But it was a powerful part and it really framed the values we wrote into our administration and into development proposals."[7]

Community development is a significant area of public policy particularly as it relates to urban politics. Revitalizing urban areas like Newark and other post-industrial cities has become a key concern for many involved in the public policy and sustainability fields and especially in planning, architecture, and engineering. Frequently, cities contain fundamental elements and infrastructure features that suburban and rural areas lack. Recently, cities like Newark have undergone significant redevelopment as Americans recognize the potential an urban landscape offers in terms of community sustainability, mixed-use development, and transportation alternatives. Mixed-use development, for example, allows for commercial and residential zoning in the same general area. Even the city's industrial sector, with over 400 manufacturers employing 10,000 workers, could blossom further if businesses recognize Newark's potential since so many large land parcels are available for redevelopment, according to one Brookings Institution study. Often, cities give developers the flexibility to create residential areas near office or retail spaces; this planning feature is critical for walking, bicycling, or public transit. New Jersey, like most heavily suburbanized states, has been overbuilt and running out of usable land, especially in the last 20 years; therefore, much of the policy and planning focus has been centered-around rebuilding and reinvesting in cities like Newark. The Garden State has been instrumental in offering various policy incentives and design approaches that emphasize less automobile dependence and more mixed-use development initiatives. Transit Oriented Development (TOD) has become a signature initiative that gives grant, tax, and loan incentives to developers, architects, and engineers in order to make urban and, often, suburban areas become more sustainable. For instance, New Jersey has reinforced Transit Villages as a TOD-related initiative; this initiative encourages development around an existing transit station because it is critical for mixed-use development and to create a sustainable community. In addition, the state government supports grants like Green Acres, which funds and preserves open spaces and public parks. Also, the state's Neighborhood Revitalization Tax credit program gives businesses that invest in neighborhood projects a significant tax credit.[8] In addition, Urban Enterprise and Empowerment Zones (UEZ) have remained critical for commercial corridors to thrive because they lower sales taxes. At the local level, a number of New Jersey's cities also advance new development initiatives in blighted or brownfield (former industrialized) areas through Payment in Lieu of Taxes (PILOT) and tax abatements where developers enter into agreements with local governments to pay lower property taxes for a certain number of years; this lures potential renters or property owners to an underdeveloped community. A number of these concepts are critical elements in public policy, community development, city planning, and sustainable design. With suburban sprawl and limited green space, revitalizing New Jersey's cities through various policy incentives has been at the forefront of many public officials' and developers' minds. Many cities close to Newark, such as Jersey City (downtown and Journal Square in particular), Harrison (surrounding the PATH train station), Rahway, and New Brunswick, have become beneficiaries of these policies and ultimately serve as textbook examples of sustainable communities.[9]

Booker, like many twenty-first century mayors, recognized the potential Newark holds for reconfiguring and redeveloping its city and, in particular, its downtown. As a newly arrived resident and mayoral candidate, he promised to resolve many of the zoning and economic investment barriers that prevented Newark from thriving as a viable and sustainable city. For example, seeing that few tourists or residents frequented venues and restaurants downtown, Booker pushed for a mixed-use development Master Plan as well as "24/7" corridors, where more people would visit and live in the city's core, enabling the downtown to stay busy throughout the day and night. Booker also introduced the Living Downtown initiative to attract new residents to live downtown. Sadly, downtown Newark hardly offers a 24-hour-a-day, 7-day-a-week atmosphere; there are only a handful of residential complexes in downtown Newark. Moreover, there are few retail and dining options for residents and tourists that are open at night. Newark has little cityscape or desirable walking, sidewalk eating, or shopping areas, or even viable public spaces.[10] "We need more people living around here, more residential development," says Sean McGovern, owner of McGovern's Bar in downtown Newark. "We need people on the streets."[11]

By pushing for both commercial and residential development, the mayor advocated for retail spaces on the ground level in buildings and residential units on upper floors of new complexes. Yet Adam Zipkin, the city's deputy mayor, acknowledges it's harder than it sounds. "It's the chicken and the egg thing, where people want to move where there's amenities but the retail is not going to come until the people come," states Zipkin. "So what we're trying to do is create a critical mass almost all at once by just dropping it all in—the residential and retail—and building around transit hubs like Broad Street Station and Penn Station."[12] Within six months of taking office, Booker tried to demolish some 600 abandoned properties the city owned; he wanted to use the land for redevelopment purposes, especially in downtown. His downtown housing plan allowed developers to build in areas that were not slated for residential development as many of the abandoned properties were zoned for commercial use.[13] At the same time, the city faced difficulties in trying to seize properties, even from agreements signed years prior to the Booker administration. For example, property owners sued the city because the Booker administration upheld the James administration's use of eminent domain to claim 166 lots or 14 acres that spanned eight blocks surrounding Mulberry Street in downtown; this land was to be used for the proposed Mulberry Street Redevelopment Project, which included 2,000 apartments and stores near the Prudential Center. According to the city, about 60 percent of the properties were parking lots and were designated as blighted and thus needed redevelopment (however, the property owners argued the amount was closer to 30 percent). While Booker was against using eminent domain unless it was absolutely necessary, in this instance he supported the city's cause because the proposed condo developer donated over $53,000 to council members' campaigns. But the Superior Court ruled against the city, claiming that the city misused the state's definition of blighted and an area needing redevelopment.[14]

The fact that so many parcels of land surrounding downtown Newark remain vacant demonstrates the city's potential and also how much it remains a work in progress. Just by walking or driving on the city's main streets, and in particular its side streets downtown, a person can see the great variation in land use and development. The heart of the city lies around its transit hubs—from the legendary international airport just south of downtown to the Newark Pennsylvania Station and Gateway Center office complex (with its indoor walkways connecting buildings but not city streets) to its east and Newark Broad Street Station to its north; its downtown is a significant transportation center for the region. Immediately to the west of downtown is an area called University Heights where the city's universities are located—Rutgers University–Newark, New Jersey Institute of Technology (NJIT), University of Medicine and Dentistry of New Jersey (UMDNJ), and Essex County College. On weeknights, it's noticeable how many people leave the city's core in automobiles and buses as traffic downtown becomes a significant problem during rush hour. Surrounding the Broad Street commercial corridor and even its side streets are vast surface parking lots, vacant buildings, and empty lots, as well as several tall office towers where many white-collar employees work during the day. Many of them work for Prudential Insurance Company, which is headquartered in the heart of Newark, only blocks from Broad and Market Streets near the Prudential Center sports venue.

One redevelopment idea, which was conceived by the James administration, was to somehow link the entertainment centers—the New Jersey Performing Arts Center, Bears Stadium, and the Prudential Center—to create something similar to Times Square in downtown Newark. Booker eventually supported this cause and said that with all the complexes nearby, "[t]hey'll all resonate with each other."[15] However, the Newark Bears were in financial trouble by 2008: They filed for bankruptcy protection because the owners owed back rent to the county. Eventually, the team was put up for sale.[16] Many people also doubted the financial viability of a minor league baseball team considering that the New York Red Bulls of Major League Soccer in nearby Harrison drew more city residents, particularly Latino and Portuguese fans.[17] However, of all the disputes surrounding local sports, the conflict between City Hall and the owners of the New Jersey Devils about the Prudential Center was and has remained the most contentious.

Prudential Center Dilemma

One of Booker's most significant problems was to resolve the construction and promotion of the Prudential Center (also called the Rock). The National Hockey League hockey and entertainment arena was to be the largest venue in Newark. For better or worse, the project was a leftover initiative from, and significant centerpiece of, the James administration. Booker and many others in Newark were adamantly against the entertainment arena and forged coalitions to challenge the project because it would cost over $210 million in public money (with $100 million coming from the NHL New Jersey Devils' owners) and because the city would be responsible for millions in new infrastructure costs.[18] Yet the Rock was a political lightening rod for the city and the mayor, and it remains a sore spot for many residents, tourists, and investors as the project continues to draw national attention. Just as Booker was about to embark on his first mayoral term in 2006, he advocated stopping construction of the arena. Booker wanted to live up to his campaign promises, but this was not the most pragmatic policy approach because the deal had already been made a couple of years prior during the James administration and had statutory authority with state government support. Besides, the arena's foundation and early steel framing were already underway because contractors were trying to meet an aggressive construction schedule in order for the arena to open for the hockey season in fall 2007.

The 30-year contract between the Devils' owners and the Newark Housing Authority appeared problematic from the very beginning. The housing agency already faced federal investigation for purchasing property for the arena with money meant for low-income housing. The head of the Newark Downtown Core Redevelopment Corporation, Richard Monteilh, who was James' business administrator, was to help oversee the project. But Monteilh only lasted several months into Booker's first term before he decided leave the agency. While Booker suggested ending the construction project, which could lead to a lawsuit, the *Star-Ledger* urged City Hall to renegotiate the terms of the contract now that there was a new administration in City Hall.[19] The initial deal had required the Devils to lease the arena from the city for $2 million annually and be responsible for construction cost overruns; the city would receive seven percent of luxury seat and concession sales as well as general advertising revenue and naming rights. The city would also receive four percent of all gross revenues from other events at the arena. The income would range from $2 million to $6 million a year, but the arena's base rent, maintenance, and sports and job training programs would cost $2.5 million. Booker hired an arena consultant, Paul Fader, for $175 an hour to evaluate the existing agreement. Fader, a lawyer for former Governor Richard Codey and an attorney for the Jets-Giants who worked on the new Meadowlands Stadium deal, had also contributed a significant amount, some $10,000, to Booker's campaign.[20]

By October 2006, it appeared that Booker had become a supporter of the arena. He publicly stood alongside former Lehman Brothers banker and current Devils owner Jeff Vanderbeek at a press conference and stated that he would back the project. Interestingly, Vanderbeek donated $7,200 to Empower Newark, a political action committee that supports local candidates and has ties to Booker's (the mayor's former law firm serves as the organization's legal adviser).[21] Both men agreed to changes in the initial agreement, including hiring more minority-owned vendors and having the team fund Newark projects such as parks and recreation initiatives and provide for training and apprenticeship programs.[22] Still, as the

Star-Ledger said in an editorial, "the arena is still an unfortunately lopsided deal for a city that has better things to do with its money. The city is still on the hook for 'extras' such as land acquisition, infrastructure and road improvements that could easily drive the city's contribution to $300 million."[23] Vanderbeek said that he had no ill feelings toward Booker for his earlier stance against the project, and the mayor proclaimed himself a Devils fan and held a Devils' jersey with "Booker" and "07" printed on it.[24]

The chair of the commission that examined the arena development zone, Seton Hall Law School Dean Patrick Hobbs, said that with the mayor's endorsement, development surrounding the arena would be key. "There are 24 acres to be developed and they are the most important pieces of real estate in the city," Hobbs stated. However, a very important utility line that served as an underground transmission wire for the northeast electrical grid was buried under the land that would house the arena, so the project's backers had to negotiate with the power company.[25] Because of land swaps between a number of other developers, landholders, and the Newark Housing Authority (NHA), all the land deals in the 24-acre zone were placed on hold by the federal government.[26] In addition, the NHA director, Keith Kinard, refused to sign the redevelopment agreement because it would expose the authority to additional costs; therefore, in reality, the deal Booker had made with Vanderbeek was simply a gentlemen's agreement and Kinard had to sign off on this agreement.[27] It would take nearly ten months for the landholders to resolve the property agreements.[28]

Within weeks of signing the agreement, Booker's support for the arena started to falter. According to Fader's report for the city council and mayor, Newark was responsible for additional costs, including $18.8 million to repair streets surrounding the arena, $6.5 million for completing the Market Street Plaza, and $19.3 million for Triangle Park—both entry points to the arena zone. In addition to costs for upgrading and creating roads, and other infrastructure related to the arena, there were further costs associated with the project, including a pedestrian bridge from Newark Pennsylvania station estimated at $50 million that the city decided to wait to build until state or federal funding could assist with costs.[29] Also, Fader's analysis showed that the city might have to cover more than $102 million.[30]

Not surprisingly, in January 2007, the city council approved a $44.7 million bond to finish the street projects, increasing the city's financial burden from an approved $210 million to nearly $255 million[31] (later estimates put the amount closer to $300 million).[32] Ultimately, the entrance plaza ran behind schedule and required using land acquisition and Urban Enterprise Zone funds to cover extra costs.[33] "It's going to be an initial hit for us, with the hopes for paying it off later on," assured Booker.[34] Also in January, the state Attorney General's Office issued subpoenas for the Newark Downtown Core Redevelopment Corporation that was overseeing the project. The state Department of Transportation received subpoenas for the road projects surrounding the arena. Newark had received $30 million from the state DOT to redesign roadways, but the James administration had used over $3 million to purchase the Mulberry Street Mall while only a small portion of that land was used for street widening and most of the parcel went to the arena. The DOT suggested that the Devils' owner reimburse the state for that money, but no one could decide who would cover the expenses.[35] The city also spent closer to $2 million over the arena's first seven months for police, fire, and engineering inspectors on overtime because securing the permanent certificate of occupancy took months, even though the mayor assured the public that the costs would decrease over time.[36] Additional costs included protecting a largely suburban clientele since they became a key concern for many local officials. According to one poll, 14 percent of respondents said that because of the new arena they would stay away from Newark, even though more police patrolled the area on game and event days to ensure public safety. Expenses for the first year was $3 million for police overtime (or $10,000 to $15,000 in police overtime per event).[37]

While cost estimates increased, many Newarkers remained skeptical that such an arena, especially designed around hockey in a majority Black and Latino city, would draw local interest, even though there had been attempts made to create a small hockey team in the city's East Ward.[38] Furthermore, the front of the complex and its main entrance faced east toward Newark Pennsylvania Station, beckoning suburbanites and tourists, and the arena's back walls ignored the city's main thoroughfares, Broad and Market Streets. "They turned their backside to Broad Street," argued City Council President Mildred Crump. Yet hockey team owner Jeff Vanderbeek and supporters of the arena claimed that the blank wall facing Broad and Market Streets would eventually have an entrance and building in front of the complex and that the arena was merely a part of the city's greater development plan.[39]

Vanderbeek had been disappointed with the turnout for his hockey team in the distant Meadowlands Continental Airlines Arena (which was later renamed the Izod Center in 2007). Only 8,200 fans attended hockey games in the outdated venue, even though it had seats for more than double that amount. Vanderbeek hoped to see the hockey team thrive in a downtown urban area instead.[40]

The new downtown arena was to seat 17,625 people for hockey games, 19,500 for basketball games, and 1,000 more for concerts. With a 350-seat restaurant, 78 luxury suites, and 2,200 club seats, Newark's arena was going to be significantly more modern and spacious than the Meadowlands complex.[41] But the competition between the Newark arena and the Izod Center for other sports events and concerts became a bone of contention for many public officials including the state's New Jersey Sports and Exposition Authority, which operates the Meadowlands arena.[42] While the Izod Center offered lower-cost events and was one of the highest-grossing facilities in the nation, the Newark arena had better transit access, acoustics, and technology, and Vanderbeek had to book over 150 events beyond the Devils' games to keep it financially solvent.[43] However, most public officials saw the potential for sports and entertainment complexes in cities like Newark. "Everybody is always talking about how we needed to revitalize our cities," stated Essex County Executive Joe DiVincenzo. "Here's a chance to do it. The arena is critical to the health of the state's largest city, and we should be doing every possible thing to make sure in succeeds."[44] If fact, officials tried to broker an agreement between the arenas so that the state's sports authority would also have oversight of the operational management of the new arena.[45] When George Zoffinger resigned as the authority's head, the *Star-Ledger* predicted that "it's over" for the Izod Center.[46] (In a letter to Governor Jon Corzine, Booker later criticized that plans to upgrade the Izod Center were "fiscally irresponsible" and would harm the Prudential Center. So many politicians and political candidates chimed into the debate once the letter became public that the mayor said it was his "J.V. mistake" to have written the letter at all.[47])

While questions lingered about the arena's success, city officials made an agreement to name the arena the Prudential Center, or "The Rock," and announced future event plans. Prudential Financial—the hometown insurance company headquartered only blocks away—agreed to pay Devils' owners $5 million annually for at least 20 years. Typically, naming rights have gone for significantly more money, and many agreed it was a modest amount for a large New Jersey–New York media market.[48] In March 2007, the "top off" ceremony was held to recognize the setting of the 2,500-pound beam that comprised the highest structural point of the arena. Booker attended the event and led spectators and construction workers in a moment of silence for Newark resident and ironworker Jamal Lawson, who had fallen to his death from an 85-foot high steel frame in September.[49] As early as summer 2007, more information about the progress of the arena was made public. The Rock would open in October as workers were meeting construction deadlines, and the first event would be a concert by New Jersey's own Jon Bon Jovi.[50] In addition, several bars in the area around the Rock opened during the years of its construction, including Hell's Kitchen, the Arena Bar, Devil's Advocate, and Dinosaur Bar-B-Que. Adjacent to the arena is a $35 million, 150-room Courtyard by Marriott Hotel; of the construction workers who built the hotel, 30 percent were from Newark, and 50 percent of the hotel's staff were Newarkers (this was the first hotel in downtown Newark in nearly 40 years). Also, a planned boutique Hotel Indigo would occupy a nearby historic bank building. Marriott received $9 million from local and state sources while five additional commercial projects were granted almost $400 million in tax incentives, the largest amount granted by any one city.[51] A number of investors contacted the deputy mayor and the city's Brick City Development Corporation to offer incentives to existing or prospective businesses interested in the area, even though development around new arenas can perform well or poorly depending on the city and the neighborhood's existing vitality.[52] There were a number of small stores near the arena, and many of Brick City's incentives would help them to target potential customers, but rents would likely increase.[53] Finally, in September, arena owners announced nearly 1,200 job openings and organizers expected over 5,000 candidates to attend the job fair.[54] In fact, the Devils hired closer to 1,400 employees, 577 of whom were Newarkers.[55]

Despite the positive results of the arena, the relationship between the Devils' owner and the city soured. Some council members questioned why the city did not have access to a luxury box, and a number of them were planning to boycott the Bon Jovi concert on the arena's opening day. At a council meeting just weeks before this event, Council President Mildred Crump said, "To me, the height of disrespect is the city of Newark has put into the project $210 million—which is the baseline—and the Devils have not given us a box. They're dissing us at a level that's disrespectful."[56] But Vanderbeek claimed that the city never requested a suite, even though some cities with venues similar to the Rock have a box for public officials' use, particularly if clients, contractors, or dignitaries are in town for business.

In addition, the city had to hire additional traffic-control officers so visitors could arrive safely from the nearby train station. While car parking was plentiful around downtown, the city emphasized public transportation instead. "We want to make this the most accessible arena in the nation," stated Booker.[57] But a nearby pedestrian bridge connecting a parking deck and the Rock had not been completed because a permit had not been issued and a stop-construction order was enforced.[58] Another issue was that the arena was built too close to the nearby streets and could possibly be susceptible to terrorist attacks. Considering that terrorists reportedly cased the nearby Prudential Financial's headquarters, it was surprising that the Department of Homeland Security did not perform a security survey of the site.[59]

After months of various concerns, on opening day in October 2007, Booker recognized James for his efforts in getting the arena started and the two shook hands and embraced in a full hug. "If it wasn't for my predecessor, Mayor Sharpe James, Senator Sharpe James, we would not be here today," acknowledged Booker. While James attended the ribbon-cutting ceremony, he was not invited to speak. Yet Booker remained optimistic about the arena's potential for the city and its redevelopment initiatives. "I know it will continue to fuel and energize the resurgence of Newark," said Booker. "Indeed, this is a testimony to hope."[60] Many restaurants in the nearby Ironbound community felt the affects of the Prudential Center's events—some even reported a 40 to 60 percent increase in business, especially if they offered patrons a discount. There was even discussion about establishing a bus service to the arena from Ironbound district businesses.[61]

While the arena's opening night appeared promising, the area around the Rock appeared more problematic. Like Newark itself, much of the surrounding blocks remained overwhelmingly undeveloped, containing parking lots or abandoned buildings. While there were plans to revitalize the area with new amenities, the reality was that there were few dining and shopping options for visitors and residents. There were a variety of proposals to build more bars and cafés and even to create a children's museum as well as to complete the pedestrian bridge from Newark Pennsylvania station. However, lack of funding and legal battles delayed many of these projects.[62] And some stores, like Borok's, a furniture store on Broad Street near the arena, were forced to close because their properties were key parcels for redeveloping around the Rock since the city planned to acquire properties or facilitate land swaps for the arena.[63] Still, Booker remained optimistic that the downtown area would be transformed in due time. "I want the public to go to our downtown and spend an entire day eating, going to shows, museums and other types of entertainment," said the mayor. "I see thousands of more residential units so it is a 24-hour district."[64] But the nation's financial downturn was one of the realities in 2008, and Newark's redevelopment, even around the arena, was affected. Even though Newark might have appeared to attract visitors to the Rock on game and event nights, the "once-ambitious plans for new downtown hotels and sky-scrapers have faltered as lending for such project[s] have dried up."[65] Ultimately, redevelopment surrounding the stadium remains stalled since the administration has been unable to acquire a dozen properties for future redevelopment.[66]

Keeping visitors in Newark after the event or game became a serious problem for city officials; this was largely due to the city's crime-ridden image. National commentators still portrayed the post-industrial city as a forgotten and destitute place. In March 2008, for example, ESPN hockey commentator Barry Melrose said on the cable sports network that visitors should not go beyond the arena "espe-cially if you have a wallet or anything because the area around the building is awful." But the *Star-Ledger* disproved that fear; their analysis concluded that there was no correlation between crime and arena events. And Vanderbeek claimed that visitors were "getting more comfortable with downtown Newark."[67] In fact, the number of fans taking public transit was 50 percent, 15 percent higher than initially thought, according to various surveys conducted by Vanderbeek and the *New York Times*.[68] But a number of council members also sought to make money for the city by urging police to give parking tickets to visitors, knowing that extra expenses for the arena would reach nearly $6 million annually.[69] Using the fact that events at the arena were heavily attended by fans, City Hall and Vanderbeek tried to lure the Nets basketball team and owners to the Rock. But Bruce Ratner, the principal owner of the team, already had plans to complete a mixed-use project and arena in Brooklyn, although there were a series of delays and setbacks on that complex. Reportedly, few investors and financers were on board with the Brooklyn proposal. But Ratner's executives brushed aside the speculations because he was able to secure financing for other real estate projects, including the Frank Gehry tower in the lower end of Manhattan; the same architect would design the pro-posed arena in Brooklyn.[70] Instead, the Nets chose to play their preseason games at the Prudential Center in 2009, with 13,000 in attendance,[71] and agreed to a two-year stay at the Rock before moving to Brooklyn[72] (projections estimated that the Nets' 39 home games would generate about $5 million in extra business around the area[73]).

Thus, the Rock appeared to draw fans and interest to downtown Newark; however, in reality, the arena faced closure several times because the owners had only received temporary, not permanent, certificates of occupancy. This was because officials failed to resolve problems with the emergency systems for clearing smoke from stairwells. This would be a sticky point for the Newark Housing Authority, as they were the leaseholders to the arena. In addition, the Newark Downtown Core Redevelopment Corporation called for a financial performance review of sales at the Rock. The firm hired for this purpose also reviewed how the arena compared in ticket sales to its competitors.[74] By year's end, Devils' team owners had defaulted on their lease because they failed to pay $2.4 million in rent. But Devils' owners argued that the NHA owed them $800,000 in penalties because of construction delays and a $210,000 credit for the following year's rent. Even though the team owed the city money for sports and job training programs per the agreement, they wanted to send this money directly to community groups and not the housing authority. But the authority blamed the Devils for the delays. City officials also said that the hockey team owed over $41,000 for installation of sewer lines and that a number of subcontractors had not been paid. Per the contracted agreement, if the disputes were not resolved within 30 days, team owners and city officials were to go to arbitration and a panel chosen by both sides would issue a decision.[75]

In May 2010, the NHA made the dispute more official by sending a "notice of dispute" to Devils management over the back rent owed on the Rock. The letter, written by NHA lawyers, suggested that as they had received no response to earlier correspondence, they would take steps toward arbitration. Vanderbeek claimed that he was "confused" about the letter and that, even after contacting the mayor's office, "they seemed equally confused as to why the letter was sent."[76] But NHA officials argued that $4 million was a "substantial amount of money," and they were carrying out the public's interest.[77] By June, Devils' owners had submitted a new offer to the city saying they would immediately pay $3.9 million in back rent after a deduction of $1.7 million in capital expenditures and they would make a separate payment of $346,576 for jobs and youth programs. However, the NHA asked a judge to declare a 2005 agreement about parking revenues, which would have given the hockey team $2.7 million a year in parking revenues, void. Also, Booker and Kinard argued that the agreement was not approved by NHA commissioners or its director and it was not ratified by the city council. In other words, the Devils payment dispute only became worse in 2010.[78] Toward the end of the year, Superior Court Judge Patricia Costello finally ruled that the parking agreement between the NHA and Devils management was an unenforceable contract and the questions surrounding the revenue should go to arbitration.[79] In an effort to get around the judge's decision and arbitration matters, Vanderbeek and his vice chairman and partner, Michael Gilfillan, wrote a *Star-Ledger* op-ed piece that stated that their arena and others in cities helped provide economic growth in overlooked urban areas. They presented examples of cities such as Washington, DC, and San Diego where sports facilities have spawned revitalized communities and created new businesses. They argued that "the same is starting to occur in Newark. Since opening in late 2007, the Rock has hosted more than 4 million guests, primarily at night, creating a vibrancy downtown. This should lead to some of them investing and living in Newark, as has happened in other cities."[80]

One of the positive events at the arena was the National College Athletic Association's eastern regional basketball tournament, which was held at the Rock in March 2011. For nearly a week, the city was buzzing with visitors and tourists. The NCAA had 1,000 volunteers to help with organizing, planning, and showing events and programming related not only to March Madness but also Newark. These volunteers were staffed at public locations like the airport, transit stations, hotels, and communities. Many of them, in fact, came from city businesses and even Booker's new community volunteering nonprofit, Brick City SERVES. As Vanderbeek said, "From a transportation standpoint, you've got everything at your fingers. We have as much, if not more, to offer than any place else."[81] There were flash mobs and packed restaurants and businesses surrounding the arena by the end of March, all due to the NCAA tournament. It was considered highly successful, especially because the games drew more than 55,000 people to Newark and officials hoped that visitors' perceptions of the city were positive.[82] Booker received close to 200 interview requests that week, and he completed over a dozen interviews within a couple of days. He stated that, as mayor, he brought a national spotlight to the city in addition to philanthropic dollars. Vanderbeek stated that he had "never been more proud of the cooperation between the city, sometimes the state, and the corporations. We want people to move in and say 'I should think about moving my business to the city.'"[83]

But team owners were able to gloat some more in the spring of 2012 when arbitrators decided in their favor in their dispute with the city about back rent. The NHA was awarded $14.7 million in back rent, relocation fees, and fines, while the Devils were awarded $15.3 million in unpaid parking revenue, capital costs, and taxes. In other words, the city owed team owners $600,000. City Hall was very disappointed with the ruling, arguing that it was unfair, especially because the agreement was "entered into by the prior administration with the Devils."[84] Aside from the $600,000 the city would have to pay the team owners, Newark also had to pay $3.7 million in legal and consulting fees, of which $1.9 million was for arbitration. In a detailed *Star-Ledger* analysis, their investigation showed poor communication, mistrust, and stubbornness between team owners and city officials, even though "the city had a chance to cut a better deal than it ended with on a least five occasions." And the newspaper's review showed that "many of Booker's post-arbitration statements are at odds with the facts and blame for failed deals belongs as much with the mayor as anyone."[85] Booker did try to meet with team owners before the dispute went into arbitration, but he proved largely unsuccessful at reaching a comprise with the Devils. The parties met six times since the mayor took office, and they were reportedly close to a deal, but they failed to resolve matters.[86] Booker largely blamed Vanderbeek and Devils management for taking the city into arbitration, but PolitiFact New Jersey determined that the mayor was "wrong" in his statements about team owners when Booker said they were resolved to take the city on and that city officials had "no choice."[87] PolitiFact also discovered that Booker's claims that Vanderbeek had refused to pay any funds to charitable causes (as they were required to do under the agreement) were true. The Devils did not give $1.5 million over the three years of the lease agreement for youth, community sports, and job training programs, although they did make a $346,000 payment for the programs in the first year of their lease.[88]

Likely the most dramatic moment of the entire Newark–Devils saga was when Booker went public—or essentially went rogue—after the arbitration ruling. At a bombastic press conference staged right in front of the arena, the mayor shockingly called Vanderbeek "a high-class, high-falutin huckster and hustler" and said that Vanderbeek was a "Wall Street millionaire that played into every stereotype that's out there." Moreover, according to the mayor, the Devils' owner was "one of the most despicable owners" in the NHL. According to Booker, Vanderbeek "came into this city with a mouthful of promises and a pocketful of lies." For example, according to the mayor, Vanderbeek did not fulfill the agreement to build a recreation center near the arena; "He suddenly picks up his papers and walks away like a kid taking his marbles or his basketball," Booker said. Instead, Vanderbeek was "sitting pretty in his fancy office waiting for us to write him more checks? Hell no. It is time that we had justice from this building." But Vanderbeek argued that, "clearly the mayor has not spent a lot of time on this." He also said that he hoped that "cooler heads [would] prevail" and that he had "no doubt the facts [would] speak for themselves."[89] In the past, the mayor had called the team owner a mensch, or a person of integrity, as well as a good friend and partner of the city, and then suddenly he referred to Vanderbeek as a huckster and hustler.[90] The *Star-Ledger* called the mayor's rampage "over the top," but recognized that the city had made a poor deal under the former administration, especially because parking revenue for the city was significantly less than predicted. This $210 million deal had not been decided by the city council but instead by James' officials merely through a letter between the Newark Housing Authority and Devils owners. "And in an odd move, the arbitrators chose to enforce that letter, even though they acknowledged it wasn't legally binding."[91]

Days after the bombastic press conference, the mayor wrote an op-ed piece to explain his public criticism. Booker stated that he had "every expectation" that Vanderbeek "would be a man of his word." Instead, according to the mayor, "I've watched him employ a host of legal maneuvers and bad-faith negotiation tactics in order to evade his public commitments." Booker went on to outline several examples of the team owner's tactics to avoid making annual contributions toward the city's job training and youth organization funds as well as the recreation center.[92] But the battle over the Rock only became worse after the arbitration decision. Suddenly, just as the Devils were heading into playoff season, fewer police were on hand to help fans cross streets, making it especially dangerous to attend games. Booker acknowledged that some police had been reassigned so more officers were present in Newark's communities but that the decision had had nothing to do with the Vanderbeek dispute.[93] Since the city had paid nearly $11 million for police around the Rock for nearly five years, city officials publicly announced that if team owners wanted more security then the Devils should pay for the police. With the city's fiscal problems, Newark could no longer afford to station nearly four dozen officers at the arena, according to police officials. But many area business owners grew concerned that the image of fewer police and the ongoing feud between the mayor and Vanderbeek might have an impact on their businesses.[94] In fact, a roving band of teenagers assaulted and robbed several visitors outside the arena at a Red Hot Chili Peppers concert only weeks after the police reassignment, even though Booker claimed more police were assigned to events like the concert.[95] Because the Devils were in the 2012 hockey playoffs that spring, additional police were suddenly seen on the streets, and police confirmed "more than a dozen arrests" for robberies and assaults.[96] It appeared as though Devils management returned fire against Booker by publicly disclosing that the mayor's office requested tickets to Bruce Springsteen's upcoming sold-out concert at the Prudential Center. But City Hall officials denied the team owners' claim. While the blame games continued between team management and Booker, the mayor decided to take up poetry and present some of his to the public in honor of the 2012 Dodge Poetry Festival, which came to the city in October. Not surprisingly, some of his poetry was in reference to the feud with Devils owners to which the *Star-Ledger* said that Booker's attacks were now becoming "poetry slams" and "Booker hardly seems like a man in need of yet another form of literary release. One would think his nonstop Twitter habit would provide all the catharsis one mayor could need."[97] But this drama continued into the NHL 2012 playoff series. The media frequently asked the mayor if he planned to attend any Devils games at the Rock, considering that, after the arbitration ruling, he vowed he would not enter the arena (even though he offered the team a parade if they won the Stanley Cup). One reporter asked Booker if he would attend the first Devils–Kings Stanley Cup finals, but he said he would be in Washington. When the reporter pointed out the game was not on the same day, the mayor said he would attend. But the mayor was in the "midst of a precarious dance" after publicly rebuking Vanderbeek.[98] For the team owner's part, Vanderbeek told the *New York Times* that Booker's rant was a mayoral meltdown or a "Mel Gibson moment or a Charlie Sheen moment."[99] However, Vanderbeek was also not out of the woods, at least financially speaking, because team management had not paid nearly $80 million owed to their banks, they had $200 million in overall debt, and they were looking for additional investors. Yet the Devils were still able to bring in over $32 million of additional revenue due to the playoffs and 11 sold-out home games. Plus, the post-season run brought nearly $4 million to area bars and restaurants.[100]

    The entire Prudential Center dilemma finally came to an official end almost six years later; as the mayor called it, it was "an enraging five year saga."[101] Following outside arbitration between Devils' owners and Newark in late February 2013, the ruling required the city to build a new parking deck and receive a 1.37 percent tax on ticket sales. The city would also pay the Devils $2.7 million a year for parking revenue and a new $1.25 facility fee would be added to every ticket for all events with a gradual increase after the second year. The fees are expected to raise $2 million a year and city officials estimated that the new deal could bring in $50 million over the term of the lease. Even though the ordeal ended all litigation between both sides in late spring 2013, it cost some $4 million in legal fees. The Newark Housing Authority would not be nearly as engaged in the new agreement, but the parking authority would help with new development initiatives surrounding the arena. The city council approved the deal 7-1, with only Councilwoman Crump voting against the decision. Although Councilman Augusto Amador supported the agreement, he reminded the public, "We're going to get about $50 million for an investment of $250 million."[102] Booker felt that the dramatic affair and specifically his public rant had gained public attention and enabled city officials to complete the deal. "For us the untold story was that it may seem that I was losing my temper or something like that, but it was a very strategic decision that we had to figure out a way to create fire and controversy again to get everyone back hopefully to the table working constructively," claims the mayor.[103]

Booker and his supporters remain hopeful about the Prudential Center, and that the negotiated deal will spur future development. "It's connected to development around the arena," offers the mayor. "It's connected to parking; it's connected to a long term sustainable relationship that's going to help us in a lot of different fronts—most importantly for me, the budget." As for how long it took to complete the deal, Booker admits that, "it was a long ugly affair and it shouldn't have taken so long but it all stems from two of the biggest mistakes that Sharpe made, in my opinion, in the stewardship of this city: the disposition of land and the settlement with the Port Authority over Newark International Airport payments owed to the city." He further adds that

> Sharpe settled for pennies on the dollar in order to get a quick infusion of cash to build the arena. That was the only time in my four years outside of city government that I lobbied the council. I said, "don't do this deal. We can get enough revenue into the city to double our police force and create 100 new parks." It was just unbelievable. And the land the city use[d] to own—these lots—hundreds and hundreds of millions of dollars of revenue was just given to friends [of Sharpe James].[104]

Clearly the city's agreement with the Devils was one of the most problematic sagas of the Booker administration. Not only did the mayor give a diatribe against the owner, the episode left the city with a costly financial agreement. Booker was presented with a very difficult challenge because he was not initially in favor of the $210 million agreement as it was a holdover from the previous administration. While blaming the NHA for the agreement would be "inappropriate" according to former director Harold Lucas, the agency had the statutory authority to raise and pay for bonds and became the chief facilitators of the project because the NHA had a significant financial stake in the deal. The team owners, on the other hand, were a part of the deal, and they paid a good share of the construction costs, which was highly unusual.[105] But the team faced $200 million in debt and in August 2013 Vanderbeek sold the Devils to Philadelphia 76ers owners Joshua Harris and David Blitzer for a reported $320 million. Long term, however, economic spinoffs and in particular opening new businesses related to the arena has been challenging during the Great Recession era, according to Michael Meyer.[106] Booker hoped to amend the flawed agreement and appeared optimistic that adding community-related initiatives would resolve some of the chief concerns. But once additional expenses like new roadways and infrastructure were added to the city's share of the bill, it became increasingly clear that the city as well as the administration were over their heads as they entered into arbitration.

Newark as Themed Villages

As mayor, Booker, along with his administration, advanced community development through a major master plan. Booker envisioned the potential Newark held if the city planned along smart growth lines or predetermined elements based on land use, environmental conditions, and transportation uses. Interestingly, the city had not advanced a master plan in years. "We had zoning ordinances that had not been comprehensively reexamined in half a century and a master plan that hadn't been touched in decades," claimed Deputy Mayor Zipkin.[107] Booker was determined to see that Newark not only had a plan but that his administration also carried out development initiatives, particularly in the downtown area, that either already existed or had yet to be developed. Michael Meyer, director of Housing and Real Estate, suggested that the master plan had two core components: (1) to address equitable growth by maximizing opportunities for current residents, particularly for those of color and in poverty, and (2) to center on physical development to maximize housing opportunities in various communities, especially relating to sustainability. "First class planners and thinkers were directly involved in the plan and it was a big picture and testimony to the administration to maximize community vision that will survive this administration and beyond with proscriptive policies that will test over time," according to Meyer.[108] The master plan was considered bold, detailed, and impressive; the plan was delineated in a 106-page document that had 76 pages of colorful illustrations and a bibliography that was available online.[109] Many community leaders found the plan very impressive and thought that the administration had been very responsive to balanced development.[110] For example, the administration tried to address mixed-housing in the city's downtown by supporting a number of condominium projects. From January to May 2007, there were 22 condo projects with more than 770 units before the Newark planning board, whereas the year before, only 155 condo units were approved. Long term, 1,000 units would be completed during the administration's tenure, and another 1,000 units would be added to the downtown area.[111] "This is a sign of revitalization," claimed Booker. "There wasn't a condominium market in the city of Newark and now, in a matter of months, we are seeing a market."[112] But nearby population-rival Jersey City saw more than 15,000 units approved within five years and is also expected to see that many a few years into the future. "Newark is still a frontier location, similar to where Jersey City was in the 1980s," acknowledged James Hughes, Dean of the Edward J. Bloustein School of Planning and Public Policy at Rutgers University.[113]

One of the first concepts the mayor and his administration embraced included community-themed villages. These small communities or community villages would ideally draw specific vocational or area residents into privately and publicly invested emerging neighborhoods. From Warren Street Village for NJIT fraternity and sorority residences to Teachers Village for educators and Arts Village near NJPAC for artists, Booker and his administration saw areas in and around downtown as mixed-use communities for specific groups. Through the application of some of the community development policy initiatives used in other cities (like TODs, PILOTs, UEZs), the mayor thought to attract potential residents and existing Newarkers to a viable and livable downtown. Newark was not the only New Jersey city to consider this approach, as many area cities were carrying out similar village initiatives to create mixed-income and mixed-development communities.[114] For the Booker administration, supporting mixed-income housing, particularly in and around Newark's downtown, was essential. "The challenge in our downtown is to get the affordable units; the challenge in our neighborhoods is to get the market rate units so it's constantly getting mixed income in both areas," stated Deputy Mayor Zipkin. "A huge focus from day one from the mayor was making sure we aren't just making development activity just for development activity but that we're connecting it on all levels to our residents. So in the housing component, making sure we're building housing that is affordable to Newark residents."[115]

Teachers Village

Teachers Village became one of the first and most important of these villages because outside funding and significant fundraising was already taking place for education-related initiatives. Booker and his administration consider Teachers Village a signature initiative, especially because it would bring high-quality design to downtown and replace surface lots while displacing few Newarkers.[116] Between Facebook's $100 million donation in 2011 and other corporate investments as well as government and public foundation grants and loans, Teachers Village was well funded, and it would house Newark's educators in convenient downtown quarters. What made Newark's proposed Teachers Village in the Four Corners Historic District especially unique is the city's medium-size population and the notion of workforce housing for teachers within a specified downtown district. It's been estimated that just 17 percent of the city's teachers live in Newark, and new incentives are needed for public sector employees to live in the city.[117] While the plan appeared controversial to some, it could serve as an effective and necessary model for downtown revitalization for Newark and other cities. Newark's Teachers Village could become an enlightened paradigm of effective urban redevelopment so long as the incentives are beneficial for all those involved in the process. Mayor Booker and developer Ron Beit pushed for a specific area of downtown to be completely revitalized; this area is conveniently near City Hall and is home to three potential charter schools. Through public financing and private investment, this Teachers Village project would center around a proposed school area—Halsey and William Streets and Meridian and Treat Places. One of the key components of the project was to provide workforce housing for Newark's teachers in downtown. The project's groundbreaking occurred on February 9, 2012, with great fanfare, and the mayor, developers, and investors attended the event. Nearly 1,000 construction and permanent jobs will result from the project.[118]

In 2007, Beit believed the city held redevelopment potential and encouraged investors to construct Teachers Village. The 38-year-old attorney-developer and his firm, RBH Group, already owned more than 25 properties in Newark's downtown.[119] In fact, Beit has been a landlord in that area for over two decades. After acquiring 32 contiguous parcels in the Four Corners Historic District of the area south of Market Street, Beit has been anxious to complete the redevelopment process. For example, a 12-block area contains many parking lots, blighted buildings, and unused land, and even the abandoned, but stunning, Paramount Theater. Almost 91 percent of the land is parking lots, and the remainder is dilapidated properties.[120] By creating 15 million square feet of mixed-use downtown space, the redevelopment would serve as a magnet for teachers and other Newark residents and shoppers.[121] "The addition of retail, schools, and a daycare center will turn an underutilized section of downtown into a vibrant, 24/7 neighborhood—all from the mind of international starchitect and Newark native Richard Meier," according to Booker. "A game changer like Teachers Village would never break ground without the unique collaboration between the City, the State, Ron Beit, and countless other partners."[122]

Two buildings (totaling 90,000 square feet) will serve three relocated charter schools (Great Oaks, Discovery Charter School, and Team Academy) and a daycare center (CHEN School Daycare). These schools will serve 950 students (150 pre-K and 800 K–8 students).[123] The remaining eight buildings (about 200,000 square feet) will be rental apartments with 221 units for qualified teachers paying monthly rents at $700 for studios, $1,100 for one bedrooms, and $1,400 for two bedrooms. Almost 70,000 square feet will be dedicated for retail and commercial space, which will include a specific area for a major grocery store[124] (since 38 percent of Newark residents' spending on groceries happens outside the city[125]). A number of unique amenities will be available for residents, including a gymnasium and a sports club.[126] By creating a range of newly constructed retail spaces or a new retail corridor, city officials hope to make Teachers Village a magnet for teachers as well as a draw for young professionals and middle-class consumers and residents.[127]

One of the key areas for development adjacent to the proposed Teachers Village is the Four Corners Millennium Project. For an estimated $410 million, the four block area surrounding Broad and Market Streets would be converted from empty office and warehouse space into more than 800 apartments and a 130-room hotel as well as 150,000 street-level retail spaces spread among several buildings. Beit and RBH Group are also heading this project and are applying for $33 million in Urban Transit Hub tax credits. Even though new apartments have opened in the area at the Bowers Building and Rock Plaza Lofts, additional housing above downtown retail space, particularly in the area near Teachers Village, was crucial to the administration.[128]

One of the most important components for the Teachers Village project is its public- and private-sector backing. From a mixture of local, state, and federal grants and tax credits to private and public financing, the project has an unusual mix of funding and has raised $150 million. Of this amount, $40 million is from the state's Economic Development Authority through the Urban Transit Hub Tax Credit, which served as a very important primer for investing in urban communities.[129] This incentive encourages developers to construct projects near public transit and particularly in existing cities (whereas most new construction projects are financed in exurbs or sprawling suburban communities and subdivisions). Several smaller cities in New Jersey have been the recipient of this tax credit, including New Brunswick, Harrison, and Rahway.[130] During the Booker administration, Newark has used the state's Urban Transit Hub Tax Credit program—a tax benefit initiative for developers and corporations to encourage redevelopment near public transit in nine qualifying areas. Newark, being one of the qualified cities, lured Panasonic Corporation to its downtown from nearby Secaucus so they could be closer to public transit and receive over $102 million through the Hub tax credit.[131] But the Urban Transit Hub Tax Credit has been criticized for helping larger corporations and not small businesses or businesses outside of New Jersey. Panasonic as well as Prudential have benefited from the tax credit as they are constructing additional buildings in downtown Newark. But critics charge the tax credits have helped these corporations with intrastate moves and creating few jobs.[132]

Another $60 million in federal and private-sector aid will come from New Markets Tax Credits (NMTC) to help with new school construction. Most of the tax credits will go to investors from Goldman Sachs through its Urban Investment Group.[133] Congress established the NMTC program to allow individual and corporate taxpayers to receive a credit against income taxes by investing in qualified projects. This incentive has been very popular in rebuilding many inner-city and rural communities from California to Maine. The NMTC initiative has spurred growth in numerous sectors, most particularly in real estate reinvestment.[134] It is administered by the United States Treasury Department's Community Development Financial Institutions fund (CDFI). As of January 2010, the CDFI's fund has allocated $26 billion for the NMTC program, and New Jersey has been one of the top ten recipients. But the Government Accountability Office found that the CDFI Fund Director needs to collect additional data to improve overall program performance.[135] Additional financing for the Teachers Village project will come from the city government, the state Casino Reinvestment Development Authority, and federal bonds from the Qualified School Construction Bonds. A significant share of the private-sector financing will come from loans and investments through Goldman Sachs, Prudential Financial, TD Bank, and New Jersey Community Capital.[136]

In terms of actual construction requirements, there are several important considerations. Because Teachers Village is planned in a recognized historic district (even though the district is currently blighted), lead architect Richard Meier plans to limit the buildings' heights and incorporate some historical elements into the buildings. "I was born in Newark and have vivid memories of visiting my family's business in downtown Newark," said Meier. "This is a sort of homecoming for me and an opportunity for me to apply a lifetime of skills learned in the world arena to the revitalization of a major area of the city's downtown."[137] The Newark Living Downtown Plan requires that all new building fronts facing Halsey Street be four stories tall, which Meier will follow; however, other buildings set back from the street will be six stories high.[138] Meier's plans also include generous windows open to light, elevated courtyards with green terraces, and gardens. Sustainable designs, new landscaping, and streetscape improvements will also be important elements to the community, according to Meier.[139]

Since the proposal's public unveiling in February 2012, several concerns have been raised, typically about redevelopment and gentrification issues. Even though the area is now largely vacant, Teachers Village will likely draw more teachers and white-collar professionals, and living expenses in nearby downtown districts may increase. In addition, City Hall's natural ties to developers, architects, and investors for this project may have many political watch-dogs, policy savants, and gadflies worried. Danny Weil is among the numerous individuals concerned with the project. "The issue of gentrification and urban removal cannot be separated from the new turnaround artists and their plans for increasing charter schools," claims Weil.[140] Several community organizations and activists have also voiced concerns that they were not a part of the planning process of Teachers Village. For example, Newark community activists Donna Jackson and Cassandra Dock argue that the public was largely disengaged at the public meetings before the planning board and the Newark Preservation and Landmarks Committee. According to the activists, the project has not involved enough local people, and the majority of its supporters are from the corporate sector. "The problem is this new development continues to drive out Newarkers," argues Jackson. "Most of us in Newark feel that again this is another prime example of segregation and building for only a certain few."[141] While former housing director Harold Lucas sees "nothing new" with the idea of mixed-development projects, he remains critical of how residents will interact and truly become a part of the whole project.[142] Another concern about Teachers Village is the possible perception that conventional public schools and their staffs were excluded. Several Newark public schools have closed and been reorganized in recent years; does adding charter schools in the Teachers Village project demonstrate exclusivity to a certain sector? Some see Teachers Village as reinforcing a segregated community in downtown Newark and little investment in area public schools. "Rather than investing in new charter schools, why not invest in real change for schools that have been serving Newark's youth for decades?" states New Jersey Teacher Activist Group member Kathryn Strom. Beit argues that Teachers Village apartments will be marketed to teachers in all sectors and that developers are flexible about considering additional schools whether they are public, private, or charter.[143] And Mo Butler, the mayor's chief of staff, states that the suspicion about gentrification is unnecessary.[144]

Supporters of Teachers Village are looking to federal government policies and other city governments' approaches for examples of how to promote affordable workforce housing. One of the most notable is the US Department of Housing and Urban Development's subsidies for teachers, police, firefighters, and other public servants to help them purchase property where they work. Often, they can receive favorable terms and interest rates if they choose to own and work in the same city. Several cities have engaged in unique community workforce housing policies. In fact, supporters of Newark's project point to the widely known Harlem Children's Zone project in New York City and Chicago's Grow Your Own Teachers models.[145] While Harlem's initiative through Geoffrey Canada's stewardship has received notable accolades for a community raising children holistically, it has had several setbacks related to test scores and cost overruns[146] (the proposed Team Academy charter school will be run by the KIPP schools, the same firm featured in the film "Waiting for Superman"[147]). In addition, Baltimore's Charles Village features apartments in Millers Court that rented to teachers at a substantial discount. Similar to Newark's Teachers Village, the New Markets Tax Credit helped finance Baltimore's project.[148] Finally, the Los Angeles Glassell Park complex has been the ultimate model of teacher and public sector workforce housing. In an area desperate for new schools and infrastructure, the Los Angeles Unified School District partnered with developer Abode Communities of Los Angeles to build housing for educators.[149]

Warren Street, Artists, and Eco Villages

One of the significant university- and city-related projects included an initiative called Warren Street Village also popularly dubbed Greek Village, which is the first phase of the New Jersey Institute of Technology's billion-dollar Campus Gateway Redevelopment Plan to coincide with the Broad Street Station District Redevelopment Plan. The idea was to have students live in defined urban spaces near college campuses. The interesting feature unique to Newark is the fact that the college campuses are all near one another—something any American city would desire because having access to nearby universities is imperative in community development. Yet, in Newark, there were a number of parcels and properties left undeveloped, especially between the campuses. "The university area of the city and creating a college town—where and how we zone that area—is important," said Deputy Mayor Zipkin. "One doesn't think of Newark as a college town and we have 40,000 students living in the area and a small percentage living here in the city."[150]

Many NJIT and Rutgers fraternity and sorority houses were originally located on Dr. Martin Luther King Jr. Boulevard near Central Avenue. But these houses were in poor shape. Relocating the Greek houses closer to campus through mixed-development while redeveloping other areas became a key goal for area colleges.[151] In phase one of NJIT's redevelopment, a four-acre site on Warren Street would be created to hold eight Greek houses, student honor residences, retail spaces, and a parking garage complex costing $80 million. The university wanted to create a "seamless neighborhood" around the college campus. The additional three phases would include adding some 19 acres surrounding parts of NJIT near Baxter Terrace and the historic James Street Commons. As radical as the phases appeared on paper, it was a true example of what an urban space is and should be: a combined population of area students and residents for a mixed-development community.[152] Moreover, since nearby Baxter Terrace projects were demolished to make room for future mixed-income residences, the administration sought to transform the area completely. "Now you have Baxter Terrace demolished and the first phase open and we're working with the Newark Housing Authority for the next phase. Their model has been to build dense low income housing," said Deputy Mayor Adam Zipkin. "What we're working with them on is to make a mixed-use, mixed-income neighborhood there with retail and possibly a supermarket."[153]

Also adjacent to Rutgers and NJIT are the New Jersey Performing Arts Center, Bears Riverfront Stadium, and Washington Park, which are located in the northern edge of downtown. This area became a critical centerpiece to downtown's redevelopment, and Booker recognized that the area, between two commuter transit stations and new light rail access, held development potential. Newark's Master Plan called for rebuilding around the Broad Street New Jersey Transit station and the terminus of the city's light rail. Just to the west of Washington Park are the historic James Street Commons, the Newark Museum, the Newark Public Library, and Rutgers University–Newark, but several parcels of land in the area remain underdeveloped. City Hall wanted to revitalize this unique area, particularly for artists by specifically creating an Artists Village. Considering the interest in areas of downtown shown by many artists who had relocated there from nearby New York City, many local artists already recognized Newark's potential for artists' space.[154] But this part of downtown contained various businesses that were very eclectic, ranging from a fried chicken take-out to a small jewelry store to a sex cinema to a Halal butcher. Also located in this district were the former Westinghouse factory and the deserted "magnet [for] nefarious activity," the Lincoln Motel, which was a former Holiday Inn and also a former disco hall called Club Zanzibar.[155]

In October 2007, the mayor climbed into the cab of an excavating machine and destroyed part of the Lincoln Motel's exterior at a public event to promote razing and redeveloping the area. A shopping center builder planned to create a mixed-use project on the four-acre site. Deputy Mayor Stefan Pryor envisioned an area thriving with commuters, college students, and downtown office workers. "It won't happen overnight, but we think the area has one of the greatest development potentials in the city," he said.[156] Booker's administration also pushed for the nearby abandoned Westinghouse factory to be demolished only four months later. However, even though the building had possible environmental contaminants, the city did not inform nearby James Street residents of the demolition, and many were concerned about air quality. In addition, the owner of the site said construction of the mixed-use development project could not take place for a number of years until the site's environmental cleanup was complete.[157]

But the most important complex that would anchor the Artist Village concept was the proposed 2 Center Street apartment tower near NJPAC. In early 2008, City Hall, NJPAC officials, and the Philadelphia developer announced the project, which would include a swimming pool, wine storage, and other luxury amenities. Most importantly, 20 percent of the 200 market-rate rental units would be for artists, whose rents would be subsidized. The tower itself would be 28 stories high and cost $200 million with 328 rental units. NJPAC selected Dranoff Properties to develop the project partly because they had built a luxury apartment tower near Philadelphia's Kimmel Center for the Performing Arts. While the developers hoped to break ground in 18 months, partners and investors still had to agree on the design and financing of the project.[158] NJPAC President and CEO, Lawrence Goldman, finally unveiled to the public the proposals for One Theater Square in the spring of 2010. The New Jersey Economic Development Authority approved $38 million in Urban Transit tax credits over ten years, and, by designating 20 percent of the units as affordable housing, officials also hoped to receive federal tax credits. Nevertheless, the largest share of the financing for the project was to be privately funded, and the housing was mostly geared to middle-class residents. As Booker stated at the public unveiling of the project, "I pledge to you we will build this building. We stand in a building they said couldn't be built. I'm telling you now. Quiet on the set. Lights. Camera. Action. Let the show begin."[159] But developers would not break ground for the project until 2013.[160]

By late 2008, the city was looking to redesign and rezone the area around the Broad Street Station. Because the station would serve as a linchpin for the entertainment complexes and proposed villages, it was imperative that the area be rezoned, especially as the city was pitching redevelopment proposals to some 25 lending institutions. The city's decades-old zoning rules set aside significant swaths of the area around the train station for industrial development, which barred new home and retail construction. Since the Lincoln Motel and Westinghouse factory were demolished, City Hall had planned for the construction of over 3,000 residences and offices as well as retail and restaurant businesses.

City officials claimed that they tried to progress with plans for this redevelopment, and they were hopeful that the area around the train station would be transformed in several phases; this transformation would begin in two years and be complete within a decade. However, some residents from nearby James street were against these development plans because they were concerned about noise coming from proposed commercial establishments.[161]

Just to the south of the train station on Broad Street and only a block from NJPAC were overlooked properties on the west side of Broad Street facing Military Park. This is a significant area for redevelopment not just because of its location but because the blocks are also sizable and historic. Known as Ladies Mile, the worn storefronts were once home to a variety of unique stores that catered to housewives and workingwomen.[162] The owner of these properties (including the Hahne's and Griffith buildings), Arthur Stern, also owned and restored the nearby National Newark Building at 744 Broad Street and 1180 Raymond Boulevard. His revitalization of Newark's tallest buildings was a significant feat as it cost nearly $250 million. But transforming the empty parcels and dilapidated buildings on Broad Street proved to be a difficult task, especially because he faced resistance from the new administration in City Hall. The Hahne's project, for example, was supposed to have 3,200 residential units and more than 200,000 square feet of retail space, yet it was on the planning board for over ten years while the administration pushed for redeveloping similar properties. As much as Booker talked about redeveloping the area surrounding Stern's properties, he did not consider Stern's proposed projects as part of the downtown transformation. Stern blamed politics for this as he's from New York and not a part of Booker's inner circle and could not secure financing for the projects; hence, he became an outsider to Newark's downtown redevelopment plans.[163] By the end of 2009, Stern sued Hanini Group for contracts on properties surrounding the Prudential Center.[164] He also faced foreclosure on 744 Broad Street from Bank of America for $72 million they were due.[165] So Miles Berger, owner of the Robert Treat and Carlton Hotels on the east side of Military Park, acquired the Hahne's and Griffith buildings and planned to rehabilitate these former stores. Near these hulking complexes, the Booker administration supported the demolition of parcels west of Military Park for the expansion of Prudential headquarters as construction began on the $444 million, 20-story office tower. Preserving some of the old storefronts proved to be an impossible challenge because many of the abandoned properties were in very poor condition. Aside from demolition of additional properties, future plans for the area also call for more pedestrian-friendly and connected streets for an improved streetscape.[166] Still, securing financing has remained the most significant problem for many of these downtown projects, especially during the Great Recession. According to Michael Meyer, several of these projects would have taken off five years earlier with more financing and a better economy.[167]

Finally, one of the most significant village projects along Broad Street was Eco Village in the farthest southern edge of the downtown area at Lincoln Park. While the area's location appeared ideal for redevelopment, as it's close to the civic center and near the airport, many public officials have often overlooked the community for urban revitalization. The Lincoln Park area not only has a vast public park, it also contains many historic features and unique architecture. The city announced in 2010 that developer Baye Adofo-Wilson was to design a Leadership in Energy and Environmental Design (LEED) certified residential complex, and he was able to secure financing to create 66 units at four locations near the South Park Presbyterian Church ruins using local labor. Families living in the LEED and sustainable-energy project could not earn more than 50 percent of the Essex County median income (from $32,000 to $45,000). Adofo-Wilson's initiative, through his nonprofit organization, has advocated for more sustainable urban housing. In fact, his offices, located at nearby Washington Street are alongside several green houses. Adofo-Wilson has spoken extensively about innovative ways to make housing more environmentally friendly.[168]

Beyond the village concepts, several loft-style apartment complexes also opened around downtown Newark during the Booker administration. The Studebaker Lofts, located on the farthest northern area of downtown on Broad Street near the transit station, has 68 apartments that are LEED certified. And Packard Lofts, on the farthest southern edge of downtown on Broad Street near Lincoln Park, has 28 condo lofts. In addition, a couple blocks from the Rock is the LEED-certified Richardson Lofts, a former jewelry factory turned apartment complex, that has 67 units (34 market-rate and 33 affordable apartments). All three upscale complexes are examples of rebuilding former industrial or commercial spaces for residential use. They also demonstrated downtown living redevelopment that modeled the mayor's Living Downtown Plan with mixed-income units. "They have all been very well received and quickly rented in the marketplace," said Deputy Mayor Adam Zipkin. "All mixed income complexes including market rate apartments in Studebaker and Richardson Lofts are 50 percent and Rock Plaza Lofts are 20 percent" for low and middle income renters.[169] Resolving zoning restrictions was key to these developments because these zoning restrictions prevented productive residential growth, especially with 50,000 office workers and 50,000 students and faculty commuting daily to the downtown area.[170] But one of the most significant problems renters and owners face in these new complexes is the fact that few amenities—like grocery stores, restaurants, bars, and retail stores—are immediately nearby. As one real estate expert put it bluntly about downtown, "Newark doesn't have it yet—a place to buy toilet tissue, a quart of milk."[171]

Public Housing Community Development

One of the chief concerns surrounding housing policy in Newark has been finding policy approaches to address low- and middle-income rentals and homeownership options. The city has been notorious for problematic public housing, particularly with its sordid history of warehousing many low-income and working poor families in tall housing projects. As a councilman and mayoral candidate, Booker advocated for providing more solutions to the housing problem, and because he was a tenant lawyer, he had added concerns about this issue. He was well aware of the myriad problems Newark families confronted in obtaining affordable and modern housing. But finding solutions that worked across the city proved to be a difficult feat.

The Newark Housing Authority (NHA) was and remains one of the most important agencies in city government. Due to its troubled history and its infamous reputation for bureaucracy and even corruption, resolving the agency's problems would be one of the most difficult issues facing the new administration. Even though Booker appointed Keith Kinard as the authority's executive director in 2006, the NHA still remained a problematic agency; the US Department of Housing and Urban Development (HUD) had issued a memorandum of understanding that required the NHA to resolve 100 of the 139 items listed in order to avoid federal control. HUD's audit revealed that the NHA misused $20 million in federal funds. The NHA engaged in several reforms including laying off more than 270 employees (out of more than 600 employees) in 2006, which improved their standing with HUD. In addition, the authority had 8,000 units to manage for 23,000 residents and distributed over 9,000 federal rental vouchers. Finally, rent collection increased to 80 percent in 2006, up from 63 percent the year prior. But challenges remained, including addressing the physical conditions of NHA properties and finding long-term solutions for more modern housing[172] as well as replacing demolished low-income project housing; this was the subject of a federal lawsuit that was eventually dismissed but that reinforced officials' need to address the housing shortfall.[173] Thankfully for Newark, in 2009, an additional $6.3 million in federal funding from the Obama administration went toward repairing vacant townhouses for many families seeking housing.[174]

Part of the problem with Newark's housing policy and the NHA has been planning newer low-income units because many of the older low-income units were never replaced. While the James administration razed numerous project complexes, getting many of Newark's low-income families into the city's newer units has remained a significant problem. As much as the city tried to offer new low-rise apartments and townhouse style housing, the NHA met various barriers. While former housing director Harold Lucas says that the agency was never meant to warehouse so many families who relocated to Newark, clearly there was a housing shortage.[175] Moreover, ensuring that builders followed codes and regulations and passed inspections proved to be difficult for the housing authority. For instance, Tony Gomes was removed as developer for 88 townhouses on 11th and 12th Avenues because the NHA accused him of not completing plumbing and electrical inspections. In turn, Gomes blamed the city for not having enough inspections. At the time he was awarded the city contract, Gomes had hired state senator Ronald Rice as a paid employee and as Rice was also deputy mayor, he was able to directly lobby the NHA, Mayor James, and the city council for Gomes to receive the contract. Gomes in turn promised to complete a townhouse complex on Elizabeth Avenue or the NHA would not pay him. Interestingly, this particular project was to replace one of the razed projects, Columbus Homes, but the Newark Coalition for Low Income Housing sued the NHA to force the authority to replace the demolished low-income units. Thus, the agency had a poor record for replacing low-income units let alone completing new low-income housing units, and many families were waiting for apartments.[176] However, years later, the NHA and a detailed *Star-Ledger* analysis found the new complexes Gomes had erected were "poorly built and structurally deficient" and would not pass a city inspection for a certificate of occupancy. At that time, the authority's waiting list was surpassing 16,000 names, and the newspaper largely blamed Gomes and city and federal officials for not complying with local building permits and code requirements.[177] As a result, a number of families were forced to relocate to nearby cities or even states like Pennsylvania. So many Newark families moved to Altoona, PA, that US Representative Bill Shuster of Pennsylvania asked then New Jersey Governor Jon Corzine to address the issue. Even the mayor of the small town wrote to Kinard to tell his staff to stop referring families to Altoona, even though many of the families had moved there after discovering fliers advertising shorter waiting lists for housing in the Pennsylvania town.[178] It would not be until late 2009 that the NHA would agree to pay Gomes $2.4 million to complete the affordable housing project; Kinard would also have to assess how much money and time it would take to bring the units up to code and finally place the 10,000 people waiting for housing.[179] Even the Millennium Way complexes in the South Ward did not open until years later in 2011. These 56 units were a part of Kinard's outside inspection that discovered roofs that did not meet ceilings, uneven floors, and mold even though Gomes claimed that the NHA "didn't change nothing." As Kinard said of the housing issues with Gomes, "When it's all said and done, I want to write a book about this particular project."[180] Whereas former housing director Harold Lucas says he remains unsure whether Gomes was "the victim or cause" of the housing construction projects' problems.[181]

Besides passing out housing vouchers and relocating families, Newark continued to raze low-income housing projects, including Baxter Terrace. While it had been one of Newark's first public housing complexes, only 355 of the 502 units in 2006 were occupied, and crime was rampant. The condition of Baxter Terrace was so bad that it would cost an estimated $67 million and a year and a half to repair the development. Instead, in late 2007, the NHA announced the scheduled demolition of the project along with the future razing of other public housing complexes, including Booker's former residence, Brick Towers, and Felix Fuld Houses. Residents could choose to receive housing vouchers or they could move permanently or temporarily to privately owned residences. By razing these complexes, the NHA and City Hall were hoping to replace the projects with mixed-income housing.[182] The US Department of Housing and Urban Development announced that the NHA would use $11 million in federal stimulus aid to demolish the development.[183]

Beyond providing modern public housing, the administration also supported green amenities such as solar-powered and high-tech features. The New Community Corporation and the mayor attended the 2009 groundbreaking of Roseville Commons, a $14 million mixed-use residential and commercial development on Orange Avenue that would feature solar panels and other green technological advancements and would be certified as a LEED project. The five-story complex is located in the West Ward's Roseville Community Revitalization Area and would accommodate low-income families, including special-needs populations such as homeless veterans and visually impaired individuals.[184] In 2009, the 45-unit Park Place townhouse complex opened in the city's Central Ward; this complex contained solar-powered panels, which would reduce energy costs by 35 percent. The city's first solar-powered affordable housing complex, City View Landing, actually opened a year ago, but their panels only partially delivered power to the development. "There are some of the highest quality construction units you will find across the county, sitting right here in the middle of the central ward," claimed NHA director Keith Kinard. Booker claimed that over 65 percent of the subcontractors were local and many of them were minority- or women-owned businesses.[185] A townhouse complex identical to Park Place, called Oak Brook Square, also opened in the city's South Ward. Rent for a unit in both complexes averages $650 monthly. Unquestionably, these housing complexes were a welcome change from the superblock projects built in the 1940s, but many residents were worried that there would not be enough units for those originally displaced by the low-income housing demolition years earlier.[186]

The NHA gave out $10 million in Section 8 housing vouchers in summer 2010. Through the voucher program, a family ideally pays 30 percent of its annual income for housing, while the authority pays the remainder of the rent and utilities or about $800 a month per family. Kinard tried to help the 19,000 people on the voucher waiting list, and the NHA was able to reduce that number to 4,000 within two years; now there are only 1,000 people on the waiting list for housing vouchers. As Kinard stated, "Leaving families without a home is unacceptable."[187] In addition, the authority relied heavily on subsidized rental buildings owned by private landlords who were paid directly through Section 8 vouchers. While HUD routine inspections are conducted annually, many units go uninspected or are often in poor condition. Many investors and companies invest in subsidized housing in Newark because of the housing demand, but they have few incentives to maintain their properties.[188]

The city also prioritized public employee workforce housing in addition to low-income housing. Because the state's Department of Community advocated low-interest loans and workforce housing in cities, Newark was actively engaging in such initiatives.[189] In late January 2008, for example, City Hall announced a new program to move city employees, such as police and firefighters, to 700 discounted apartments in an existing housing complex in Newark's Weequahic community. Although public safety employees are required to live in Newark for their first year of service, interestingly, only 20 percent of firefighters and 40 percent of police live in Newark. In fact Apollo Real Estate Advisors paid $43 million for rental apartments for public workforce housing. "We can now bring our police back into our community, our firefighters back into the community, our teachers back into the community," Booker said. "This will give strength to our neighborhoods and it will give us added security and protection."[190] Live-where-you-work initiatives were already popular in many American cities, and Newark tried to advance similar public policy approaches even though housing values remained high in northern New Jersey.[191]

Another housing initiative the administration endorsed was to offer builders five-year property-tax abatements. Ideally, they would convince builders to rent or even sell houses to qualifying families that were eager for newly constructed homes. The abatements, for example, would reduce an annual property tax bill of $10,000 on a new multifamily home to approximately $4,000 or $6,000, and the rent would be lessened; thus, a new property owner would see a significant cost savings over the term of the abatement.[192] Under the old law, only buyers could qualify for a tax abatement, which was two percent of the value of improvements to the land in lieu of property taxes (PILOT). The new changes would allow developers to pay the same amount plus an additional one percent fee and is still transferable to a buyer for the remainder of the five-year period. The PILOT program would defer taxes in the first year and charge 20 percent the following year, 40 percent the third, 60 percent the fourth year, and 80 percent in the fifth year. Any remaining time on the tax abatement would be transferable to a potential buyer.[193]

Additional Community Development Initiatives

One of the first completed community development projects during Booker's first term was the revitalization of Ferry Street in Newark's Ironbound neighborhood. Located in the city's East Ward just southeast of downtown, it is one of the most heavily visited areas in Newark and is home to many Latino, Portuguese, and Brazilian Americans. The Ironbound Business Improvement District and City Hall designated a 26-block stretch for redevelopment along the neighborhood's main roadway, Ferry Street. Planters, benches, streetlights, and new designs and uses for the Peter Francisco Park were part of the $5 million Ferry Streetscape project. The Ironbound neighborhood was overdue for redevelopment as it's a high-traffic area. "That corridor needs improvement," stated the community's councilman, Augusto Amador. "It's a shot in the arm for the area and the community."[194] In addition, a luxury condominium project called "The Continental" was added to the corner of Ferry and Magazine Streets; this edifice had 67 residential units and a dozen retail spaces. The project was designed by architect Dean Marchetto, who confirmed that the mixed-use development complex would complement the area: "It's a welcome alternative and signals a new urban approach."[195]

Similar to the Ferry Street makeover, various streets around downtown were transformed with new lighting, signage, and plantings through a three-year project financed by a Special Improvement District from the Newark Downtown District. The New Jersey Economic Development Authority approved $10 million in bonds for the Newark Downtown District with nearly $8 million coming from the city, Public Service Gas and Electric (PSEG), and the Newark Urban Enterprise Zone.[196] Newark's main roadway in downtown, Broad Street, also received significant redesigning as the city added plant-filled center medians, bump-out intersections, and tree-lined curbs. Part of the reason for the transformation was to make the street more pedestrian-friendly because Broad Street is a six-lane roadway and it can be dangerous to cross on foot. The new medians helped pedestrians and also beautified the street. At the same time, however, adding a median blocked drivers traveling south on Broad Street from entering Edison Place, and this prevented cars from accessing the Ironbound neighborhood. This caused many businesses to protest the change, and they organized a petition against the proposal.[197] Beyond the downtown and East Ward streets, many residents in Newark's outer neighborhoods also saw new streetscapes. For example, many Central and West Ward main streets that were once home to a number of variety stores and community businesses were in desperate need of street restoration. In 2007, developers were invited to submit proposals for revitalizing these wards around South Orange and Central Avenues.[198]

One of Booker's main community development initiatives was to contact national retailers directly about Newark's development progress. Because Newark has only one big-box retail store, Home Depot, and a few chain retailers such as Applebee's, Old Navy, and Ashley Stewart, the city lacks major commercial chains. In fact, one study indicated that almost 40 percent of the money Newakers spend on groceries and building materials goes outside the city. For full-service restaurants that number is closer to 25 percent, 35 percent for electronics and appliances stores, and 30 percent for office supply stores. Even in an area like University Heights, teeming with college students and staff, people spend virtually all their dining-out money in restaurants outside the city. The negative perception of Newark and inner-city disinvestment (due to concerns about image, crime, and lack of potential customers with disposable income) have been significant barriers for retailers to invest in Newark.[199] Hoping to dispel the negative image associated with Newark and recruit retailers to the city, Booker attended the International Council of Shopping Centers' annual convention in Las Vegas in May 2007. This was the city's first time sending representatives to the convention, and they had a booth promoting Newark at the event. But as the *Star-Ledger* stated, "much of the selling has hinged on Booker, banking on his national celebrity."[200] Booker and Deputy Mayor Stefan Pryor presented data, pictures, and images of various properties, trying to lure retailers. The mayor said that the city would be willing to offer discounted property if retailers hired Newarkers and complied with environmental regulations.[201] As Booker said about Newark to a couple of developers, "This is undiscovered country right now. We're looking at retail and developers and asking, why are you not here?"[202] And the mayor and his staff would return to another Council of Shopping Centers conference the next year still trying to sell Newark and its potential and trying to attract a Whole Foods store and a Barnes and Noble, even though the city would lose Old Navy, Starbucks, and Kinko's.[203] Although a city should have certain conveniences, like retail stores, the reality is that, for many residents in New Jersey's largest city, having a grocery store in the neighborhood is a rarity. Newark is second only to New York City in the percent of population without car. "So we have more than half of our residents that are without a car and so add that to the fact that there are so few local supermarkets," states Deputy Mayor Adam Zipkin. For example, in Newark's Central Ward, for decades, there was only one large Pathmark grocery store for numerous communities. "We have put a lot of energy into attracting a lot of supermarkets here," says Zipkin. "But large supermarket corporation owners tend to have suburban mindsets and models and they are often obsessed about parking ratios, rents and demographics. So it was a challenge."[204]

Beyond attracting large chain supermarkets, Booker brought in a team of officials specializing in food policy, urban farming, and sustainability. For the first time, a five-member staff helped address food concerns and developed agricultural-related projects in Newark through a number of different of community input meetings and policy initiatives.[205] From hosting a green conference and green summit to having adopt-a-lot and leasing public parcels or vacant lots, the Booker administration planned to resolve urban blight through urban agriculture and open space. The staff even issued a Sustainability Action Plan on air quality, energy, recycling, community greening, and healthy food access. "The City has leveraged state and federal resources and organizational partnerships to promote energy efficiency, boost recycling, plant trees, increase urban farming, reduce air pollution, clean up brownfields, and more," states the report.[206] Using stimulus grants from the federal government and private grants, Newark's City Hall emphasized the importance of creating sustainability and agriculture plans.[207] "The mayor came into office with sustainability as part of the transition team, particularly with the city's long history of environmental and social justice concerns," says Stephanie Greenwood, the city's Sustainability Director. "Growing urban agriculture alongside neighborhood projects was key."[208] In fact, the administration started a program to give grants to bodega owners so they could offer more fresh produce options, and this program was highly popular among shop owners and shoppers. Finally, creating local food systems to grow produce locally became a key part of giving food options to residents. "So our Clean and Green Program that is a transitional jobs program started off cleaning and greening city owned lots in the neighborhoods that were often eyesores," states Zipkin. "So after a couple of years we then went from just cleaning and greening these lots onto some bigger lots to growing produce." The deputy mayor further states that by partnering with Rutgers University and the Newark Conservancy, the city created a farm stand program that employed local high school students to maintain, distribute, and sell fresh produce.[209] According to Greenwood, "Sustainability offers interest in the community and we used various models with a number of neighborhood groups. We examined proposals at the national level about community sustainability and connected various resources at the community level."[210]

As a vegetarian, Booker knew firsthand the difficulty of finding fresh and organic foods, which partly explained his zeal to address food desert concerns in Newark. He lobbied to have a Whole Foods store in Newark as the chain store was looking to open several hundred new markets in North America. The mayor even gave the company's CEO and regional president a personal tour.[211] Hence, three new full-service supermarkets opened within two years, and additional stores are planned.[212] Booker did eventually announce in February 2012 the opening of a 31,000-square-foot Food Depot in the Central Ward. City officials said that the $8 million store addressed the food desert where Newarkers had so few grocery store options. "They have created a food oasis in a food desert," said the mayor. Booker also stated that the store was a part of $700 million in development projects in the city.[213] Food Depot planned to hire some 100 employees, many of them local residents, and receive a $2 million loan from Brick City Development Corporation as well as a 30-year tax abatement. There were initial concerns that lawyers helping store owners used Booker's former law firm for legal advice, while many applicants for store positions needed specific qualifications and training from Brick City Development Corporation and the Victoria Foundation in order to be hired.[214] Some eight months later, Key Food, another large grocery store chain, opened a 13,000-square-foot $3 million retail space on Springfield Avenue that employed 30 residents.[215] Additional large retail development closer to downtown included a proposed Springfield Avenue Marketplace just west of downtown on a vacant parcel. The $100 million mixed-use development project would feature 164 market-rate apartments and 150,000 square feet of retail space, much of it for anchor stores with grocery stores, including a new Shop-Rite offering 300 full- and part-time jobs as well as 240 construction-related jobs.[216] According to Councilman Anibal Ramos Jr., "these are positive indicators with grocery store openings and Special Improvement Districts leading the way towards tremendous change." He pointed to the fact that his northern ward district and the Mount Prospect community were offering new retail options and said that he hopes to see additional commercial corridors beyond downtown prosper.[217]

Despite proposed and new retail stores near Newark's central business district, much of downtown still needed serious revitalization and zoning changes. Even after the renovation of 1180 Raymond Boulevard into a high-end apartment complex, the city lacked various amenities and high-end stores. Booker hoped to attract retailers and additional high-end rentals to large lots and abandoned buildings like the old Hahne's department store. While Newark drew interest during Booker's first term for the revitalization of its downtown, the city's negative past remained a barrier for many tourists and suburbanites.[218] Zoning reform efforts by the administration included removing excess signage on many buildings around the city's downtown because some 40 percent of properties did not adhere to the rules for signs. Many of these signs, especially on retail and commercial buildings, were very large, gaudy, and boldly colored. Newark officials promised zoning changes because the signage laws were outdated and lacked regulation. Many of the rules were drafted in the 1950s and had not been updated, primarily because of private-sector interests. Booker's officials proposed nine changes to zoning laws to address the signage issue, but only for future developments, not for current buildings.[219] "Poor zoning created economic development problems all over the city. So we did a series of quick fixes where we had to sort out emerging issues," said Deputy Mayor Zipkin. For example, dated zoning laws required residential units to have back and side yards as well as parking spaces. For projects like the Four Corners Millennium project, it would have been impossible to adhere to such requirements. "In a less dense part of the city, some of the zoning laws could have made sense. But clearly in downtown, it doesn't."[220]

Beyond zoning changes, in late 2007, the mayor also introduced new initiatives for selling city properties. Over 1,400 lots would be sold at market rates unless offering a discount would lead to a "public benefit" (like adding affordable housing, parks, or green design into development plans). The city considered requests for proposals from developers of more than 12 houses, while single lots for rehabs or demolition projects would be offered to contiguous property owners at public auction. The city also placed ten percent of all sales proceeds in an affordable housing trust fund and established a property disposition working group to vet all development proposals and make recommendations after reviewing applications. The group's recommendations were reviewed by an outside third party before the mayor made final approval of a lot sale. Finally, the administration supported new design efforts to curtail the esthetically unappealing Bayonne Box (a three story, vinyl-sided, multifamily house that many developers were building around Newark) and to mimic neighboring buildings and allow for increased setbacks, larger front yards, and more space between houses. "Think about the crappy looking housing thrown up all around the city," suggests Booker. "Between 2002 and 2006, the hundreds of millions of dollars worth of value that was just rushing outside of this city to well connected individuals to build awful looking housing. No idea about planning; no idea about affordability or access to housing."[221] The *New York Times* overwhelmingly supported the new proposals as progressive, transparent, and overdue: "If Newark is to enjoy a widespread, five-ward revival, it must lose its reputation as a place where business is carried out in the shadows. Mr. Booker's plan to make city land sales transparent is a giant leap in the right direction."[222]

Another strategy Booker advanced was to attract celebrities to invest in the city's revitalization efforts. Tiki Barber, former New York Giants running back and football star, founded Tiki Ventures to invest in urban development projects. Booker met with Barber and announced that areas of Newark would be rebuilt by local developers and investors. In addition to Barber, former basketball star and Newark native Shaquille O'Neal made plans to create upscale condominiums in the old Science High School and to begin a $7 million renovation of Newark's Screens movie theater. Actor Keenan Ivory Wayans, singer Queen Latifah, former basketball player Magic Johnson, and former football players Emmitt Smith and Carl Banks expressed serious interest in developing Newark as well.[223] Jon Bon Jovi supported and helped fundraise for 51 units of affordable housing with 15 of them earmarked for HIV/AIDS patients in the city's North Ward. The rock star and HELP USA chairwoman Maria Cuomo Cole introduced the idea to Booker. With fundraising efforts from Bon Jovi's JBJ Soul Homes and tax abatements, the $10.4 million project created new and stylish housing for many Newarkers.[224] Additional housing projects through Integrity House and Project Live to help women and individuals with mental health issues became landmark initiatives for the administration, especially because the mayor helped with the fundraising efforts. Key officials in the Booker administration point to special needs housing and parks projects as signature milestones.[225] "Youth and community development as well as open space and parks were critical elements for Newark, and we even had an environment commission to help advise the city on future planning," stated Sustainability Director Stephanie Greenwood.[226]

Redeveloping Newark's neighborhood parks was an awesome feat because the city had very few parks—that is, there was very little land per person, says Newark's Deputy Mayor Adam Zipkin.[227] Open space and park redevelopment became an early issue for the administration. Michael Meyer, the city's director of Housing and Real Estate, states that public parks advance healthy lifestyles in communities and, sadly, when the administration came into office "one of the most striking things was the poor condition of the parks and facilities [which was] shocking." A basic element to parks—benches—were added to many city parks in an effort to reestablish Jane Jacobs' eyes-on-the-street model of residents being alert to community problems by monitoring street activity in public spaces. Some $100 million was raised to help renovate parks, and, by the end of 2009, 21 parks were transformed through a public and private initiative that cost nearly $29 million.[228] Furthermore, a $150 million plan was created to renovate Essex County parks, many of which were located in Newark. There was also a $500,000 maintenance fund for park upgrades, and many residents saw the park renovations and updates as significant improvements over the previous administration. As Booker proudly proclaimed about his fundraising efforts, "Any connection I have, I'm trying to get a park out of a person."[229] When the Ironbound Athletic Field was closed after the Environmental Protection Agency revealed that it was contaminated by lead and much of the community had serious environmental problems, the city renovated the field at a cost of $2.2 million. After the renovations were complete, 100 children and parents paraded from Newark's Pennsylvania Station to the park. "We've turned an obstacle into an opportunity," said the mayor.[230] Booker even proved successful in getting the Mount Vernon School playground, where the four college-age students were killed, completely redesigned with a running track, basketball courts, and a community garden.[231]

In 2009, Booker announced the redevelopment of several more parks across the city. A large Ironbound community park along the Passaic River near Raymond Boulevard was a primary focus of his administration. Using the Trust for Public Land's fundraising and Green Acres and Urban Enterprise Zone funds, Booker was determined to see the park developed, especially if apartment buildings, hotels, and commercial spaces could be built in the area surrounding the proposed park. "Our riverfront has to return to be the focal point of our city," said the mayor. "It must be accessible. It must be a place where people come together."[232] As a matter of fact, the whole waterfront will be transformed to include a 40-foot walkway and bikeway, according to the new master plan, and there will be changes to zoning regulations as well. "It will be touted as a model of riverfront zoning for the state," said Deputy Mayor Zipkin. "We will require that each property, as it redevelops, will have to deed the easement and create a contiguous walkway."[233] The city also received financial support from the Trust for Public Land, the Obama administration, the state's Department of Environmental Protection, and Tiki Barber's company, Tiki Recreation, to finally open a nine-acre recreational and park facility at Nat Turner Park in Newark's Central Ward after the lot had sat vacant for 30 years. "Nat Turner Park—talk about framing something with great racial ancestral heritage," states Booker. "How symbolic is that—once a dump—a place where literally bodies have been found, and we attacked it with great partnerships trusts for public lands, philanthropists, grassroots organizations and caretakers, and they have created a transformation of our city."[234] Both the mayor and Barber threw footballs to area children at the park's opening and highlighted that the fact that at nine acres, Nat Turner Park was now the city's publicly owned park.[235] Later that summer, the city's only skateboard park opened in Jesse Allen Park in the city's Central Ward and nearby South Ward.[236] Even the West Ward's abandoned buildings were eventually transformed into public spaces with some 200 residents helping to build playgrounds and parks.[237] Finally, Booker announced an overdue makeover of Military Park. The city dedicated $2 million in capital funds and $1 million from the Cooperman Family Foundation that Booker was able to secure through his fundraising efforts. Plans included offering free WiFi, food kiosks, and outdoor movies—similar amenities to midtown New York's Bryant Park. In fact, Dan Biederman, who helped redesign Bryant Park, agreed to remake Newark's downtown park and help begin the 501c-3 non-profit Military Park Partnership for fundraising purposes to pay for much of the park redesign costs. Work began in spring 2013 with a scheduled re-opening and park programming in spring 2014. [238] "With new office towers on the way from Prudential and Panasonic, and new residents moving downtown, a revitalized Military Park will be the central community public space," states Booker.[239]

During Booker's last term, the city also attracted tourists, singers, and notable figures. Widely popular television shows, such as *American Idol* and *America's Got Talent*, were filmed in downtown Newark at the Prudential Center[240] and the New Jersey Performing Arts Center.[241] Also, the Geraldine R. Dodge Poetry Festival occurred in downtown Newark at various venues for four days in late 2012[242] and featured notable poets, including Newark resident Amiri Baraka, who recounted the 1967 riots.[243] In addition, international figures, such as British Prime Minister David Cameron, met with Booker and took tours of the city. Cameron was especially interested in Newark's urban development and economic investment as a model for English cities.[244] The national and international attention centered on downtown Newark was a significant result of the mayor's plans to portray the city as a positive example of urban resurgence for tourists, entertainers, and dignitaries.

Community Development Considerations

Newark is on the threshold of modern community development approaches. But implementing many of these concepts remains very complex. There are several barriers to redevelopment in Newark, even though the city is primed for it. As New Jersey's largest city, Newark is the county seat of Essex County, is home to the state's international airport, and offers many transit options from light rail to bus to train (NJ Transit, PATH, and Amtrak). However, the city's efficient subway system is often overlooked by many outsiders even though it has been featured in a recent blockbuster movie.[245] Newark also has direct automobile access to the Garden State Parkway and New Jersey Turnpike. The city's location is ideal for air, train, and port shipping and travel because it is only 20 minutes from New York City; thus, it should be a developer's and investor's dream. But three factors remain problematic for holistic community development: *economic stratification, racial segregation,* and *Newark's image.*

One of the main concerns surrounding the city's development is Newark's blatant economic stratification. With residents' average income at $36,000 (and 25 percent of residents classified at poverty level or below it), only 12 percent of residents earning an undergraduate diploma, and only 25 percent owning homes, Newark is one of the poorest cities in America.[246] And with the Great Recession continuing to affect many homeowners, housing costs have become a significant burden for many Newarkers, particularly in the city's minority communities. Some 40 percent of Newark homeowners spend more than half their income on housing, and many of them are first-time homeowners who have subprime loans.[247] While some banks offered small grants to help with the foreclosure crisis in the midst of the Great Recession, high unemployment and longstanding urban problems remain in Newark.[248]

Unemployment, particularly for community-development related jobs, also remains a pressing economic concern for Newark. According to Councilman Anibal Ramos Jr., "the real divide is in economic development and jobs. Unemployment is exceptionally high in Newark, and it has been dividing many communities."[249] Moreover, Councilwoman Mildred Crump argues that the Booker administration rarely includes key Black leaders in discussions about future development projects and jobs. "At least under the James administration there were more opportunities for Black and Brown residents. Under the Booker administration even with the master plan, little happens for actual residents."[250] Unemployment remains a longstanding problem for the city and the mayor, according to other leaders. "We have not been able to demand for more," says Councilman Luis Quintana. "Who works on the downtown projects or in downtown offices or at the airport? I often ask around the airport to find Newark residents and I rarely find any."[251] Considering the state of the economy and Newark's economic potential, other leaders stress that administration officials should do more to help Newarkers. "A pro-Newark economy only helps the city, so put the people back to work," remarks former housing director Harold Lucas. He further asks, "[W]hy does the city not prosper more?"[252] Richard Cammarieri of the New Community Corporation states that he sees few mechanisms to ensure that Newarkers receive community-development related jobs. [253]

However, the Booker administration argues that construction jobs are a chief priority for community development and employment policy. "If we give a tax abatement, if we sell land, in almost anything we do, we're making that there's requirements built in wherever we have leverage points that minority, women-based contractors and Newark-based contractors have opportunities," says Deputy Mayor Zipkin. "We just finished an analysis of all the projects since the mayor has been in office, and all the projects that have gotten tax abatements have these kinds of requirements of local minority participation." A proposed minimum of 30 percent of workforce hours went to Newarkers, according to Zipkin. And yet, 40 percent or some 40,000 hours went to Newark residents exceeding 10 percent more workforce hours than initially planned. Also, employers with permanent job openings must notify Newark Works training agency to have prescreened and prequalified residents apply for open positions. While the administration acknowledges that job training, readiness, skills, and literacy remain barriers for many residents, Newark Works has had notable victories, such as finding jobs for 60 percent of employees in the program at Dinosaur BBQ, First Street Market, and the new movie theater and new downtown hotel.[254]

In addition to economic stratification, racial segregation in Newark remains a significant concern. De facto, or residential, segregation reached its apex in the 1950s and 1960s, but it still has an impact on Newark. In fact, due to the increase in Latino, Portuguese, and Brazilian residents since the 1970s, racial issues have become more nuanced. The city remains a very racialized space since few wards are heterogeneous. Considering Newark's modern racial history and political experience, race and ethnicity have been significant barriers for effective community development since residential segregation has been a key issue in the city's history.[255] Administration officials remain firm that they do not intend to segregate along racial and class lines. "The challenge is as much as you don't want racial segregation, you also really want to be conscious you don't have economic segregation."[256]

Finally, one of the most significant problems facing Newark as it relates to community redevelopment is the stigma associated with the city. Again, this is interconnected to the city's modern history. Newark's image is largely associated with riots and urban decay, and the city remains overwhelmingly undeveloped in many wards. Unfortunately, many outsiders view the city as a dystopia that is beyond repair. While residents largely disagree with this image, a vast majority outside the city, particularly suburbanites and tourists, identify Newark as a negative place.[257] By providing a viable district in its city center, Newark officials are banking on new development approaches to help remove the city's stigma.[258] According to Councilman Anibal Ramos Jr., "I give the mayor credit for working hard to improve the image of the city. There's been a lot of attention nationally on Newark's economic development projects, and the administration should be commended for doing these initiatives especially during an economic recession."[259] However, even though Councilman Ras Baraka is supportive of downtown development and making the downtown area a 24/7 space, he also remains concerned that "the mayor has not made a direct commitment to communities outside the master plan, and it may lead to arbitrary development. The city cannot just attract other people; we must consider those who are indigenous to the area otherwise gentrification will take place."[260]

For the Booker administration to provide a very detailed master plan and to do so within three years of the mayor taking office was ambitious. Unquestionably, the plan and zoning reforms were impressive changes.[261] Streamlining the permit process was also a start, but more needs to be done, according to some elected officials.[262] At least many of Booker's foes "give him credit" for the master plan, zoning changes, and downtown development.[263] But many council members, including Councilwoman Crump, who believes that Springfield Market Village and Teachers Village "tax credits suggest a free ride for investors, and they're exclusive projects," remain concerned. Councilwoman Crump also suggests that the mayor has been like a "hammer with the city council when it comes to plans and revitalization. He'll slam the table on what projects he wants and demands."[264] There have also been concerns related to continuity within the administration since Deputy Mayor Stefan Pryor accepted the position as Connecticut's education commissioner. As much as Pryor, Booker, and other officials tackled future planning, it proved to be a challenging process as the Great Recession affected investment and development in Newark.[265] Many Newarkers faced foreclosures, and the Booker administration attempted to address distressed mortgages through New Jersey Community Capital, a nonprofit Community Development Financial Institution.[266] At $56 million in additional city services to maintain abandoned homes and $630 million in underwater mortgage debt as well as $1.9 billion in lost property values, Newark was clearly slammed by the Great Recession.[267] At the same time, Deputy Mayor Pryor was often criticized for his myopic downtown development plans as he engaged little in neighborhood development outside the city's center.[268] Whereas others questioned his ability to bring actual jobs to local residents.[269] The city's newest deputy mayor, Adam Zipkin, remains focused on community development throughout the city and finding ways to complete ongoing projects as well as creating a vibrant downtown.[270] Projects costing over $1 billion were completed in 2011 and 2012, with another $1.5 billion in the pipeline for 2012–2013. "It tends to be portrayed at times that there's a downtown boom, but the truth is of the billion dollars worth of projects, more than half are outside of downtown and more than half are in the neighborhoods," states Zipkin.[271] If City Hall demonstrated one area of public policy effectively, it was community development, and it remains an ongoing hallmark of the Booker administration.

5

The 2010 Election and Booker's Second-Term Honeymoon

As early as fall 2008, Booker and other possible candidates were strategizing for the 2010 mayoral election. The election was a year and a half away, and it was unusual for potential mayoral candidates to consider running for office let alone begin organizing fundraisers and campaign staff that early. In previous mayoral elections, candidates had not made their campaigns official until six months before the May nonpartisan election. Yet, for the 2010 race, there appeared to be serious interest in challenging Booker. Many Newarkers, and in particular James supporters and anti-Booker gadflies, hoped to recruit and support a formidable candidate. Former Essex County Prosecutor Clifford Minor made his candidacy official in October 2008 with a $250-per-plate birthday fundraiser at the Robert Treat Hotel in downtown Newark. Most of Newark's older Black political guard supported Minor at the event, and several of them served as honorary co-chairs of his campaign, including former mayoral candidate and State Senator Ronald Rice Sr., former chief of staff Calvin West, Sharpe James' lead attorney Thomas Ashley, former Mayor Kenneth Gibson, and Newark Teachers Union President Joe Del Grosso. But Minor, a soft-spoken and methodical candidate, was often under-whelming at public events, and many thought Booker deserved a challenge because he was often characterized as arrogant. As Gibson said, "I don't think Booker is making friends too well. He has a tendency to act like a lone ranger—he knows it all. Cliff is a solid Newarker. He's been here all his life, and he's achieved a great deal and wants to do something to put the city back on its proper footing."[1] While overall crime rates (especially the homicide rate) decreased, rates for some crimes (such as burglaries) increased, and many Newarkers, including Minor, blamed crime-related problems on Booker's administration. Booker also got an early start on the campaign, starting to reorganize his campaign staff only a week after Minor's fundraiser. His chief of staff, Pablo Fonseca, and deputy chief of staff, Jermaine James, left City Hall to run the campaign in early November. Modia

Butler, a member of Booker's Newark Now nonprofit community organization, became the mayor's new chief of staff.[2]

In June 2009, Booker returned from nearly a two-week cross-country fundraising trip, during which he had received $200,000 in re-election campaign funds. From Silicon Valley to Los Angeles and Miami to Chicago, Booker organized numerous fundraisers and related his narrative of change for a city that has been plagued by economic, social, and political problems. While several business developers and philanthropists had donated $35 million to help the city during his first term, Booker had also raised campaign money to add to his $3.4 million re-election fund. Significant supporters often donated to both his political campaign and city foundations and nonprofit organizations that addressed education, environmental, and public safety issues. Although this was unusual for most mayors, especially in New Jersey, Booker clearly had the advantage of an influential network of supporters; in contrast, Minor only raised $121,604. Some people grew tired of Booker's constant fundraising efforts, including State Senator Rice. "He needs to stay home and be the mayor," Rice said. "He's all over the place, and we're getting gunned down every day. We've got budget problems. I'm not even sure he knows what's going on in his own administration."[3]

While the summer of 2009 proved to be the season for fundraising for the mayoral election, Newark's public safety and other public policy issues became important concerns for voters and political observers. Although Newark's homicide rate was lowest recorded for the first four months of the year since 1959, in May alone there were nearly a dozen murders.[4] In July, Booker called for an end to some of the city's worst violence in months, which raised the homicide rate to nine more than the same time the year before. In response, Police Director Garry McCarthy increased the number of police patrols, and Booker advocated for more cameras for his traffic and public safety campaign (which reduced traffic violations and brought in millions in revenue and even caught former mayor James committing a traffic violation[5]). However, many residents became concerned about illegal guns as many people were shot with unregistered firearms, even though, months later, a successful gun buyback initiative occurred.[6] As Joan Whitlow stated, "May, the cruelest month so far this year in Newark, ended with 11 homicides, compared to 14, from January to April, a record-setting start-of-the-year low for Newark. There were eight homicides last moth and the most recent madness brought this month's total to nine, with one more week to go. What happened?"[7] There were various protests in response to the shootings and to raise awareness about the violence. Several Newark grassroots organizations clogged the streets every week by late summer, and the demonstrations brought many residents out to the streets because they were concerned about what to do next. Several of these organizations and their leaders were not aligned with the mayor. In fact, some were outspoken against Booker, including councilman and high school principal Ras Baraka.[8]

The mayor called for greater curfew enforcement and unity among Newark's communities to end the violence, especially after 14-year-old Keith Calhoun was shot to death. Booker urged neighborhood associations and community groups to cooperate with the police and to increase community policing. He also wanted residents to start block watch organizations, tenant associations, and after-school programs.[9] In addition, Booker pressed for more security cameras, over 60 new police recruits, and more communication from community residents about previous murders.[10] The mayor demanded that the police enforce controversial curfew laws that required teenagers to be off the streets by 11 pm in an effort to prevent more teens from being shot.[11] However, many of the anti-crime initiatives Booker announced were just stronger versions of policies already in place, and he called on residents to aid police. "We need the community now to do more," Booker claimed.[12] Days later, however, a 4-year-old girl was shot on a neighborhood playground in the afternoon, and Booker admitted he was "frustrated and angry right now."[13] Although these preventive tactics had lowered the number of shootings 43 percent and reduced homicides by one third since Booker took office, the anti-violence groups brought some of their protests directly to downtown Newark, disrupting public events and calling for McCarthy's resignation because many of these activists blamed the mayor and the police director for the recent murders.[14] Yet again, Booker faced critics who were community leaders and protesters. Even though Booker reminded them that community partnership was critical to address the violence, many protestors questioned his leadership. At the same time, some in City Hall characterized the marches as political because Ras Baraka was often the featured speaker.[15]

Public safety and recidivism rates were top priorities for the administration during the reelection campaign.[16] In January 2010, Booker wrote an opinion piece in the *Star-Ledger* arguing that re-arrest and re-imprisonment reform required significant public policy reform from all ideological and partisan perspectives. Ex-cons have limited employment opportunities, and 62 percent of inmates became repeat offenders within three years of their release, at a cost of $48,000 per year per inmate, according to Booker. Therefore, Newark launched the Newark Prisoner Reentry Initiative to address reimprisonment, and he proposed state legislative bills to eliminate employment barriers for ex-cons and to establish a high school equivalency program for inmates.[17] The *Star-Ledger* provided their own analysis of the issue and urged state lawmakers to not only support these bills but also reduce the costs associated with reforming and educating ex-cons from $12 million to $7 million.[18] Eventually, in 2012, Newark banned city agencies and landlords from asking job applicants about their criminal history. Councilman Ron Rice sponsored the Ban the Box measure, which made attaining a job or housing less difficult for ex-convicts.[19]

In addition to concerns about crime, outside factors made the reelection especially interesting because Barack Obama had been elected president in 2008 and Chris Christie had been elected New Jersey governor in November 2009. As a result of Booker's early and continued support for Obama during the 2008 presidential election, Booker's reelection campaign received a lot of media attention.

Furthermore, Christie and Booker's relationship was not only unique, and it captured many of their followers' attention. A newly elected Republican governor and a recently elected second-term Democratic urban mayor may in theory be the "state's political odd couple," but they were amicable toward one another in their discussions about Newark.[20] Christie visited the city after defeating Democrat incumbent Governor Jon Corzine, and, even though only ten percent of Newarkers voted for Christie, his appearance and interest in Newark grabbed the media's and mayoral candidates' attention.[21] Even on his inauguration day, Christie attended mass at Newark's Cathedral Basilica of the Sacred Heart and held the inauguration at the Prudential Center.[22] However, the newly elected governor lobbied to suspend $72 million in state aid for financially struggling cities,[23] which included $42 million that had been earmarked for Newark's public schools,[24] and he made cuts to Urban Enterprise Zones funding.[25]

Thus, Booker received a great deal of attention from the media by 2010. The mayor was devoted to posting and responding to Twitter posts, and he famously shoveled a constituent's driveway after a January snowstorm.[26] But there was some negative press, which came mostly from Booker gadflies and, in particular, many Black Newarkers who favored Minor as mayor. While he did not officially launch his bid until late January, Minor did line up several council candidates for his "Newark's Choice" ticket, yet he did not immediately have any candidates for the North and East Wards. One of his council candidates included Sharpe James's son, John James, who was a decorated Afghanistan war army veteran. As the younger James said at the kick-off event, "Since 2006, we've been disrespected—there's no reason why we don't have the jobs and the contracts give[n] out since 2006."[27] Even poet Amiri Baraka (whose son Ras Baraka was on Minor's ticket) stated that Booker's administration did little for Newark residents. So the Minor team introduced early concerns about Booker giving favorable contracts and consulting positions in City Hall to his contacts, campaign supporters, and donors. The *Star-Ledger* also reminded many readers that the city council favored their former members for certain city contracts as well.[28] And Booker's campaign argued that City Hall had remained concerned with addressing Newark's crime rates, creating affordable housing, and investing in open space. While the number of shootings was lower, Minor questioned the fact that the administration's and the county prosecutor's numbers (77 versus 80) differed.[29]

On the campaign trail, Booker collected nearly $6 million in donations, while Minor barely had a quarter-million dollars by the end of January. Even though Minor had a smaller campaign operation, he was determined to cause an upset in the nonpartisan May elections by going from one Newark community to the next and engaging with residents through neighborhood meetings and campaign gatherings.[30] Because he had gained significant support among Newark's Black traditional leadership and had some familiar names on his ticket (Baraka, James, Gibson, Ronald Rice Sr.), Minor hoped that his hometown credibility would enable him to surpass Booker. At the same time, Booker had the support of

Councilmen Donald Payne Jr. and Ronald Rice Jr., so the election appeared to be more of a generational struggle.[31] Still, Minor seemed to have a difficult challenge considering the Booker campaign machine. Aside from Booker's financial domination and campaign organization, which easily outweighed Minor's, incumbency also favored the mayor. Through mayoral events and speeches, including his February State of the City address, Booker spoke of his record and future plans. The mayor cited crime reduction statistics to show that shootings were down 46 percent, murders were down 28 percent, and overall crime was down 21 percent. Booker also spent much of his time highlighting his economic development achievements and proposals. He mentioned his financial empowerment centers that are based on economic assistance and his administration's partnership with both large and small businesses to employ more Newarkers. Minor responded that Booker did little to provide for more city jobs but instead eliminated hundreds of government positions, and, at the same time, the city faced a $73 million deficit from the year prior that required state aid, Port Authority funding, pension deferral, furloughs, and pay cuts for 2,000 employees to ameliorate.[32] Some community leaders thought that the budget plugging approaches could have been avoided if the mayor had lobbied Trenton for more state aid and additional taxes on parking and other items.[33]

Unfortunately for the mayor, however, a scandal involving his former deputy mayor, Ronald Salahuddin, came to the public's attention during the campaign. Booker's deputy mayor was indicted on federal charges just days after Booker's State of the City Address; US Attorney Paul Fishman claimed that the deputy mayor had had numerous meetings with Nicholas Mazzocchi, an undercover consultant and owner of a demolition firm, who recorded proof that Salahuddin illegally steered city demolition contracts to various firms in exchange for donations to certain nonprofit groups and political action committees. In taped recordings, Salahuddin stated that everyone in City Hall was corrupt except for Booker, and the mayor himself warned the deputy mayor not to engage in any inappropriate behavior. Even though the deputy mayor had resigned the summer before for health reasons, he had maintained important ties with city contractors, especially during the early days of the Booker administration.[34] For instance, Sonnie Cooper's businesses, which included a restaurant and trucking and street cleaning companies, donated $6,300 to the mayor's campaign in 2008 and 2009; Cooper was also indicted. Yet a 2007 executive order by the mayor prohibited city contractors from donating to municipal campaigns. The campaign office returned Cooper's donations after the fact even though the executive order exempts contracts awarded through competitive bidding and Cooper had won snow removal and street sweeping bids. However, Cooper owned several businesses; if one of his businesses made donations and his other businesses received city contracts, did that mean he was circumventing Booker's executive order?[35] In any event, the federal government charged Salahuddin with steering demolition contracts to Cooper, Nicholas Mazzocchi, Joseph Paralavecchio (an East Ward political boss), and the mayor's chief of staff, Pablo Fonseca. Assistant US Attorney Zahid Quraishi accused Fonseca of pressuring people to collect $10,000 in contributions as Salahuddin told Fonseca that Fonseca could not get contributions from Mazzocchi because Mazzocchi had not "eaten yet," a euphemism for getting contracts.[36] Thus, even though the mayor had vowed to end the corrupt practice of giving political contributions in exchange for city contracts, Salahuddin not only allowed it to happen, he also participated in it. The deputy mayor even solicited a $5,000 contribution from Mazzocchi for Booker's nonprofit group, Newark Now. Salahuddin told Mazzocchi that the donation made him a "strong" ally with City Hall.[37] Mazzocchi claimed that in New Jersey there was no real difference between a bribe and a political donation because he also donated to Governor Christie and Bayonne Mayor Joseph Doria as well as Booker. Mazzocchi felt the deputy mayor was "shaking him down" on Booker's behalf to get money in order to raze buildings.[38] As Salahuddin knew, demolition was also needed around the Prudential area, and the mayor wanted hundreds of abandoned properties razed. Hoping to cash in on this, Salahuddin also tried to solicit contracts for the potential demolition around the hockey arena.[39] Booker, on the other hand, testified that while Salahuddin was a friend and adviser, Booker was unaware of any deals his deputy mayor made between contractors and nonprofit organizations regardless of what the deputy mayor said. "I knew nothing about Ron Salahuddin giving special privilege to anyone for any matter," stated Booker. "That would be unacceptable."[40] Even Salahuddin denied that he received any kickbacks from the contracts or donations.[41] Ultimately, a couple of years later, a jury found the deputy mayor guilty of conspiring to commit extortion but not guilty of attempted conspiracy and bribery.[42]

Additional campaign finance concerns remained a focal point of the 2010 election. An advocacy group named Citizen's Campaign claimed that the mayor had violated the executive order because political action committees had accepted donations from various city contractors and had spent funds on political campaigns. For instance, Empower Newark accepted over $35,000 from ten city vendors, and, within a year, five of the firms were awarded $5 million in no-bid contacts and another five received $8.2 million in amended contracts. The advocacy organization argued that the executive order should be strengthened to exclude all contractors from making donations to any political action committee, especially because Sonnie Cooper had donated to Empower Newark. But Booker denied having any control over Empower Newark.[43]

Other campaign concerns related to the way candidates used literature and signs around the city to publicize their campaigns. Booker had banners posted on city buildings stating, "Cory Booker, Newark: building a stronger, safer, prouder city"; some found this questionable because the city was essentially spending money to promote the administration during an election year (this was eerily similar to the 2002 race when James used billboards paid for with city funds to feature his administration, something the Booker campaign filed a complaint about with the state Election Law Enforcement Commission).[44] In addition, city-paid T-shirts for youth basketball and other recreational sports stated on the back, "Mayor Cory A. Booker—here to win in 2010." City recreation employees grew concerned, and the city eventually stopped production of the shirts.[45] At the same time, Minor put together some of *Star-Ledger* columnist Joan Whitlow's pieces that appeared to support his campaign and challenge Booker's administration and its policies to create a newspaper-like campaign ad. However, Booker refused to debate Minor, and there were few public events related to the mayoral election.[46] Interestingly, the first and only debate between Minor, Booker, and two minor candidates, Yvonne Garrett Moore and Mirna White, would not be held until the following month, only days before the election.[47]

Finally, in early April 2010, Booker held his reelection kick-off event at New Hope Baptist Church, saying to almost 1,000 supporters, "Let the work I've done speak for me." Booker defended charges that city jobs were going to outsiders, stating that, "Everyone of God's children is important." As for his frequent travel, the mayor argued that he did it to obtain philanthropic donations for Newark.[48] At a press conference with Police Director Garry McCarthy, Booker reminded Newarkers that there had not been any murders in the city in March. As it was an election year, this proved to be a crucial statistic.[49] The day after the press conference, former mayor Sharpe James was released from the Petersburg, Virginia, jail and traveled by Greyhound Bus to Newark; he was welcomed by hundreds of Newarkers. James claimed that he wanted to work with Booker and that "Booker would rather be seen on Oprah's couch than in City Hall." James would go on to serve his remaining sentence of several months at a halfway house in Newark and to work as a mentor at Irvington's Christian Love Baptist Church.[50]

By early May, Booker had campaigned heavily on his record, and he had little competition. By avoiding several candidate forums and only participating in one televised debate, the mayor and his campaign machine were successful at dodging the media and his opponents. The mayor also received the *Star-Ledger*'s endorsement because he could easily fundraise $100 million for Newark's causes, including charter schools, recreation centers, security cameras, and numerous social causes. But Booker, said the newspaper, still remained "aloof," according to his own supporters because he traveled a great deal to raise funds for his campaign and to promote himself as mayor instead of spending time in Newark's communities.[51] With campaign donors such as movie director Steven Spielberg and Craigslist founder Craig Newmark offering thousands of dollars to the Booker team, the mayor clearly had advantages of money and name recognition that Minor did not. By election day, Minor had raised only $300,000; in comparison, Booker had almost $7.5 million (Booker outspent Minor 20–1). However, some claimed that Booker's increasing national publicity tours were undertaken not so much for Newark's sake but for his own political interest.[52] Aside from the media attention on election day, Booker's campaign received some notable interest in implementing voter-mobilization technology in the North Ward as a test to monitor voter turnout on election day. Campaign Connect allows information to be logged in from netbook computers or iPhones manned by volunteer poll watchers to monitor voting and challenge any suspected voter fraud.[53]

Not surprisingly, Booker won the May 11 election with 59 percent of the vote while Minor attained only 35 percent. The remaining six percent went to minor candidates Yvonne Garrett Moore and Mirna White. But voter turnout was light at barely 35,000; therefore, a couple of Booker's city council candidates had to participate in runoff elections in June, and two of them lost seats to Darrin Sharif and former councilman and high school principal Ras Baraka (Amiri Baraka's son), one of Booker's harshest critics.[54] In fact, a year after the election, Baraka's anti-violence community coalition continued to gain momentum against crime, gangs, the mayor, and the police chief.[55] The anti-Booker contingent and old guard lost the mayoral election, but many still felt emboldened to challenge the mayor and question his future in the city. As Newark Teachers Union President Joseph Del Grasso said, "I don't think Mayor Booker's going to come out of this election having a political future."[56]

Several months following the election, Minor was accused of accepting bribes to help a client avoid gun charges.[57] In April 2011, the former mayoral candidate pled guilty. The United States Attorney for New Jersey, Paul Fishman, argued that Minor took $3,500 from Abdul Williams while acting as a lawyer for Jamal Muhammad. A grand jury indicted Williams on the gun charge, and FBI agents discovered that Minor lied to them about his involvement and found the bogus retainer agreement showing that he had worked for Muhammad, not Williams.[58] The former police officer, judge, prosecutor, defense lawyer and mayoral candidate

Second-Term, First-Year Challenges

Despite his reelection, Booker faced significant challenges immediately into his second term. Public safety and urban development remained consistent concerns for the administration. With the continued economic recession turned Great Recession, the city government faced an economic downturn in tax revenues and financial resources. This increasingly affected city services and the city's overall budgetary operations and deficit. Unfortunately for Booker and his administration, they made the difficult decision in early June to double the number of furlough days to help reduce the deficit. The year prior City Hall had closed operations for several days, and this time city employees were asked to take two days off per month during the summer to save almost $3 million and prevent any further layoffs. But this cost saving measure only put a dent in the $100 million estimated deficit. The mayor's chief of staff, Mo Butler, considered the furlough program "one part of a more comprehensive approach to guide us through these very difficult financial times."[59] But few council members were aware of the furlough program, even though the city was waiting for state approval and unions were being briefed about the proposal. Some even called the timing of the furloughs political because they occurred just weeks after the mayoral election. According to union president Rahman Muhammad, if the administration was aware of the budget problems, city workers were political pawns.[60]

In addition to the proposed furloughs, the administration made the difficult but politically problematic decision to restructure the water management operations in order to raise money. The administration wanted to create a new city water system to collect on bills and find more ways to increase revenues, including selling water to other cities. The new water authority would increase water rates for a minimum five percent every year for ten years.[61] The city already owned the property and reservoirs in West Milford, and the city's water agency needed about $500 million to replace and repair pipes under the city's streets. Few cities own their water sources, but Newark had invested in the property generations ago. The proposed Municipal Utility Authority (MUA) could raise tens of millions of dollars over the next 30 years by selling as much as $70 million in bonds that the city could use for its budgetary problems. However, people were concerned that a special authority, which was not subject to public scrutiny, could lead to patronage politics.[62] Still, Booker introduced the new authority proposal, hoping to provide $50 million to pay down the city's deficit. His budget also required additional cuts to city services. Booker formally presented the budget to the city council in late June prior to the inauguration. The spending plan called for a seven percent property tax increase (or an increase averaging $292 per property) and 651 additional layoffs as well as significant cuts to public institutions such as the library and the Newark Museum. But Booker threatened that property taxes could increase by as much as 35 percent if the MUA was not created and bonds were not sold. The administration faced resistance, however, toward the MUA proposal as well as the suggested police and fire department layoffs. "For the next few months there are going to have to be very difficult decisions to be made," Booker said. "For that, we need everyone to come to the table to work together, especially the public safety unions." But union representatives claimed that there were few, if any, communications with City Hall about the proposed cuts to their workforces and benefits.[63]

The timing of Booker's budget plan, at the same time as the 2010 inauguration, hardly convinced council members to agree with Booker's financial proposal. In fact, several members were publicly outspoken against the plan at the New Jersey Performing Arts Center's gathering on July 1. Councilman Ras Baraka said that it was wrong for the mayor to use his office to reward privileges and "give away power" by "selling out" city services and creating the MUA. And Councilman Augusto Amador said that the council "will say yes, and will say no. And yes, Mr. Mayor, sometimes that means disagreeing with you." In addition, Booker had not supported Councilwoman Mildred Crump for council president (she thanked Sharpe James instead at the inauguration), and now she appeared to lose favor with her so-called "political godson," the reelected mayor.[64] In fact, she started to have serious concerns about the mayor before the inauguration because he "did not keep his word and he constantly hired people outside of the city." According to the councilwoman, the mayor also demonstrated poor communication skills by failing to return officials' phone calls.[65] Also, the newly chosen council president, Donald Payne Jr., stated that the city government would not be "one branch dictating to another."[66] Council members were offering just a taste of things to come; the mayor–council relationship would be a rocky one.

By mid-July 2010, it was apparent that City Hall had to consider extreme solutions to address the financial deficit, and the council proved resistant to Booker's suggestions. The mayor pressured the city council to pass the MUA proposal; otherwise the city would lose $70 million in bond revenue and city residents would face a revised 37 percent tax hike. Interestingly, the mayor was against creating an authority when he was a councilman resisting then Mayor Sharpe James' proposal.[67] But the idea of putting the city's water into an independent authority concerned many council members. Councilman Ras Baraka led the charge against the mayor's proposal and said that Newarkers needed to weigh in on the decision, even though the mayor was calling for immediate change so bonds could be issued by September. Councilman Luis Quintana also added that the MUA proposal did not have the five votes necessary for adoption. "He needs to talk to the people who elected him," stated the senior council member. But Booker argued that the council was aware of the MUA proposal when he suggested the authority idea in 2009, and he urged that the plan be considered immediately. Still, council members were resistant to an immediate adoption of the MUA idea because the public had had little time to consider and respond to the proposal; the council twice voted to defer the plan until weeks later because many residents attended council meetings to voice their concerns. Booker, according to Councilwoman Crump, underestimated how proud Newarkers are of water rights, and the mayor "thought he could turn around Newarkers on this issue. He could have, but he didn't know how."[68]

Sadly, the MUA was a missed opportunity for Newark, the mayor, and coalition politics. It should have been a key reason for sustainable coalition building in Newark between residents, officials, and the mayor. Instead, Booker's opponents and even some of his allies joined against the proposal in a backlash coalition effort. "It became a key moment, and it was truly a grassroots effort," states Richard Cammarieri.[69] According to the New York Times, the mayor was "far less aggressive in selling his propsoals ... When opponents of the plan packed churches and neighborhood meetings, Mr. Booker made almost no effort to counter them, said members of the Municipal Council who were elected on Booker's platform."[70] So many Newarkers were against the MUA initiative that even some of Booker's former allies and Newark's old guard prevented the proposal from passing the city council.[71]

In addition to the water authority debate and the failure to pass the legislation in 2010, many city employees and residents were very anxious about the library closures and police layoffs. A number of residents, in fact, signed petitions against closing libraries, which would have saved the city $2.45 million.[72] The city also considered laying off 263 police officers to fix a $16.7 million police department deficit. However, Booker claimed that if the police union negotiated for furloughs and ended uniform and gas allowances, then there would be no layoffs. But the union chief argued that the contracts were already negotiated and he refused to make concessions to the mayor. "I'm not going to be the culprit in this political game that he's playing," Newark's Fraternal Order of Police President Derrick Hatcher stated about the mayor. "He's going to have to answer to his constituents for the lack of police services that are provided to them." But Booker argued that the state had cut much of the aid they received from Trenton and revenue had fallen short for the fiscal year—by almost $60 million. He also said that any mention of crime increasing due to police layoffs was "fear mongering." Police Director Garry McCarthy said that if the layoffs were to happen, the department would do more with fewer police officers and still bring crime rates down.[73] Still, residents remained fearful about the state of the city with fewer police officers, and the *Star-Ledger* encouraged unions to make concessions. "The real priority is protecting the city, and givebacks will keep cops on the street."[74]

Due to the conflicts about police cutbacks and the financial troubles facing the city, Booker claimed that the city council was failing to do its job. He held several press conferences suggesting that deferring the MUA proposal was financially problematic. "We are in crisis mode," he suggested. "We all need to come together."[75] But the council proved resistant to the mayor and charged back that the city could not function under Booker's proposed budget cuts. Council President Donald Payne Jr. and four council members held a press conference arguing that while the council advises and agrees to a budget, it's the mayor's responsibility to draft the budget; the council members also stated that they found the cuts draconian.[76] The mayor also threatened to close public pools and the city's 250-children day camp (Watershed Camp) as well as institute furloughs.[77] Keeping Newark's pools maintained became a critical concern, and pool servicing company Hayward Industries donated $150,000 so public pools would remain open until Labor Day.[78] Even having toilet paper in city offices was an issue because Booker had threatened that his administration would no longer buy basic supplies if the council failed to pass the budget. The toilet paper war was clearly a media stunt as thousands of toilet paper rolls were donated by Marcal Manufacturing and Justtoiletpaper.com.[79]

But the mayor had other concerns besides receiving toilet paper donations. Once Booker organized public meetings about the MUA proposal, it became clear that Newark residents were concerned about the plan. At the first meeting at West Side High School, nearly 200 people attended, many holding signs protesting the MUA.[80] The Newark Water Group, a grassroots association, continued to organize protests at the events and held several community gatherings to criticize the proposal. For some, the rallies against the plan were similar to those that challenged the 1960s UMDNJ proposal.[81] The *Star-Ledger* said that even if the authority were managed carefully, they were concerned about the plan because "it's unwise to borrow money to cover current operating costs rather than for capital projects with long-term benefits."[82] The city council had to make a decision about the MUA plan because it was the linchpin of the mayor's budget. Even though many on the council accused the mayor of mismanaging the budget before the May elections, council members were clearly up against the wall. "The mayor is playing a chicken game," argued Councilman Baraka.[83] By an 8–0 vote, the council defeated the MUA plan, but they also agreed to consider alternative proposals to address the unbalanced budget. These alternatives included collecting money the city was owed from the Passaic Valley Sewage Commission, setting up tolls on McCarter Highway, getting an advance on the annual $70 million Port Authority payment, and selling city properties and then leasing them; however, council members were resistant to these reform measures.[84] It would not be until 2012 that Booker would succeed in his efforts to get the council to consider creating the MUA as they did not want to jeopardize $24 million in state aid for the fiscal year. By approving an application for the aid, the council at least agreed to create the authority. In 2012, while Booker wrote letters and newspaper op-eds arguing against the "distortions" to his plan[85] and disagreeing with the charge that his proposal would create patronage,[86] several council members were against the creation of the authority;[87] instead, the council adopted a resident-generated ordinance for the creation of a municipal utilities authority by referendum.[88] But Booker stated that the MUA battle was "so over exaggerated and I know so. First of all, polls show you that people would want their water. We always laugh because we get 99.9 percent of the things we want through our council. 99.9 percent! And the press is latching onto this as a great policy failure, when it was an electoral failure."[89]

For some observers, it appeared Booker lost favor with many of his supporters on the city council just after he was reelected. The failed MUA plan and the continued financial crisis were serious blows to his political agenda. And the MUA proposal created a political backlash, even a backlash coalition against the mayor. According to historian Clement Price, Booker has "considerably lost his ability to galvanize support for something that he considered absolutely essential to the city's fiscal health." Or as the *Star-Ledger* put it, "Booker has lost his mojo with the city council."[90] The community outcry through the Newark Water Group was highly organized, and protesters frequently attended public events, meetings, and council hearings, allowing for a coalition against the mayor and his proposal and causing backlash coalition politics.[91] Residents were worried that authority heads and bond investors would profit at Newark's expense.[92] "After the insurrection in the late '60s, most people who could leave did leave," said Council President Payne. "Outsiders have always come in and used our resources and gotten wealthy. It appears they just take and go home, and you're left here with almost nothing. I think that's the way residents of Newark see this. It's the outsiders who have taken everything else, and doggone it, they're not going to take our water."[93] According to Councilman Anibal Ramos Jr., public water is sacred territory for many

Newarkers: "Water has an incredible history in this city. Residents see an asset with public water, and they have legitimate fears about privatizing water. But there are so many infrastructure problems with the city's water systems and so many budgetary problems facing Newark at the same time."[94]

In contrast, after winning reelection, reducing crime, and raising $100 million for the city, Booker believed that the council would support proposals like the MUA even though they clearly had concerns about the proposal, and he appeared blindsided by the political backlash. As observer Joan Whitlow stated, "Booker didn't like a similar water-borrowing scheme when it was proposed by his predecessor. Booker might have realized that people would not like his version, either. Citizens organized. Political heat was applied." Booker postponed the matter until after the elections, which seemed "an attempt to back the city in the corner."[95] In addition to Booker's shortsightedness about the proposal, many council members and constituents did not take the mayor seriously because he admitted that seeking a third term would require drastic measures. "I've asked my friends to get a weapon, preferably a gun or a knife, and shoot me," he told the *Star-Ledger* after the inauguration. Booker later said that he was disappointed that his comment was framed that way in the newspaper, and he was unsure as to whether he would run for another term.[96]

In any event, Booker had to immediately find solutions to address the budget gap. For years, City Hall, and in particular previous administrations, had relied on payments from the Port Authority or other large entities that leased land or had made sizable financial agreements with the city. Councilman Anibal Ramos Jr. stated that "Newark, for a better part of 15 years, was able to balance their budget with gimmicks to fill in gaps and now suddenly police have to be laid off."[97] One of the first initiatives the mayor considered, especially following the initial rejection of the MUA plan, was to sell city properties. At a special council meeting that Councilman Ron Rice Jr. suggested to discuss land sales, a paid budget consultant laid out a plan to have the Essex County Improvement Authority bond the sales of city buildings and then lease the buildings back to Newark. Now that consultants estimated the deficit to be $83 million for 2010, the administration hoped city land sales would garner $40 to $50 million.

The land appraisals, bonding, and sales still had to be approved by the council, the Improvement Authority, the Essex County Freeholders, and the State Local Finance Board before mid-November. Booker said that he would include the council in the decisions about which buildings would be considered for sale.[98] The city had not considered selling buildings and then leasing them for generations. And a number of individuals would profit from the sales, including consultants, lawyers, and bondsmen—all within a very short time span.[99] "This is a new frontier," said James Hughes, Dean of the Edward J. Bloustein School of Planning and Public Policy at Rutgers University. "To get it done in that time frame, all of the bureaucratic stars have to be in perfect alignment and that rarely happens." California, New York, and Arizona have enacted similar policy measures to raise revenue. But the difference in Newark's case was that City Hall was looking to institute the sales immediately, which was very unusual. In fact, Newark missed the County Freeholders' deadline for posting the sales for the September meeting.[100] The city did plan to sell 16 city-owned buildings, including police headquarters and Symphony Hall, and lease them back. The leaseback initiative would generate $75 million, with $40 million going to the 2010 budget and the rest to capital improvements. But Newark would have to pay nearly $4 million a year for the plan, and the city could not rely on similar budget fixes in the future.[101]

Besides the leaseback proposal, another significant budget solution was layoffs of city employees. The mayor and council appeared to underestimate the city's financial problems, and unions were continually pressured to renegotiate for benefits and pay raises.[102] By the end of September, 2,200 layoff notices had been issued to city employees. Union president Rahaman Muhammad challenged Booker to step away from the media limelight he was basking in as a result of the $100 million donation Facebook's founder had given the city on the Oprah Winfrey Show. "We want Mayor Booker to step away from the cameras, do some soul-searching, and come clean with the City of Newark." Privatizing, or essentially outsourcing, the sanitation department was seriously considered because doing so could save the city $7 million a year, but it would also slash a good share of jobs[103] (the city later decided against privatization of its sanitation services[104]). Meanwhile, the firefighters union, who remained supportive of Booker throughout his political career, grew concerned about 90 possible layoffs, and their leaders warned that visitors would have second thoughts about Newark being a destination city. However, laying off 165 cops, demoting 112 more, and hiring new recruits and then firing them, even though there had been 35 homicides that summer (more than in the summer of 2006), appeared political because the mayor said that union leadership had refused to make the smallest concessions.[105] With the cuts and transfers, homicide detectives couldn't keep pace with the number of murders and almost half of the homicides went unsolved. At the same time, the anti-violence movement coalition continued to organize weekly protests against the ongoing murders.[106] The Fraternal Order of Police President Derrick Hatcher said, "There's no way in hell that any officer should be laid off here in the city of Newark especially with the incidents that are occurring more frequently. There have been some major shootings and homicides in the last few weeks and I think that causes alarm to citizens." The police union had already started attacking the mayor by paying for billboards around the city stating: "Welcome to Newark— Stop Laying Off Cops and Call Cory Booker."[107] In other words, it was a difficult time for the mayor and the police.[108]

Unquestionably, Newark's police union was busy addressing layoffs and the increased murder rate, but the end of summer the police also had to contend with accusations by the American Civil Liberties Union (ACLU) of false arrests, improper searches, excessive force, and other corrupt practices. The ACLU, through a 96-page petition, listed 407 allegations covering a two-and-a-half year period and requested a federal investigation into the Newark Police Department, citing troubling statistics and dozens of lawsuits. In 2008 and 2009 alone, there were 261 complaints involving excessive force, and the petition suggested that there were substantial ongoing systemic failures. The Booker administration, however, said that the petition actually undermined the city's efforts to address crime. And police officials argued that "people are looking for money" and that criminals make allegations regularly. But ACLU of New Jersey's executive director, Deborah Jacobs, said that, "You're going to tell me 200 people made internal affairs complaints and the majority made it up? That doesn't make sense."[109] In addition, she wrote in an op-ed in the *Star-Ledger* that the ACLU supported Booker and Police Director Garry McCarthy's new era of reform, but Booker and McCarthy had failed to establish an independent monitor to oversee the police department's operations and mandate the necessary reforms. Jacobs also stated that the ACLU had exhausted other avenues to resolve the persistent problems within the department, but the problems were too large for a city like to Newark to handle with its "starved resources."[110] Even worse, the *Star-Ledger* discovered that one out of every ten internal affairs complaints filed against Newark police from 2000 to 2008 were not reported to the state's Attorney General's Office. In addition, a large share of the internal affairs cases, some 1,315, went missing because they were not carried over from one year to the next, according to the Attorney General.[111] Ultimately, New Jersey Attorney General Paula Dow and Acting Essex County Prosecutor Robert Laurino launched a joint review of the police department's internal affairs division.[112] One study even indicated that the department's misconduct had cost the city more than $4 million in lawsuit settlements and damage awards within just three years.[113]

The criticism of the Police Director became so great that one of Newark's police unions, the Superior Officers Association, had a vote of no confidence in McCarthy only days after the ACLU's petition and the state and county began their investigation into the internal affairs division. McCarthy responded that the vote was the union's way to undermine his authority. Even the Fraternal Order of Police considered a vote of no confidence in the police director. The timing of these events was crucial, as shortly thereafter McCarthy had to go before the city council for his reappointment and he was narrowly confirmed.[114] Finally, the police director admitted that it was difficult to operate a bureaucracy that was resistant to change and claimed that he would address police brutality and similar concerns.[115] Weeks later, McCarthy made an effort to improve community relations by proposing improved police training and a performance monitoring system; he hoped these efforts would improve residents' faith in the police in light of the ACLU's accusations.[116] Years later, in an unprecedented move, the police department also agreed to publish the sex, race, and age of every individual that officers stop and frisk.[117]

However, the city council added further pressure on the police and the mayor. Six council members signed a letter to the US Justice Department asking the federal government to honor the ACLU petition and investigate the police department for misconduct and use of excessive force. Councilman Rice drafted the letter, which said, "The ACLU petition makes clear that the NPD is not able to correct itself and our personal observations bear that out."[118] Council members who agreed with Rice included Ras Baraka, Augusto Amador, Luis Quintana, Mildred Crump, and Council President Donald Payne Jr. Although many of these council members supported McCarthy's reappointment as police director, they were still concerned about police brutality and misconduct. In fact, one councilman, several officials, and a number of community leaders spoke with the Justice Department as the federal government started investigating the ACLU's claims. But McCarthy was critical of civic leaders for supporting the ACLU and not inquiring about police reforms: "Have they come and looked at what we've been doing in the Newark Police Department in the past four years? Have they come and tried to work collaboratively with us?"[119]

Nevertheless, the worst aspect of the Newark police department's struggles was the layoffs that occurred in October 2010. It was already problematic to lay off police, but firing 19 newly graduated academy recruits did not help Booker's claims that he cared about public safety. Yet the mayor blamed the union for not negotiating. "The union leadership should apologize to their members for selfishly refusing to make even the smallest concessions," claimed Booker. Several recruits commented that they were "done" and did not want to join the force again especially because many of them were "going to lose everything." As one recruit commented, "Booker's main thing when he took office was cops and law enforcement. Now it's turned to teachers. He turned his back on us."[120] In addition, Newark's mounted police patrol was suspended, forcing the city to sell 18 horses to other cities and ending a widely popular police presence on Newark's streets.[121] Four unions, nonetheless, filed suit to prevent the city from laying off police and firefighters, claiming that doing so would affect public safety and that the city had not been engaging in meaningful negotiations. The unions' lawyer, David Fox, called the layoffs "massive and dangerous" and said that Booker did not have the authority to make these cuts. But Superior Court Judge Patricia Costello stated that she did not have the authority to prevent 167 police officers and 24 firefighters from being laid off and that it was the responsibility of the mayor and the state Civil Service Commission to hear the request.[122] Only days later, another judge ruled that the city had given little information about contract concessions to the Fraternal Order of Police (FOP); Superior Court Judge Kenneth Levy said that the city was not forthcoming about negotiations with the union, and he granted a ten-day stay preventing police layoffs. The other unions (the Superior Officers Association and the Newark Firefighters' Union) reached last-minute deals with the city that protected their union members from layoffs.[123] During that ten-day period, however, the FOP claimed that their members offered $9 million in givebacks and other cost saving proposals, including pay deferrals. Yet the mayor's office argued that the deferrals provided no real savings to the city and would not prevent layoffs. "This is becoming a circus," asserted FOP's President Derrick Hatcher. "Does the mayor want to keep these officers or not?" The politics only got worse as the state's appellate division granted the city's request for a hearing to lift the order, but the judge upheld the stay. The city also argued that delaying the layoffs threatened the city's finances. And city council members, including Ras Baraka, called the administration's inability to negotiate with the unions "unconscionable."[124]

Hatcher and the FOP decided not to continue negotiations with the administration. Even though the FOP had offered $2.7 million in concessions and $6 million in pay deferrals until 2013, city officials said the deferrals would have to be paid at some point and thus did not count as true savings. Yet, FOP members did not vote on the city's counteroffer of a one-time salary deferral, an overtime cap, and five unpaid leave days in addition to the $2.7 million in concessions because Hatcher did not agree to the language, and, thus, he only discussed the deal with a few union members, even though 167 officers were going to be laid off.[125] But the political differences between the two leaders seemed to be personal. The mayor stated that Hatcher was not a man of his word and that Hatcher was "a guy who was sitting in a bubble." On the other hand, Hatcher argued that the mayor had hired the new police officers, not the police department. "He should put on his big-boy pants and say 'I'm going to take this on the chin.'"[126] However, the *Star-Ledger* argued that although the mayor should have recognized the city's financial problems, the blame lay with the union for refusing to return to the negotiating table and not supporting temporary cuts and concessions (which were never voted on by the union's executive board or members).[127] Many of Newark's laid off police officers were forced to relocate to other cities in the state and across the country.[128] With 13 percent of its officers laid off—the largest reduction in 32 years, Newark's police department and the mayor had increasing problems to address, including spikes in shootings and carjackings only weeks after the layoffs.[129]

By March 2011, the number of carjacking arrests increased and carjackings declined sharply.[130] Booker offered a radical approach to gangs and youthful offenders: Either gang members chose to address their problems through education, employment, or drug treatment programs, or the gangs would be dismantled. The new strategy was based on "Operation Ceasefire," a violence reduction program that had been used in other cities and would involve a series of meetings with community leaders, city officials, and police who would sit down with some of the city's most violent groups. Some critics called the initiative "hug-a-thug" and were concerned because the police would be directly involved. "Nobody from the streets or the community will be there because the people here do not trust the police," said Lamont Vaughn, a member of the Bloods. Booker remained optimistic, however, and announced the initiative's success rate in other cities during his State of the City Address. He was outspoken about the city's recidivism rate and said that, "our new initiative seeks to end this."[131] Booker remained particularly concerned about the prison rates of minorities in New Jersey. "We have savage disparities including the prison population where the prison population in New Jersey is 60 something percent [Black] even though our population is 13 percent statewide."[132] Police Director McCarthy stated that this new form of policing was proactive because it involved community and city leaders and that Newark would be the first New Jersey city to begin the initiative. Because other cities, such as Boston, Cincinnati, and Stockton had had some success with the program, conceived by John Jay College's David Kennedy and Rutgers–Newark's Anthony Braga, city officials hoped to see a decrease in Newark's crime activity even though New Jersey's gangs are far less structured than other state's gangs.[133]

Sadly, though, the Operation Ceasefire initiative would not fully come to fruition under Police Director McCarthy as he would leave his post a month later. He was one of the final candidates for the post of superintendent of the Chicago Police Department, and, according to the *Chicago Sun-Times*, he was considered one of the most-qualified candidates for the position, after being a finalist in 2003 for the same job. Once it was known that McCarthy was being seriously considered for another position elsewhere, Councilman Baraka and Councilwoman Crump urged the city to hire a Newark native as the next police director. "We need to look for a homegrown police director," said Crump. "We need somebody from the community to understand the community."[134] Within days, McCarthy confirmed that he was leaving Newark for Chicago. Immediately, his supporters and even some critics responded to the news, saying that his four-year tenure as the Newark police director had been challenging. "I don't ever think he really got the support of the community that you need to be successful in this town," stated Council President Payne. "It was kind of a double-edged sword with him."[135] Interestingly, the *Star-Ledger* editorial board wrote in a supportive editorial that "McCarthy's departure is a big loss for the Brick City, as its own bloody summer approaches."[136]

Deputy Chief Samuel DeMaio was immediately named the acting police director because he had to quickly deal with the department's various problems, ranging from layoffs to staff restructuring to the increasing homicide rate that summer.[137] But five council members and a pastor group challenged DeMaio's appointment and wanted to see his disciplinary record because he questioned journalists at a crime scene about their immigration status and confiscated a camera and photographs. Even the ACLU of New Jersey urged the mayor to voluntarily release disciplinary records of any candidates for police director; the organization had already questioned DeMaio's record and reputation.[138] "Booker must embrace a transparent process if he has any hope of earning public support for his pick," warned the ACLU.[139] DeMaio remained defiant about not releasing his records, while Council President Payne called for a national search for the new police director. Still, DeMaio suggested further restructuring the police department by reviving the mounted and motorcycle units and possibly rehiring half of the police officers who had been laid off the year prior.[140] Within days of DeMaio's appointment, however, the *Star-Ledger* discovered that the US Department of Justice's investigation of the

ACLU's accusations against Newark's Police Department for police brutality and misconduct had already been underway for several months. The federal agency examined police practices and internal affairs policies and was considering whether an outside monitor should be put in place. Booker, at a lighthearted press conference, suddenly appeared to be "welcoming" the investigation,[141] even though, as the media reminded many residents, the mayor had initially resisted it.[142] By the end of summer 2011, when police were accused of harassing Carl Sharif, Booker's former adviser and son of Councilman Darrin Sharif, Booker appeared to underestimate police harassment, while the media and the city council were growing concerned about officers threatening area residents. Sharif claimed that police officers had visited his office and suggested that he was the person who had created a faxed flier critical of DeMaio; the officers' visit to his Irvington office was described by the acting police director as "unwarranted." Still, the image of police harassing a respected citizen caused alarm and suggested even more reasons for the federal government to investigate the department.[143]

Both Booker and DeMaio had to plan for the upcoming summer despite the ongoing federal investigation. Since Officer William Johnson was murdered in a driveby shooting at a fried chicken take-out restaurant in May, the administration had faced pressure to prevent further incidents. With shootings up 40 percent, 163 police layoffs, and less state aid—thanks to Christie's financial cuts, Booker had to prepare for another problematic summer.[144] The mayor and acting police director unveiled the "Safe City Task Force" to recruit churches, recreation centers, and campus and nonprofit groups to provide alternative activities for Newark's youth. In fact, now teens who violated the 11 pm curfew would have to go to area churches or community groups and be enrolled in summer programs. Considering the increase in murders during the spring and the previously murderous summers, Booker resolved to plan ahead.[145] "It is time that we as a community take a greater responsibility for what is going on," vowed the mayor. "This summer we have something to prove to ourselves again." DeMaio emphasized that the new initiative would require positive interactions between the community and the police.[146] But the original antigang initiative, Operation Ceasefire, was delayed until the end of September to coincide with a $2 million US Department of Justice grant to help start the program and support community policing initiatives.[147]

Like clockwork, the Newark Anti-Violence Coalition efforts continued and grew even larger during the summer of the first year of Booker's second term. The group held their 100th weekly vigil against violence and continued to march at corners and housing complexes throughout the summer.[148] The coalition also held a 24-hour peace event later in the summer.[149] One of Booker's most outspoken critics in the coalition, Councilman Ras Baraka, continued to question the administration's approaches to address crime. "Obviously there's something wrong," he said about finding ways to protect late-night take-out restaurants in the wake of Officer Johnson's murder. But the administration's idea to require small restaurants to hire armed guards for late nights would be costly and do little.[150] Moreover with a shrinking police force and council members' continued pressure against the administration to do more about crime, several attempted initiatives took place.[151] In an effort to build stronger relations with the South Ward, where much of the crime was occurring, Booker appointed Sheilah Coley as police chief; he felt it was a good start toward active community policing because the South Ward community recognized her as a valuable asset as acting captain of the 5th precinct. Coley was the first female police chief for Newark's Police Department. Although the police chief position was dissolved in 2008, residents pressured the city to recreate the post, especially as Coley was the head of Internal Affairs. At the same time, interim Police Director DeMaio was relieved to share some of his responsibilities with the new chief. In addition, many on the city council supported her appointment, and even the ACLU agreed with the change.[152]

Despite these positive changes, however, the police faced one of their most controversial issues when allegations were made that the New York Police Department was spying on Muslim residents as part of a counterterrorism operation. Public officials discovered that former police director McCarthy was informed of the NYPD actions as early as 2007 and even gave the NYPD tours of the city. By early 2012, Booker was informed that the NYPD had conducted surveillance of citizens without his knowledge. "I have deep concerns, and I am very disturbed that this might have been surveillance that was based on no more than religious affiliation," said the mayor.[153] Once again, the ACLU became concerned and wanted to ensure that NYPD actions would not be repeated. A detailed 60-page NYPD report stated that NYPD plainclothes officers took pictures and mapped out and eavesdropped on Newark mosques, businesses, and student groups. According to the NYPD, the purpose of the surveillance program was to trace information about Newark's Muslim communities should someone not from Newark stay, eat, or communicate with a Newarker. Yet hundreds of American citizens were cataloged by an outside police force, often inaccurately, and no actual criminal allegations were made. Even though the report claimed that the NYPD was cooperating with Newark police, Booker said he never authorized the program, and the new police director claimed that Newark police's intelligence unit was unaware of the surveillance even though the police department had some "minimal involvement" with the NYPD.[154]

While New York Mayor Michael Bloomberg argued that surveillance gathering was critical after 9/11 as a counterterrorism strategy, Booker immediately stated that the NYPD's initiatives were "deeply disturbing," and his office and, eventually, the state Attorney General would launch an investigation of the NYPD program, particularly after a number of Muslim leaders became worried that the program was still in operation.[155] In fact, at one news conference at Rutgers University–Newark, Nadia Kahf, chairwoman of New Jersey's Council on American-Islamic Relations, said that the Muslim community felt "betrayed."[156] At the same time, some leaders supported the program, including M. Zuhdi Jasser, founder of the American Islamic Leadership Coalition. "They talk about us as if we are monolithic," he stated before organizing a rally supporting the NYPD.[157] Interestingly, the surveillance program also caused strain between New Jersey state officials and New York City officials. New Jersey Governor Chris Christie stated that the NYPD had a reputation for not revealing too much information to other government agencies. NYPD Commissioner Ray Kelly countered that "[anyone] who intimates that it is unlawful for the police department to search online, visit public places, or map neighborhoods has not read, misunderstood or intentionally obfuscated" legal guidelines.[158] In addition, NYPD Deputy Commissioner Paul Browne specified that there was always a Newark police officer with NYPD officers "AT ALL TIMES."[159] Months later the Christie administration finished a three-month review, concluding that New Jersey laws were not violated by the NYPD surveillance program. Following the review, NYPD and state officials agreed to meet regularly and adhere to notification rules when outside agencies conduct operations in New Jersey. The findings, however, meant that New Jersey Muslim residents had no recourse within the state to stop NYPD surveillance. State officials discovered that New Jersey has no laws barring outside law enforcement agencies from secretly conducting operations in the state.[160] A week later, Muslim Advocates, an advocacy organization, held a press conference announcing that they would file a lawsuit in federal court in Newark against the NYPD. But NYPD officials referred to the earlier state findings that the agency did no wrong. Muslim Advocates' executive director, Farhana Khera, commented, "With New York officials refusing to look into the NYPD's abuses, the New Jersey Attorney General saying his hands are tied, and the US Department of Justice dragging its heels, this lawsuit is the victims' last resort for justice to prevail."[161]

Education Policy

One of the key issues facing Booker during his second term was education policy. Even before he was mayor, Booker was weary of the James administration and their handling of education policy as the former mayor argued that the public school system was not a part of City Hall's responsibilities. "Well we just would not accept that in this administration," said Booker.[162] And with hundreds of Newark students protesting in downtown, the Booker administration felt pressured to improve the city's learning facilities. For example, there was an organized protest and walk out from Barringer High School where students claimed their building was unsafe and unsanitary.[163] In addition, in 2006, 2010, and 2013, thousands protested Christie's proposed cuts to state education funding. Not only did the protests create traffic delays and receive media attention, they also stirred interest about education reform among politicians, including the mayor.[164] But Booker appeared more focused on creating charter schools than "getting his hands dirty when it comes to public school problems," argued Councilwoman Mildred Crump. "Booker is in favor of destroying our school system."[165] Although the city received $22 million in donations to create the Newark Charter School Fund, only ten percent of students actually benefited from the fund because the vast majority of students attended conventional public schools. As a matter of fact that the public school budget was nearly $1 billion, or $24,000 spent per pupil, Newark students still performed poorly on high school exit exams because many of them faced a variety of challenges caused by poverty. In addition to federal grants to help offset the rehabilitation and construction of schools, five Newark public schools received another $21.9 million.[166] Yet with school budget cuts and layoffs of 357 nontenured teachers, Newark public schools had challenges as well.[167]

Because the new public school superintendant, Clifford Janey, replaced Marion Bolden in 2008, he was the center of education policy initiatives. Janey was interested in teacher performance, tenure reform, and staff cuts. But making some of these changes in Newark's bureaucratic school system proved to be a challenging feat.[168] Janey pushed to increase literacy and other basic skills in elementary school. He also wanted students to not just pass the state test but to complete advanced-level courses.[169] In fact, Science High School started its new AP with Summer Institute with 335 students taking Advanced Placement classes as the superintendent advocated. The district received $300,000 in federal grants and hired eight consultants to train teachers.[170] Janey also went ahead with his "Great Expectations" plan to address the reading and writing gap as well as Newark's 54 percent high school graduation rate. Other initiatives included hiring teacher recruiters and building new classrooms and preschool centers.[171] One significant idea the administration proposed was to create a special zone for education by having seven low-performing schools join together and partner with colleges and community groups organized by New York University. Central High School and six elementary and middle schools would be a Global Village School Zone, similar to Harlem Children's Zone, where a network of social and community services would be offered to children and residents. The district would receive $20 million over three years to help rehabilitate schools, offer professional development, and increase teacher compensation. Committees of principals, teachers, parents, college educators, and community leaders would make daily decisions about operations and policies. This model has operated in certain neighborhoods in New York City, Syracuse, and Cleveland. Although Booker had always sought mayoral control of the city's schools, he supported the proposal. Governor Christie also backed the plan, as did the Newark Teachers Union.[172]

Critics argued that although proposals like the Global Village School Zone and the Great Expectations plan were taking shape, Janey's record was relatively thin. By the end of summer 2010, Janey's contract status became the focus of Newark's education politics. His three-year contract was not going to be renewed, which left the city to search for a new school superintendant. And Newark's education statistics remained largely unchanged—46 percent of high school students failed to graduate and only 40 percent of third graders could read and write at grade-level. Some 98 percent of Newark's high school graduates who attended Essex County College, for example, had to take remedial math courses before they were able to complete college classes.[173] Many Newark parents found the results dismal and decided that they must be outspoken at public events and advance proactive initiatives.[174] Governor Christie was particularly unsatisfied with the superintendant and his supposed reforms. "Newark's children, and those around the state, simply cannot wait any longer," said the governor. "It is my expectation that new leadership will move quickly, aggressively and with accountability to implement the kind of fundamental reform that is urgently needed to improve Newark's school system." However, Janey had little political backing.[175] As the *Star-Ledger* editorial board stated, the superintendant "failed to [score] the kind of substantial improvement the city must have. A good superintendant is fine in a place that already has decent schools. But Newark needs a star." Interestingly, a coalition of parents and reformers hoped to fill the position with a visionary candidate, and even the new president of Newark's advisory school board, Shaver Jeffries; the Newark Teachers Union; and the governor seemed to agree about finding a candidate who would create school reform.[176] Janey's dismissal was also apparently critical to negotiations between the mayor, the governor, and a potential major philanthropist.[177]

Although the superintendant search was crucial to Newark's public schools, another education-related issue took the spotlight: the $100 million donation from Facebook's founder and chief executive, Mark Zuckerberg, to the city schools. Attention was centered on Newark, Booker, Zukerberg, and Christie because the national media highlighted the donation in various newspapers, periodicals, on cable news shows, and even on the Oprah Winfrey Show. In fact, the mayor and the governor met Zuckerberg on the Oprah Winfrey Show to announce the donation. The front pages of New Jersey's newspapers the last week in September 2010 featured pictures of Winfrey, Zuckerberg, Booker, and Christie, an unusual pairing of personalities and egos. The announcement also included the fact that Christie would cede some control of the state-run school system to Booker. Considering the urgency of finding a new school superintendant, the governor agreed to give the mayor a significant role in the search. Giving a Newark mayor more control over the city's school system was an unusual proposal, but Christie felt that Booker could institute several education reforms.[178] Moreover, the donation appeared to be ideally timed because the state also lost a $400 million federal education grant from the US Department of Education's Race to the Top initiative due to a clerical error (as a result, former Jersey City Mayor and Education Commissioner Bret Schundler was forced to leave his state post). Interestingly, Booker and Zuckerberg met at a conference, discussed plans for Newark's schools, and agreed to the donation, which would be handled by Facebook's new education foundation in Newark called Start Up: Education, led by former teacher and principal Jennifer Holleran.[179] Zuckerberg's donation was by the far the largest amount received from a single philanthropist, as he was worth nearly $7 billion. But the donation had some strings attached, including the fact that the $100 million would come from Zuckerberg's private Facebook stock, which could be turned into cash when necessary. And, in addition, Newark officials would have to match the $100 million through their own fundraising efforts (the city's education budget was almost a $1 billion annually). In fact, Microsoft founder Bill Gates, investor William Achman, and Newark native Ray Chambers had already agreed to donate as well.[180] Finally, the mayor would gain substantial control of the school system through his education reform plans. Interestingly, the timing of the donation also coincided with the scathing depiction of Zuckerberg in the movie "The Social Network," where he's portrayed as an abrasive and insecure prodigy seeking social acceptance. At the same time, the movie "Waiting for Superman," about Harlem's Children's Zone, debuted, and Christie and Booker planned to attend a showing of the film followed by a panel discussion.[181]

But the announcement of the donation brought more questions than answers. The Newark Teachers Union only supported limited expansion of charters, even though the mayor clearly favored them politically and financially. And several community advocates questioned the governor's ability to cede control of the schools to the mayor, claiming that it was an improper use of his power. However, Zuckerberg thought it essential that Booker somehow have some control over the operations of the school system even if alternative approaches could be used (such as naming the mayor a special assistant to the governor for education in the city as the state legislature or voters decide the management structure of the school district). And at a press conference after the announcement, Zuckerberg and Booker seemed to hint that closing poorly performing schools was an option.[182] Many residents questioned why Booker did not publicly criticize Christie's state budget cuts and his stay of Newark's school construction.[183] Notably, the Newark Teachers Union was not told about the donation prior to the public announcment, and the union president was not given details about the agreement.[184] The newly elected president of the city's school advisory board, Shaver Jeffries, supported the donation, but charged that City Hall had to better communicate proposed school reforms to Newarkers.[185]

Communication between the administration and residents was difficult because Booker had alienated key community leaders and residents by making a local issue a national one. As Reverend Reginald Jackson, head of the Black Ministers Council, stated, "The mayor has to do a better job connecting to the people of Newark." And Jackson suggested that former Washington, DC, Mayor Adrian Fenty could serve Booker as an example because Fenty also alienated many residents as he tried to lead his city, and Fenty was not reelected.[186] As a matter of fact, Booker said that because of the Facebook donation he would consider running for a third term so he could help monitor the money over a longer period.[187] Also, because the city and state would have to spend time finding a new superintendant to carry out the initiatives, Booker wanted to be a central player in the school system in his second and possibly third term.[188] However, many questioned the way that Booker handled the announcement as well as the governor's intentions in suggesting that the mayor play a significant role in choosing a new superintendant and implementing significant education reforms. New Jersey Acting

Commissioner of Education Rochelle Hendricks testified at the state legislature's Joint Committee on the Public Schools in early October that the Quality Single Accountability Continuum (QSAC) does not authorize a governor or mayor to reform a district under state control. Since the announcement of the donation, there had been some community opposition and legal concerns about Booker's direct involvement with the public schools, particularly if Christie appointed him a special assistant to develop a comprehensive education reform plan. State Senator Ronald Rice Sr. led the charge because he helped write the original law. Both he and Hendricks agreed that a mayor could not play a direct role in school reform if the state government had taken over its public schools.[189] As a matter of fact, the Institute on Education Law and Policy at Rutgers University–Newark issued a study in October that found "no conclusive evidence" that having greater mayoral participation harmed to a state-controlled school district. The authors, including law Professor Paul Tractenberg, argued that mayoral control does not necessarily solve urban education problems. But it can bring stability, attention, and increased funding for a school district. "Mayoral involvement, if not control, should at the very least be considered as part of an overall district improvement strategy," stated the report.[190] There were also rumors that the controversial school superintendent of Washington, DC, Michelle Rhee, would become Newark's new school superintendent or New Jersey's next commissioner of education. Newark City Hall and the state became interested in Rhee because she had a reputation for forcing tenure reform through the Washington, DC, school system as Mayor Fenty's school superintendent.[191] Christie showcased Rhee at his State of the State Address, and she praised Christie as a no-nonsense politician who understands that people "want to hear the truth."[192] Both Rhee and the governor agreed that eliminating tenure would bring needed school reform. Yet Rhee would go on to dedicate more time to her lobbying organization, Students First, which researches education reform measures.

Likely the most significant concern about the donation was how the money would be spent. Newark had 54 emergency projects related to school construction and facility updates, and the city's schools were in desperate need of repair.[193] One of the first initiatives was to implement a survey to ask Newarkers their ideas on how to use the $100 million. Booker suggested that residents would be directly involved in the process because paid survey takers would go door-to-door and ask for recommendations. The shortlived organization created to help promote the events, the Partnership for Education in Newark (PENewark), estimated it would cost $1 million to pay for advertisements and host 30 coffee klatches and ten town hall meetings in a movement of "relentless outreach"; the campaign was scheduled to end in late January of 2011.[194] Many residents informed pollsters that the city's schools needed reforms, including more parental involvement, better teachers, and additional afterschool programs. Several respondents also stated that it was a rare for Newark residents to be asked about Newark's schools. Interestingly, Cory Booker participated in the door-to-door polling as well.[195] However, there was a great deal of criticism surrounding the community canvassing. Many residents who were questioned simply reiterated the known problems in Newark's public schools, and a lot of the money went to pay the PENewark staff. Former Elizabeth, NJ, Board of Education member and politico Jeremiah Grace led the survey initiative, but he refused to disclose how much the survey cost, and an actual accounting of the organization's expenses was not released.[196] Many people questioned the purpose of this $1 million "suggestion box" and wondered whether the initiatives were rushing to create civic engagement, but not steering real civic engagement.[197] By January 2011, it was apparent that the survey and the data were flawed. Pollsters had knocked on only 66,000 doors in Newark (even though their aim was over 90,000), and only 23,000 surveys were actually completed. And the survey instrument itself was vague and contained only a handful of questions. Sadly, a brief examination of the questionnaire suggests few approaches to address specific problems. In fact, the *Star-Ledger* stated that PENewark and Newark "could have spent a whole lot less on this effort."[198] As a result of the initial survey's flaws, PENewark was shortlived, and, ultimately, a new questionnaire was introduced in late January 2011. This time two universities, Rutgers University–Newark and New York University, were directly involved in the survey process and in analyzing the data. Professor Alan Sadovnik agreed to take charge of the survey results and post them online. The goal was to get 1,500 respondents by polling 5,000 residents through anonymous online polling and canvassing door-to-door. In addition, and most importantly, the new survey had 23 parts and measures with a number of new issues, ranging from mayoral control of schools to the parents' role in education and respondents' knowledge about the issues. Survey results indicated that most Newarkers wanted local control, but few respondents wanted mayoral control.[199]

The community survey outreach was a start toward some kind of reform, and, in December 2010, the district's advisory board unanimously voted that the school system satisfied the legal prerequisites for more autonomy from the state. The board demonstrated in its biannual report to the state that it had passed four of the five benchmarks, including governance, fiscal management, personnel, instruction, and operations. The district failed in instruction, which included student achievement measures, and the state did not agree with the district's self-assessment.[200] Both Booker and the Acting Education Commissioner, Christopher Cerf, said that "incremental change" toward school reform was not enough and that the district needed radical change to get free from state control. Serious reforms were necessary to address some of the problems a study done by Cerf's organization, Global Education Advisors (GEA), had found. The study raised several issues ranging from the fact that Newark's schools had almost twice as many administrators per student than the state average to the fact that only 22 percent of students entering high school in Newark graduated after four years (having passed the High School Proficiency Assessment) and the fact that principals had little authority over staff and budgets in their own schools. The GEA also proposed opening 11 new charter schools. The study was conducted using money Booker raised from private donors and a $500,000 Board Foundation grant, but it drew significant criticism because of Cerf's connections to the GEA.[201]

While Cerf acknowledged that he helped to establish the GEA and he donated $1,000 to Booker's reelection campaign, he said he was no longer involved in leading the organization.[202] In fact, Cerf's formal nomination as state education commissioner was delayed for months because some legislators, including State Senator Ronald Rice Sr., withheld approval because Cerf had ties to Booker that appeared to "smell."[203] In response, Governor Christie refused to appoint any new Superior Court judges in Essex County while Cerf's nomination was unconfirmed.[204] State Senator Rice went so far as to organize a coalition of officials and educators from Paterson, Jersey City, and Newark to challenge state control of urban school districts, calling it "a racist policy" and stating that a federal inquiry into the Department of Education was imperative.[205] Clearly, politics was a significant part of Cerf's nomination, and his affiliation with the GEA and Booker's relations to that organization became issues due to the GEA's study. Still, Booker agreed with much of the report's findings and advanced the idea to consolidate and close some public schools and create new themed schools because 14 percent of Newark's students attended charter schools[206] and that number would increase to 19 percent the next year.[207]

However, the GEA study was not released to the public and remained confidential because it proposed shifting hundreds of students to different schools. This became a significant issue for Booker to address as many critics challenged this secrecy, as well as the funding for the report and Booker's political connections to the GEA, which generated the report. The Star-Ledger obtained and published the report, and many parents and educators felt angry and misled by Booker and his administration.[208] Many public officials, including district advisory board members and several state officials, wanted to create greater transparency in local government. Even though Booker had received a large number of donations to help evaluate public sector services like education, the mayor did not appear to circumvent state laws. But the study's secrecy introduced concerns that he was operating a shadow government. While Booker argued that other cities also fundraise for their school districts, the difference was that the mayor's fundraising efforts made it seem as if he was operating the school district when in fact it had long ago been taken over by the state and was not operating under mayoral control.[209] Therefore, many community and union leaders were disturbed by any hint of secrecy. "What happened last week was a huge step backward," stated American Federation of Teachers President Randi Weingarten. "It reconfirmed the community's distrust of their leaders."[210]

Considering the community and political pressure, Booker decided to make his actions more transparent as he raised money for political causes like education. The mayor admitted to the *Star-Ledger* editorial board that "if I need to sacrifice my political viability on the altar of what is best for our children, that is fine." He "bemoaned" to the editorial board what happened after the the report was leaked, saying that it drew attention away from his proposed school reforms. The next day, Booker finally acknowledged in his State of the City Address that any private money raised for Newark's public schools would be publicly accounted for and each donor would be named. He clearly would use his mayoral bully pulpit to introduce school reforms, including longer school days and changed firing and retention practices for teachers. "Sometimes after years of persistent failure, you have to hit the reset button," Booker said. Yet some 40 people protested outside the New Jersey Performing Arts Center, arguing that the education reform process lacked community involvement. The crowd frequently chanted "No more lies," and the protest gained a lot of media attention.[211] Bob Braun's column in the *Star-Ledger* reminded many that the mayor really had no role in school reform because the school district was state controlled and said, "[I]t is disingenuous for Booker to say he is merely exercising a 'bully pulpit' to urge reform. He is doing far more than that. Foundations and other entities over which he has control have donated more than $143 million to promote his efforts."[212]

The timing of Booker's suggestions also appeared to coincide with Christie's gubernatorial task force's report, which recommended an overall review of New Jersey's teacher evaluation process. The nine-member committee, which included two teacher union members as well as state and national experts, argued that they were not simply rubber-stamping Christie's ideas. They proposed that teachers be measured by their classroom performance and their students' test scores. This would then influence teachers' salaries and tenure. By forwarding this plan on to the legislature, the governor hoped the suggested reforms would be instituted in the fall of 2011. The New Jersey School Boards Association supported the recommendations, but the New Jersey Education Association (NJEA) advocated against any measure that tried to connect teacher performance to student test scores.[213] Later that week, at Ann Street School—one of the city's highest-performing elementary schools—Christie announced that Newark's next superintendent would be selected by May. The governor also said that in addition to the $100 million Facebook donation, Newark had already raised $50 million in matching funds (however, raising money past that amount proved to be difficult because many donors chose to give to specific causes, schools, or programs as opposed to a general fund[214]). Christie also publicly supported Booker, calling him "my partner," and said that Booker would play an "integral advisory role" in the school reform decision-making process as well as efforts to increase student performance.[215] Cerf also stated in an op-ed that as interim commissioner he would involve the governor, the mayor, and other officials to engage "a cross-section of community members and community leaders to help find the next superintendent. While Mayor Booker is not in the statutory 'chain of command' led by the governor, he actively supports the governor's and the district's efforts to transform Newark's schools."[216] Obviously, Cerf was trying to quash any concerns about the mayor's and the governor's involvement in hiring a new superintendent and in reforming schools, but he also continued to advocate consolidating and closing public schools.

In addition to closing and merging schools, Cerf and Booker wanted public schools to share facilities with charter schools. This proposal was introduced publicly through community meetings and was also discussed by many educators and administrators. In fact, the Newark Teachers Union members urged teachers to refuse to share public school facilities with charter schools.[217] In late March, the outcry at Barringer High School auditorium was so great that over 1,000 parents, students, and educators attended the public forum while dozens were turned away. Many of those in attendance criticized the expansion of charter schools as well as the idea of sharing public school facilities with them. However, others, including Booker and Cerf, wanted to reform the school system by increasing the number of charter schools. "It simply makes no sense for some Newark public school buildings to sit half-empty while public charter schools are forced to use their scarce operating dollars to seek and pay for private facilities," suggested Cerf. He also reminded the audience that former Newark Superintendents Marion Bolden and Clifford Janey were in favor of the initiative.[218]

In addition to this conflict, in early April, Newark's Public School Advisory Board became embroiled in its own controversy about whether to create additional schools. The school board was faced with voting to add six new alternative high schools, but board members were largely divided. Board Chair Shavar Jeffries blamed North Ward boss Steve Adubato Sr. for manipulating members to vote against the new schools because the politico was revered for operating two charter elementary schools, a preschool, an elderly day-care center, and recreation programs. Adubato made certain that his employees voted in the majority Latino North Ward where "he treat[ed] politics like a knife fight,"[219] and public officials praised his education standards.[220] But a number of board members argued that Jeffries could have corralled votes better and that the vote should have taken place after the board election, which was only weeks away. In addition, others said that they voted against the new schools because of inconsistent information, the confidential reform report that was leaked in February, and their exclusion from the decision making process in creating new schools. Nonetheless, Jefferies accused the ward boss of using his supporters to serve his interests and not the childrens', while Adubato suggested that Jeffries was being unprofessional. "What he did to the board members was very unethical," stated Adubato. "He's talking publicly, saying his colleagues are unlawful. I believe Shavar votes his conscience, but accusing other people of not voting their conscience is wrong. It's sad."[221] While the board consults with the mayor and only has advisory powers because the state operates the city's schools, board members still voted to open the alternative schools, and the state rebuked the board's decision. As the *Star-Ledger* said, the vote demonstrated "Newark's petty politics" and did "tangible damage to the reform movement by undercutting Newark's reputation at a critical time" while signaling "that the politics around school reform in Newark remain dysfunctional. And that undermines the city's position in the competition for talent and philanthropy."[222] The newspaper urged the board to vote on the proposal again. Weeks later, Adubato's candidate, Eliana Pintor Marin, was named the board's new chair, ousting Jeffries in a 5–4 vote.[223] And, ultimately, Newark's interim superintendent, Deborah Terrell, reversed the board's vote by week's end.[224]

The mayor entered the fray in the only way he knew: by attaining money for the new schools while gaining national attention. The first $1 million award came from Zuckerberg's foundation, Start Up: Education, which donated the money to help the five new public alternative high schools. The grant would go toward recruiting new principals and staff and helping design curriculum.[225] But concerns were raised about adding more consultants and foundation staff due to the Facebook donation. For example, the mayor, the Foundation for Newark's Future board members (who each donated more than $10 million), and the Foundation's CEO Gregory Taylor (whose salary was $382,000) made all decisions about where and how the money would be administered (the mayor was the only Newark resident who had any role in the decision making).[226] Thus, it appeared as though there was a shadow government deciding the fate of the Facebook donation and matching funds, even though surveys were conducted to supposedly help with the decision-making process. As former Newark Public Schools Advisory Board member Richard Cammarieri noted, "I'm not really clear what the Foundation for Newark's Future is supposed to do."[227] And Newark Teachers Union President Joseph Del Grosso stated, "[W]e don't know what the foundation is doing or how they intend to spend the other money. With that money comes a responsibility to the public to be clear about its use."[228]

Clearly, the proposals to create alternative schools while closing and merging several existing Newark schools caused deep divides. Few administrators and teachers were aware of the proposed changes, and many parents were left out of the decision about where their children would attend schools should existing schools close or merge.[229] This led some Newarkers to question the changes and to wonder what actions parents could take.[230] However, supporters of these reforms, including US Department of Education Secretary Arne Duncan, argued that the education reform movement in Newark could lead to a national standard. "If it can happen in Newark it can happen anywhere," Duncan stated. "The eyes of the country are here." The education secretary visited Newark in mid-April 2011, cheerleading reform efforts and promoting President Obama's initiative to recruit one million teachers nationally within four years. Duncan argued that there were over two million high-skill and high-wage positions that were unfilled because Americans are not graduating from high schools with specific private-sector skills. He stated that changes to our school systems had to happen now, and a city such as Newark should recruit high-quality educators and begin education reform measures.[231] One such measure that Booker considered was merit-pay salary incentives, based on student performance and test achievement standards, for

Newark's teachers. The mayor examined various similar salary initiatives for junior teachers in New York and Washington, DC, public schools. However, these salary incentives were not fully supported by the Newark Teachers Union.[232]

While national attention was focused on Newark's attempts to reform the city's schools, the superintendent search took center stage at the local level. The new superintendent would not be chosen until after the school board election, but the two finalists were mentioned in an audio recording of a search committee meeting. Many committee members were upset that one of their colleagues had recorded the meeting and that, ultimately, the *Star-Ledger* published the candidates' names. On the recording, some members commented that the decision-making process was taking longer than expected and involved too much community engagement. Also on the recording, Cerf blamed the long process on politics, while an assemblyman observed that the candidates were probably discouraged by the "circus between the governor and the mayor, [which took] all the oxygen out of the room."[233] Committee members were also afraid that the candidates' racial backgrounds would be a problem because one candidate, Maria Goodloe-Johnson, was Black, and the other, Cami Anderson, was White. Considering Newark's history in light of race and education, the candidates' races was a potentially a volatile issue. In addition, Anderson had served as a paid consultant for the mayor's first campaign.[234]

Yet, ultimately, the governor chose Newark's new school superintendent, and he picked Cami Anderson because she had previously served as director of New York's Teach for America and she was a New York City school official willing to institute school reforms.[235] At a press conference, the governor welcomed Anderson but made a controversial remark: He commented that if his family had remained in Newark when he was a child, "I don't think I'd be governor if I went to school in Newark. How many students are sitting in classrooms with God-given gifts to be whatever they want to be, but won't because of the status quo? As governor, I can't live with that."[236] Christie's controversial speech generated a lot of response from public officials, including Assembly Speaker Sheila Oliver, who had graduated from Newark's public schools. She said that his statement was "symbolic of the governor's lack of understanding of education. Everyone agrees that improvements are needed in our urban schools, but I've got news for the governor—people don't fail simply by walking into a Newark school classroom."[237]

Thus, Anderson's appointment caused a great deal of media attention due to the governor's words about Newark's schools, and the *New York Times* stated that her chance to reform Newark's schools was "the ultimate high risk opportunity."[238] She immediately faced stiff opposition from many residents because she was appointed by the state, did not have roots in Newark, and was the first White school superintendent in over 40 years. Friends described Anderson as someone willing and able to transcend race and embrace diversity as she did in her both her professional career and her personal life, living in a multiracial family. Anderson agreed to move from Harlem to Newark, but the new superintendent would have to win over cynical local officials and residents, especially because the Facebook donation had divided Newarkers. Even during the governor's announcement of the new superintendent, Anderson was heckled by parents who told her to go back to New York. "We don't want her here," said one parent. Booker attempted to ease residents' concerns, but the public perception of the closed decision-making process remained an issue.[239] Anderson, however, was willing to take up the challenges, and she reminded the public, "[J]udge me by actions. Let me roll up my sleeves and dive in. Then we'll talk."[240] Community activist Robert Curvin reminded residents that it was no longer 1960s when racist practices prevented qualified applicants from occupying the superintendent position and stated that he was impressed by Anderson's experience working with disadvantaged populations as well as her spunk.[241] Both Booker and Christie spoke glowingly of Anderson. The governor said that he was impressed with "her spirit," while the mayor said Anderson was a "get-it-done" manager who brought a "level of love" to her work.[242] The *Star-Ledger* editorial board stated that "Newark's success now hinges on her success," and they went on to remind readers that bringing any change to Newark was a difficult feat for local officials including the mayor to the former police director. The newspaper said, "Politics in Newark is not for wimps" and "[o]ur hope is that Anderson is prepared in the end to knock her head through brick walls to create change."[243]

Clearly then, there was wide support for Anderson, but the governor reminded watchers that neither the mayor nor the city's school advisory board would regain control of the district even though many were hoping to hasten local control. Christie warned that the state, including his administration, would remain in charge and that they would enforce "success and excellence" for public schools. But the newly chosen chairwoman of the advisory board argued that Newark "deserve[d]" local control because local officials knew the city's issues better than Trenton bureaucrats. Booker also believed in local control even though he understood the state's oversight measures,[244] and he believed that local politics played a significant role in advancing reforms, particularly if ward bosses like Steve Adubato did not support the changes.[245] By the end of the month, the state Board of Education voted unanimously to formally appoint Anderson as superintendent of Newark's public schools, and Anderson later lobbied the state Board of Education for local control as well.[246]

Weeks after Anderson started as superintendent, she allowed only two of the six alternative high schools to open in September because several of the schools required additional planning and staff.[247] She also pushed for significant reforms but received negative public responses to her proposals especially during a Rutgers University–Newark forum in early 2012. Many parents and teachers were outspoken, if not belligerent, in their opposition to closing seven failing schools, and Anderson took the brunt of the audience members' negativity.[248] Despite the teachers' union's objections, she also wanted both principals and teachers to agree on any new classroom placements, meaning that no principal would be forced to accept a problematic tenured teacher.[249] Anderson also received outside support from consulting firms and nonprofits to hire some new principals,[250] and she suggested teacher buyouts or early retirements for nearly 400 low-performing educators.[251] In addition, because public schools had nearly 10,000 empty seats and the district could save over $4 million by renting unused space to charter schools, Anderson pushed ahead with the idea to have public schools share space with charter schools; the *Star-Ledger* also supported this idea.[252] And the newspaper reminded residents that with the mayor, school superintendent, and donors supporting school reform, Newark's advisory board members should try to be on the same page and not resort to "revenge and petty politics... Reform must be a democratic conversation, but weak governance works against that principle. Test this district's ability to sustain its progress and avoid political games, then return power to the board."[253] Finally, Anderson pushed charter schools to enroll low-performing students and follow similar expulsion rules as conventional schools. Charters that agreed to these changes would receive help with fundraising efforts and space for their schools.[254] Not surprisingly, considering the early changes and proposals Anderson advanced and Booker supported, by spring 2012, the superintendent was named one of *Time* magazine's 100 Most Influential People and Booker praised her as a "modern day freedom fighter."[255]

But by the end of the first year of Booker's second term, just as Newark's education policies appeared to be headed in a reform-oriented direction, the ACLU sued the city over the $100 million donation. The organization represented a parent group called the Secondary Parent Council, who claimed that they were denied access to correspondence between the mayor, the governor, and Mark Zuckerberg even though they had filed an Open Public Records Act (OPRA) request. For nearly three months, the group demanded documents related to the deal between city officials and Facebook, and the ACLU charged that the agreement lacked transparency. The city asked for a three-month extension before complying with the request and then argued that the OPRA request was overly broad and any correspondence was protected by executive privilege. Although Booker had pledged that any grants related to the Facebook donation to help schools would be made public as they were awarded, he admitted that there were no documents between himself, the governor, and the Facebook founder about the actual donation. "They're using Mark Zuckerberg and me to attract publicity for themselves," Booker said about the ACLU.[256] The organization claimed that they were seeking transparency and that the city was creating lawsuits "by taking unconstitutional actions" and not complying with the parent group's OPRA requests.[257] But City Hall claimed that there were no emails, letters, or official correspondence regarding the deal[258] and that all that was said between the parties was that Zuckerberg's donation would come from his stock options and Newark would then use the donation as cash from the Start Up: Education foundation. Even after Facebook's poor initial public offering in 2012, the value of the gift remained valued at $100 million.[259] The ACLU ultimately succeeded in obtaining a court order for Newark to turn over emails from Zuckerberg. "Newark's arguments to skirt '... public disclosure laws simply haven't added up from the start," claimed ACLU attorney Frank Corrado.[260] As a result, the emails, which were the closest form of an agreement between City Hall and Facebook, were publicly released in late December 2012. The emails revealed the administration's and Facebook's executives' concerns about gaining support for the donation from Newark residents. For example, Booker stated in one email that "this is our biggest concern right now as we must be ahead of the game on community organizing by next week." Planning would have to include polling, focus groups, mailings, and consultants, which would cost over $300,000 total. The mayor's aides assured Facebook executives that the donation would not go into classrooms but instead would fund a variety of education and teaching incentives. But Facebook and other donors were concerned about who the new school superintendent would be as it made fundraising a difficult challenge. This was especially true because the mayor, the governor, and Zuckerberg announced the donation through national media, and residents were suspicious of outside money. Finally, the emails revealed that aides were looking for extremely wealthy donors, such as Bill Gates, who could potentially give tens of millions of dollars to the Foundation for Newark's Future.[261]

Although it took years before the details of the agreement between the city and Facebook were made public, newspapers had mixed views about the donation. The *New York Times* was optimistic about the Facebook donation and they urged politicians to put aside their differences.[262] And the *Star-Ledger* discovered that although residents were disappointed with how some of the early Facebook money was spent, reform efforts continued despite the rocky public relations and political missteps. Considering the leaked $500,000 "secret plan" to close and merge schools, many residents still doubted that the money would actually help Newark's school-children. But with a new superintendent and a nonprofit group overseeing the project, "the first Facebook dollars are showing up in Newark classrooms," claimed the newspaper. By late September, almost $9 million of Zuckerberg's $100 million donation was spent, and another $48 million was raised from private donors to match the Facebook donation.[263] Also, in February, 25 teams of teachers at 19 Newark schools received $200,000 grants (paid for by the Facebook donation through the Teacher Innovation Fund) to create programs for their schools.[264]

At first, many teachers and even the Newark Teachers Union were leery of the Facebook donation, uncertain of the financial backers and their political aims, especially because teachers' contracts were under negotiation. In fact, the Newark Teachers Union president said that many members called it "blood money."[265] However, the union eventually approved a new form of merit pay, called bonus pay, using the donation's funds. Teachers evaluated as "effective" or "highly effective" on a reformed four-tier scale would be considered for pay increases, which in the past were connected to years of service. Those teachers rated in the lower categories of "partially ineffective" or "ineffective" would not receive any extra pay. Teachers could also earn "bonuses" for teaching in the city's lowest-performing schools.

In fact, Florida, Indiana, and Idaho state governments have passed similar laws to require districts to assess teacher performance to determine pay scale. According to education experts, the new proposal would allow for fewer appeals and lawsuits. But NTU's sister organization, the New Jersey Education Association, had traditionally been against any merit pay due to competition and cost concerns, and they did not favor the bonus pay approach. However, the NTU president agreed to support the proposal if it included peer review, even though the contract did not define what was a bonus-worthy rating or identify which specific schools had the poorest academic performance records.[266] Under the newly instituted three-year teaching contract, annual bonuses ranged from $2,000 to $12,500 for those teachers rated "effective" or "highly effective" or who taught in struggling schools or hard-to-staff areas.[267] Some of the money would come from the Facebook donation as well as additional fundraising sources. Each school would have a three-person evaluation committee comprised of a school administrator, the principal, and a similarly ranked teacher. The new contract also included $31 million in retroactive pay for union members for those teachers who had been working without a new contract. In mid-November, union members voted in favor of the contract by nearly 62 percent (1,767 to 1,088).[268] By various accounts, it was a progressive but experimental approach toward merit pay and forced retirement[269] even though some detractors found the proposal divisive and publicly lied about the contract's provisions.[270]

Booker stated that America has "a teacher compensation problem" and "Newark has the opportunity to be a national leader in compensating teachers fairly, and has a chance to show that unions and school districts can work together in the interest of both teachers and students."[271] And Christie suggested at a news conference that the new contract would be a "transformational change in education in America." At the same time, the governor said that the mayor was an "indispensable partner" and that Booker "ha[d] stood up strongly and eloquently every step along the way."[272] However, the mayor was not invited to the governor's news conference even though he attended it; as the *Star-Ledger* wrote, "[T]he governor knows Booker deserves a chunk of the credit here." The editors also said, "[S]o remember, whatever conspiracy theorists say about the evils of private money in public schools, it was the private philanthropy that helped make this advance for public schools possible."[273]

Nearly a month after the contract was completed, the state announced that between 2011 to 2012 the percentage of graduating high schools students increased 7 percentage points to nearly 69 percent.[274] However, because the state used a new federally mandated formula to calculate the number of graduates, many observers remained cautious about the number of graduates in the next year and subsequent years to come.[275] Also, according to a 2012 report, the longstanding problem that was affecting the most Newark students, particularly elementary and middle school students, was a failing school system. Almost 14,000, or 43 percent, of K–8 students were classified as "highest need" in terms of home lives, English proficiency, and special education classification, and nearly 60 percent of K–8 schools are "falling further behind" as a result of low test scores. While the report outlined critical needs for Anderson and local officials to address, Newark's public schools still remain problematic.[276]

By the final year of Booker's term, the superintendant not only lost favor with many officials, but the city's charter schools were subjected to further scrutiny. Fredrica Bey, the founder of Adelaide L. Sanford Charter School in Newark, was placed under investigation for misusing state and federal funds. While many in Newark's Black communities supported the school's founder and charged that the media was conspiring against their community charter school, the state closed the school agreeing with the *Star-Ledger* that "the school has long failed to comply with state regulations, refusing to release even basic information about its finances."[277] With the closing of schools like Adelaide L. Sanford Charter School and the public school system's advisory committee voting no confidence in the superintendent, Anderson was losing support in 2013. Even the city council passed a resolution opposing all school reforms for the next school year. In other words, any reforms the superintendant and the mayor wished to advance for Newark schools gained little political backing form local officials.[278]

6

Newark, Booker, and Post-Racial Reality

Although Mayor Cory Booker brought many of Newark's longstanding urban problems to state and national attention, the city remains in a precarious place. As many voters and students of urban studies know well, it would take more than one leader to resolve all of the city's social, economic, and political ills. But Booker was never shy about broadcasting Newark's issues as well as his victories for the city. Like many idealistic post–civil rights generation leaders, Booker not only introduced urban issues to the media, he also found revolutionary methods to highlight and fundraise for many of Newark's problems. Always good for a story about an event in Newark, Booker introduced the general public to a number of unique instances and challenges that a post–racial era mayor faced in a post-industrial city. However, many public officials, activists, scholars, and journalists challenged Booker's post-racial approach of basking in the limelight, particularly during his second term as mayor.

In addition to the increased media coverage generated by the Facebook donation, Booker seemed more eager to be on the national stage during his second term. In spring 2012, he received significant attention for comments he made on NBC's *Meet the Press* that appeared to support Bain Capital and Republican Presidential Candidate Mitt Romney. Booker called both parties' attacks on the other candidate "nauseating" and said that Democrats' criticisms of the private equity firm "undermine[d]" the real issues of the election.[1] Even though he tried to clarify his comments, saying that Obama's campaign had every right to condemn Romney's record as a job creator, the Republican National Committee organized an online petition using Booker's comments, and the Romney campaign created a web ad featuring the mayor. However, the *Star-Ledger* argued that the mayor "was right to speak the truth."[2] Interestingly, Booker received almost $500,000 in campaign funds from the financial services industry, while private equity firms invested $1.3 billion in greater Newark. Between campaign donations and philanthropists' dollars, Booker and the city have benefited from the financial sector.[3] Thus, many people thought he was selling out to large-scale financial investors and Republicans and that he was somehow a secret Republican, especially because of his "genial relationship" with Governor Christie.[4] Some press accounts even suggested that Booker had lost his chance to be appointed to a cabinet position in the Obama administration.[5]

Despite the private equity flap, Booker still served as co-chair of the Democratic platform committee at the 2012 Democratic National Convention and spoke on the president's behalf; this was one of Booker's key moments. Booker and Democrats had faced a great deal of criticism because the party did not include "God" and failed to refer to Jerusalem as Israel's capital in their platform; however, they downplayed this issue, saying that it's "not a controversial issue in American politics."[6] And, in Booker's speech, the mayor reminded Democrats that their party was about "inclusion" and "growing together" and that the president was not only motivated to help as many voters as possible, but to also help "people and businesses in Newark." While the supportive speech lasted nearly 12 minutes, Booker chose not to emphasize his own background or challenges, which was rare.[7] In contrast, Booker's attempts to grab national attention before the convention was more of a swag campaign; delegates were given bags, hats, and t-shirts with Booker's name and the slogan "Building a Better Newark. Building a Better New Jersey."[8] Noticeably absent from Booker's speech, however, was any mention of US Senator Frank Lautenberg; the senator did not even attend his own event the first night of the convention. There was already early speculation that Booker would challenge Lautenberg for his senate seat or run for governor.[9]

By fall 2012, the mayor not only had the attention of the conventional press, blogs, and Twitter, but also the senator and governor. This attention affected Newark in several ways. First, the mayor's decision became a primary focus for many outside Newark, while the city continued to face ongoing urban problems. Second, the intricate but personal politics between Booker and Governor Christie became more delicate. City Hall requested state aid for $24 million while planning to cut 1,000 municipal jobs and reduce spending by a large amount. Christie replied that his administration would help the city, partly because it was their responsibility but also due to politics. "I've been trying to keep these negotiations quiet because I want to get something resolved with the city and because I have a good working relationship with Cory."[10] Interestingly, during October, the city and the state went back and forth over an appropriate figure for state aid because Christie stated that he did not want "to pay a nickel more than" necessary; ultimately, Newark received only $10 million in transitional aid for 2012 because city officials had failed to pass a municipal budget on time as they had been required to do by the state. Some observers thought that Booker would be plagued by the fact that the city had failed to meet this agreement should he run against Christie for governor. Still, others thought that Christie's negotiating tactic was an example of state government flexing its political muscle.[11]

By mid-October 2012, it became increasingly clear that Booker was not interested in a third term as mayor; would he challenge Christie in the gubernatorial race? Journalists, pundits, and pollsters focused their attention on a supposed Booker–Christie showdown. In a Quinnipiac University poll, 46 percent favored Christie and 42 percent Booker.[12] The mayor would not only be the most formidable potential candidate among a number of Democratic hopefuls, he also had an enviable campaign war chest. In fact, Booker traveled for the majority of October and November to raise even more money from potential supporters in California. As the *Star-Ledger* noted, "[T]he trip west underscore[d] Booker's sizable advantage over a crowded Democratic field: his relationships with celebrities, and his ability to raise enough cash to compete with a large Christie campaign and to pay for crucial statewide advertising." Between the media attention and advertising costs, the race would be expensive and wide ranging and Booker would face a popular and nationally recognized incumbent.[13] Christie had a variety of donors contribute to his 2009 gubernatorial campaign, especially advocacy groups. These organizations had spent nearly $14 million, and if the mayor were to enter the 2013 gubernatorial race, costs for that campaign were estimated to be well over $25 million, especially because of undisclosed donors and unrestricted financing from Super Political Action Committees (Super PACs).[14]

Booker's focus on fundraising and deciding which office he wanted to pursue, however, was not the primary concern of many Newarkers because most of the political jockeying in Newark in 2012 surrounded the city council. During the 2012 budget approval process, in his State of the City Address, the mayor asked city council members to cut many of their expenses. The council's budget was nearly $4 million (including a salary of $85,000 for each council member, which was a part-time position), and Booker wanted to cut their budget in half because the council's expenses were the highest in the state and were six times as much as nearby Jersey City, the second largest city in the state. Several council members agreed with some cuts, even though members had already cut 16 percent of their expenses since 2008. But others defended the current expenses, particularly their constituent service resources, almost 50 staffers, leased cars, and $20,000 annual gas expenses.[15] To some observers, it appeared the mayor was picking a fight with the council instead of trying to work with them, and he seemed duplicitous for accepting longevity pay raises for himself and his staff at the same time he was urging the council members to cut their pay.[16]

Thus, in early 2012, relations between the council and the mayor were strained and getting worse. Vacancies in the city council and US Congress only led to more problems for City Hall. Unfortunately, one of the most respected New Jersey members of Congress, US Representative Donald Payne, died in March 2012. Not only was the Newark congressman seen as a statesman who was particularly concerned with human rights and international aid, Payne was one of the most "squeaky clean" politicians.[17] His son, Council President Donald Payne Jr., was elected to his father's former seat following a multiple-candidate primary election in the summer.[18] Who, and more importantly how, to fill the city council seat vacated by Donald Payne Jr. after November's general election brought Newark's politics to a crescendo at the end of 2012 in what many called the "November surprise" council meeting. Some of the same anti-Booker residents packed city council chambers to support Sharpe James' son, John Sharpe James, because he had been one of the runner up candidates in the council race two years prior.[19] Recognizing that the James camp and the Black old guard were planning to introduce James as a nominee, Booker and his chief of staff, Modia Butler, introduced a new nominee, Shanique Davis Speight, a former school board member and ally of North Ward boss Steven Adubato Sr. What should have been a customary nomination process turned into a dramatic political episode, and some called it a near-riotous meeting. No debate or discussion was allowed about the nominee. Moreover, the council did not have quorum as Councilman Ron Rice boycotted the meeting concerned about the appointment process, leaving three Black members who supported James and four Latino members who backed Speight. "I have voted with the mayor [in the past], but I don't recognize this guy," claimed Rice. "[The mayor]'s shown us, like a lot of his predecessors, that it's either my way or the highway."[20]

But the administration saw Rice's boycott as a "no" vote, and one additional vote was necessary to appoint Speight. Therefore, Booker entered the council chambers to cast the deciding vote, arguing that state law was on his side; meanwhile, residents stood nearby chanting, "Cory's gotta go!" As YouTube videos show, Speight entered council chambers for her swearing in escorted by police, but a number of residents, including union president Rahaman Muhammad, approached and lunged at her and her young son. Muhammad later claimed that he was reaching for the Bible being used to swear in Speight, stating that he would "never hit a woman."[21] But a police officer used pepper spray on the group, injuring Amina Baraka (wife of Amiri Baraka and mother of Councilman Ras Baraka). "Of all the issues that have been a lot more pressing ... [the mayor] comes down there and makes sure that he votes on an empty seat because it's a political move for him," said Councilman Baraka.[22] The mayor argued that his vote was "in the interest of good government" and ensured "efficient operation" of City Hall. The *Star-Ledger* stated that "the mayor won" and that the meeting turned into a "schoolyard brawl" as Muhammad, a "burly union man," intimated Speight, and "this was clearly thuggery."[23] However, Booker claimed that the people who had attended the November and MUA meetings were his political opponents. "And that was the thing people didn't realize is that the media were saying it was near riots," said the mayor. "And when I saw that on film, I could name 75 percent of the people in the room."[24]

That council meeting was a harrowing moment for Booker's legacy. Many analysts claimed that the mayor had demonstrated that he could use executive authority and that this could be to his advantage if he ran for governor against Christie. But others thought it was a misstep, making Booker appear more political than necessary.[25] And politics might have been part of the goal because Booker possibly had a gubernatorial or a senatorial campaign to run. However, his chief of staff, Modia Butler, said that state law was on the mayor's side and besides that, Rice's decision harmed the nomination process since he chose not to attend the council meeting.[26] Even though Superior Court Judge Dennis Carey III ordered all council members to the chamber to vote again days later in early December, Speight received four yes votes, two no votes, and two abstentions as the same four council members supported the nominee. This council meeting appeared even more intense than the one in November: a SWAT team was present in the council chambers, a council member was censured, and the city clerk was asked to resign. As the *Star-Ledger* acknowledged, "[T]he long fight over a vacant city council seat is quintessential in Newark politics: familial dynasties, simmering grudges and a sudden vacuum of power all in the same volatile brew." In fact, James supporters reportedly told Councilman Luis Quintana that he would get their support for council president if he voted for John James, but the James camp instead backed another councilman for council president. Quintana, a former aide to Sharp James, probably felt betrayed, and he supported the mayor's nominee so that he could gain four Booker council allies and become council president. Ultimately Councilman Anibal Ramos was chosen as the interim council president.[27]

Despite the political calculations that occurred during the votes for the empty council seat and for council president, Judge Carey had the final word in the lawsuit Councilman Baraka brought against the mayor, protesting his vote. The judge stated there was no direct precedent for this situation, but he ruled in favor of Baraka and reversed Booker's vote, forcing a special election in November 2013 for the open council seat and keeping the council split 4–4 (with the mayor voting on proposals during a tied vote). Following the decision, Booker and his camp stated that they had "successfully blocked" James' appointment, and, thus, it was a "partial victory," while Baraka and his supporters argued that, "Justice is done." If there was one thing both sides agreed on, it was that each camp schemed behind closed doors. Butler said, "[I]t was obvious that Sharpe James and certain council people were trying to arrange a back room deal to place his son on the council." Rice countered that it was the mayor, Butler, and their allies who "decided in the dark of night to engineer a deal which fell through under the light of the justice system in America."[28] While the council drama reminded the city how alienated the mayor was from certain council members, it also reinforced the harsh reality that Booker was growing further estranged from Black leaders. Many of the old Black guard kept their distance from the mayor, but Black council members who were former Booker allies were further entrenched against the mayor. Council members Rice and Crump, previous Booker supporters, were outspoken against the mayor during the nomination debacle. As a matter of fact, after the court decision, Crump said, "Mayor Cory Booker does not care about Newark" and suggested that opponents would prevent him from seeking office as senator or governor in light of the council maneuvering.[29]

Booker's decision to run for state-wide office was a major focus of local and state media in November and December of 2012 because he was supposed to announce which race he would enter following Thanksgiving. Several potential Democratic candidates were vying to run against Christie—assuming Booker did not run for governor—and Booker's final decision would begin a political chain reaction in New Jersey.[30] Even though Booker called Christie "vulnerable," regardless of the fact that Christie was an incumbent with high approval numbers (particularly after Hurricane Sandy), Booker said, "I am trying to make the decision based on where I can make the most difference in the city I love and the state I love and the nation I pledge my life to."[31] Finally, days before Christmas, Booker announced that he would run for the US Senate, which would mean that he would have to challenge five-term Senator Frank Lautenberg for the Democratic nomination or force the senator to retire. At the same time, one poll indicated that Booker would receive 59 percent of Democratic primary votes, and Lautenberg would receive only 22 percent.[32] Although Booker might have reached out to Lautenberg's office before deciding to run, the senator did not announce whether he would seek another term until months later.[33] As a way to compare himself to the senator, the mayor discussed his support for gun control laws requiring universal background checks and sharing data about people who have mental health issues as well as laws tightening illegal gun trafficking. This was similar to Lautenberg's position, but nowhere near his earlier statements, made when he was a councilman, in favor of banning all guns.[34]

Booker's early announcement caused some concern that Booker had preempted the veteran lawmaker's decision and discouraged other potential Democratic candidates from running, including US Representative Frank Pallone and State Senate President Stephen Sweeney. Even State Assembly Speaker Sheila Oliver commented, as she stood several feet away from Booker at a political event, "I don't feel that an assumption should be made that because Cory has national celebrity translates into who should be our next US Senator."[35] Councilwoman Crump said that Booker seemed to feel as though he was the "heir apparent" by trying to run for the seat.[36] Similarly, Assembly Speaker Sheila Oliver called Booker's public announcement self-entitling: "The notion that there is an heir apparent to replace Senator Lautenberg, I just don't believe in that."[37] By all indications, Lautenberg was considering another term, even though he would be 90 years old by 2014. Lautenberg's office responded to Booker's announcement by saying that the senator was busy with public policy and "this is not the time for political distractions, and the senator will address politics next year."[38] Weeks later, the senator stated that the mayor needed a "spanking" for announcing his candidacy; the *Star-Ledger* suggested that Lautenberg should be disciplined for making such comments but agreed that the mayor "could have been more graceful."[39] Moreover, at the annual New Jersey Chamber of Commerce's dinner in Washington, Lautenberg commented that he was "surprised but not disappointed" that the mayor did not attend the event. "I thought traveling out of the city was one of his favorite activities; perhaps we're too close to Newark," the senator quipped.[40]

Clearly, Lautenberg and Booker's relationship was icy in early 2013. By the middle of February, however, Lautenberg announced he would not seek a sixth term but would place as much energy as possible into his remaining two years in the US Senate.[41] In early June, the 89-year-old Lautenberg died, leaving the US Senate seat in peril among a number of officials and potential candidates. Lautenberg's family announced in a news release and took a swipe against the mayor saying that they would not support Booker and that New Jersey needs a "workhorse, not a show horse...gimmicks and celebrity status won't get you very far in the real battles that Democrats face in the future."[42] Even his son, Joshua Lautenberg said that, "it was a simple request" for the mayor to wait and not challenge his father in a primary race but "Booker didn't want to abide by that."[43]

Aside from Booker's early interest in Lautenberg's seat, several Democrats announced that they wanted to run to finish the senator's one-year term and then for a full six-year term in 2014. US Representatives Rush Holt and Frank Pallone as well as Assembly Speaker Sheila Oliver expressed their early interest before Booker for the Democratic ticket, while former mayor Steve Lonegan sought the Republican nomination. In fact, Christie, as governor, nominated his state Attorney General Jeffrey Chisea to fill the seat temporarily. He also decided for an August primary election with a special election on a Wednesday in October since there were conflicting state statutes about when special elections could be held. "Without question, the Governor was authorized to call a special election in this circumstance," ruled Superior Judge Jane Grill in a Democratic official's lawsuit concerned about voter confusion with multiple elections.[44] Many grew concerned that the governor wanted his upcoming November reelection go uninterrupted since Democratic turn out would be significant for Booker for US Senate and few Democrats would support Christie for governor leaving him with a small gap against his Democrat opponent, Booker-backed state Senator Barbara Buono. At an estimated $24 million for the primary and special elections, the *Star-Ledger* argued that Christie's move to have a special election before the November election was "naked self-interest."[45] At the same time several opinion polls revealed that Booker had easy name recognition since he polled 40 points ahead of his closest Democratic rival and he raised nearly $5 million within weeks of his announcement (with 2,027 New Jersey donors and almost 5,000 out of state donors).[46] Not surprisingly then, the mayor agreed to only three Democratic candidate debates and chose not to attend the first debate as he was attending fundraising events. Moreover Booker easily won the special primary election in August with 59 percent of Democratic voters.[47]

Many speculated that Booker was more interested in the governor's office but that challenging Christie at that time would be difficult financially and politically. Running for the US Senate was a safe alternative even though Booker had said in the past that being a senator with all the usual political bickering was "less attractive. I would be discussing rules of procedure until I'm nauseous." But Booker said that, now, as a senatorial candidate, "[I]t's all about purpose and not position." In addition, Booker and Christie might have their policy disagreements, but they do respect one another and have even agreed not to take cheap shots at each other. In fact, they have such a cordial relationship that they text each other "like teenagers," claims Booker.[48] Running against each other in a statewide election would not only challenge their relationship, it would also be costly, and Booker would "have to stop being full time mayor today" even though he was "very interested in the idea [of running] for governor."[49] Still, this is not to say that Booker would never want to run for governor, but the opportunity was not ripe in 2013.[50] However, some officials and observers have grown concerned about how much attention Booker can give to managing the city while simultaneously running for the US Senate.[51] Despite this, Booker stated in an editorial that while he would run for the US Senate, he would also continue his "hard work" as mayor because "there is still much work to do." He boasted that "Newark is in its biggest period of economic development since the 1950s" and that "in the coming months there are transformative development projects that can bring thousands of jobs to Newark."[52] Even the *Star-Ledger* came out to endorse Booker for the US Senate because of his mayoral record. "He's done a great job as mayor, with measureable progress on economic development, reducing violent crime, building affordable housing and parks. He deserves credit for removing the vestiges of Newark's corrupt former mayor, Sharpe James, and making huge progress on ethics reform in this city."[53]

Unquestionably, Booker has been an effective mayor as it relates to the city's philanthropic efforts and urban development goals. The mayor has raised over $400 million for a variety of projects and initiatives. From housing to parks to education, Booker proved beyond successful at fundraising for community efforts. "As a city, we're fighting above our weight class in terms of attracting those resources that are enabling us to do everything from affordable housing to transforming our parks," said the mayor. "Philanthropists told me that they didn't want to get involved with the city." In fact, Booker transformed the process of getting donors to negotiate with the city: "So there's this meeting when I first started as mayor when we brought together a huge philanthropy round table and folks said that this was the first time we ever sat together and listened to a mayor give priorities that we could all believe in and get behind." In addition to Booker's fundraising success, public safety has and remains a serious concern in Newark (as it is many American cities) and major crimes did decrease significantly during his tenure as mayor. Even property taxes were reported to be to cut 13 percent just as he leaves City Hall. There is little question that Booker will continue to achieve success in community development and education policy during his last term. "This could be arguably our most productive year when it comes to economic development," said Booker. "So you'll see dynamic economic development and exciting things happening for our schools especially with projects like Teachers Village."[54] Even one of the mayor's critics offers a similar assessment of Booker, saying that "he's made undeniable progress on schools, economic development, crime and parks." But when it comes to the city council and working with a number of key public officials, "Booker is losing control politically, to the point that riot police were in recently to maintain order at a city council meeting."[55]

Where does this political disconnect stem from, however? How is it that such a dynamic and charismatic mayor loses allies and political control, as demonstrated in the "November surprise" council meeting? Booker had managed difficult circumstances before the council meeting, but slowly over time, and in particular during his second term, the mayor lost allies and gained more opponents in addition to the growing James faction. In other words, Booker spent little time shepherding or even working with the city council. Of course, many of the same council members had refused to work with him from the beginning, but he slowly lost alliances, and it all came to a crashing point in November 2012. More importantly, Booker was unsuccessful at maintaining coalition building after the mayoral elections. In fact, Booker's electoral coalition efforts backfired as Black council members and Latino council members became racial voting blocks opposing or supporting the mayor's nomination of Speight (Latino council members supported the mayor and his nominee while Black council members did not support the mayor and his nominee). While Booker had appointed and hired a variety of officials and staff in his administration who were Black, Latino, and White, he lacked credibility among many Black Newarkers and, in particular, among Black old guard officials. Booker failed to find ways to maintain sustainable coalition politics among many Black officials and their supporters. This is a critical lesson toward sustainable coalition building, particularly during an era of post-racial politics. Racial politics has hardly ended in a city like Newark, certainly not for many Black Newarkers and their public officials. But Booker stated that he thinks Newark "is maturing to the point to where voters don't think race first. They really want qualified people to represent them who will deliver the basics. There are coalitions around issues and around poverty issues, housing issues and great coalitions around economic development."[56] However, for many, post-racial idealism is elusive, and overlooking key Black officials and not building bridges with residents in Newark's Black communities proved detrimental for Booker and the city.

Instead of focusing his attention on maintaining sustainable coalition building, Booker was more invested in emphasizing Newark's ongoing issues through unorthodox approaches. While he was genuinely interested in issues such as crime, homelessness, and poverty, the mayor typically drew media attention to himself by talking about significant urban problems. In December 2012, for example, he challenged himself to eat only $33 worth of food in one week; this was based on what a single individual on food stamps received as part of the Supplemental Nutrition Assistance Program (SNAP), and Congress was considering $16 billion in cuts to the program. He wanted to "dispel the stereotypes that exist" about food stamp users and make his Twitter followers recognize the difficulties of surviving on so little money,[57] even though SNAP is meant to supplement a recipient's food budget and not comprise it entirely. As the Star-Leger stated on the newspaper's front page, "[H]e is using the experiment to raise awareness for the plight of the working poor, like 850,000 other New Jerseyans who receive food stamps each month." In the accompanying picture, the mayor is shown with the food he purchased from an area grocery store. But, some of the items, like a bottle of organic olive oil and a bag of expensive mixed greens, drew attention to his food choices.[58] "The media-savvy mayor may have lived on a meager diet of beans and yams, but he created a feast of publicity, both for himself and for the issue of government-assisted nutritional programs for the nation's poor."[59] While the challenge introduced the public to some of the realities of food stamps and food costs, the media continued to focus on the mayor and the sparse food items he purchased as he was forced to eat burned food.[60] In addition to newspaper articles, the mayor also appeared on CNN, CBS, and the Daily Show with Jon Stewart, and he Tweeted his experiences to followers.

Clearly, his efforts to highlight the problem of food insecurity created media buzz, but pragmatically, as mayor, was Booker able to work with policy officials at the local, state, or even federal level to address the issue? From a local standpoint, did Booker work with officials in city government or try to partner with other public officials about the issue? Booker has been branded a media darling because he is undeniably charismatic and regularly communicates with the public through the media and his Twitter account. As one observer stated, "Booker has the annoying habit of transforming others' personal distress into fuel for his personal marketing machine."[61] This may be a weakness of Booker's, but it speaks volumes about how a post-racial era mayor can underestimate sustainable coalition building because sustainable coalition politics demands that the mayor work with other officials and not operate as an individual by capturing the attention of the media and people on social media.

Booker's public approaches and post-racial politics have received critical attention, particularly during his second term. In a front page New York Times article printed at the end of the 2012, for example, there was a blistering assessment by a growing number of Newarkers that Booker "has proved to be a better marketer than mayor, who shines in the spotlight but shows little interest in the less-glamorous work of what it takes to run a city."[62] The mayor responded on Twitter that the article was merely "a hard-nosed but fair look at my administration." Booker admitted that he and his staff were initially concerned about the article and the negative attention his opponents offered to the press, but his internal polls revealed that his popularity remained high, at nearly 80 percent.[63]

Essentially, Booker relishes the positive press accounts—despite recent negative media attention—and he convinces others that he is widely popular and "not hated" and that "it's a weird reality" that detractors appear to get so much attention.[64] By doing heroic deeds like rescuing a neighbor from a burning building and helping a constituent shovel snow, Booker portrays himself as the quintessential mayor,[65] but too often he is "eager to tweet his good deeds to the world." However, Newark has far bigger problems as the city was unable to remove snow for days because there was no snow removal contract and City Hall has eliminated three fire departments, which has led some to think that "Booker sells the sizzle, not the steak."[66] But there's a larger concern in these instances. Booker has lost touch with supporters and, to a greater degree, Newark's issues even though he argues that few mayors are more responsive to individual constituent complaints.[67] There's little doubt that he responds to questions (and even flirtatious banter with a Portland, OR, vegan club stripper) through his Twitter account, performs rescues, and fulfills individual constituent's needs,[68] but he lacks credibility with many officials, especially among his political opponents. After Booker rescued a woman from a fire, the *Star-Ledger* stated in an editorial that "Mayor Batman deserves nothing but praise and gratitude for this move." At the same time, they also said,

> Booker is one of the most popular politicians in New Jersey, but he also has inspired a small army of detractors, mostly in Newark, who can't give him credit for anything—including the drop in crime and corruption, the refurbished parks or the new building cranes working downtown. This time they're stuck. There is simply no way to spin this story as anything less than heroic. Is the mayor a publicity hound? Without a doubt.[69]

In other words, Booker enjoys the anecdotal and small victories that are glowingly emphasized by the media more than sustainable coalition politics or building bridges with his opponents. In contrast, Booker said, "So that when I can bump into a guy, as I did coming into City Hall today, who benefited from our prison reentry program that didn't exist before; and when I can bump into somebody who hugs me and says 'you saved my life' because of our financial empowerment center; or the average Newark resident walks out with 10 percent more in income or benefits; or I bump into a grandparent who benefited from our Grandparents Support Center … All these things to me, that's the substantive stuff."[70]

Booker uses the press and social media to announce these types of policy triumphs. In addition to his popular Twitter account, the mayor also launched his own social media news site on Waywire that aggregates news features and targets Millennial Generation computer users. While the mayor was a board member of Waywire, he was also an active participant on the website. However, many questioned his ability to serve as mayor and, at the same time, serve as a board member and active user of a social media site. Several journalists scrutinized Booker for serving on the Waywire board and he eventually stepped down during the special senatorial election.[71] Yet Booker enjoys taking part in many aspects of social media and does not even mind parodying himself. For example, Booker and Christie were featured in a three-minute YouTube video produced by the governor's office that shows the men trying to outdo each other. The mayor solves New Jersey residents' problems by doing various things from fixing a flat tire to catching a falling baby; Christie tries to play catch up while Booker acts the hero. And Christie sputters, similar to *Seinfeld*'s character Jerry about Newman, bitterly stating, "Booker!"[72] Finally, the mayor has been featured in a number of prominent lifestyle and national magazines, particularly during his second term. In 2011, Booker was chosen as one of *Time* magazine's 100 World's Most Influential People. In a magazine article titled "Saving Newark with a Smile," Oprah Winfrey tells how Booker "defines [the term] *servant leader*" and says that "he is a man of, for and about the people."[73] Featured in *Men's Heath* magazine's "Celebrity Fitness" column, the mayor discussed his fitness routines and mantras of "don't run from hard; run toward it" and "be the change you want to see in the world." Booker is portrayed as a "conversational chameleon who can talk credibly on Wall Street, Main Street, or Mean Street."[74] In *Vogue* magazine, Booker was described as "America's most influential mayor" and his governing style was depicted as "collective parent and urban superhero" with "applications of a theory of civic revitalization, which says that a single leader, visibly doing the right thing, can influence a whole community's behavior."[75]

Besides these positive images of Booker, however, the lasting effects of the Newark elections were the attacks by many old guard Black leaders against Booker's racial authenticity. In fact, these attacks may deter future Black leaders who were raised outside cities from running for public office in urban areas. Walter Fields, the former director of the National Association for the Advancement of Colored People (NAACP) pointed out, "If you want places like Newark to grow, you want the Cory Bookers of the world to be an active part of the city. To have black elected officials question his legitimacy, to have him penalized for his own success, that's the tragedy of this election."[76] Yet James' strategy to challenge Booker's background proved successful, particularly in gaining Black voters' support during the 2002 election. Even though he lost by six percent, "Booker's ability to mount a serious campaign gave evidence that the political waters in urban American were shifting course."[77] Journalists and political scientists observed this phenomenon, and it became increasingly clear that Booker challenged the civil rights generation's style of urban politics.[78] James' politics proved disconcerting and divisive for Blacks, and yet the 2006 election demonstrated uncanny similarities. As the *New York Times* pointed out, Booker introduced the "prickly dynamics of interracial politics."[79]

A number of council members, public officials, and supporters grew weary of the attention, both positive and negative, that Booker received, and they became concerned that Booker was out of town too often and that the media had distracted him from managing City Hall. The *Star-Ledger*, for example, discovered that he was out of town nearly a quarter of the time during a year and half period in 2011–2012.[80] And the mayor was often more focused on the media attention and traveling than on coalition building with key officials and city council members. One councilman said, "[W]henever there's a real issue in the city to be resolved, he's nowhere to be found. The real issue is we need a mayor."[81] In fact, this partly explains why Assembly Speaker Oliver was running against Booker for the US Senate in the special election: to speak towards his weakness as a mayor, according to one Oliver supporter who is also a councilman. "He's been a no-show mayor. He's got all kinds of problems in city hall," stated Rice.[82] Despite his controversial absenteeism, Booker has an awesome ability to capture the national spotlight, and many people outside Newark view him as the quintessential mayor.[83] However, others, particularly many Newark residents, viewed the mayor as aloof and politically disconnected. In other words, there seem to be two Cory Bookers: the national media show horse and the opportunistic workhorse .[84]

But the public's most important concern—besides the media attention, problematic political relations, and dismal coalition building efforts—was what will become of Newark's politics in the future. With the special election pushing Booker to his senatorial rise a year earlier than planned, how would the city operate without the mayor? Between Councilmen Baraka and Ramos running for mayor in May 2014, concerns centered on who would be council president let alone interim mayor since Ramos served as interim president and could be mayor for eight months with Booker winning higher office. The council eventually voted to have Councilman Quintana as council president in September 2013, but some viewed the vote as political since Baraka supported Quintana in an effort to gain Latino support for his mayoral election. For a council that remained so divided internally, this political calculus only further divided Newark politics. "It makes what's already going to be a contentious mayoral fight downright medieval," said Councilman Rice. "I think the city will be rudderless if that is the case, in a very critical time, a time that we may be having our first budget in a number of years without the need for state aid."[85]

Aside from the politics of an interim mayor, the Booker-James clash continued over council seats and familial legacy. Booker frequently reminded Newarkers, he inherited a $180 million deficit from the James administration, and he was able to decrease it to $60 million. But James and his son, John Sharpe James, as well as the Newark First team (largely made up of old guard Black Newarkers) remained critical of Booker and his administration, even with a budget surplus in 2013.[86] Booker's campaign for the US Senate left a significant vacuum in City Hall; potential mayoral candidates came from local family political dynasties, particularly in Newark's Black communities (the James, Paynes, Rices, Sharifs, Barakas), which brought a familial showdown.[87] For Councilwoman Crump, Booker's decision not to seek a third term left City Hall "not in a vacuum but allows for freedom when Cory's gone."[88] In fact, political lines were drawn for the mayoral election. Many elder Black leaders backed Councilman Baraka under the Essex County Independent Democrats, a grassroots organization that is separate from and opposes the Essex County Democratic Committee.[89] While Newark school advisory board member, Shavar Jeffries, tried to gain—if not split—Black voters by running for mayor and advocated for school reform.[90] At the same time, many Latinos vying for city council and the mayoral post, including Councilman Ramos, relied increasingly on party bosses like Stephen Adubato Sr. and Essex County Executive Joseph DiVincenzo as many candidates had in the past.[91] "With stakes that high, the city could see a fractious battle," said the *Star-Ledger* about the potential conflict between the Black family dynasties and Latinos and party bosses.[92] According to Councilman Baraka, Newark has been divided along racial and ethnic lines for generations "while many party leaders and community bosses center much of their power around social stratification. Newark is still a deeply segregated city—like so many cities."[93]

As a result of Newark's sordid racial history and Booker's post-racial politics, many city officials remain engaged in divisive politics. Although Booker articulated coalition politics during the election 2006 season, after the election, he did little to maintain sustainable coalition building. "Politicians have often splintered based on the elections and getting elected and that's it," said Councilman Luis Quintana.[94] According to the councilman, the MUA debate, unemployment, and various downtown projects should be reasons for coalition building between officials and constituents. Whereas other officials see redeveloping Newark as a coalition opportunity. For example, Councilman Anibal Ramos Jr. argues that retail stores, in particular major department stores, is key for downtown. "But our constituents grow suspicious of us if it's just downtown development." He states that he plans to stress more growth outside downtown areas and in large-scale commercial corridors in each ward, especially if he chooses to run for mayor in the future. "People want to see development beyond downtown."[95]

Despite local officials seeing some opportunity to coalition build, Booker's foes politicized and engaged in backlash coalition politics for their respective communities while the mayor campaigned for municipal elections and media attention. The City Hall layoffs, MUA debates, Facebook donation, and antiviolence movement became watershed moments for coalition building for the city because demonstrations and grassroots efforts mobilized thousands of residents across all color lines and social classes. "So many city issues transcend race," said Councilman Baraka. "Issues of crime and police forges people to come together, and it establishes sustainable coalition building efforts." In fact, Baraka played a significant role in organizing many demonstrations. "Blacks and Latinos were in so many rallies in so many wards that issue-based coalition building propelled people to rally. Newarkers are starving for some kind of coalition," stated the councilman. "People can see when it's a genuine response." He went on to suggest that, at the local level, coalition building has been difficult in many cities compared to the national-level coalition building between Congress and the president. At the grassroots level, "it's hard and not an easy task for local coalition building and it takes a level of commitment. Booker was more stuck on community based politics for elections, which fosters communities' differences only further."[96] Many Black old guard leaders and Booker foes led the charge to address key community issues while Booker remained in the shadows. Booker appeared distant, and he rarely reached out to community leaders, especially during his second term as he was traveling a great deal. People's expectations of the mayor were high, but the old guard and their supporters were leading the way for coalition politics.[97] In other words, these were missed moments for coalition building for the mayor *and* his city, and, instead, backlash coalition politics occurred as opposed to sustainable coalition building. It was mostly Booker's opponents who galvanized Newarkers concerned about the Facebook donation, City Hall consultants, privatization of public water, government layoffs, and rising homicide rates through grassroots coalition building.

These backlash groups emerged largely because of Booker's post-racial politics. However, Booker and his officials saw the anti-Booker coalition methods as political. Early in Booker's tenure, some of the Black old guard worked with the mayor on increasing Latino representation in City Hall, addressing key community issues such as crime, and opening more parks, but Booker's political relations during his second term have been "deteriorating."[98] Even though Latinos were appointed to various City Hall positions during Booker's tenure, some leaders thought more should be done. "This administration has had no Hispanic department head," said Councilman Luis Quintana. "At least under Sharpe James there were many more [Latino] agency officials."[99] At the same time, Booker offered many appointments and contracts to outsiders beyond Newark, particularly White officials and consultants. These appointments and contracts only furthered the divide between Booker and the Black communities and created a lot of distrust for Booker among Newarkers. While the anti-Booker coalition politicized race, they also attempted backlash coalition building. Facing racial politics in Newark proved especially difficult for a post-racial mayor like Booker as certain politicians energized their coalition. The administration recognized the problem, but saw racial politics as fear mongering. "It's a concern and it shows how misinformation can spread especially among older Black Newarkers," said the mayor's chief of staff, Modia Butler. "Some politicians demagogue issues especially related to race to play to their base … Navigating racial politics with their own vision especially with a shrinking pie of resources and finances proves challenging for just about anyone."[100] Booker remained steadfast when it came to the social and economic issues facing the city, particularly the James administration's plot to sell city land to their supporters, and Booker claimed that his detractors politicized race at the expense of Newarkers. "So talk about hurting African Americans, talk about hurting the long-term environmental health of the city," argued Booker. "So this is why when people look at me saying, 'Sharpe had people's back'—Mildred Crump and others. Where's your understanding of policy of what our community really needs in the long run?"[101]

Clearly, the lines had been drawn, and, by Booker's second term, relations between Booker and council members had soured. Even his own council member allies acknowledged that the mayor's focus on fundraising and the media was a significant problem because he was away from City Hall so much during his second term. Much of the time the mayor made dozens of speeches outside of Newark, raising $1.3 million within a five-year period claiming to donate much of the money to community nonprofits and recruiting potential donors for the city's philanthropic initiatives.[102] But the mayor "has not spent the time necessary to manage the city and that has only contributed to the divide in this city and it is his weakness," said Councilman Anibal Ramos Jr. "This city is used to having strong local mayors and now the city has a superstar mayor and it's even tough on the city council."[103] But Booker suggested that council relations with his administration are amicable "99.9% of the time" and "when you live in the crucible the council lives in—particularly when I was on the city council—and you have these people coming to the council meetings, it's very non-representative of this city. That's the crazy thing I found out when I ran for mayor the first time. And you sit there and you keep listening to vindictive and angry comments. And then you take polling and the city is completely counter to that. It's tough ... this is historically mild and is not respective of what it is. It's performance politics."[104]

Thus, Booker thinks that his opponents are a small and vocal minority trying to grab media attention and that his administration *never* experienced a backlash, especially because he had a 70% approval rating and received 60% of the votes during the 2010 election. "If there was a backlash against our leadership it was in 2010 after we made a lot of unpopular choices. Otherwise I would not have gotten reelected by a thunderous 20 points—and we were 24 points ahead [of] our closest opponent," says the mayor. While Booker was reelected by a landslide, he still lacks credibility not just among a supposed small cadre of anti-Booker Black old guard residents, but also among some of his former council allies and supporters. They have frequently made cracks about the Booker administration through press accounts, in interviews, and during protests. The mayor, though, mostly disregards this supposed backlash and argues that, "in any place in America people would say, 'this guy has got a dominant fix on winning elections.' But somehow this counter narrative is fueled by people like Sharpe James, Ron Rice Sr., and Mildred Crump that people actually believe." He also suggests that there's a "media fascination" with many of these Black old guard leaders who are "stuck in their bitterness that's gone beyond rational," and it's largely because they were unsuccessful mayoral candidates. Booker says that the media seems to focus their attention on his opponents, even though he is widely popular and has the same approval rating as Governor Chris Christie—70 percent. "But no one is looking at the backlash or the people against him. But here consistently even before I got into office there was always this account—and always characterized in racial terms." Booker argues that "there is a laziness in analysis that allows people to think these are massive moments."[105] Therefore, Booker sees the old Black guard as being envious opportunists who have the ear of the press even though polls show significant support for his leadership. But Booker's opponents have remained focused on attacking him, particularly during his second term, albeit as a backlash movement that he insists does not exist. Even if he views his opponents as a small and irrelevant group because he is so popular (statistically speaking), Booker has a credibility gap to effectively coalition build on significant issues with many Black Newarkers.

While gaining attention for various issues and problems in Newark on the national stage, in the process Booker became politically detached from Newark and lost whatever support he had had from the local Newark Black civil rights generation. Clearly, Booker was alienated from many Black voters as was demonstrated during the mayoral elections, and, by his second term, relations between the mayor and several Black officials had grown tense. In fact, former supporters of the mayor grew weary of his politics and the media's fixation on him.

Councilwoman Crump said that Booker has a "character flaw" in maintaining political relations. "He's the Trojan horse of Essex County, and the attention is always on him, and he inserts himself as heir apparent."[106] But Booker countered that Crump has "a wounded sense of anger."[107]

Another public official stated that it was not just Booker's "character flaw" that led to politicizing coalition politics in City Hall. Councilman Baraka suggests it was more of a generation gap that exists in cities such as Newark. Moreover, veteran leaders rarely share power with younger leaders while post-racial leaders like Booker are so ambitious that they often fill the vacuum when seasoned officials leave office. "While any government is subject to incompetence and corruption—no matter which generation—the reality of City Hall is that there's been a serious gap between the 1960s generation and the generation coming of age in the 1990s," said the councilman. "There have been systemic problems for generations." He also stated that as a mayoral candidate in 2014, he plans to run on a platform of coalition politics and he recognizes that "it will be hard but it has to be done. This city needs it. So many City Halls have so many problems in so many cities … I can't pick up the pieces by myself and we need people to get together."[108]

Once again, coalition politics comes back to haunt Newark and its officials. It's as though the city has not only missed awesome opportunities for coalition building among leaders and constituents, but for so long its officials have squandered various opportunities to fully develop sustainable coalition building approaches. Instead, many embrace politicizing coalition building during election season or, as was the case with Booker and his gadflies, create opportunities for backlash coalition building to flourish. According to Baraka, Councilman Luis Quintana understands that it is necessary to practice coalition politics beyond the election season and also understands sustainable coalition building because he has worked with both Black and Latino Newarkers as an at-large official.[109] Quintana says, "[C]oalitions really need to go beyond personal politics, and we need to work toward similar goals." He also describes how the Black and Puerto Rican Convention in Newark attempted grassroots coalition building in the 1970s because it helped foster trust, empowerment, respect, and, ultimately, brotherhood between the two communities. Quintana suggests that becoming familiar with one another is the key to understanding cultures, religions, foods, and dreams of another community; these were the basic tenets of coalition building decades ago. Unfortunately, Newark has lost much of that basic camaraderie between its communities, and Quintana states that political officials, clergy, and other community leaders need to inspire trust because "so many groups in this city are so splintered. Let children and their education, safety and health concerns be the bridge for the future and for successful coalition building."[110]

Thus, race and class remain significant dilemmas for a post-racial mayor like Cory Booker and a city like Newark. Because Booker sought to be the quintessential post-racial mayor, many Black officials and old Black guard leaders frequently defined Booker's politics in the voting booth, City Hall, and on the streets. This, unfortunately, led to undermining his leadership, politics, and agenda and cemented backlash coalition politics, not sustainable coalition building. In truth, in several key areas, Booker has been one of the city's most effective mayors. Crime has been reduced significantly, and education reform is finally taking shape in Newark. Booker's greatest achievement was clearly advancing progressive community development initiatives. But, along the way, and particularly during his second term, the mayor often overlooked the political connections that are critical for a city to flourish. Relying on elections and social media have been useful for Booker, but understanding the city's racial politics and maintaining sustainable coalition politics were essential for post-racial politics to thrive in Newark.

Appendix*

Table A1 Survey Results from 2006 Mayoral Election

	Voted for Booker in 2002 (%)	Planned to Vote for Booker in 2006 (%)	Percent Change	Disagreed Booker an Outsider in 2002 (%)	Disagreed Booker an Outsider in 2006 (%)	Disagreed Booker not "Authentically" Black (%)	Favorable Booker (%)	Percent Range
Whites	77	92	15	76	84	71	71–92	19
Latinos	56	53	−3	57	57	73	53–73	20
Blacks	35	52	17	44	52	57	35–57	22

Newarkers' Issue Priority

Issue	Resident (267 respondents)	Star-Ledger Poll (401 respondents) July 10, 2006
Crime	1 (46%)	1 (53%)
Education	2 (20%)	2 (16%)
Unemployment	3 (11%)	3 (14%)
Housing	4 (12.4%)	5 (4%)
Healthcare	5 (6.4%)	N/A
Entertainment/Attractions	6 (0.4%)	N/A
Other	7 (3.7%)	7 (1%)
Government Reform	N/A	6 (2%)
Not Sure/Refuse	N/A	4 (8%)

Figure A1 2006 Survey Results of Newark's Most Pressing Issues (by Percentage).

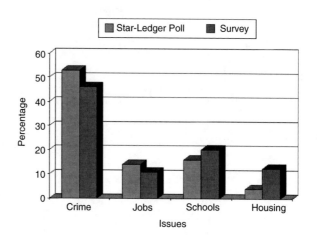

* Figures A1 and A2 were by Ryan Bennick. Images A1–16 were by Russell Nadler.

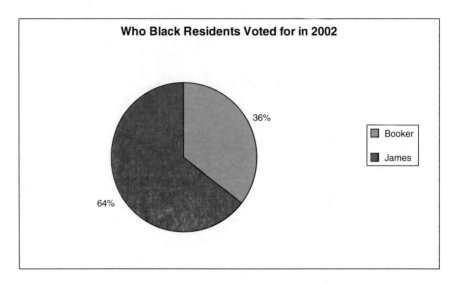

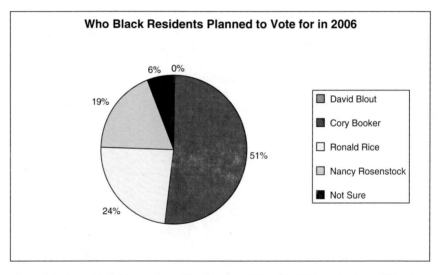

Figure A2   How Black Respondents Voted in the 2002 and 2006 Newark Mayoral Elections

Image A1 Newark's main street, Broad Street, and Prudential headquarters with northern blocks behind the tower being razed for additional office buildings that will overlook Military Park. This area will also be the future home to the Four Corners Millennium Project at Broad and Market Streets as well as the Teachers Village just a couple of blocks away.

Image A2 The Prudential Center plaza (*center*), Rock Plaza Lofts, and Dinosaur Barbeque Restaurant (*left*) with the PSE&G office tower in the background. With restaurants and shops at street level and apartments on upper floors, Rock Plaza Lofts typifies future mixed-use development for downtown Newark.

Image A3   The back of the Prudential Center, with no entrance facing Newark's main artery, Broad Street (adjacent to the center on the right side are the parking garage and the new Courtyard by Marriott Hotel on Broad Street).

Image A4   Prudential Center entrance (facing east toward commuter Pennsylvania Station).

Image A5   Panasonic Corporation of North America's tower on Raymond Boulevard, a block from Newark Pennsylvania Station. A large part of financing this project came from New Jersey's state HUB tax credits.

Image A6   The Gateway Center office complex (*center*), the Hilton Hotel (*left*), and its walkway (*right*). Many office workers walk between complex towers and Newark Pennsylvania Station in walkways, not on Newark streets.

Images A7 and A8 New Jersey Performing Arts Center (NJPAC), located near the north end of Broad Street, and Newark Symphony Hall, at the southern end of Broad Street.

Image A9   The Newark Broad Street train station (in front, the demolished Westinghouse plant and, in back, the Colonnade Apartments complex).

Images A10 and A11 Adjacent to Newark Broad Street Station is the James Street Commons historic district on the northern edge of downtown. Following budget cuts in 2011, Newark's Mounted Police unit was shut down, but it was later reinstated; the Mounted Police unit patrol many areas of Newark, particularly around James Street Commons.

Image A12   While the James Streets Commons historic district is only a few blocks long, its location near the city's universities means that it is ripe for future residential and commercial development. Adjacent to the James Street Commons is Frat Row where many fraternity and sorority houses for students from nearby New Jersey Institute of Technology and Rutgers University–Newark are located. A couple of short blocks away is the redeveloped Baxter Terrace area (former housing projects turned into mixed-income housing). NJIT and the city will continue to raze and redevelop this area, and Frat Row will be relocated to the newly designated Warren Street Village on NJIT's campus several blocks away.

Image A13   Empty super blocks surround Springfield Avenue in the city's Central Ward, reminders of Newark's 1967 riots; this area is the future home of the Springfield Avenue Marketplace.

Image A14   Once former high-rise housing projects, this Central Ward area on Dr. Martin Luther King Jr. Boulevard was turned into mixed-income and low-income townhouse complexes (including the nearby Montgomery Heights Apartments). The Brick Towers complex, the former home of Mayor Booker, was only a few blocks away. Replacing low-income project towers with townhouses in a number of Newark's neighborhoods has been a redevelopment plan since the 1990s.

Image A15   Richardson Lofts, near the city's East Ward, typifies many of the new high-end loft-style apartments in Newark. Like many newer loft complexes, 50 percent of its units are available for low-income and moderate-income residents.

Image A16   Adjacent to Newark's Pennsylvania Station in the city's East Ward is the renowned and bustling Ironbound neighborhood. Formerly an Italian American enclave, this area is home to many Portuguese, Brazilian, and Latino Americans.

Notes

Introduction

1. Paula McClain and Joseph Stewart, *"Can We All Get Along?": Racial and Ethnic Minorities in American Politics*, Fourth Edition (Boulder: Westview, 2006); Rufus Browning, Dale Rogers Marshall, and David Tabb, *Protest Is Not Enough: The Struggle of Blacks and Hispanics for Equality in Urban Politics* (Berkeley: University of California Press, 1984); John Mollenkopf, "New York: Still the Great Anomaly" in *Racial Politics in American Cities*, ed. Rufus Browning, Dale Rogers Marshall, and David Tabb (New York: Longman Publishers, 2003); and Raphael Sonenshein, *Politics in Black and White: Race and Power in Los Angeles* (Princeton: Princeton University Press, 1994).
2. Jonathan Tepperman, "Complicating the Race," *New York Times Magazine*, April 28, 2002.
3. Georgia A. Persons, "From Insurgency to Deracialization: The Evolution of Black Mayoralities," in *Perspectives in Black Politics and Black Leadership*, ed. John Davis (Lanham: University Press of America, 2007), 92–93.
4. William Nelson and Philip Meranto, *Electing Black Mayors: Political Action in the Black Community* (Columbus: Ohio State University Press, 1977), 184.
5. Marguerite Ross Barnett, "A Theoretical Perspective on American Racial Public Policy" in *Public Policy for the Black Community: Strategies and Perspectives* (New York: Alfred Publishing Co, 1976), 5–6, 13.
6. Richard Keiser, *Subordination or Empowerment?: African-American Leadership and the Struggle for Urban Political Power* (New York: Oxford University Press, 1997), 20.
7. Marion Orr, *Black Social Capital: The Politics of School Reform in Baltimore, 1986–1998* (Lawrence: University of Kansas, 1999), chapter 1.
8. William Nelson, Jr. and Philip Meranto, *Electing Black Mayors: Political Action in the Black Community* (Columbus: Ohio State University Press, 1977), 178–179.
9. William Sales, Jr. and Roderick Bush, "Black and Latino Coalitions: Prospects for New Social Movements in New York City," in *Race and Politics*, ed. James Jennings (New York: Verso Books, 1997). See also John Mollenkopf, David Olson, and Timothy Ross, "Immigrant Political Participation in New York and Los Angeles" in *Governing American Cities: Inter-Ethnic Coalitions, Competition, and Conflict* (New York: Russell Sage Foundation, 2001), 64 and Karen Kaufman, *The Urban Voter: Group Conflict and Mayoral Voting Behavior in American Cities* (Ann Arbor: University of Michigan Press, 2004), 119.

10. Heather Parker, "Tom Bradley and the Politics of Race," in *African-American Mayors: Race, Politics, and the American City*, ed. David Colburn and Jeffrey Adler (Urbana: University of Illinois Press, 2001) and Mike Davis, *City of Quartz: Excavating the Future in Los Angeles* (New York: Vintage Books, 1992).
11. Persons, 59.
12. Ibid., 78.
13. Ibid., 90–94.
14. William Nelson and Philip Meranto, 90.
15. Roger Biles, *Richard J. Daley: Politics, Race, and the Governing of Chicago* (DeKalb: Northern Illinois University Press, 1995) and William Grimshaw, *Bitter Fruit: Black Politics and the Chicago Machine, 1931–1991* (Chicago: University of Chicago, 1995).
16. J. Phillip Thompson III, *Double Trouble: Black Mayors, Black Communities, and the Call for a Deep Democracy* (New York: Oxford University Press, 2006), 30–36.
17. Andra Gillespie, *The New Black Politician: Cory Booker, Newark, and Post-Racial America* (New York: New York University Press, 2012), chapter 1.
18. Michael Jones-Correa, "Comparative Approaches to Changing Interethnic Relations in Cities," in *Governing American Cities: Inter-Ethnic Coalitions, Competition, and Conflict* (New York: Russell Sage Foundation, 2001), 2.
19. Davis, *City of Quartz*, 102.
20. Raphael Sonenshein, *The City at Stake: Secession, Reform, and the Battle for Los Angeles* (Princeton: Princeton University Press, 2004), chapter 5.
21. Sonenshein, *Politics in Black and White*, 27.
22. Davis, *City of Quartz*, 161–169.
23. Paula McClain, "Coalition and Competition: Patterns of Black-Latino Relations in Urban Politics," in *From Polemics to Practice: Forging Political Coalitions Among Racial and Ethnic Minorities*, ed. Wilbur C. Rich (New York: Praeger, 1996), 58.
24. Sonenshein, *Politics in Black and White*, chapter 7. See also Heather Parker.
25. Sonenshein, *Politics in Black and White*, chapter 8.
26. Kaufman, 113.
27. Ibid., 116–117.
28. McClain and Stewart, 203.
29. Mike Davis, *Magical Urbanism: Latinos Reinvent the U.S. City* (New York: Verso Books, 2000), chapter 5.
30. McClain and Stewart, 182.
31. Mollenkopf, 141.
32. Browning, et al., *Protest Is Not Enough*, chapter 3.
33. Mollenkopf, 116–117.
34. Sonenshein, *Politics in Black and White*, chapter 14.
35. Thompson, 169.
36. Ibid., 153 and Davis, *Magical Urbanism*, chapter 12.
37. Roger Biles, "Mayor David Dinkins and the Politics of Race in New York City," in African-American Mayors: Race, Politics, and the American City, ed. David Colburn and Jeffrey Adler (Urbana: University of Illinois Press, 2001), 133 and Thompson, 249.
38. Kaufman, 128.
39. Mollenkopf et al., 64.

40. Kaufman, 119.

41. Ibid., 132–145. See also Mollenkopf, 130–131.

42. Sales and Bush, 139.

43. Cory Booker interview, April 5, 2013, with author.

44. Paul Peterson, *City Limits* (Chicago: University of Chicago Press, 1981), 20.

45. Thomas Sugrue, *The Origins of the Urban Crisis: Race and Inequality in Postwar Detroit* (Princeton: Princeton University Press, 1996), 9. See also Susan Welch, Lee Sigelman, Timothy Bledsoe, and Michael Combs, *Race and Place: Race Relations in an American City* (New York: Cambridge University Press, 2001).

46. Neil Smith, *The New Urban Frontier: Gentrification and the Revanchist City* (New York: Routledge Press, 1996), chapters 1 and 5.

47. Sugrue, 271. See also Heather Ann Thompson, *Whose Detroit? Politics, Labor, and Race in a Modern City* (Ithaca: Cornell University Press, 2001), 2.

48. Dennis Judd and Susan Fainstein, ed., *The Tourist City* (New Haven: Yale University Press, 1999), 12.

49. Alice O'Connor, Chris Tilly, and Lawrence Bobo, ed., *Urban Inequality: Evidence from Four Cities* (New York: Russell Sage Foundation, 2001).

50. Kevin Delaney and Rick Eckstein, *Public Dollars, Private Stadiums: The Battle Over Building Sports Stadiums* (New Brunswick, NJ: Rutgers University Press, 2004), 203.

51. Peter Dreier, John Mollenkopf, and Todd Swanstrom, *Place Matters: Metropolitics for the Twenty-First Century*, Second Edition (Lawrence: University of Kansas Press, 2004), 47.

52. Manning Marable, *How Capitalism Underdeveloped Black America: Problems in Race, Political Economy, and Society* (Boston: South End Press, 1999).

53. Joanna Cagan and Neil deMause, *Field of Schemes: How the Great Stadium Swindle Turns Public Money into Private Profit* (Monroe: Common Courage Press, 1998), 36.

54. Joan Whitlow, "Mayor's Review of Arena Deal Is a Safe Bet," *Star-Ledger*, July 31, 2006.

55. James Jennings, ed., *Race and Politics* (New York: Verso Books, 1997), 8. See also David Bender, *Poverty: Opposing Viewpoints* (San Diego: Greenhaven Press, Inc., 1999).

56. Robert Dahl, *Who Governs? Democracy and Power in an American City* (New Haven: Yale University Press, 1961), 7, and Clarence Stone, *Regime Politics: Governing Atlanta, 1946–1988* (Lawrence: University of Kansas Press, 1989), chapter 1.

Chapter 1

1. Robert Curvin, "The Persistent Minority: The Black Political Experience in Newark," dissertation (Princeton: Princeton University, 1975), 2.

2. Modia Butler interview, November 26, 2012, with author.

3. Komozi Woodard, "It's Nation Time in NewArk: Amiri Baraka and the Black Power Experiment in Newark, New Jersey" in *Freedom North: Black Freedom Struggles Outside the South, 1940–1980*, ed. Jeanne Theoharis and Komozi Woodard (New York: Palgrave MacMillan, 2003), 309.

4. Clement Alexander Price, "The Afro-American Community of Newark" dissertation (New Brunswick: Rutgers University–Newark, 1975), ii–iii.

5. Brad Parks, "Crossroads Part I: Before 1967, a Gathering Storm," *Star-Ledger*, July 8, 2007.

6. Barbara Kukla, *Swing City: Newark Nightlife: 1925–1950* (New Brunswick: Rutgers University Press, 1991), Introduction.

7. Price, 48–49.

8. Kevin Mumford, *Newark: A History of Race, Rights, and Riots in America* (New York: New York University Press, 2007), 1–3.

9. John T. Cunningham, *Newark*, Third Edition (Newark: The New Jersey Historical Society, 2002), 309.

10. Price, 50–52

11. Cunningham, 312.

12. Cunningham, 262 and 307.

13. Price, 156.

14. Ibid., 57–58.

15. William B. Helmreich, *The Enduring Community: The Jews of Newark and Metrowest* (New Brunswick, NJ: Transaction Publishers, 1999), 38.

16. Ibid., chapter 1.

17. Price, 8.

18. Ibid., 11.

19. Ibid., 158.

20. Curvin, 29, and Price, 156.

21. Curvin, 24.

22. Cunningham, 307.

23. Curvin, 31; Price, 89; Mumford, 70; and Harold Kaplan, *Urban Renewal Politics: Slum Clearance in Newark* (New York: Columbia University Press, 1963), 153–154.

24. "A Newark Reformer," *Star-Ledger*, November 12, 1999.

25. Curvin, 39. He quotes an observer in Gerald Pomper's "A Report on Newark Politics," Urban Studies Center, Rutgers University.

26. Curvin, 110. See also Ronald Porambo, *No Cause for Indictment: An Autopsy of Newark* (Hoboken: Mellville House, 2006), 60–61.

27. Porambo, chapter 5.

28. Woodard, 291.

29. Wilbur C. Rich, *Black Mayors and School Politics* (New York: Garland Publishing, 1996), 92; and Cunningham, 312.

30. Woodard, 291.

31. Porambo, 6.

32. Price, 176.

33. Woodard, 76. See also Curvin, 21.

34. Curvin, 20–21. See also Brad Parks, "Crossroads Part I: Before 1967, a Gathering Storm," *Star-Ledger*, July 8, 2007.

35. Price, 174.

36. Kaplan, 111.

37. Ibid., 10–11.

38. Price, chapters 4–5.

39. Kaplan, chapter 2 and page 25.

40. Ibid., 36.

41. Kenneth Jackson, *Crabgrass Frontier: The Suburbanization of the United States* (New York: Oxford University Press, 1985), 225. See also Curvin, 151.

42. Kaplan, 153–157. Kaplan states that many of these middle-class leaders or "silk-stocking leaders of the NAACP and Urban League" severed most of their ties to the Central Ward once they left Newark but remained involved in the city's politics.

43. Michael Immerso, *Newark's Little Italy: The Vanished First Ward* (New Brunswick: Rutgers University Press, 1997), 140–141; and Cunningham, 309.

44. Mumford, 61.

45. Curvin, 25.

46. Kaplan, 114. "Not until 1955 did Newark hire a professional city planner."

47. Brad Parks, "Crossroads Part I: Before 1967, a Gathering Storm," *Star-Ledger*, July 8, 2007. See also Mumford, 50, and Jackson, *Crabgrass Frontier*.

48. James E. Blackwell and Philip Hart, *Cities, Suburbs, and Blacks: A Study of Concerns, Distrust, and Alienation* (New York: General Hall, Inc., 1982), chapter 1. See also Helmreich, 42, and Jackson, 156.

49. Jackson, chapter 10.

50. Brad Parks, "Crossroads Part I: Before 1967, a Gathering Storm," *Star-Ledger*, July 8, 2007.

51. Ibid. and Porambo, 5.

52. Ibid. See also Jackson, chapters 10–11.

53. Jackson, 217. See also Mumford, 55.

54. Brad Parks, "How the Good Will Inside a City Gave Way to Long Goodbyes," *Star-Ledger*, July 10, 2007.

55. Ibid.

56. Kenneth B. Clark, *Dark Ghetto: Dilemmas of Social Power* (New York: Harper and Row, 1965), 12. See also Price, 170.

57. Brad Parks, "Crossroads Part I: Before 1967, a Gathering Storm" *Star-Ledger*, July 8, 2007.

58. Willa Johnson, "Illusions of Power: Gibson's Impact Upon Employment Conditions in Newark, 1970–1974" dissertation (New Brunswick: Rutgers University, 1978), 37.

59. Cunningham, 312–316.

60. Price, chapter 4. See also page 160 where he compares Blacks in Jersey City and Mayor Hague's machine and his handling of protests.

61. Price, 149–168.

62. Curvin, 46.

63. Mumford, 85–86.

64. Andrew Jacobs, "With 40-Year Prism, Newark Surveys Deadly Riot," *New York Times*, July 8, 2007.

65. Robert Curvin, "PBS Distorts Newark Riot History," *Star-Ledger*, July 8, 2007. See also *Revolution '67*.

66. Ibid. See also Alan Sepinwall, "What Brought Newark to the Edge," *Star-Ledger*, July 10, 2007; Porambo, 80.

67. Mumford, 87, 95, and 172. See also Barry Carter, "Documentary Stirs Strong Feelings," *Star-Ledger*, July 10, 2007. See also *Revolution '67*.

68. Mumford, 109.

69. Brad Parks, "Crossroads: A Neighborhood's View of Despair, Riot and Recovery in Newark," *Star-Ledger*, July 9, 2007. See also Mumford, 109.

70. Porambo, 83, and Woodard, 291.

71. Curvin, 152, and Brad Parks, "Crossroads: A Neighborhood's View of Despair, Riot and Recovery in Newark," *Star-Ledger*, July 9, 2007. The application was filed on April 25, 1967, just months before the riot. See application available online at http://blog. nj.com/ledgernewark/2007/06/model_cities_report.html

72. Brad Parks, "Crossroads: A Neighborhood's View of Despair, Riot and Recovery in Newark," *Star-Ledger*, July 9, 2007.

73. Ibid. See also "Revolution '67" panel discussion, June 27, 2007.

74. Brad Parks, "Crossroads: A Neighborhood"s View of Despair, Riot and Recovery in Newark," *Star-Ledger*, July 9, 2007.

75. Ibid.

76. Kaplan, 135, and Porambo, 84.

77. Curvin, "The Persistent Minority," 153.

78. Johnson, 61.

79. Andrew Jacobs, "With 40-Year Prism, Newark Surveys Deadly Riot," *New York Times*, July 8, 2007. See also Curvin, 152.

80. Rhoda Lois Blumberg, *Civil Rights: The 1960s Freedom Struggle* (Boston: Twayne Publishers, 1991), 165–166.

81. Brad Parks, "Crossroads: A Neighborhood's View of Despair, Riot and Recovery in Newark," *Star-Ledger*, July 9, 2007.

82. Ibid.

83. Dylan Foley, "Speaking Volumes When Newark Burned" (interview with Kevin Mumford), *Star-Ledger*, July 8, 2007.

84. Alan Sepinwall, "What Brought Newark to the Edge," *Star-Ledger*, July 10, 2007.

85. Cunningham suggests that Smith was never beaten but bruised. Whereas Woodard argues that he was "beaten like an animal" and "while Smith was being beaten the black community was gathering outside [the precinct], fearing that the worst would happen to Smith, and demanding to see him," page 194 in "It's Nation Time."

86. Brad Parks, "Crossroads: A Neighborhood's View of Despair, Riot and Recovery in Newark," *Star-Ledger*, July 9, 2007. See also Charles V. Hamilton, "The Politics of Race Relations" in *Urban Violence*, ed. Charles U. Daly (Chicago: University of Chicago Press, 1969), 44. See also Porambo, 22.

87. Cunningham, 165, and Clark, chapter 5, as well as Curvin, 63.

88. Brad Parks, "Crossroads: A Neighborhood's View of Despair, Riot and Recovery in Newark," *Star-Ledger*, July 9, 2007; Mumford, chapter 5.

89. Ibid.

90. Porambo, 113.

91. Brad Parks, "Crossroads: A Neighborhood's View of Despair, Riot and Recovery in Newark," *Star-Ledger*, July 9, 2007.

92. Ibid. See also Mumford, chapter 4, and Porambo, 113.

93. Ibid. See also *Revolution '67*.

94. Ibid.

95. "Newark Civil Disorders 1967," WBGO Radio Gallery and reception, April 27, 2006.

96. Brad Parks, "Crossroads: A Neighborhood's View of Despair, Riot and Recovery in Newark," *Star-Ledger*, July 9, 2007; Cunningham, chapter 28.

97. Cunningham, 28.

98. Woodard, 309.

99. Mumford, 133. See also Brad Parks, "Crossroads Part I: Before 1967, a Gathering Storm," *Star-Ledger*, July 8, 2007.

100. Helmreich, 41–42.

101. Blumberg, 167.

102. Porambo, pages 64 and 76.

103. Albert P. Blaustein and Robert L. Zangrando, eds. *Civil Rights and the American Negro: A Documentary History* (New York: Trident Press, 1968), 619.

104. Ibid., 620.

105. Blumberg, 92–93.

106. Edward G. Carmines and Paul M. Sniderman, "The Structure of Racial Attitudes: Issue Pluralism and Changing the American Dilemma," in *Understanding Public Opinion*, Second Edition, ed. Barbara Norrander and Clyde Wilcox (Washington, DC: CQ Press, 2001), 106 and 111.

107. Doug McAdam, *Political Process and the Development of Black Insurgency, 1930–1970* (Chicago: The University of Chicago Press, 1982), 190.

108. Komozi Woodard, *A Nation within a Nation: Amiri Baraka and Black Power Politics* (Chapel Hill: University of North Carolina Press, 1998), 94.

109. Adam Fairclough, *Better Day Coming: Blacks and Equality, 1890-2000* (New York: Penguin Books, 2002), 297. See also McAdam, 191 and 214.

110. Mildred Crump interview, January 28, 2013, with author.

111. Thomas K. Shannon et al., *Urban Problems in Sociological Perspective*, Third Edition (Prospect Heights: Waveland Press, 1997), 26.

112. Hamilton, "The Politics of Race Relations," 53.

113. Brad Parks, "Crossroads Part I: Before 1967, a Gathering Storm," *Star-Ledger*, July 8, 2007. See also Brad Parks, "How the Good Will Inside a City Gave Way to Long Goodbyes," *Star-Ledger*, July 10, 2007.

114. Ibid.

115. Mumford, 194. Originally from Charles V. Hamilton, "No Truce with Oppressors: Black Americans and the American Political Struggle," *Black World*, May 1970, 5–9.

116. Mumford, 170.

117. Paul Goldberger, "Tony Imperiale Stands Vigilant for Law and Order" in *Takin' it to the Streets: A Sixties Reader*, Second Edition, ed. Alexander Bloom and Wini Breines (New York: Oxford University Press, 2003), 313.

118. Ibid.

119. Porambo, 35.

120. James Haskins, *A Piece of the Power: Four Black Mayors* (New York: The Dial Press, 1972), 146.

121. Porambo, 32.

122. Woodard, It's Nation Time in NewArk, 118 and 290.

123. Curvin, "The Persistent Minority," 199.

124. Alphonso Pinkney, *Red, Black, and Green: Black Nationalism in the United States* (New York: Cambridge University Press, 1976), chapters 6–8, and Woodard, "It's Nation Time in NewArk."

125. Pinkney, 130.

126. Woodard, *A Nation within a Nation*, 75.

127. Woodard, "It's Nation Time," 295–297.

128. Ibid., 299.

129. Mumford, 195.

130. Ibid., 5.

131. Pinkney, 139.

132. Woodard, *A Nation within a Nation*, 2.

133. Luis Quintana interview, February 6, 2013, with author.

134. Mumford, 197, and Harold Lucas interview, November 14, 2012, with author.

135. Curvin, "The Persistent Minority," 60. See also Pinkney, 138, and Woodard, *A Nation within a Nation*,115.

136. Woodard, *A Nation within a Nation*, 145.

137. Ibid., "It's Nation Time," 121 and 301.

138. Haskins, 147 and 152.

139. Curvin, "The Persistent Minority," 78.

140. Ibid., 82.

141. Alan Sepinwall, "What Brought Newark to the Edge," *Star-Ledger*, July 10, 2007.

142. Curvin, "The Persistent Minority," 107.

143. Harold Lucas interview, November 14, 2012, with author.

144. Richard Cammarieri interview, December 3, 2012, with author.

145. Curvin, 71 and 89. See also Haskins, 150 and 163, as well as Johnson, 148.

146. Haskins, 161, and Curvin, 96.

147. Cunningham, 336.

148. Mumford, 198.

149. Haskins, 159.

150. Ibid., 151.

151. Curvin, 100, and Steve Golin, *The Newark Teacher Strikes: Hopes on the Line* (New Brunswick: Rutgers University Press, 2002), 123; as well as Woodard, 103, and Haskins, 160.

152. Rich, 94.

153. Anyon, chapters 5 and 6, as well as Rich, 100.

154. Rich, 98.

155. Mumford, 186.

156. Cunningham, 337, and Golin, 175.

157. Curvin, 173.

158. Haskins, 161.

159. Golin, chapter 5, and Haskins, 137–139.

160. Johnson, 65–85, 97–98, 121, 131.

161. Ibid., 147–154, and Curvin, 119.

162. Curvin, 113–121.

163. Ibid., 192.

164. Ibid., "The Persistent Minority," 227–228.

165. Cunningham, 341, and Mumford, 213.

166. Mumford, 178.

167. Cunningham, 340.

168. Mumford, 209.

169. Rod Bush, *We Are Not What We Seem: Black Nationalism and Class Struggle in the American Century* (New York: New York University Press, 1999), 211, and Mumford, 8.

170. Curvin, 124–127, and Cunningham, 344.

171. Johnson, 101.

172. Curvin, "The Persistent Minority," 131–133.

173. Rich, 104–111.

174. Georgia A. Persons, "From Insurgency to Deracialization: The Evolution of Black Mayoralities" in *Perspectives in Black Politics and Black Leadership*, ed. John Davis (Lanham: University Press of America, 2007), 89.

175. Johnson, 175. See also pages 176 and 177 where total assets and revenues are listed for downtown corporations like Prudential Life and PSE&G and several banks.

176. Brad Parks, "How the Good Will Inside a City Gave Way to Long Goodbyes," *Star-Ledger*, July 10, 2007. Richard Cammarieri, a Newark resident active in community development, noted these policy shortfalls.

177. Curvin, "The Persistent Minority," 185 and 187. See also Persons, 89.

178. Cunningham, 349; and Woodard, *A Nation within a Nation*, 252.

179. Rich, 116 and 117.

180. Persons, "From Insurgency to Deracialization," 89, and Rich, 116 and 117.

181. Georgia A. Persons, "Black Mayoralties and the New Black Politics: From Insurgency to Racial Reconciliation," in *Dilemmas of Black Politics: Issues of Leadership and Strategy*, ed. Georgia A. Persons (New York: Harper Collins, 1993), 59.

182. Andrew Jacobs, "A Mayor Is His Own Inspiration: James Trumpets His Record and Newark's Future," *New York Times*, April 25, 2005. See also Jeffrey Gold, "Newark Mayor Running on His Record Fifth Term," *Associated Press*, March 28, 2002.

183. Harold Lucas interview, November 14, 2012, with author.

184. Cunningham, chapters 29 and 30.

185. Sharpe James and Richard Monteilh, "Managing Metropolis," in *New Jersey Profiles in Public Policy*, ed. Silvio Laccetti (Palisades Park: Commonwealth Books, 1990), 134.

186. Ibid., 135.

187. Andrew Jacobs, "A Mayor Is His Own Inspiration: James Trumpets His Record and Newark's Future," *New York Times*, April 25, 2005. See also Cunningham, 378–379.

188. Cunningham, 331. Also Richard Cammarieri interview, December 3, 2012, with author.

189. Cunningham, 355.

190. "McGreevey Links Newark Mayor's Re-election to Arena Project," *Associated Press*, January 22, 2002. See also response from the governor in Richard Lezin Jones, "Arena and Vote Are Not Linked, Governor Says," *New York Times*, January 23, 2002.

191. Silvio Laccetti, *New Jersey Profiles in Public Policy* (Palisades Park: Commonwealth Books, 1990), 132.

192. Andrew Jacobs, "A Mayor Is His Own Inspiration: James Trumpets His Record and Newark's Future," *New York Times*, April 25, 2005.

193. Richard Cammarieri interview, December 3, 2012, with author.

194. Andrew Jacobs, "A Mayor Is His Own Inspiration: James Trumpets His Record and Newark's Future," *New York Times*, April 25, 2005. See also Cunningham, 388–389.

195. Harold Lucas interview, November 14, 2012, with author.

196. Anyon, 139.

197. Rich, 123.

198. Anyon, 144.

199. *Jersey Journal* editorial, "Needed: Informed Young Citizens," March 23, 2005. See also the survey by the New Jersey Center for Civic and Law-Related Education at Rutgers University.
200. Cunningham, 389–390.
201. Rich, 123.
202. Jeffrey Gold, "Newark Mayor Running on His Record Fifth Term," *Associated Press*, March 28, 2002.

Chapter 2

1. Andrew Jacobs, "A Political Neophyte in Newark Challenges a Shrewd Incumbent," *New York Times*, March 29, 2002.
2. Greg Sargent, "City's Power Chic Backs New Mayor—in Newark," *The New York Observer*, February 18, 2002, 1.
3. Andrew Jacobs, "Newark Race's Contrasts Extend to the Volunteers," *New York Times*, May 12, 2002.
4. Andrew Jacobs, "A Political Neophyte in Newark Challenges a Shrewd Incumbent," *New York Times*, March 29, 2002; and Matthew Purdy, "Our Towns: A New Tale of 2 Cities, But Both Are Newark," *New York Times*, May 15, 2002.
5. Paul H. Johnson, "Ex-Bergen Athlete Eyes Mayoralty in Newark," *The Record*, January 9, 2002. See also George Will, "NJ Mayoral Race Weighs Claims," *The Times Union*, March 17, 2002.
6. Richard Lezin Jones, "Race, Writ Large," *New York Times*, May 5, 2002; and Jonathan D. Tepperman, "Complicating the Race," *New York Times Magazine*, April 28, 2002, 69; as well as Andrew Jacobs, "A Fierce Race Leaves Deep Bruises in Newark," *New York Times*, May 20, 2002.
7. Paul H. Johnson, "Political Tale of Two Cities; Newark: James Survives Tough Challenge by Booker; 4-Term Veteran Boasted of Role in City's Recovery," *The Record*, May 15, 2002.
8. Jeffrey Gold, "Newark Mayor Running on His Record Fifth Term," *Associated Press*, March 28, 2002. See also Andrew Jacobs, "A Political Neophyte in Newark Challenges a Shrewd Incumbent," *New York Times*, March 29, 2002.
9. Paul H. Johnson, "Showdown in Newark: Mayor Faces Stiffest Competition in 16 Years," *The Record*, April 13, 2002. See also Paul H. Johnson, "James Back at Work; Booker Vows to Run Again; Newark Mayor Thinks Budget; Challenger Regroups for 2006," *The Record*, May 16, 2002.
10. Andrew Jacobs, "A Fierce Race Leaves Deep Bruises in Newark," *New York Times*, May 20, 2002. See also Richard Lezin Jones, "Newark Hasn't Heard the Last of Booker," *New York Times*, May 16, 2002.
11. *New York Times* editorial, "Cory Booker for Mayor," May 6, 2002.
12. Daniel Baer, "Cory Booker, Standard Bearer of the New Politics," *Christian Science Monitor*, May 16, 2002, 9. See also Paul H. Johnson, "Battle in Newark Nearing End: Mayoral Post Hotly Contested," *The Record*, May 12, 2002, 3; and Andrew Jacobs, "Newark Relives Day of Machine in Mayor's Race," *New York Times*, April 9, 2002.
13. John T. Cunningham, *Newark*, Third Edition (Newark: The New Jersey Historical Society, 2002), 389. See also Paul H. Johnson, "Ex-Bergen Athlete Eyes Mayoralty in Newark," *The Record*, January 9, 2002.

14. Jeffrey Gold, "Newark Mayor Running on His Record Fifth Term," *Associated Press*, March 28, 2002. See also Paul H. Johnson, "Showdown in Newark: Mayor Faces Stiffest Competition in 16 Years," *The Record*, April 13, 2002.

15. Andrew Jacobs, "A Political Neophyte in Newark Challenges a Shrewd Incumbent," *New York Times*, March 29, 2002.

16. Jonathan D. Tepperman, "Complicating the Race," *New York Times Magazine*, April 28, 2002, 69. See also Alexandria Marks, "New Game in Urban Politics," *Christian Science Monitor*, May 20, 2002.

17. Andrew Jacobs, "Youth, Money and Ambition Fuel Rival to Newark Mayor," *New York Times*, April 24, 2002.

18. Matthew Purdy, "A Mayor Runs on His Record (Well, Nowadays It's Called a CD)," *New York Times*, May 5, 2005.

19. Matthew Purdy, "Our Towns: A New Tale of 2 Cities, But Both Are Newark," *New York Times*, May 15, 2002. See also Jonathan D. Tepperman, "Complicating the Race," *New York Times Magazine*, April 28, 2002, 69.

20. Andrew Jacobs, "Youth, Money and Ambition Fuel Rival to Newark Mayor," *New York Times*, April 24, 2002. See also Jeffrey Gold, "Newark Mayor Running on His Record Fifth Term," *Associated Press*, March 28, 2002.

21. Alexandra Marks "New Game in Urban Politics," *Christian Science Monitor*, May 10, 2002.

22. Andrew Jacobs, "Youth, Money and Ambition Fuel Rival to Newark Mayor," *New York Times*, April 24, 2002. See also Matthew Purdy, "A Mayor Runs on His Record (Well, Nowadays It's Called a CD)," *New York Times*, May 5, 2005.

23. Paul H. Johnson, "James Getting a Run for His Money; Booker Is Raising Big Funds in Newark," *The Record*, May 10, 2002. See also Andrew Jacobs, "A Political Neophyte in Newark Challenges a Shrewd Incumbent," *New York Times*, March 29, 2002.

24. Matthew Purdy, "A Mayor Runs on His Record (Well, Nowadays It's Called a CD)," *New York Times*, May 5, 2005.

25. Andrew Jacobs, "Newark Race's Contrasts Extend to the Volunteers," *New York Times*, May 12, 2002. See also S. Craig Watkins, *Hip Hop Matters: Politics, Pop Culture, and the Struggle for the Soul of a Movement* (Boston: Beacon Press, 2005), 195.

26. Jonathan D. Tepperman, "Complicating the Race," *New York Times Magazine*, April 28, 2002, 69.

27. Andrew Jacobs, "Youth, Money and Ambition Fuel Rival to Newark Mayor," *New York Times*, April 24, 2002.

28. Matthew Purdy, "A Mayor Runs on His Record (Well, Nowadays It's Called a CD)," *New York Times*, May 5, 2005.

29. Paul H. Johnson, "Battle in Newark Nearing End," *The Record*, May 12, 2002.

30. Andrew Jacobs, "Vitriol of Newark Campaign Steeps into Debate," *New York Times*, May 9, 2002. See also Andrew Jacobs, "A Fierce Race Leaves Deep Bruises in Newark," *New York Times*, May 20, 2002; Watkins, 193.

31. Andrew Jacobs, "A Political Neophyte in Newark Challenges a Shrewd Incumbent," *New York Times*, March 29, 2002. See also Paul H. Johnson, "Ex-Bergen Athlete Eyes Mayoralty in Newark," *The Record*, January 9, 2002.

32. Jeffrey Gold, "Newark Mayoral Race Spotlighted After Years in the Shadows," *Associated Press*, May 11, 2002; Richard Lezin Jones, "Race, Writ Large," *New York Times*, May 5, 2002.

33. Andrew Jacobs, "Newark Relives Day of Machine in Mayor's Race," *New York Times,* April 9, 2002. See also Andrew Jacobs, "In Newark, a Rainy Day Ends a Stormy Campaign," *New York Times,* May 14, 2002. See also Amy Westfeldt, "Harassment Charges Fly Early in Bitter Newark Mayor's Race," *Associated Press,* May 14, 2002.

34. Paul H. Johnson, "Showdown in Newark: Mayor Faces Stiffest Competition in 16 Years," *The Record,* April 13, 2002; Watkins, 193–194.

35. Paul H. Johnson, "Showdown in Newark: Mayor Faces Stiffest Competition in 16 Years," *The Record,* April 13, 2002.

36. Andrew Jacobs, "Youth, Money and Ambition Fuel Rival to Newark Mayor," *New York Times,* April 24, 2002; Paul H. Johnson, "Ex-Bergen Athlete Eyes Mayoralty in Newark," *The Record,* January 9, 2002.

37. "Records Show Newark Mayor With Holdings Outside City," *Associated Press,* April 18, 2002.

38. Paul H. Johnson, "Political Tale of Two Cities; Newark: James Survives Tough Challenge by Booker; 4-Term Veteran Boasted of Role in City's Recovery," *The Record,* May 15, 2002. See also Matthew Purdy, "A Mayor Runs on His Record (Well, Nowadays It's Called a CD)," *New York Times,* May 5, 2005; Andrew Jacobs, "In Newark, a Rainy Day Ends a Stormy Campaign," *New York Times,* May 14, 2002.

39. Andrew Jacobs, "Youth, Money and Ambition Fuel Rival to Newark Mayor," *New York Times,* April 24, 2002.

40. Andrew Jacobs, "Opponent Says Newark Is Using City Funds for Ads," *New York Times,* February 23, 2002.

41. Greg Sergent, "City's Power Chic Backs New Mayor—in Newark," *The New York Observer,* February 18, 2002, 1.

42. George Will, "NJ Mayoral Race Weighs Claims," *The Times Union,* March 17, 2002; Jonathan D. Tepperman, "Complicating the Race," *New York Times Magazine,* April 28, 2002, 69.

43. Georgia A. Persons, "From Insurgency to Deracialization: The Evolution of Black Mayoralities," in *Perspectives in Black Politics and Black,* ed. John Davis (Lanham: University Press of America, 2007), 89.

44. Ted Sherman and Kimberly Brown, "In a Divided Vote, James Played to His Strength," *Star-Ledger,* May 16, 2002. See also Andrew Jacobs, "In Newark, Newcomer's Allure Can't Topple Local Favorite," *New York Times,* May 15, 2002.

45. Richard Lezin Jones, "The Newark Election: News Analysis; As Civil Rights Battles Recede, Generational Fights Replace Them," *New York Times,* May 15, 2002.

46. Matthew Purdy, "Our Towns: A New Tale of 2 Cities, But Both Are Newark," *New York Times,* May 15, 2002.

47. Andrew Jacobs, "Newark Race's Contrasts Extend to the Volunteers," *New York Times,* May 12, 2002.

48. Richard Lezin Jones, "The Newark Election: News Analysis; As Civil Rights Battles Recede, Generational Fights Replace Them," *New York Times,* May 15, 2002. See also Andrew Jacobs, "Newark's Competing Visions of Itself: Reborn or Struggling? Each Review Is Reflected by a Mayoral Candidate," *New York Times,* May 10, 2002.

49. Andrew Jacobs, "Youth, Money and Ambition Fuel Rival to Newark Mayor," *New York Times,* April 24, 2002.

50. Watkins, 194.

51. Amy Westfeldt, "Sharpe James Re-elected in Close Race After Nasty Campaign," *Associated Press*, May 14, 2002. See also Andrew Jacobs, "The Newark Election: Overview; James Wins 5th Term in Newark as Challenger Is Rebuffed," *New York Times*, May 15, 2002.

52. Jeffrey C. Mays and Nikita Stewart, "Candidates in Newark Ask Who's Authentic," *Star Ledger*, April 7, 2002.

53. Jonathan D. Tepperman, "Complicating the Race," *New York Times Magazine*, April 28, 2002, 69.

54. Andrew Jacobs, "The Newark Election: Overview; James Wins 5th Term in Newark as Challenger Is Rebuffed," *New York Times*, May 15, 2002.

55. Watkins, 195.

56. Richard Lezin Jones, "Race, Writ Large," *New York Times*, May 5, 2002.

57. Cory Booker interview, April 5, 2013, with author.

58. Matthew Futterman and Jeffery Mays, "Newark Devils Are Still Apart on Arena," *Star-Ledger*, January 10, 2006. See also "Cash Crisis Puts Arena on Thin Ice in Newark," by the same authors, *Star-Ledger*, January 12, 2006; and "Devils Barely Beat Newark Deadline," *Star-Ledger*, January 25, 2006.

59. Jeffery Mays, "Newark's Mayor Walks and Talks Like He's Running for 6th Term," *Star-Ledger*, January 4, 2006.

60. Tom Moran, "Round Two: Booker Jabs, but James Stays Low," *Star-Ledger*, February 15, 2006.

61. I attended the speech, and, throughout it, James acted as though he wanted to continue the city's "renaissance" urging audience members to respond to his question: "Is Newark better off now than in 1986?" when James was first elected. See also Joan Whitlow, "The Mayor Boasts Like a Man in the Race," *Star-Ledger*, February 14, 2006.

62. Jeffery Mays, "Could Change Be Coming Newark?" *Star-Ledger*, March 5, 2006. See also Jonathan Casiano, "Petitions in, Rice Running for Mayor in Newark," *Star-Ledger*, March 5, 2006.

63. Katie Wang and Jeffery Mays, "James a Mystery as Filing Deadline Nears," *Star-Ledger*, March 16, 2006. See also Jeffery Mays and Katie Wang, "The Guy on the Bike? Seems to be a Candidate," *Star-Ledger*, March 17, 2006; Damien Cave, "Mayor Is Vague, but 10,000 Signatures Say He's Running Again," *New York Times*, March 17, 2006.

64. *Star-Ledger*, "Big Wheel Keeps on Turning," March 17, 2006.

65. Katie Wang, "James' Deputy Staying in Mayoral Race Against Boss," *Star-Ledger*, March 18, 2006.

66. Damien Cave, "All but on the Ballot in Newark, but Not Yet on the Stump," *New York Times*, March 19, 2006. See also Jeffery Mays and Brad Parks, "This Mayoral Race Will be Shorter and Sweeter," *Star-Ledger*, March 19, 2006.

67. Joan Whitlow, "The Mayor Is Drawing on His Future," *Star-Ledger*, March 24, 2006.

68. Jeffery Mays, "Routine Newark Ballot Drawing: No-Show James and Defamation Suit," *Star-Ledger*, March 25, 2006.

69. Jeffery Mays, "Sharpe Drops Out," *Star-Ledger*, March 28, 2006.

70. Joan Whitlow, "Hard to Get Nostalgic Over Sharpe," *Star-Ledger*, March 28, 2006.

71. Jeffery Mays, "Sharpe Drops Out," *Star-Ledger*, March 28, 2006.

72. Clement Alexander Price, "James' Legacy: A Proud Newark," *Star-Ledger*, April 2, 2006. "James held Newark in a tight personal embrace over the last 20 years," says Price.

73. Josh Benson, "Newark Is Up for Grabs," *New York Times*, May 7, 2006. "Mr. James's decision not to run this year, widely considered to be an acknowledgment of Mr. Booker's political strength, has created a political vacuum."

74. Damien Cave, "For First Time in 20 Years, Newark Looks to a Future Without Sharpe James as Mayor," *New York Times*, March 29, 2006.

75. Jeffery Mays, "Newark's Mighty Machine Is Left Leaderless," *Star-Ledger*, March 29, 2006.

76. Ibid.

77. Josh Benson, "The Challenger Is Now the Favorite, and He Has the War Chest to Prove It," *New York Times*, March 28, 2006. See also Katie Wang, "Booker Resists Counting Chickens," *Star-Ledger*, March 28, 2006.

78. Brad Parks and Katie Wang, "With James Out, Rice Picking Up Where He Left Off," *Star-Ledger*, March 29, 2006.

79. Damien Cave and Josh Benson, "In Newark, Candidate Takes Cues from Mayor," *New York Times*, April 1, 2006.

80. Jonathan Schuppe, "Booker Leading Rice by 43 Points," *Star-Ledger*, April 2, 2006.

81. Jeffery Mays, "Rice Isn't Familiar to Most Voters," *Star-Ledger*, April 4, 2006.

82. Katie Wang, "Rice Makes It Official," *Star-Ledger*, April 9, 2006.

83. Damien Cave and Josh Benson, "Voucher Issue a Touchy Topic in Newark Race," *New York Times*, April 16, 2006.

84. Joan Whitlow, "'Guns and Hoses' and Election Poses," *Star-Ledger*, April 12, 2006.

85. *Star-Ledger* editorial, "Same as the Old Boss?," April 12, 2006.

86. William Jacoby, "Core Values and Political Attitudes," in *Understanding Public Opinion*, Second Edition, ed. Clyde Wilcox and Barbara Norrander (Washington: CQ Press, 2001).

87. Andrew Jacobs, "Newark Relives Day of Machine in Mayor's Race," *New York Times*, April 9, 2002.

88. Andrew Jacobs, "Newark Relives Day of Machine in Mayor's Race," *New York Times*, April 9, 2002. See also Nikita Stewart and Jeffery C. Mays, "Black Firefighters Give Boost to James," *Star-Ledger*, April 23, 2002.

89. Andrew Jacobs, "Newark Relives Day of Machine in Mayor's Race," *New York Times*, April 9, 2002.

90. Nikita Stewart and Jeffery C. Mays, "Firefighters Union Stands Alone with Booker," *Star-Ledger*, April 19, 2002.

91. Damien Cave and Josh Benson, "Voucher Issue a Touchy Topic in Newark Race," *New York Times*, April 16, 2006.

92. Brad Parks, "Why Newark Matters," *Star-Ledger*, April 16, 2006. See also Brad Parks and Jeffery Mays, "Man vs. Machine: Would Booker Become James?" *Star-Ledger*, April 14, 2006.

93. Ibid.

94. Michael Patracuolla, "Newark Can't Blame Benefactors," *Star-Ledger*, letter-to-the-editor, April 20, 2006.

95. Steve Strunsky, "In Newark, a Rail Line Downtown Is Viewed as Crucial," *New York Times*, April 16, 2006.

96. Ian Shearn, "Rivals Differ Sharply on Newark's Development," *Star-Ledger*, April 17, 2006.

97. Katie Wang and Jeffery Mays, "College Brings Back James for Two Posts," *Star-Ledger*, April 20, 2006.

98. Jeffery Mays, "James Eyed to Head Up Urban Issues Institute," *Star-Ledger*, April 18, 2006.

99. Jeffery Mays, "James Accuses N.J. of Meddling with $80 Million Newark Windfall," *Star-Ledger*, April 22, 2006.

100. Damien Cave and Josh Benson, "Newark Is Ordered to Freeze Private Funds Linked to Departing Mayor," *New York Times*, April 21, 2006. See also Damien Cove, "Newark Mayor Rebukes State in Fund Dispute," *New York Times*, April 22, 2006.

101. *New York Times* editorial, "Newark's Deep Freeze," April 30, 2006.

102. David Chen, "Corzine and James Face Off Over Newark Fund Dispute," *New York Times*, April 27, 2006.

103. Joan Whitlow, "Newark Is Unconvincing in Victim Role," *Star-Ledger*, April 28, 2006. See also Jonathan Casiano, "Newark, State Go to Mat About City's Intent for Funding," *Star-Ledger*, April 27, 2006; and Tom Moran, "A Serious Accusation, Made Cheap in Newark," *Star-Ledger*, April 28, 2006.

104. Jonathan Schuppe, "Mayor Sounds Off on Benefit for Booker," *Star-Ledger*, April 18, 2006.

105. Katie Wang, "Booker Criticizes City Sale of Properties," *Star-Ledger*, April 19, 2006.

106. Damien Cave, "Booker Says Newark Mayor Is 'Giving Away Our Land,'" *New York Times*, April 19, 2006.

107. Katie Wang, "Booker Criticizes City Sale of Properties," *Star-Ledger*, April 19, 2006.

108. Damien Cave, "Booker Says Newark Mayor Is 'Giving Away Our Land,'" *New York Times*, April 19, 2006.

109. Ibid.

110. Katie Wang, "Booker Criticizes City Sale of Properties," *Star-Ledger*, April 19, 2006.

111. Damien Cave and Josh Benson, "Newark Mayoral Candidate Tries to Escape Shadows," *New York Times*, May 5, 2006; Josh Benson, "Newark Is Up for Grabs," New York Times, May 7, 2006; and Damien Cave, "Booker Says Newark Mayor Is 'Giving Away Our Land,'" *New York Times*, April 19, 2006.

112. Josh Benson, "Who Is Ronald Rice Anyway?" *New York Times*, April 23, 2006.

113. Damien Cave and Josh Benson, "Newark Mayoral Candidate Tries to Escape Shadows," *Star-Ledger*, May 5, 2006.

114. Joan Whitlow, "Rice Running Late, Maybe a Dozen Years," *Star-Ledger*, March 21, 2006.

115. Josh Benson, "Who Is Ronald Rice Anyway?" *New York Times*, April 23, 2006.

116. Brad Parks and Jeffery Mays, "For Would-be Mayor, the Mission of a Lifetime," *Star-Ledger*, April 23, 2006.

117. Joan Whitlow, "Rice Running Late, Maybe a Dozen Years," *Star-Ledger*, March 21, 2006.

118. Brad Parks and Jeffery Mays, "For Would-be Mayor, the Mission of a Lifetime," *Star-Ledger*, April 23, 2006.

119. Josh Benson, "Who Is Ronald Rice Anyway?" *New York Times*, April 23, 2006.

120. *Star-Ledger* editorial, "Cory Booker for Newark Mayor," April 30, 2006.

121. *New York Times* editorial, "Cory Booker for Mayor," April 23, 2006.

122. Brad Parks, "Newark and Former Inmates' Future Tied," *Star-Ledger*, May 7, 2006.

123. Jonathan Schuppe, "Booker, Rice Vow to Make Newark Safer," *Star-Ledger*, April 21, 2006.

124. Kasi Addison, "Newark Candidates Differ on Schools," *Star-Ledger*, April 27, 2006.

125. Jean Anyon and Alan Sadovnik, "Beyond Newark's School Yard," *New York Times* Op-Ed, April 23, 2006.

126. Jeffery Mays and Brad Parks, "Tenants Want a Mayor Who'll Clean up Mess," *Star-Ledger*, April 25, 2006.

127. Katie Wang, "Unsung Newark Candidate Urges Workers' Rights," Star-Ledger, May 2, 2006; and Jeffery Mays, "A Newark Upstart Eyes an Upset," *Star-Ledger*, May 3, 2006.

128. Katie Wang, "Candidates Get 60 Minutes on Issues," *Star-Ledger*, May 3, 2006. Also, May 2, 2006, Newark Student Voices Forum, Rutgers University-Newark; and Katie Wang and Brad Parks, "'Debate' in Newark Draws Criticism from Rice Rivals," *Star-Ledger*, April 26, 2006.

129. *Star-Ledger*, "Reflections on a Changing of the Guard in Newark," May 7, 2006.

130. Jeffery Mays and Brad Parks, "Mayoral Hopefuls Face Off on TV," *Star-Ledger*, May 4, 2006.

131. Damien Cave, "In a Debate of Newark Candidates, Some Agreement and a Lot of Discord," *New York Times*, May 4, 2006.

132. Brad Parks, "Rice Calls for Election Monitoring," *Star-Ledger*, April 28, 2006.

133. Tom Moran, "Reflections of Booker in Yesterday's Rising Star," *Star-Ledger*, May 5, 2006.

134. Jeffery Mays and Katie Wang, "In Newark Race, the Mud Flies," *Star-Ledger*, May 5, 2006.

135. Ibid.

136. Katie Wang, "'Outsider' Booker Slowly Makes Way into Newark," *Star-Ledger*, April 30, 2006.

137. Cory Booker interview, April 5, 2013, with author.

138. Damien Cave and Josh Benson, "In Newark, Booker Runs Against His Own Fame," *New York Times*, May 4, 2006.

139. Jeffery Mays and Katie Wang, "Booker and Rice's Stunted Campaign Enters Its Final Leg," *Star-Ledger*, May 9, 2006.

140. Brad Parks, "Rice Calls for Election Monitoring," *Star-Ledger*, April 28, 2006.

141. Damien Cave and Josh Benson, "Booker's Race Takes on Air of Coronation," *New York Times*, May 8, 2006.

142. Josh Benson, "Newark Is Up for Grabs," *New York Times*, May 7, 2006.

143. Surveyors were Ed Aguilar, David Byrne, Ray Kirchhoff, Danny Kwok, Chris Lin, Jon Matos, Patrick Nolan, Vidya Rao, Ami Shah, Ricardo Slatter, Greg St. Louis, Ryan Telford, James Watkins, Jonathan Wharton, Devon Williams, William Young, and Xiaoxu Zhao. Many also assisted with Excel and SPSS entry including Ryan Bennick, Matt Gray, Eddie Kastrat, Murat Kocak, Manny Marasigan, and Manny Rios.

144. Ted Sherman and Kimberly Brown, "Mayor Triumphant: In a Divided Vote, James Played to His Strength," *Star-Ledger*, May 16, 2002.

145. Damien Cave, "In Victory Laps, Booker Greets Newark's Hopeful and Doubtful," *New York Times*, May 11, 2006.

146. Jeffery Mays, "Booker Sees Success for Himself and the City," *Star-Ledger*, April 28, 2002.

147. *Star-Ledger* editorial, "Cory Booker for Mayor," May 5, 2002. See also *Street Fight* for the "golden boy" comment made by one Black Newarker.

148. Ted Sherman, "Newark Mayor's Race Is Run in Political Arenas in and Outside City," *Star-Ledger*, March 21, 2002.

149. George Jordan, "Booker Blasts James on City's Development," *Star-Ledger*, April 30, 2002.

150. Jonathan D. Tepperman, "Complicating the Race," *New York Times Magazine*, April 28, 2002.

151. *Street Fight.*

152. Matthew Purdy, "Our Towns: A New Tale of 2 Cities, But Both Are Newark," *New York Times*, May 15, 2002. See also *Street Fight.*

153. Damien Cave and Josh Benson, "In Newark, Candidate Takes Cues from Mayor," *New York Times*, April 1, 2006.

154. Cory Booker interview, April 5, 2013, with author.

155. Tom Moran, "Reflections of Booker in Yesterday's Rising Star," *Star-Ledger*, May 5, 2006.

156. Damien Cave and Josh Benson, "In Newark, Booker Runs Against His Own Fame," *New York Times*, May 4, 2006.

157. Cory Booker interview, April 5, 2013, with author.

158. Katie Wang, "'Outsider' Booker Slowly Makes Way into Newark," *Star-Ledger*, April 30, 2006.

Chapter 3

1. Jeffery Mays and Katie Wang, "The Guy on the Bike? Seems to Be a Candidate," *Star-Ledger*, March 17, 2006. See also James' State of the City address, February 22, 2006 and James' resignation letter, March 28, 2006.

2. John T. Cunningham. *Newark*, Third Edition (Newark: The New Jersey Historical Society, 2002), chapter 31.

3. Jeffery Mays, "An Often-Troubled City Loses a Leader of Endless Spirit," *Star-Ledger*, March 28, 2006.

4. Damien Cave, "After 5 Terms as Newark Mayor, James Opts Not to Run Again," *New York Times*, March 28, 2006.

5. Cunningham, 371.

6. Marshall Curry, director and producer, *Street Fight* documentary, 2003.

7. Jeffery Mays, "Booker to Ban Gifts from City Contractors," *Star-Ledger*, February 8, 2007. I also attended the State of the City address in 2006 and, admittedly, James' speeches were stirring and memorable.

8. S. Craig Watkins, *Hip Hop Matters: Politics, Pop Culture, and the Struggle for the Soul of a Movement* (Boston: Beacon Press, 2005), 194.

9. David Kocieniewki, "Jury Selection Starts in Corruption Trial of Mayor Who Ran Newark for 20 Years," *New York Times*, February 27, 2008.

10. Luis Quintana interview, February 6, 2013, with author.

11. Tom Moran, "A Serious Accusation, Made Cheap in Newark," *Star-Ledger*, April 28, 2006.

12. Joan Whitlow, "Newark Is Unconvincing in Victim Role," *Star-Ledger*, April 28, 2006.
13. Tom Moran, "A Serious Accusation, Made Cheap in Newark," *Star-Ledger*, April 28, 2006.
14. Jonathan Casiano, "Newark, State Go to Mat About City's Intent for Funding," *Star-Ledger*, April 27, 2006.
15. Jeffery C. Mays and Nikita Stewart, "Candidates in Newark Ask Who's Authentic," *Star-Ledger*, April 7, 2002.
16. Jonathan D. Tepperman, "Complicating the Race," *New York Times Magazine*, April 28, 2002.
17. Jeffery Mays, "An Often-Troubled City Loses a Leader of Endless Spirit," *Star-Ledger*, March 28, 2006.
18. Jonathan D. Tepperman, "Complicating the Race," *New York Times Magazine*, April 28, 2002.
19. Paul H. Johnson, "Showdown in Newark: Mayor Faces Stiffest Competition in 16 Years," *New York Times*, April 13, 2002.
20. *Street Fight*. See also Andrew Jacobs, "Vitriol of Newark Campaign Steeps into Debate," *New York Times*, May 9, 2002.
21. Andrew Jacobs, "A Political Neophyte in Newark Challenges a Shrewd Incumbent," *New York Times*, March 29, 2002. See also Andrew Jacobs, "A Fierce Race Leaves Deep Bruises in Newark," *New York Times*, March 20, 2002.
22. Jeffery C. Mays and Nikita Stewart, "Candidates in Newark Ask Who's Authentic," *Star-Ledger*, April 7, 2002.
23. Andrew Jacobs, "A Fierce Race Leaves Deep Bruises in Newark," *New York Times*, March 20, 2002. See also Jonathan D. Tepperman, "Complicating the Race," *New York Times Magazine*, April 28, 2002.
24. Paul H. Johnson, "James Getting a Run for His Money; Booker Is Raising Big Funds in Newark," *The Record*, May 10, 2002.
25. Matthew Purdy, "A Mayor Runs on His Record (Well, Nowadays It's Called a CD)," *New York Times*, May 5, 2002.
26. David Chen and Nate Schweber, "For James's Companion, Real Estate Proved Very Lucrative in a Hurry," *New York Times*, July 14, 2007. See also Mark Mueller and Kate Coscarelli, "Sweetheart Deals for Mayor's Friend Are Key to Charges," *Star-Ledger*, July 13, 2007; and John P. Martin and Ian T. Shearn, "James Indicted on 25 Counts," *Star-Ledger*, July 13, 2007.
27. Jeffery Mays, "An Often-Troubled City Loses a Leader of Endless Spirit," *Star-Ledger*, March 28, 2006. See also Matthew Purdy, "A Mayor Runs on His Record (Well, Nowadays It's Called a CD)," *New York Times*, May 5, 2002; and Jonathan D. Tepperman, "Complicating the Race," *New York Times Magazine*, April 28, 2002.
28. Ian T. Shearn, "Dirt-Cheap Land Deals in Newark: New Details," *Star-Ledger*, December 4, 2006; and Jeffery Mayes and Katie Wang, "Judge Suspends Bargain Sales of Newark's Land," *Star-Ledger*, June 1, 2006.
29. Ian T. Shearn, "Dirt-Cheap Land Deals in Newark: New Details," *Star-Ledger*, December 4, 2006; and Ian T. Shearn, "Newark Official Involved in Land Deals Resigns," *Star-Ledger*, February 6, 2007.

30. Ian T. Shearn and John P. Martin, "New Player in Newark Land Deals," *Star-Ledger*, January 14, 2007. See also David Kocieniewski, "Inquiry into Ex-Mayor of Newark Turns to Cheap Sales of City Land," *New York Times*, January 15, 2007.

31. Joan Whitlow, "Sharpe Isn't Showing His Cards," *Star-Ledger*, August 23, 2006. See also Tina Kelley, "Booker Praises Freeze on No-Bid Sales of Newark Property," *New York Times*, June 1, 2006.

32. Ian T. Shearn and Jeffery Mays, "From A.C. to Rio, City Picked Up James' Tab," *Star-Ledger*, August 20, 2006. See also Richard G. Jones, "Federal and State Investigators Seek Credit Card Records of Newark's Ex-Mayor," *New York Times*, August 22, 2006; and Ian T. Shearn, "2 Probes Launched into James' Travel Fund," *Star-Ledger*, August 22, 2006.

33. Ian T. Shearn and John P. Martin, "Feds' Probe of James Now Takes Close Look at Newark Land Deals," *Star-Ledger*, November 28, 2006.

34. Ian T. Shearn, "Absent Computers Sought in Widening James Probe," *Star-Ledger*, December 23, 2006.

35. Ronald Smothers, "With Usual Flourish, Sharpe James Pulls Curtain on a Career and an Era in Newark," *New York Times*, April 11, 2007; and Ian T. Shearn, "Two Testify in Corruption Probe," *Star-Ledger*, June 29, 2007.

36. The Associated Press, "Grand Jury Indicts Former Newark Mayor," *New York Times*, July 13, 2007. See also John P. Martin and Ian T. Shearn, "James Indicted on 25 Counts," *Star-Ledger*, July 13, 2007.

37. David Kocieniewski, "Former Mayor of Newark Is Indicted," *New York Times*, July 13, 2007. See also John P. Martin and Ian T. Shearn, "James Indicted on 25 Counts," *Star-Ledger*, July 13, 2007.

38. Jeffery C. Mays, "Some Call July 12th a Bad Day for the City," *Star-Ledger*, July 13, 2007; and Katie Wang and Peter Filichia, "An Indicted James Hits 'Campaign' Trail to Trumpet Innocence," *Star-Ledger*, July 14, 2007.

39. Bob Braun, "The Right Man for James Trial," *Star-Ledger*, March 16, 2008.

40. David Kocieniewki, "Jury Selection Starts in Corruption Trial of Mayor Who Ran Newark for 20 Years," *New York Times*, February 27, 2008.

41. Richard G. Jones, "Affair Is Cited at Fraud Trial of Ex-Mayor of Newark," *New York Times*, March 4, 2008. See also John P. Martin and Jeff Whelan, "James' Corruption Trial Under Way," *Star-Ledger*, March 4, 2008.

42. John P. Martin and Jeff Whelan, "James' Corruption Trial Under Way," *Star-Ledger*, March 4, 2008.

43. Jeff Whelan and Maryann Spoto, "James' Secretary Tells of Girlfriend's Access," *Star-Ledger*, March 5, 2008.

44. Jeff Whelan and Maryann Spoto, "Graft Trial Focuses on James Memo," *Star-Ledger*, March 6, 2008.

45. John O. Martin and Jeff Whelan, "Ex-Aide: James Pushed Riley Deal," *Star-Ledger*, March 8, 2008. See also Bob Braun, "Sharpe James' Newark: No City for Little Guys," *Star-Ledger*, March 9, 2008; and Peter Applebome, "Scenes from Newark's City Hall, Replayed in Federal Court," *New York Times*, March 9, 2008.

46. Ted Sherman and Jeff Whelan, "Prosecutors Attack Their 'Turncoat' Witness," *Star-Ledger*, March 12, 2008.

47. Maryann Spoto and Jeff Whelan, "Former Newark Aide Says Her Boss Bowed to James' Wish," *Star-Ledger*, March 13, 2008.

48. Maryan Spoto and Jeff Whelan, "Riley Said to Have an 'Inside Track' on City Properties," *Star-Ledger*, March 15, 2008.

49. Jeff Whelan and Maryann Spoto, "James' Friend: Mayor Oversaw City Land Sales," *Star-Ledger*, March 19, 2008.

50. Jeff Whelan and Maryann Spoto, "Official: Riley Got Housing Subsidies," *Star-Ledger*, March 21, 2008.

51. Richard G. Jones, "Defense Takes Its Turn in Former Mayor's Trial," *New York Times*, April 2, 2008.

52. Richard G. Jones, "Former Mayor Guilty of Fraud in Newark Sales," *Star-Ledger*, April 17, 2008.

53. Kareem Fahim, "Ex-Mayor of Newark Is Spared a 2nd Trial," *New York Times*, May 13, 2008.

54. *New York Times* editorial, "Leniency Pleas for Ex-Mayor Are a Last Hurrah in Letters," July 30, 2008.

55. Alan Feuer and Nate Schweber, "Former Newark Mayor Is Sentenced to 27 Months," *New York Times*, July 30, 2008. See also Peter Applebombe, "Our Towns: In Newark, More Weariness Than Anger at Sentence," *New York Times*, July 31, 2008; Bob Braun, "A Judge Who Chaffed at the Advice He Got," *Star-Ledger*, July 30, 2008; and *Star-Ledger* editorial, "The Harm James Did His City," July 30, 2008.

56. Jeff Whelan and John P. Martin, "The James Sentence Shows Shift in Judiciary," *Star-Ledger*, July 31, 2008; and Joan Whitlow, "Corruption Isn't a Victimless Crime, Judge," *Star-Ledger*, August 1, 2008.

57. Joe Ryan, "Sharpe James' Lawyer Asks Appeals Panel to Throw Out Conviction," *Star-Ledger*, June 20, 2009.

58. Jeff Whelan, "James Takes a Step to Appeal Conviction," *Star-Ledger*, August 12, 2008. See also Jeff Whelan, "James Hires New Attorney for Appeal," *Star-Ledger*, August 20, 2008.

59. Jason Grant, "U.S. Attorney Says Juror in Sharpe James Fraud Trial Did Not Attempt to Mislead Court," *Star-Ledger*, May 13, 2011.

60. David Giambusso, "James' Bid for New Trial Rejected by Federal Judge," *Star-Ledger*, October 26, 2011.

61. Richard Perez-Peña, "Ex-Newark Mayor Is Accused of Misusing Campaign Funds," *New York Times*, May 26, 2011. See also David Giambusso, "Ex-Newark Mayor Sharpe James Accused of Using Nearly $100,000 in Campaign Funds for Legal Defense," *Star-Ledger*, June 1, 2011.

62. Matt Friedman, "Ex-Politicians Wield Clout with Their Coffers," *Star-Ledger*, May 13, 2012.

63. David Giambusso, "Ex-Newark Mayor Sharpe James Now Part of Group Looking to Reform City's Politics," *Star-Ledger*, November 15, 2010.

64. Mildred Crump interview, January 28, 2013, with author.

65. Kevin Mumford, *Newark: A History of Race, Rights, and Riots in America* (New York: New York University Press, 2007), 219.

66. Damien Cave and Josh Benson, "Voucher Issue a Touchy Topic in Newark Race," *New York Times*, April 16, 2006.

67. Mumford, 220.

68. *Street Fight.*
69. Mumford, 219.
70. Jonathan D. Tepperman, "Complicating the Race," *New York Times Magazine*, April 28, 2002, 69.
71. Mumford, 221.
72. Jonathan D. Tepperman, "Complicating the Race," *New York Times Magazine*, April 28, 2002, 69.
73. Brad Parks, "The Hard-won Grounds for Hope," *Star-Ledger*, July 11, 2007.
74. Andrew Jacobs, "A Mayor Is His Own Inspiration," *New York Times*, April 25, 2002.
75. *Star-Ledger* editorial, "Cory Booker for Mayor," May 5, 2002.
76. Damien Cave and Josh Benson, "Newark Mayoral Candidate," *New York Times*, May 5, 2006.
77. Mumford, 220.
78. Cory Booker, "Why Have I Lost Control," *The Stanford Daily*, reprinted from May 6, 1992, on January 24, 2013. See also Janelle Griffith, "A Younger Booker Worried His Race Would Overshadow His Achievements," *Star-Ledger*, January 24, 2013.
79. Ted Sherman, "Cory Booker Wrote About His Homophobic Past While Attending Stanford," *Star-Ledger*, January 10, 2013.
80. Jacob Weisberg, "Local Hero: Cory Booker," *Vogue*, January 2013.
81. Mumford, 219.
82. Tom Moran, "Booker Views a Landscape Even More Bleak Than He Thought," *Star-Ledger*, June 11, 2006.
83. *Street Fight.* See also Jessica Durando, "There's a Lot to Learn from Newark," *Star-Ledger*, July 11, 2007. When South Africans visited City Hall, Booker said that "what goes on in South Africa actually goes on here. Our struggles are your struggles are our struggles." Also Cory Booker interview, April 5, 2013, with author
84. Mumford, 221.
85. Jeffery C. Mays and Katie Wang, "For Booker, Often-told Tales Turn into Trouble," *Star-Ledger*, August 6, 2007.
86. Mumford, 220. See also *Street Fight.*
87. Cory Booker interview, April 5, 2013, with author. Booker states that coalitions are no longer based on race but on issues. "But it's not … a convention like the Black and Puerto Rican Convention [of the 1970s] where it's about the disadvantaged minority. Then, you had an Italian machine that excluded opportunity. They wouldn't let Black and White police officers even ride in the same car. Those are understandably people rallying around racial empowerment."
88. Cory Booker interview, April 5, 2013, with author.
89. Cory Booker interview, April 5, 2013, with author.
90. *Street Fight.*
91. Luis Quintana interview, February 6, 2013, with author.
92. Jeffery C. Mays and Katie Wang, "For Booker, Often-told Tales Turn into Trouble," *Star-Ledger*, August 6, 2007.
93. Ibid.
94. Ibid.
95. Ibid.
96. Ibid.
97. Ibid.

98. Jeffery C. Mays, "Newark Gets $2M Federal Grant for Prisoner Re-Entry Programs," *Star-Ledger*, September 10, 2008.

99. Tom Moran, "Booker Redirects His Anger at the War on Drugs," *Star-Ledger*, June 24, 2007.

100. Cory Booker interview, April 5, 2013, with author.

101. *Star-Ledger* editorial, "Let Newark Remember the Past and Rise Above It," July 8, 2007.

102. Mumford, 221.

103. Mildred Crump interview, January 28, 2013, with author.

104. Andrew Jacobs, "Newark's Mayor Battles Old Guard and Rumors," *New York Times*, July 3, 2007.

105. *Revolution '67* film forum, Newark Museum, June 27, 2007.

106. Andrew Jacobs, "Newark's Mayor Battles Old Guard and Rumors," *New York Times*, July 3, 2007.

107. Ibid.

108. Cory Booker interview, April 5, 2013, with author.

109. Ibid.

110. Jonathan Schuppe, "Sad Twist as Newark Talks Jobs for Ex-Cons," *Star-Ledger*, March 15, 2007; and Jonathan Schuppe, "City Aims to Break Cycle for Ex-Cons," *Star-Ledger*, May 2, 2007. See also Tom Moran, "Booker Redirects His Anger at the War on Drugs," *Star-Ledger*, June 24, 2007.

111. Katie Wang and Jeffery Mays, "Booker, Taking Oath, Urges City Onward," *Star-Ledger*, July 2, 2006.

112. Cory Booker interview, April 5, 2012, with author.

113. Richard Cammarieri interview, December 3, 2012, with author.

114. Jeffery C. Mays and Katie Wang, "Newark Voters Back Booker's Council Choices," *Star-Ledger*, June 14, 2006.

115. Joan Whitlow, "Questions About the City Where I (at least) Live," *Star-Ledger*, September 15, 2006.

116. Modia Butler interview, November 26, 2012, with author.

117. Damien Cave, "Team Booker Sweeps Municipal Races in Newark," *New York Times*, June 14, 2006.

118. Ronald Smothers, "Booker Has 100-Day Plan for Newark's Reorganization," *New York Times*, July 11, 2006. See also Katie Wang, "Booker's 100-day Plan for Newark 'Ambitious,'" *Star-Ledger*, July 11, 2006.

119. Andrew Jacobs, "New Mayor Tests His Promises on Newark's Reality," *New York Times*, October 19, 2006.

120. Damien Cave, "Booker Has Unity in Newark; Trick Now Is to Keep It," *New York Times*, June 15, 2006.

121. Jeffery C. Mays, "His Good Deeds Became His Resume," *Star-Ledger*, June 18, 2006.

122. Jeffery C. Mays, "Newark Agency Will Slash 425 Jobs," *Star-Ledger*, August 31, 2006; and Ronald Smothers, "Drastic Layoffs at Newark Housing Agency Are Defended," *New York Times*, September 1, 2006. See also Jeffery C. Mays, "Booker and Healy Protest HUD Cuts for Their Cities," *Star-Ledger*, January 31, 2007.

123. John Holl, "Booker Names 6 to Top Jobs in Newark," *New York Times*, June 30, 2006; and Andrew Jacobs, "Booker Losing 2 Key Officers in Newark," *New York*

Times, January 5, 2008. See also Jeffery C. Mays and Katie Wang, "Role of Booker Consultants Questioned," *Star-Ledger*, January 13, 2008.

124. Katie Wang, "Newark Names Deputy Mayor," *Star-Ledger*, August 2, 2006. See also Robin Finn, "Public Lives: Go West Young Man, to the Other Side of the Hudson," *New York Times*, August 4, 2006.

125. Jonathan Schuppe, "Booker Taps NYPD Ace to Lead Newark Police," *Star-Ledger*, September 7, 2006; and Andrew Jacobs, "New York City Crime Strategist Picked as Director of Newark Police Force," *New York Times*, September 7, 2006.

126. Andrew Jacobs, "New Mayor Tests His Promises on Newark's Reality," *New York Times*, October 19, 2006.

127. Kareem Fahim, "In Effort to Cut Homicide Rate, Newark Mayor Creates Narcotics Unit," *New York Times*, January 9, 2007.

128. Jonathan Schuppe and Jeffery C. Mays, "Booker to Appoint Acting Chief to the Post," *Star-Ledger*, August 14, 2007.

129. Jonathan Schuppe, "Newark's Police Is Suspended," *Star-Ledger*, March 11, 2008. See also *Star-Ledger* editorial, "End the Newark Police Feud"; Jonathan Schuppe and Jeffery C. Mays, "Substitute Newark Police Chief Retracted," *Star-Ledger*, March 12, 2008; Jeffery C. Mays and Jonathan Schuppe, "As Newark Police Succeed, There's Trouble at the Top," *Star-Ledger*, March 16, 2008; and Joan Whitlow, "Booker's Brew of Police and Politics," *Star-Ledger*, March 21, 2008.

130. Joan Whitlow, "Questions About the City Where I (at least) Live," *Star-Ledger*, September 15, 2006; and Katie Wang and Jeffery Mays, "Booker Makes Choices for Top Newark Posts," *Star-Ledger*, June 29, 2006.

131. Katie Wang, "Newark Hires Firm with Ties to ex-Booker Aide," *Star-Ledger*, January 5, 2007. See also Katie Wang and Jeffery C. Mays, "Newark Staff's Salaries Have Increased," *Star-Ledger*, January 14, 2007.

132. Joan Whitlow, "Newark Needs a New Start, Not More 'Added Starters,'" *Star Ledger*, July 24, 2006.

133. *Star-Ledger* editorial, "No Rubber Stamp in Newark," September 12, 2006.

134. Katie Wang, "Newark Hires Firm with Ties to ex-Booker Aide," *Star-Ledger*, January 5, 2007.

135. Joan Whitlow, "Florida Swamp to Newark Morass," *Star-Ledger*, January 8, 2007.

136. Andrew Jacobs, "New Mayor Tests His Promises on Newark's Reality," *New York Times*, October 19, 2006.

137. Richard E. Benfield, "The City Life: A Mayor Goes One-on-One," *New York Times*, February 25, 2007.

138. Alan Sepinwall, "'Brick City' Review," *Star-Ledger*, September 15, 2009. See also Katherine Santiago, "'Brick City' Documentary Premieres Before Diverse Audience," *Star-Ledger*, September 15, 2009; and Joan Whitlow, "'Brick City': Reality TV Comes to Newark," *Star-Ledger*, September 17, 2009.

139. Rohan Mascarenhas, "YouTube Spat Breaks Out Between Late-Night Comedian Conan O'Brien, Newark Mayor Cory Booker," *Star-Ledger*, September 20, 2009; and *Star-Ledger* editorial, "Conan O'Brien Invites Newark Mayor Cory Booker on Tonight Show to Settle Differences," October 1, 2009.

140. David Giambusso, "Newark Middle Class Is Overshadowed by Brick City Documentary," *Star-Ledger*, October 16, 2009.

141. Cory A. Booker, "The New City," *Esquire*, October 2006, 179 and 232.

142. Katie Wang, "In Newark, the Supporting Cast Questions Booker's Starring Roles," *Star-Ledger*, November 26, 2006.

143. Katie Wang, "City Residents Have a New Place to Call Home," *Star-Ledger*, October 15, 2006.

144. *Star Ledger* editorial, "Booker on the Move?," October 1, 2006.

145. Jeffery C. Mays and Katie Wang, "Booker's Latest Deal: Razing His Own Home," *Star-Ledger*, October 25, 2008. See also Katie Wang, "Brick Towers Goodbye Is Bittersweet," *Star-Ledger*, October 26, 2006, and Andrew Jacobs, "Evicted, Newark's Mayor Finds Another Blighted Street," *New York Times*, November 9, 2006.

146. Andrew Jacobs, "Evicted, Newark's Mayor Finds Another Blighted Street," *New York Times*, November 9, 2006.

147. Joan Whitlow, "Verdict Not Yet in on Booker's First Year in Office," *Star-Ledger*, July 1, 2007.

148. Kevin Manahan, "Let's Find Newark Mayor Cory Booker a House: Bachelor Pad Shopping for Newark's Renting Mayor," *Star-Ledger*, April 19, 2009.

149. Joan Whitlow, "Only Neighborly to Be Concerned about Mayor's Property," *Star-Ledger*, August 12, 2011, about Booker's 132 Court Street property. See also Joan Whitlow, "Who Is Dumping on Newark," *Star-Ledger*, October 28, 2011; and David Giambusso, "Newark Mayor Cory Booker's Property Damaged by Fire," *Star-Ledger*, March 2, 2012.

150. Jeffery C. Mays, "Newark Joins Task Force to Reduce Killings," *Star-Ledger*, July 4, 2006.

151. Damien Cave, "Newark: Mayor to Deploy More Police," *New York Times*, July 6, 2006. See also Jonathan Schuppe, "Booker Unveils His Tough-Love Plan for Newark," *Star-Ledger*, July 6, 2006.

152. Damien Cave, "Week One for Mayor Booker Inspires Hope in Newark," *New York Times*, July 6, 2006.

153. Jonathan Schuppe, "City Crime Campaign Falls Short of Victory," *Star-Ledger*, September 6, 2006.

154. Joan Whitlow, "Crime Charts Don't Make Newark Feel Any Safer," *Star-Ledger*, September 8, 2006.

155. Kasi Addison, "Booker Plan Adds Security Around Schools," *Star-Ledger*, September 19, 2006; and Katie Wang, "Keeping a High-Tech Eye on Downtown Newark," *Star-Ledger*, December 13, 2006.

156. Barry Carter, "Booker Expands Initiative to Schools," *Star-Ledger*, September 7, 2006.

157. Jeffery C. Mays, "Audits Find Failures in Newark City Hall," *Star-Ledger*, February 7, 2007. See also Andrew Jacobs, "Newark Squandered Millions, Audit Sought by Booker Shows," *New York Times*, February 8, 2007.

158. Andrew Jacobs, "Campaign Vows Meet Reality in Newark," *New York Times*, September 11, 2006.

159. Jeffery C. Mays, "Newark Considering Pink Slips for 800," *Star-Ledger*, September 12, 2006; and Andrew Jacobs, "New Mayor Tests His Promises on Newark's Reality," *New York Times*, October 19, 2006.

160. Jeffery C. Mays, "Booker Meets Resistance on Layoffs," *Star-Ledger*, September 13, 2006.

161. Joan Whitlow, "Sharpe Isn't Showing His Cards," *Star-Ledger*, August 23, 2006.

162. Katie Wang, "Booker to Ban Some Contributions," *Star-Ledger*, October 19, 2006. See also Katie Wang, "Newark to Wait on Pay to Play," *Star-Ledger*, November 2, 2006.

163. Andrew Jacobs, "Ethics Bills Up for Vote in Newark," *New York Times*, November 1, 2006. See also Katie Wang, "Newark Council to Vote on Ethics Package," *Star-Ledger*, November 1, 2006.

164. Jeffery C. Mays, "Booker to Ban Gifts from City Contracts," *Star-Ledger*, February 8, 2007.

165. Joan Whitlow, "Reasons to Question the State of Booker's City," *Star-Ledger*, February 9, 2007.

166. Jeffery C. Mays, "Newark's Case for $2.45M in Contracts," *Star-Ledger*, April 1, 2007.

167. Jeffery C. Mays, "Law Contracts Go to Booker Supporters," *Star-Ledger*, May 6, 2007.

168. Jeffery C. Mays and Jonathan Schuppe, "City Workers Feel Pushed to Aid Booker," *Star-Ledger*, April 29, 2007.

169. Katie Wang and Jeffery C. Mays, "Cory Booker's First 100 Days," *Star-Ledger*, October 8, 2006. See also "November 8th Call Out Time to Hit the Streets," e-mail, November 3, 2006.

170. Katie Wang and Jeffery C. Mays, "Cory Booker's First 100 Days," *Star-Ledger*, October 8, 2006.

171. Andrew Jacobs, "New Mayor Tests His Promises on Newark's Reality," *New York Times*, October 19, 2006.

172. Katie Wang, "Newark Hires 'Image' Consultant," *Star-Ledger*, November 22, 2006.

173. *Star-Ledger* editorials, "End Waste on the Website," October 20, 2008, and "Hold the Applause in Newark," October 23, 2008.

174. Joan Whitlow, "A Campaign Donation Is Powerful Medicine," *Star-Ledger*, May 25, 2007.

175. *Star-Ledger* editorial, "Openness on Police Reform," May 23, 2007.

176. Ted Sherman, "City Loses Bid for Return of Leaked Report on Cops," *Star-Ledger*, May 26, 2007; and Ted Sherman, "Newark Retracts Suit Against Newspaper," *Star-Ledger*, June 6, 2007.

177. John Mooney and Kasi Addison, "Bolden Resisting Pressure to Quit Newark School Job," *Star-Ledger*, November 18, 2006.

178. Suleman Din, "Hosting First Event in New Job, James Lauded and Applauded," *Star-Ledger*, November 19, 2006.

179. Jonathan Schuppe, "Surge in Gunfire Blamed for Leap in Newark Killings," *Star-Ledger*, December 31, 2006; and *Star-Ledger* editorial, "Newark's Dreadful Number," December 6, 2006. See also Andrew Jacobs, "With 101 Homicides, Newark Nears a Bleak Milestone," *New York Times*, December 17, 2006.

180. Andrew Jacobs, "With 101 Homicides, Newark Nears a Bleak Milestone," *New York Times*, December 17, 2006.

181. Kasi Addison and Jonathan Schuppe, "Newark Teachers Send City a Deadly Serious Message," *Star-Ledger*, January 26, 2007. See also The Associated Press, "Wanted: Help to Stop Killings," *Jersey Journal*, February 2, 2007.

182. Kasi Addison, "Teachers Union Billboard Makes 'Political Statement,'" *Star-Ledger*, February 24, 2008.

183. Katie Wang, "Merchants and Mayor Say Billboards Are Hurting Business," *Star-Ledger*, March 26, 2007.

184. Andrew Jacobs, "Crime Drops in Newark, but Murders Are Flat," *New York Times*, April 2, 2007.

185. Jeffery C. Mays, "Newark Mayor Fined for Late Campaign Fund Reports," *Star-Ledger*, December 8, 2006.

186. Katie Wang and Jeffery C. Mays, "Booker Maps Out Road to an Improved Newark," *Star-Ledger*, February 9, 2007.

187. Andrew Jacobs, "Access to Mayor Doesn't Solve All Problems," *New York Times*, March 8, 2007.

188. Katie Wang and Jeffery C. Mays, "In Essex County, a Truce Is Broken," *Star-Ledger*, March 15, 2007. See also Joan Whitlow, "A Striking Shift in Politics for Newark," *Star-Ledger*, March 16, 2007.

189. *Star-Ledger* editorial, "New Ideas Challenge Old Guard in Newark," March 16, 2007.

190. Jeffery C. Mays, "Law Contracts Go to Booker Supporters," *Star-Ledger*, May 6, 2007.

191. Richard Cammarieri interview, December 3, 2012, with author.

192. Jeffery C. Mays and Jonathan Casiano, "In Democratic Party, a Battle for Power," *Star-Ledger*, January 7, 2007.

193. Andrew Jacobs, "Booker Tries to Unseat Legislators, Dividing Party," *New York Times*, March 20, 2007. See also David Porter, "In Newark, Billboards Becoming Free-Speech Venue of Choice," *Star-Ledger*, March 30, 2007.

194. Katie Wang, "Booker's Political Agenda Becomes a Daily Grind," *Star-Ledger*, March 22, 2007. See also Joan Whitlow, "Newark Ought to Fight Crime, Not Battle Over Signs," *Star-Ledger*, March 30, 2007.

195. Katie Wang, "Booker Team Takes 5 out of 6," *Star-Ledger*, June 6, 2007. See also Andrew Jacobs, "After the Fight, Booker's Top Antagonist Is Still Standing," *New York Times*, June 7, 2007; and Katie Wang, "Sen. Rice Still Sounds Nice to Essex Voters," *Star-Ledger*, June 7, 2007.

196. *Star-Ledger* editorial, "Newark's Step Forward," April 26, 2007.

197. Cory Booker interview, April 5, 2013, with author.

198. Andrew Jacobs, "Facing Gap in Budget, Newark Plans Buyout Offers," *Star-Ledger*, June 9, 2007. See also Jeffery C. Mays, "Newark Buyout Offer Includes up to 60% of Pay," *Star-Ledger*, June 12, 2007; Jeffery C. Mays, "Uncertainty Roils Newark City Hall Workers," *Star-Ledger*, June 17, 2007; Jeffery C. Mays, "Booker Facing Budget Gap, Considers 500 Layoffs or More," *Star-Ledger*, June 29, 2007; and Katie Wang, "Newark Cash Crunch Hits Cops, Firefighters," *Star-Ledger*, June 30, 2007.

199. Jeffery C. Mays, "Newark Retains Its Moody's Rating," *Star-Ledger*, April 29, 2007. See also Jeffery C. Mays, "Booker Facing Budget Gap, Considers 500 Layoffs or More," *Star-Ledger*, June 29, 2007.

200. Andrew Jacobs, "Newark on Times on Budget, but a Fiscal Crisis Looms," *New York Times*, April 6, 2007. See also *Star-Ledger* editorial, "Newark's Step Forward," April 26, 2007.

201. Katie Wang, "Newark Cash Crunch Hits Cops, Firefighters," *Star-Ledger*, June 30, 2007. See also Andrew Jacobs, "Newark's Mayor, in Office a Year, Says Major City Job Cuts Are Likely," *New York Times*, June 30, 2007.

202. Katie Wang, "Newark Seeks Approval to Cut 400 Jobs," *Star-Ledger*, July 19, 2007.

203. Jersey Journal, "200 Jobs to Be Cut in Newark Budget Plan," August 28, 2007.

204. Andrew Jacobs, "Newark's Mayor, in Office a Year, Says Major City Job Cuts Are Likely," *New York Times*, June 30, 2007. See Professor Bridget Harrison's and Rahaman Muhammad's quotes.

205. Jeffery Gold, "Former Newark Mayor Won't Seek Re-Election to State Senate," *Star-Ledger*, April 9, 2007. See also Katie Wang and Jeffery C. Mays, "James Won't Seek Re-Election to the State Senate," *Star-Ledger*, April 10, 2007.

206. Jeffery C. Mays, "James to Leave College Post After Just a Year," *Star-Ledger*, June 19, 2007. See also The Associate Press, "Ex-Newark Mayor to Resign College Post," *Star-Ledger*, June 19, 2007.

207. The Associated Press, "After 37 Years, Sharpe James Offers His Swan Song to Politics," *New York Times*, April 10, 2007.

208. Katie Wang, "Newark Council Members Question Mayor's Tactics," *Star-Ledger*, June 8, 2007.

209. Katie Wang, "Newark Seeks Approval to Cut 400 Jobs," *Star-Ledger*, July 19, 2007.

210. Katie Wang, "Pay Hike Sought for 63 Newark Employees," *Star-Ledger*, August 24, 2008; and Dunstan McNichol and Katie Wang, "Newark Receives a $45M Boost," *Star-Ledger*, August 14, 2008.

211. Jeffery C. Mays, "Many Teens Still Waiting for Payday," *Star-Ledger*, August 1, 2007. See also Katie Wang, "Booker Apologizes to Teens in Person," *Star-Ledger*, August 2, 2007; and Jeffery C. Mays, "Pizza and Paychecks," *Star-Ledger*, August 3, 2007.

212. Jeffery C. Mays, "Newark Paycheck Headache Persists," *Star-Ledger*, August 15, 2007.

213. Jonathan Schuppe, "TV Show Based on Newark Shootings Troubles Victims' Families," *Star-Ledger*, December 13, 2007. *Law & Order: Criminal Intent* had an episode dramatizing the triple murder.

214. Jonathan Schuppe and Mark DiIonno, "24-Year-Old Nicaraguan National with Rap Sheet Wanted in Killings," *Star-Ledger*, August 12, 2007.

215. Jeffery C. Mays, "Booker Won't Push to Arrest Migrants," *Star-Ledger*, August 17, 2007. See also Kareem Fahim, "Newark Triple Murder Fuels Debate on Treatment of Illegal Immigrants," *New York Times*, August 19, 2007.

216. Kareem Fahim and David Chen, "Police Voice Concerns Over a Directive on Immigrants," *New York Times*, August 23, 2007.

217. Brian Donohue, "'Are You Legal?' Bringing Fear to Immigrants," *Star-Ledger*, September 18, 2007.

218. *New York Times* editorial, "Politicizing a Triple Murder," August 26, 2007.

219. Andrew Jacobs, "Booker Comes Under Siege After Bloodshed," *New York Times*, August 7, 2007.

220. Julia Terruso, "Final Defendant in Newark Schoolyard Slaying Sentenced to 195 Years," *Star-Ledger*, January 9, 2013.

221. Julia Terruso, "$5 Million Settlement Ends 6-Year Ordeal for Newark Schoolyard Victims' Families," *Star-Ledger*, February 13, 2013.

222. Alexi Friedman, "A Foreboding Memo: Newark Councilman Warned of Potential for Violence Before Schoolyard Killings," *Star-Ledger*, June 7, 2012; and Julia Terruso, "Newark Councilman Testifies He Warned School District of Open Gate Days Before Murders," *Star-Ledger*, January 17, 2013. See also Julia Terruso, "Graffiti Expert: Gang Tags Were an Invitation for Gang Activity in Newark School Yard," *Star-Ledger*, January 16, 2013; Julia Terruso, "Survivor in Newark Schoolyard Slayings to Take Stand in Civil Trial," *Star-Ledger*, February 4, 2013; Julia Terruso, "Schoolyard Survivor Describes Lingering Injuries, Paranoia 5 Years After Attacks," *Star-Ledger*, February 5, 2013; and Julia Terruso, "Survivor of Newark Schoolyard Triple Murder: 'I Was Just Praying They Were Going to Stop,'" *Star-Ledger*, February 4, 2013.

223. *New York Times* editorial, "Deaths in Newark," August 10, 2007.

224. Jessica Durando, "After Killings, Newarkers Take the Pledge to Stop Shootin'," *Star-Ledger*, August 9, 2007.
225. Andrew Jacobs, "After Killings, Sense of Unity Surprises Newark," *New York Times*, August 13, 2007.
226. Jeffery C. Mays and Katie Wang, "Newark Activists Seek Group Unity Against Violence," *Star-Ledger*, September 2, 2007.
227. Mark Di Ionno, "'Dear Mayor Cory Booker, I Was Afraid to Go to Sleep Saturday and Sunday,'" *Star-Ledger*, August 11, 2007.
228. Katie Wang, "Booker Recall Bid Moving Forward," *Star-Ledger*, August 15, 2007.
229. Katie Wang and Jeffery C. Mays, "Booker's First Year a Wearying Journey," *Star-Ledger*, July 1, 2007.
230. Andrew Jacobs, "Newark's Mayor Battles Old Guard Rumors," *New York Times*, July 3, 2007.
231. Bruce Lambert, "43 Days Without a Homicide, and Then a Newark Man Is Shot," *New York Times*, February 27, 2008. See also Kareem Fahim, "A Calm Stretch Ends in Newark, but Officials Claim Progress on Crime," *New York Times*, February 28, 2008.
232. Andrew Jacobs, "After Killings, Sense of Unity Surprises Newark," *New York Times*, August 13, 2007.
233. Andrew Jacobs, "A Pivotal Moment for Booker," *New York Times*, August 12, 2007. See also Manny Fernandez and Andrew Jacobs, "Sorrow and Anger as Newark Buries Slain Youths," *New York Times*, August 12, 2007.
234. Ras Baraka interview, February 11, 2013, with author.

Chapter 4

1. Cory Booker interview, April 5, 2013, with author.
2. Jeffery C. Mays and Katie Wang, "Judge Suspends Bargain Sales of Newark's Land," *Star-Ledger*, June 1, 2006; and *Star-Ledger* editorial, "End the Newark Land Grab," June 2, 2006. See also Katie Wang, "Ban Upheld on Newark Land Sales," *Star-Ledger*, June 21, 2006.
3. Katie Wang and Jeffery C. Mays, "Newark Council Kills $80 Million for Trusts," *Star-Ledger*, July 7, 2006.
4. Ian T. Shearn, "Newark Tries to Take Back City Lots Sold on the Cheap," *Star-Ledger*, July 3, 2007; and *Star-Ledger* editorial, "Right to Reclaim the Land," July 5, 2007.
5. Katie Wang, "Newark Ready to Settle with Developer," *Star-Ledger*, July 11, 2007.
6. Modia Butler interview, November 26, 2012, with author.
7. Cory Booker interview, April 5, 2013, with author. See also City of Newark press release, "Sustainability Action Plan," 2013 http://www.sustainablenwk.org/NewarkSustainabilityActionPlan_2013.pdf
8. Nawal Qarooni, "Revitalizing Cities from the Inside," *Star-Ledger*, May 7, 2007. See also Ed Beeson, "Could Newark Be a Manufacturing Hub Again? Brookings Report Explores How," *Star-Ledger*, May 29, 2013.
9. George Hawkins, "Renewing Our Cities to Save Our State," *Star-Ledger*, February 21, 2007; and http://www.njfuture.org
10. Paul Milo, "'Teachers Village' Groundbreaking Today," NewarkPatch.com, February 9, 2012; and Ian T. Shearn, "Newark Blueprint Has Lofty Ambitions," *Star-Ledger*, June 10, 2008.

11. Bob Braun, "Great Expectations Aside, McGovern's Pub in Newark Still a Hub," *Star-Ledger*, August 31, 2011.

12. Adam Zipkin interview, April 5, 2013, with author.

13. Jeffery C. Mays, "Booker Wants to Revive City's Underused Properties," *Star-Ledger*, February 21, 2007; and Ian T. Shearn, "Newark Blueprint Has Lofty Ambitions," *Star-Ledger*, June 10, 2008.

14. Katie Wang, "Mulberry Street Fight Goes to Court," *Star-Ledger*, May 6, 2007; and Andrew Jacobs, "Judge Stops Newark Redevelopment Project," *New York Times*, July 20, 2007. See also Katie Wang, "Setback for Newark Condo Project," *Star-Ledger*, July 20, 2007; and Mary Jo Patterson, "Ruling Gives Hope to Property Owners," *Star-Ledger*, June 14, 2007.

15. Dave Caldwell, "High Hopes for an Ambitious Newark Arena," *New York Times*, April 15, 2007.

16. Jeffery C. Mays, "Bears Seek Bankruptcy Protection," *Star-Ledger*, October 30, 2008; and Jeffery C. Mays, "Bears Hopeful Judge Will Say: 'Sold. Play Ball,'" *Star-Ledger*, November 11, 2008.

17. Harvey Araton, "Did Newark Bet on the Wrong Sport?" *New York Times*, August 21, 2011.

18. Richard Cammarieri interview, December 3, 2012, with author.

19. *Star-Ledger* editorial, "A New Arena Prenuptial," *Star-Ledger*, June 18, 2006; and Joan Whitlow, "Mayor's Review of Arena Deal Is a Safe Bet," *Star-Ledger*, July 31, 2006. See also Matthew Futterman, "12 Months to Faceoff," *Star-Ledger*, October 7, 2006; and Maura McDermott and Brad Parks, "The $365M Arena That Almost Wasn't," *Star-Ledger*, October 14, 2007.

20. Matthew Futterman, "Booker Hires an Arena Consultant," *Star-Ledger*, July 25, 2006. See also Jeffery C. Mays, "Helmsman of Newark Arena Steps Aside," *Star-Ledger*, October 18, 2006; and Paul Cox, "Prudential Center Has Rock Solid First Year," *Star-Ledger*, October 20, 2008.

21. Jeffery C. Mays, "Contractors Flock to PAC with Booker Ties," *Star-Ledger*, October 9, 2007.

22. Andrew Jacobs, "In Shift, Newark Mayor Backs Hockey Arena After Team Agrees to Offer Local Aid," *New York Times*, October 31, 2006; and Jeffery C. Mays, "Booker Teams Up with the Devils," *Star-Ledger*, October 31, 2006.

23. *Star-Ledger* editorial, "Helping the Arena Survive," October 31, 2006.

24. Andrew Jacobs, "In Shift, Newark Mayor Backs Hockey Arena After Team Agrees to Offer Local Aid," *New York Times*, October 31, 2006.

25. Maura McDermott and Brad Parks, "The $365M Arena That Almost Wasn't," *Star-Ledger*, October 14, 2007.

26. Jeffery C. Mays, "Mayor Warms Up to Newark's New Ice Hockey Arena," *Star-Ledger*, October 28, 2006.

27. Jeffery C. Mays, "New Boss Changes Face of Newark's Public Housing," *Star-Ledger*, August 13, 2007.

28. Jeffery C. Mays, "'Last Piece' of Puzzle in Place as Newark Finalized Arena Deals," *Star-Ledger*, July 12, 2007.

29. Maura McDermott, "Newark Goes All Out to Assure Arena's Visitors Safe Passage," *Star-Ledger*, October 17, 2007.

30. Jeffery C. Mays, "Arena Projects to Cost Newark Extra $102.4 Million," *Star-Ledger*, November 24, 2006.

31. Katie Wang, "Newark Is Seeking More Funds for Arena Area," *Star-Ledger*, January 18, 2007.
32. Jeffery C. Mays, "Additional Projects Hike Overall Tab for Newark Arena," *Star-Ledger*, October 15, 2007.
33. Ali Winston, "For Pru Center Plaza, Going Is Slow and Costly," *Star-Ledger*, April 22, 2008.
34. Jeffery C. Mays, "Additional Projects Hike Overall Tab for Newark Arena," *Star-Ledger*, October 15, 2007.
35. Jeffery C. Mays, "Subpoenas Target Land Purchases for Newark Arena," *Star-Ledger*, January 17, 2007.
36. Katie Wang, "Newark Spent $2M in OT at New Arena," *Star-Ledger*, August 10, 2008.
37. Joan Whitlow, "Layoffs, the Arena and Worries Over Police Protection," *Star-Ledger*, November 30, 2007. See also Jonathan Schuppe, "The Deputy Chief Is Determined to Show off Newark at Its Safest," *Star-Ledger*, October 21, 2007; and Brad Parks, "It's Been Built, but Will They Come?" *Star-Ledger*, October 21, 2007.
38. Kevin Coyne, "Hockey in Newark? It's Not Just for Pros," *Star-Ledger*, April 19, 2009; and Barry Carter, "Newark Teens Are First Hockey Players from High School to Play in College," *Star-Ledger*, May 25, 2011.
39. Katie Wang, "For Some, Arena's Backside Is Front and Center," *Star-Ledger*, October 24, 2007; and The Associated Press, "Newark Mayor Hopes Arena Will Be a Boon," *New York Times*, October 24, 2007.
40. Joan Whitlow, "Easier to Believe in Tinkerbell Than the Arena," *Star-Ledger*, November 29, 2006.
41. Associated Press, "Devils' New Arena to Be a Piece of the Rock," *Jersey Journal*, January 9, 2007; and Greg Saitz, "Arena Dubbed Pru Center," *Star-Ledger*, January 9, 2007. See also Mark Di Ionno, "2 Arenas Could Be 1 Arena Too Many," *Star-Ledger*, February 24, 2008.
42. Ted Sherman, "When Arenas Collide," *Star-Ledger*, March 8, 2009.
43. Peggy McGlone, "In Arena Contest, Can Two Survive," *Star-Ledger*, December 24, 2006; and Dave Caldwell, "High Hopes for an Ambitious Newark Arena," *New York Times*, April 15, 2007. See also Mary Jo Patterson, "Redevelopment Lagging Near Newark's Arena," *New York Times*, February 15, 2009; and Ted Sherman, "When Arenas Collide," *Star-Ledger*, March 8, 2009.
44. Mark Di Ionno, "2 Arenas Could Be 1 Arena Too Many," *Star-Ledger*, February 24, 2008.
45. Ted Sherman, "Deal Would Let Izod Center, 'Rock' Share the Riches," *Star-Ledger*, April 16, 2009; and Joan Whitlow, "The N.J. Nets at the Prudential Center? Ask the Lawyers First," *Star-Ledger*, April 24, 2009.
46. *Star-Ledger* editorial, "Put Redevelopment in Arena's Future," February 6, 2007.
47. Jeffery C. Mays, "Just Miles Apart, 2 Arenas Compete," *New York Times*, May 3, 2009. See also Joan Whitlow, "The Nets Are Coming to Newark! The Nets Are Coming to Newark! Maybe," *Star-Ledger*, October 25, 2009.
48. Greg Saitz and Matthew Futterman, "Newark Arena about to Become Piece of the Rock," *Star-Ledger*, December 21, 2006; and Ken Belson, "Devils' Hockey Arena, or 'Rock,' if Prudential Agrees to Pay," *New York Times*, December 22, 2006.
49. Jeffery C. Mays, "A Construction Milestone," *Star-Ledger*, March 22, 2007.

50. Jeffery C. Mays, "Newark Arena to Rock Open with Jersey's Own Bon Jovi," *Star-Ledger*, May 3, 2007.

51. Philip Read, "First New Hotel in Newark's Downtown in 38 Years Will Be Built Next to Prudential Center," *Star-Ledger*, February 4, 2010; and Heather Haddon, "Newark Displays Staying Power," *Star-Ledger*, September 21, 2012. See also Eliot Caroom, "Downtown Newark's First New Hotel in 40 Years: Courtyard by Marriott on Broad Street," *Star-Ledger*, September 25, 2012.

52. Andrew Jacobs, "Owners Push New Arena, but Residents Fear Change," *New York Times*, June 19, 2007; and Katie Wang, "Businesses Wait Patiently for Arena's Hungry Fans," October 1, 2007. As Neil deMause, author of *Field of Schemes*, mentions about arenas and public financing: "In city after city, it's been the case that only if the neighborhood was already on the upswing do you see much development."

53. Jeffery C. Mays, "Pru Center Debut Holds Familiar Promise of Revival," *Star-Ledger*, October 22, 2007.

54. Winter Miller, "Newark Arena Hangs a 'Help Wanted' Sign, and Thousands Line Up," *New York Times*, September 7, 2007; and Maura McDermott, "Prudential Center Not Yet Rock Solid on Sell-out Crowds," *Star-Ledger*, December 29, 2007.

55. Katie Wang, "Newark Hits the Jackpot with Arena Jobs," *Star-Ledger*, October 20, 2007; and Katie Wang, "Arena Doesn't Meet Newark's Suite Desire," *Star-Ledger*, September 27, 2007.

56. Katie Wang, "Arena Doesn't Meet Newark's Suite Desire," *Star-Ledger*, September 27, 2007; and Paul Mulshine, "Newark Council Has Us in a Box," *Star-Ledger*, September 30, 2007.

57. Joe Malinconico, "Forget Icing, What About Parking?" *Star-Ledger*, October 19, 2007; and Maura McDermott, "Newark Goes All Out to Assure Arena's Visitors Safe Passage," October 17, 2007.

58. Jeffery C. Mays and Katie Wang, "Newark Fines Devils Over Arena Bridge," *Star-Ledger*, March 26, 2008.

59. Jeffery C. Mays and Jonathan Schuppe, "Too Close for Comfort," *Star-Ledger*, October 11, 2007.

60. Katie Wang and Mark Mueller, "Arena Opens and Newark Glows," *Star-Ledger*, October 26, 2007; and Katie Wang, "Star of the Ribbon-Cutting: Sharpe James," *Star-Ledger*, October 26, 2007.

61. Carmen Juri, "A Feast for Ironbound Restaurants as Pru Arena Visitors Fill the Tables," *Star-Ledger*, December 7, 2007.

62. Jeffery C. Mays and Maura McDermott, "Arena Is Up. Now About the Neighborhood," *Star-Ledger*, November 21, 2007.

63. Katie Wang, "A Key Parcel," *Star-Ledger*, May 11, 2008.

64. Jeffery C. Mays and Maura McDermott, "Arena Is Up. Now About the Neighborhood," *Star-Ledger*, November 21, 2007.

65. Paul Cox, "Prudential Center Has Rock Solid First Year," *Star-Ledger*, October 20, 2008.

66. Mary Jo Patterson, "Redevelopment Lagging Near Newark's Arena," *New York Times*, February 15, 2009.

67. Jonathan Schuppe and Robert Gebeloff, "Security in and around Prudential Center has been Rock-Solid, Data Show," *Star-Ledger*, March 9, 2008. Also see Jeffery C. Mays, "Leaders of Newark Call a Foul Over Snubs," *Star-Ledger*, October 29, 2008.
68. Dave Caldwell, "For Devils Fans, Trains Seem to Work Fine," *Star-Ledger*, April 20, 2008.
69. Katie Wang, "Newark Looks to Get Tough on Illegal Parking," *Star-Ledger*, April 16, 2008.
70. Kenneth Cocuzzo, "NJ Group Explores Bringing Nets to Newark," *Star-Ledger*, May 1, 2008.
71. Ted Sherman, "Deal Would Let Izod Center, 'Rock' Share the Riches," *Star-Ledger*, April 16, 2009; and Joan Whitlow, "The N.J. Nets at the Prudential Center? Ask the Lawyers First," *Star-Ledger*, April 24, 2009. On the Nets preseason games, see Dave D'Alessandro, "Newark Mayor Cory Booker Declares Turnout for NJ Nets Preseason Game 'a Tremendous Victory,'" *Star-Ledger*, October 13, 2009; and Peggy McGlone, "N.J. Nets Pack Preseason at Newark's Prudential Center with Ticket Giveaways Discounts," *Star-Ledger*, October 20, 2009.
72. Ted Sherman, "$4M Deal Brings the Nets in Newark," *Star-Ledger*, February 19, 2010; and *Star-Ledger* editorial, "N.J. Nets in Newark: Next Steps, Decisions on Izod, NJSEA," February 21, 2012. See also Richard Pérez-Peña, "Rivals Not the Only Ones Delighted to See the Nets," *New York Times*, October 18, 2010.
73. David Giambusso, "Newark Hopes Nets' Two-Year Stint at Prudential Center Can Bring Business to City," *Star-Ledger*, October 27, 2010.
74. Maura McDermott, "Pru Center Drawing Fans, but the Work Isn't Done," *Star-Ledger*, July 14, 2008.
75. Maura McDermott, "Pru Center's Owner Demands $2.4M Back Rent from Devils," *Star-Ledger*, November 4, 2008; and Maura McDermott, "For Angry Creditors, the Devils Are in the Details," *Star-Ledger*, November 16, 2008. See also Joan Whitlow, "Prudential Center Part of Newark's Three-Ring Circus," *Star-Ledger*, February 6, 2009; and Joan Whitlow, "Newark Arena Is Looking Like a Frozen Asset," *Star-Ledger*, November 14, 2008.
76. David Giambusso, "Newark Housing Authority Says NJ Devils Owe Millions in Back Rent on Prudential Center," *Star-Ledger*, May 14, 2010.
77. Ibid.
78. Ted Sherman, "N.J. Devils, Newark Housing Authority Abandon Negotiations on Prudential Center Rent, Head to Court," *Star-Ledger*, June 15, 2010; and Joan Whitlow, "Newark Arena Rent: Some Day the Check Will Come," *Star-Ledger*, October 22, 2010.
79. Joan Whitlow, "Subpoenas. Alleged Kickbacks. Investigations. This Must Be Newark," *Star-Ledger*, October 29, 2010.
80. Jeff Vanderbeek and Michael Gilfillan, "Invest in the Cities, It's Where Growth Begins," *Star-Ledger*, November 2, 2010.
81. Simone Sebastian, "As Thousands of Tourists Arrive for NCAA East Regional, Army of Volunteers Staff Downtown Newark," *Star-Ledger*, March 23, 2011; and Mike Frassinelli, "Officials View NCAA East Regional Games as Opportunity to Show Newark as Great Transit Hub," *Star-Ledger*, March 24, 2011.
82. Aliza Appelbaum, Simone Sebastian, Meredith Galante, Mike Frassinelli, Bob Considine, David Giambusso, and Mark Mueller, "Fans Swarming into Newark for

NCAA East Regional Games Find Camaraderie, Adventure," *Star-Ledger*, March 25, 2011; and Mark Mueller, "Newark Leaves Positive Impression on Visitors During NCAA East Regional Practices, FanFest," *Star-Ledger*, March 25, 2011.

83. David Giambusso, "NCAA East Regional Games Bring Deluge of Media Focus on Newark, Mayor Cory Booker," *Star-Ledger*, March 25, 2011.

84. David Giambusso, "Newark Gets Short End in Prudential Revenue Share Ruling," *Star-Ledger*, April 4, 2012.

85. David Giambusso, "How Newark and Its First Major Pro Sports Team Fell Out of Love Over and Over," *Star-Ledger*, May 14, 2012.

86. David Giambusso, "Newark Gets Short End in Prudential Revenue Share Ruling," *Star-Ledger*, April 4, 2012.

87. PolitiFact.com, "Says New Jersey Devils Managing Partner Jeff Vanderbeek 'Took Us into Arbitration,'" *Star-Ledger*, April 4, 2012.

88. PolitiFact.com, "Says New Jersey Devils Management Partner Jeff Vanderbeek 'Froze All Those Monies During the Toughest Years in '08-'09' and 'Refused to Give the Charitable Dollars That He Was Required to Give by the Contract,'" *Star-Ledger*, April 9, 2012.

89. David Giambusso, "Newark Mayor Booker Slams Devils Owner Following Arbitrators' Ruling Against City," *Star-Ledger*, April 6, 2012.

90. David Giambusso, Ted Sherman, and James Queally, "Newark Reducing Police Outside Prudential Center Amid Feud between Mayor Booker, N.J. Devils Owner," *Star-Ledger*, April 10, 2012.

91. *Star-Ledger* editorial, "Newark, Devils Should Work Together to Fix Sour Deal," April 8, 2012.

92. Cory Booker, "Devils Owner Let Newark Down," *Star-Ledger*, April 10, 2012.

93. David Giambusso, Ted Sherman, and James Queally, "Newark Reducing Police Outside Prudential Center Amid Feud between Mayor Booker, N.J. Devils Owner," *Star-Ledger*, April 10, 2012.

94. David Giambusso and James Queally, "Newark Paid Out $10.8M for Police at Prudential Center," *Star-Ledger*, April 11, 2012.

95. James Queally, "Group of 10 or 15 'Thugs' Rob and Beat 5 People Following Prudential Center, Cops Say," *Star-Ledger*, May 9, 2012; and James Queally, "Violence May Have Been Chief Motivation in Brutal Prudential Center Assaults," *Star-Ledger*, May 10, 2012. See also *Star-Ledger* editorial, "Violence Against Newark's Prudential Center Visitors Is Unusual," May 13, 2012.

96. David Giambusso, "Cops: Hockey Series Goal Is to Keep Attendees Safe," *Star-Ledger*, May 18, 2012.

97. Peggy McGlone, "Cory Booker Lightens Mood, Amid the N.J. Devils Feud, with Poetic Words," *Star-Ledger*, April 11, 2012; and *Star-Ledger* editorial, "Newark Mayor Cory Booker's Poetry Slam…on the New Jersey Devils," April 11, 2012. See also Peggy McGlone, "2012 Dodge Poetry Festival Returns to Newark in October," *Star-Ledger*, April 10, 2012.

98. David Giambusso, "Will Cory Booker Be too Busy to Attend Devils Home Games in Stanley Cup Finals," *Star-Ledger*, May 31, 2012.

99. Richard Sandomir, "Devils' History of Success and Financial Disputes Repeats," *New York Times*, June 4, 2012.

100. David Giambusso, "Devils Take in More than $30M During Stanley Cup Run," *Star-Ledger*, June 12, 2012.

101. David Giambusso, "Newark City Council Votes to Approve Devils Arena Deal," *Star-Ledger*, February 26, 2013; and David Giambusso, "Newark, Devils End Years of Acrimony with Deal on Prudential Center," *Star-Ledger*, February 26, 2013.

102. Ibid and Heather Haddon, "Deal on Arena Helps Newark, Booker's Bid," *Wall Street Journal*, June 13, 2013.

103. Cory Booker interview, April 5, 2013, with author.

104. Ibid.

105. Harold Lucas interview, November 14, 2012, with author.

106. Michael Meyer interview, December 3, 2012, with author. Also David Giambusso, "New Devils Owners Say They Are in It for the Long Haul," *Star-Ledger*, August 16, 2013.

107. Adam Zipkin interview, April 5, 2013, with author.

108. Michael Meyer interview, December 3, 2012, with author.

109. Ralph Ortega, "Newark Draws an Ambitious Design for a Better City," *Star-Ledger*, March 11, 2009.

110. Richard Cammarieri interview, December 3, 2012, with author.

111. Michael Meyer interview, December 3, 2012, with author.

112. Jeffery C. Mays and Katie Wang, "Soaring Condo Market," *Star-Ledger*, May 6, 2007.

113. Joan Whitlow, "Newark's Rebirth Is Underway—Will It Rival Jersey City's?" *Star-Ledger*, May 9, 2007.

114. Antoinette Martin, "Attracting Residents With 'Themes,'" *New York Times*, May 19, 2010.

115. Adam Zipkin interview, April 5, 2013, with author.

116. Michael Meyer interview, December 3, 2012, with author.

117. Associated Press, "Cory Booker on Newark Creating 'Village' for Teachers," April 21, 2012. See also Dana Goldstein, "Cory Booker and Chris Christie: Teachers Should Live in Downtown Newark," *The Atlantic*, February 10, 2012. The RBH Group, which is developing Teachers Village, surveyed Newark teachers and discovered that only 19 percent of their respondents live in the city, while 29 percent reside in the suburbs, 19 percent live in New York City, and 10 percent live in nearby Jersey City.

118. City of Newark press release, "Groundbreaking Commences Construction of Teachers Village," February 9, 2012.

119. Philip Read, "Teachers Village Project in Newark Passes Historic Hurdle," *Star-Ledger*, March 11, 2010.

120. "New Life for Newark," *Business Excellence*, October 4, 2010; and Michael Rispoli, "Paramount Theater Owner Looks to Restore Venue's Glory," *Star-Ledger*, April 9, 2009.

121. Sarah Portlock, "Newark to Break Ground on Long-Awaited Teachers Village," *Star-Ledger*, February 9, 2012.

122. City of Newark press release, "Groundbreaking Commences Construction of Teachers Village," February 9, 2012.

123. Ibid.

124. Dana Goldstein, "Cory Booker and Chris Christie: Teachers Should Live in Downtown Newark," *The Atlantic*, February 10, 2012.

125. Susan Piperato, "American Cities Are Revitalizing Their Downtowns and Recreating Their Profiles," *National Real Estate Investor*, March 28, 2012.

126. "New Life for Newark," *Business Excellence*, October 4, 2010.

127. Philip Read, "Teachers Village Project in Newark Passes Historic Hurdle," *Star-Ledger*, March 11, 2010. See also Goldstein, February 10, 2012.

128. Tom De Poto, "Newark Developers to Present Plan to Make Historic Four Corners Residential," *Star-Ledger*, December 19, 2012.

129. Sarah Portlock, "Newark to Break Ground on Long-Awaited Teachers Village," *Star-Ledger*, February 9, 2012; City of Newark press release, "Groundbreaking Commences Construction of Teachers Village," February 9, 2012. Also Michael Meyer interview, December 3, 2012, with author.

130. http://www.smartgrowthamerica.org/

131. Ashley Strain, "Panasonic Corp. of North America Is Considering Leaving Secaucus for Newark, or Moving Operations Out of New Jersey Altogether," *Jersey Journal*, January 19, 2011; and David Giambusso and Sarah Portlock, "Mayor Cory Booker Confirms Panasonic Moving Headquarters from Secaucus to Newark," *Star-Ledger*, April 20, 2011.

132. Charles V. Bagli, "Christie Leaning on Tax Subsidies in Hunt for Jobs," *New York Times*, April 4, 2012; Lisa Flesiher and Eliot Brown, "Newark Lands Panasonic with Subsidies," *Wall Street Journal*, April 20, 2011. See also Sarah Portlock, "Panasonic's Move to Newark from Secaucus Is Likely to Be Supported by Tax Abatements as well as $102 Million Tax Credit from State," *Star-Ledger*, April 21, 2011; Sarah Portlock, "Panasonic Lured to Newark with City and State Incentives," *Star-Ledger*, April 21, 2011; and Sarah Portlock, "Prudential Plans to Build New, $444M Skyscraper in Downtown Newark," *Star-Ledger*, March 16, 2012.

133. Reznick Group, "NMTCs Help Build Teachers Village in Downtown Newark," Spring 2012.

134. C. Jefferson Armistead, Pratt Institute Center for Community and Environmental Development, "New Market Tax Credits: Issues and Opportunities," December 9, 2004.

135. Government Accountability Office, "New Markets Tax Credit: The Credit Helps Fund a Variety of Projects in Low-Income Communities, but Could Be Simplified," GAO 10-334, January 2010.

136. Sarah Portlock, "Newark to Break Ground on Long-Awaited Teachers Village," *Star-Ledger*, February 9, 2012. See also City of Newark press release, "Groundbreaking Commences Construction of Teachers Village," February 9, 2012.

137. Richard Meier and Partners Architects LLLP, "Revitalizing Development in Newark, New Jersey," February 15, 2012, http://archinect.com/

138. http://www.ci.newark.nj.us/. See the city's Living Downtown Plan and the city's Redevelopment Plans via the Office of Economic and Housing Development.

139. Richard Meier and Partners Architects LLLP, "Revitalizing Development in Newark, New Jersey," February 15, 2012, http://archinect.com/

140. Danny Weil, "Want to Know Who Cory Booker Is and What He Really Stands for?" *The Daily Censored*, May 23, 2012.

141. Alsion Gregor, "Newark Project Aims to Link Living and Learning," *New York Times*, March 6, 2012.

142. Harold Lucas interview, November 14, 2012, with author.

143. Alsion Gregor, "Newark Project Aims to Link Living and Learning," *New York Times*, March 6, 2012.

144. Modia Butler interview, November 26, 2012, with author.

145. *Associated Press*, "Cory Booker on Newark Creating 'Village' for Teachers: 'This Is How We Reinvent a Great American City," April 21, 2012.

146. Sharon Otterman, "Lauded Harlem Schools Have Their Own Problems," *New York Times*, October 12, 2012.

147. Reznick Group, "NMTCs Help Build Teachers Village in Downtown Newark," Spring 2012.

148. Brad Berton, "Affordability Near Employment Centers," *UrbanLand*, April 12, 2011.

149. Morris Newman, "LA Unified Project Combines Preschool and Apartments," *Los Angeles Times*, November 27, 2010.

150. Adam Zipkin interview, April 5, 2013, with author.

151. Nic Corbett, "NJIT Moves Forward on $80M Greek Village Project in Newark," *Star-Ledger*, December 21, 2011.

152. Ian T. Shearn, "Newark Seeks to Transform Housing Project Area," *Star-Ledger*, March 17, 2008; and Richard Khavkine, "NJIT Breaks Ground on Housing Project that Will Unite Greek Members, Honors Students," *Star-Ledger*, May 1, 2012.

153. Adam Zipkin interview, April 5, 2013, with author.

154. Carmen Juri, "A Haven for the Creative Set," *Star-Ledger*, April 13, 2008.

155. Andrew Jacobs, "Newark Loses Unwanted Landmark as Lincoln Motel Goes," *New York Times*, October 8, 2007.

156. Ibid.

157. Katie Wang and Maura McDermott, "Neighbors Fear Demolition Is a Health Hazard," *Star-Ledger*, January 8, 2008; and Mark Di Ionno, "Pulling Plug on a City's Past," *Star-Ledger*, January 8, 2008. See also Ian T. Shearn, "Newark Seeks to Transform Housing Project Area," *Star-Ledger*, March 17, 2008, especially about blight and the Westinghouse factory concerns.

158. Peggy McGlone, "NJPAC Sets the Stage for a High-Rise Project in Newark," *Star-Ledger*, January 18, 2008; and Andrew Jacobs, "Planning for Newark's Big Step: An Apartment Tower Near the Arts Center," *New York Times*, January 18, 2008.

159. Peggy McGlone, "A 'Game Changer' for Newark," *Star-Ledger*, May 6, 2010; and Antoinette Martin, "In Newark, Housing for Artists and Others," *Star-Ledger*, May 12, 2010.

160. Michael Meyer interview, December 3, 2012, with author.

161. John Appezzato, "Credit Crisis or Not, Newark Plans for Revival of Broad Street Area," *Star-Ledger*, December 3, 2008. See also Ian T. Shearn, "Newark Blueprint Has Lofty Ambitions," *Star-Ledger*, June 10, 2008.

162. Tom De Poto, "Chips of the Old Block in Newark as Prudential Looks to Future," *Star-Ledger*, November 11, 2012.

163. Mark Di Ionno, "A Builder Who Added Luster to Newark Feels Like an Outsider Again," *Star-Ledger*, February 10, 2009.

164. Philip Read, "Cogswell Realty Sues Developer Over Newark Venture Gone Sour," *Star-Ledger*, November 27, 2009.

165. Philip Read, "Bank of America Files Foreclosure Complaint Against Newark's Tallest Skyscraper," *Star-Ledger*, July 2, 2010.

166. Tom De Poto, "Chips of the Old Block in Newark as Prudential Looks to Future," *Star-Ledger*, November 11, 2012.

167. Michael Meyer interview, December 3, 2012, with author.

168. Philip Read, "Redevelopment Project in Lincoln Park Section of Newark Calls for 66 Homes," *Star-Ledger*, February 14, 2010.
169. Adam Zipkin interview, April 5, 2013, with author.
170. Philip Read, "Classic Car Showrooms of Newark Are Remodeled into Loft Apartments," *Star-Ledger*, November 21, 2010; and Antoinette Martin, "Turning Car Showrooms and Inspection Station into Housing," *New York Times*, April 21, 2011. For information about the Richardson Lofts, see David Giambusso, "LEED-Certified Apartment Building Opens in Newark After Years of Problems," *Star-Ledger*, June 22, 2012.
171. Sarah Portlock, "Newark in Tough Spot as Residents Want Services, But Stores Are Slow to Open," *Star-Ledger*, March 3, 2011.
172. Jefferty C. Mays, "Housing Agency in Newark Raises Its Ranking, But Still Needs Work," *Star-Ledger*, February 21, 2007; and Jeffery C. Mays, "A Year Later and Newark Residents Still Wait for Their Moving Day," *Star-Ledger*, November 8, 2006. See also Jeffery C. Mays, "New Boss Changes Face of Newark's Public Housing," *Star-Ledger*, August 13, 2007.
173. Jeffery C. Mays, "Public Housing: Case Closed," *Star-Ledger*, January 16, 2008; and *Star-Ledger* editorial, "Pressure for Housing Pays," January 23, 2008.
174. Jeffery C. Mays, "Stimulus Plan Raised Public Housing Hopes," *New York Times*, March 22, 2009.
175. Harold Lucas interview, November 14, 2012, with author.
176. Jeffery C. Mays, "A Year Later and Newark Residents Still Wait for Their Moving Day," *Star-Ledger*, November 8, 2006.
177. Jeffery C. Mays, "No One's Home," *Star-Ledger*, July 6, 2008.
178. Jonathan Schuppe, "Newarkers Take Altoona Express," *Star-Ledger*, June 1, 2007.
179. David Giambusso, "Suit's End Stirs Hope for Homes in Newark," *Star-Ledger*, December 10, 2009.
180. David Giambusso, "After 7 Years, $14M Newark South Ward Millennium Way Housing Project Opens," *Star-Ledger*, April 19, 2011.
181. Harold Lucas interview, November 14, 2012, with author.
182. Jeffery C. Mays, "Newark to Raze Housing Project," *Star-Ledger*, November 29, 2007; and Andrew Jacobs, "Cheers in Newark for a Housing Project's Downfall," *New York Times*, December 13, 2007.
183. David Giambusso, "HUD to Award $11M in Stimulus Funds to Rebuild Baxter Terrace Complex," *Star-Ledger*, September 22, 2009.
184. Chanta L. Jackson, "Newark Breaks Ground on Affordable Housing Featuring 'Green Spaces' for Veterans," *Star-Ledger*, September 3, 2009.
185. Ralph R. Ortega, "Newark Opens First Soon-to-Be Fully Solar-Powered, Affordable Housing," *Star-Ledger*, June 16, 2009.
186. David Giambusso, "Newark Unveils Second Phase of $21M Affordable Housing Project," *Star-Ledger*, August 11, 2009.
187. David Giambusso, "Newark Housing Authority Plans to Empty Waiting Lists, Hand Out $10M in Section 8 Housing Vouchers," *Star-Ledger*, June 17, 2010.
188. Antoinette Martin, "From Run-Down to Renovated," *New York Times*, September 29, 2011.
189. *Star-Ledger* editorial, "Calling a City Home," February 13, 2008.

190. Katie Wang, "Cops, Firefighters, Teachers to Get Apartment Deals," *Star-Ledger*, January 29, 2008.
191. Michael Meyer interview, December 3, 2012, with author.
192. Joan Whitlow, "Newark Home Owners, Not Builders, Need Tax Break," *Star-Ledger*, January 30, 2009.
193. Ralph R. Ortega, "Heading into the Homestretch," *Star-Ledger*, February 27, 2009.
194. Carmen Juri, "Streetscape Aims to Capture Ironbound's Flavor and Identity," *Star-Ledger*, August 8, 2006.
195. Carmen Juri, "Luxury Condos Coming to Newark," *Star-Ledger*, July 16, 2008.
196. Carmen Juri, "Newark Is Taking Change to the Streets," *Star-Ledger*, June 27, 2007.
197. Carmen Juri, "City's Epicenter Getting a $20M Broad Stroke," *Star-Ledger*, April 29, 2007.
198. Joan Whitlow, "Tearing Down Newark to Build It Up," *Star-Ledger*, September 4, 2007.
199. Jeffery C. Mays, "Newark Mayor Wants to Sell Retailers on City," *Star-Ledger*, May 16, 2007. See also Katie Wang, "Newark Has Model for Luring Retailers," *Star-Ledger*, May 27, 2007.
200. Katie Wang, "Newark's in Vegas, not to Gamble but to Sell," *Star-Ledger*, May 24, 2007.
201. Katie Wang, "Newark Has Model for Luring Retailers," *Star-Ledger*, May 27, 2007.
202. Katie Wang, "Newark's in Vegas, not to Gamble but to Sell," *Star-Ledger*, May 24, 2007.
203. Katie Wang, "Booker Markets Newark to Retailers," *Star-Ledger*, May 18, 2008. See also Kareem Fahim, "To Starbucks, a Closing; To Newark, a Trauma," *New York Times*, July 23, 2008; and *Star-Ledger* editorial, "Give Newark a (Coffee) Break," July 25, 2008.
204. Adam Zipkin interview, April 5, 2013, with author.
205. Stephanie Greenwood interview, April 3, 2013, with author.
206. City of Newark press release, "Sustainability Action Plan," 2013, p. 1. http://www.sustainablenwk.org/NewarkSustainabilityActionPlan_2013.pdf
207. Stephanie Greenwood interview, April 3, 2013, with author.
208. Ibid.
209. Adam Zipkin interview, April 5, 2013, with author.
210. Stephanie Greenwood interview, April 3, 2013, with author.
211. Heather Haddon, "Booker Pines for Whole Foods in Newark," *Wall Street Journal*, December 18, 2012; and New Jersey National Public Radio WBGO 88.3 FM, *Newark Today*, December 13, 2012.
212. Adam Zipkin interview, April 5, 2013, with author.
213. Richard Khavkine, "First Supermarket in Decades Opens in Newark's Central Ward," *Star-Ledger*, February 28, 2012.
214. Joan Whitlow, "Store Feeds Newark's Hunger for Jobs and Quality Food," *Star-Ledger*, March 2, 2012.
215. Eunice Lee, "Cory Booker Touts Newark's Newest Supermarket, Says City's Food Desert Is Shrinking," *Star-Ledger*, February 19, 2013.
216. Heather Haddon, "Wal-Mart Eyes First Store in Newark," *Wall Street Journal*, January 9, 2013 and Tom De Poto, "ShopRite to Build New Store in Newark," *Star-Ledger*, May 28, 2013.
217. Anibal Ramos Jr. interview, February 28, 2013, with author

218. Leslie Kwoh, "Tracking Newark's Renewal," *Star-Ledger*, September 30, 2007.

219. Ralph R. Ortega, "Newark Officials Trying to Update Old Zoning Laws, to Limit Large Signs and Parking Lifts," *Star-Ledger*, March 22, 2009.

220. Adam Zipkin interview, April 5, 2013, with author.

221. Cory Booker interview, April 5, 2013, with author. See also Ian T. Shearn and Katie Wang, "Booker Unveils Policy for Newark's Surplus Land," *Star-Ledger*, December 19, 2007; Jeffery C. Mays, "Newark Design Forum Seeks Thinking Outside 'Bayonne Box,'" *Star-Ledger*, November 28, 2007; and Katie Wang, "'Bayonne Boxes' May Get the Boot in Newark," *Star-Ledger*, May 8, 2008.

222. *New York Times* editorial, "The Land Is Newark's Land," December 30, 2007.

223. Jeffery C. Mays, "For Tiki, Shaq and Others, Newark's a Hot Investment," *Star-Ledger*, December 7, 2007. Read about O'Neal's 25-story proposed condominium tower in Ian Shearn, "Shaq's Development Group to Build Newark Condos," *Star-Ledger*, August 8, 2008 and Antoinette Martin, "A Native Son's Plans for Newark," *New York Times*, August 17, 2008; for information about the movie theater, see Ronda Kaysen, "With Help from Others, Newark Is Building for Business," *New York Times*, July 5, 2011.

224. David Giambusso, "Bon Jovi, Newark Mayor Booker Unveil $10.4M Affordable Housing Project," *Star-Ledger*, December 8, 2009; and "Jon Bon Jovi's New Soul Homes Attract Designer Style to Affordable Housing in Newark," *Star-Ledger*, December 9, 2009.

225. Modia Butler interview, November 26, 2012, with author; and Michael Meyer interview, December 3, 2012, with author.

226. Stephanie Greenwood interview, April 3, 2013, with author.

227. Adam Zipkin interview, April 5, 2013, with author.

228. Mark Di Ionno, "Big Dreams for Broken Parks," *Star-Ledger*, March 4, 2008; and Jeffery C. Mays and Katie Wang, "Newark Parks and Its Money at 21 Sites," *Star-Ledger*, July 27, 2008. Also Modia Butler interview, November 26, 2012, with author; and Mike Meyer interview, December 3, 2012, with author.

229. Jeffery C. Mays and Katie Wang, "Newark Parks and Its Money at 21 Sites," *Star-Ledger*, July 27, 2008.

230. Christopher DeLa Cruz, "Opening Lead-Free Newark Ballfield," *Star-Ledger*, August 3, 2008. See also David Giambusso, "Power Plant Is Approved and Newark Residents Are Outraged," *Star-Ledger*, May 13, 2012.

231. *New York Times* editorial, "A Park in Newark," October 23, 2008.

232. Ralph R. Ortega, "Newark Gets New Hope for Long-Awaited Park Along Passaic River," *Star-Ledger*, May 3, 2009.

233. Adam Zipkin interview, April 5, 2013, with author.

234. Cory Booker interview, April 5, 2013, with author.

235. Cullen Nutt, "After 3 Decades, Wait Finally Ends for Newark Park," *Star-Ledger*, July 29, 2009; and Barry Carter, "Nine Acres of Serene Green," *Star-Ledger*, September 4, 2009.

236. David Giambusso, "Newark Opens First Skate Park," *Star-Ledger*, September 2, 2009.

237. Michael Meyer interview, December 3, 2012, with author.

238. Philip Read, "Organizer Who Transformed New York's Bryant Park to Remake Newark's Military," *Star-Ledger*, November 2, 2010. Also Adam Zipkin interview,

April 5, 2013, with author. See also David Giambusso, "Construction Under Way for Newark's New Military Park, *Star-Ledger*, May 28, 2013.

239. Lisa W. Foderaro, "Revival Is Planned for a Derelict Downtown Newark Park," *New York Times*, February 5, 2013.

240. Jaime Lutz, "Newark 'American Idol' Auditions Bring Ryan Seacrest, Thousands of Singers to Prudential Center," *Star-Ledger*, June 23, 2012.

241. Peggy McGlone, "'America's Got Talent' to Film at NJPAC in Newark," *Star-Ledger*, April 8, 2012.

242. Peggy McGlone, "Dodge Poetry Fest: Melding Work on Hurricane Katrina with Jazz History," *Star-Ledger*, October 11, 2012.

243. James Barron, "A Poet Looks Back on a Bloody Week in 1967," *New York Times*, October 10, 2012. "Rebellion, I call it," said Baraka of the 1967 riots. "The idea that the city would blow up was obvious."

244. David Giambusso, "British Prime Minister David Cameron Meets with Newark Mayor Cory Booker," *Star-Ledger*, March 15, 2012.

245. Mike Frassinelli, "Holy Subway, Batman! A Hidden World of Clean, On-Time Riding Exists Beneath Newark," *Star-Ledger*, February 10, 2013.

246. Newark Census, http://quickfacts.census.gov/qfd/states/34/3451000.html

247. Kareem Fahim and Ron Nixon, "Beyond Foreclosures, Ruined Credit and Hopes," *New York Times*, March 28, 2007.

248. Sarah Portlock and David Giambusso, "$4M Revitalization Grant to Help Newark Neighborhoods Build Affordable Housing," *Star-Ledger*, December 2, 2011.

249. Anibal Ramos Jr. interview, February 28, 2013, with author.

250. Mildred Crump interview, January 28, 2013, with author.

251. Luis Quintana interview, February 6, 2013, with author.

252. Harold Lucas interview, November 14, 2012, with author.

253. Richard Cammarieri interview, December 3, 2012, with author.

254. Adam Zipkin interview, April 5, 2013, with author.

255. Jeffery C. Mays and Katie Wang, "Soaring Condo Market," *Star-Ledger*, May 6, 2007.

256. Adam Zipkin interview, April 5, 2013, with author.

257. Ras Baraka interview, February 11, 2014, with author.

258. Paul Milo, "'Teachers Village' Groundbreaking Today," NewarkPatch.com, February 9, 2012.

259. Anibal Ramos Jr. interview, February 28, 2013, with author

260. Ras Baraka interview, February 11, 2014, with author.

261. Ralph R. Ortega, "Newark Draws an Ambitious Design for a Better City," *Star-Ledger*, March 11, 2009.

262. Anibal Ramos Jr. interview, February 28, 2012, with author.

263. Ras Baraka interview, February 11, 2014, with author.

264. Mildred Crump interview, January 28, 2013, with author.

265. Modia Butler interview, November 26, 2012, with author.

266. Michael Meyer interview, December 3, 2012, with author.

267. Darrin S. Sharif and Trina Scordo, "Using Eminent Domain to Fix Newark's Foreclosure Crisis, *Star-Ledger*, May 17, 2013.

268. David Giambusso, "Newark's Deputy Mayor Leaving Administration to Become Connecticut's Education Commissioner," *Star-Ledger*, September 7, 2011.
269. Joan Whitlow, "Reduce Newark Unemployment: Bring in the Jobs, Hire the Residents," *Star-Ledger*, September 16, 2011.
270. Kavita Mokha, "'Rock' Climbing: Arena Area Sees Growth," *Wall Street Journal*, May 10, 2012.
271. Adam Zipkin interview, April 5, 2013, with author.

Chapter 5

1. Jeffery C. Mays, "Mayoral Race Kicks Off Early in Newark," *Star-Ledger*, September 14, 2008.
2. Jeffery C. Mays, "Booker Changes Staff to Ready for 2010 Campaign," *Star-Ledger*, November 2, 2008.
3. Michael Rispoli, "Newark Mayor Cory Booker Returns from Cross-Country Trip with $200K in Campaign Funds," *Star-Ledger*, June 9, 2009.
4. Joan Whitlow, "Murder to Nuisance Crimes, Newark Can Do Better," *Star-Ledger*, June 11, 2009. See also Nate Schweber, "Newark Murder Rate Dropped 30 Percent in 2008," *New York Times*, January 4, 2009.
5. James Queally, "Newark Red Light Cameras Reduce Traffic Violations, Bring in $3M in Revenue," *Star-Ledger*, March 14, 2011. See also Steve Strunsky, "Ex-Newark Mayor Sharpe James Admits Running a Red Light, after Conflicting Accounts of Violation," *Star-Ledger*, April 5, 2011.
6. Sharon Adarlo, "Day of Mayhem Renews Booker's Call to End City's Violence," *Star-Ledger*, July 22, 2009. See also Sharon Adarlo, "Newark Gun Buyback Program Ends Early After Funds Run Out," *Star-Ledger*, November 17, 2009; and Alexi Friedman, "Essex Displays Bounty from Gun Buyback Program," *Star-Ledger*, December 22, 2009.
7. Joan Whitlow, "Newark Shootings, an Aberration? We'll See," *Star-Ledger*, July 24, 2009.
8. Barry Carter, "Newark Groups Rally Against the Expectation that Gun Violence Is 'Normal,'" *Star-Ledger*, August 5, 2009.
9. Sharon Adarlo, "Shooting Spree Shakes Newark's Streets," *Star-Ledger*, August 19, 2009. See also Joan Whitlow, "Nighttime Is the Wrong Time for Kids to Be on City Streets," *Star-Ledger*, August 28, 2009.
10. Michael Rispoli, "Newark Mayor Cory Booker Vows Curfew Crackdown in Wake of 'Narcotics-Related Shootings,'" *Star-Ledger*, August 18, 2009. See also Sharon Adarlo, "Newark Welcomes Class of 64 Police Recruits," *Star-Ledger*, September 24, 2009.
11. David Giambusso and Alexi Friedman, "Newark Questions Curfew Enforcement for Juveniles," *Star-Ledger*, August 30, 2009.
12. David Giambusso, "Calling on Residents to Point Fingers," *Star-Ledger*, August 20, 2009. See also Sharon Adarlo, "Shooting Spree Shakes Newark's Streets," *Star-Ledger*, August 19, 2009.
13. Matt Dowling, "Man Is Arrested for Shooing that Injured 4-Year-Old Girl in Newark," *Times of Trenton*, September 1, 2009.

14. Matt Dowling, "Newark Shootings Prompt Increase in Patrols, Plea to Community for Help," *Times of Trenton*, August 20, 2009; and James Queally, "Newark Anti-Violence Group Holds 1-Year Anniversary March," *Star-Ledger*, August 2, 2010.

15. Joan Whitlow, "Newark Police, Protesters Have the Same Goal: Stop the Violence," *Star-Ledger*, August 21, 2009.

16. Cory Booker interview, April 5, 2013, with author.

17. Cory Booker, "Let's Break the Cycle of Re-arrest and Re-imprisonment," *Star-Ledger*, January 3, 2010.

18. *Star-Ledger* editorial, "New Jersey Legislature Should Approve Bills to Help Ex-Cons Stay Out of Prison," January 3, 2010.

19. *Star-Ledger* editorial, "Newark's Historic Choice: Arrest Records Won't Be First Hurdle for Job Applicants," September 14, 2012.

20. Richard Perez-Peña, "Booker and Christie Meet in the Middle," *New York Times*, October 1, 2010.

21. Joan Whitlow, "Newark's Democrats: Don't Blame Us for Gov. Jon Corzine's Loss," *Star-Ledger*, November 13, 2009.

22. Chris Megerian, "For Christie and for Newark, a Day to Remember," *Star-Ledger*, January 19, 2010.

23. Lisa Fleisher, "Christie Warns Cities: You Can't Look to Trenton for Aid," *Star-Ledger*, January 7, 2010. See also *Star-Ledger* editorial, "NJ Gov-Elect Says Struggling Cities to No Longer Receive State Aid," January 6, 2010.

24. Joan Whitlow, "Newark Schools: Finding Ways to Do More with Less," *Star-Ledger*, April 9, 2010.

25. Lisa Fleisher, "Cities: We'll Shrivel if Urban Enterprise Zones Are Hurt," *Star-Ledger*, April 13, 2010.

26. *Star-Ledger* editorial, "Newark Mayor Cory Booker Shovels Residents Driveway After Twitter Request," January 3, 2010.

27. David Giambusso, "Former Essex Prosecutor Kicks Off Newark Mayoral Challenge to Cory Booker," *Star-Ledger*, January 27, 2010.

28. *Star-Ledger* editorial, "Newark Council's Move on Contract Echoes the Bad Old Days," December 31, 2009.

29. David Giambusso, "Former Essex Prosecutor Kicks Off Newark Mayoral Challenge to Cory Booker," *Star-Ledger*, January 27, 2010.

30. Joan Whitlow, "Can Laid-back Clifford Minor Upset Cory Booker in Newark Mayoral Race," *Star-Ledger*, January 29, 2010.

31. David Giambusso, "In Newark, Political Family Connections Play Prominent Role in Campaigns," *Star-Ledger*, January 31, 2010.

32. David Giambusso, "Mayor Cory Booker in State of the City Address Says Newark Is Poised to Recover, Thrive," *Star-Ledger*, February 9, 2010. See also Richard Mascarenhas, "Newark Furlough a Surprise for Many Residents," *Star-Ledger*, September 9, 2009; and Associated Press, "Newark Mayor Cory Booker's National Prominence Is on the Rise," *Star-Ledger*, May 11, 2010.

33. Richard Cammarieri interview, December 3, 2012, with author.

34. *Star-Ledger*, "Former Aide to Newark Mayor Cory Booker Is Indicted on Extortion, Corruption Charges," February 18, 2010.

35. Joan Whitlow, "Newark's Pay-to-Play Ban: Gaps Linger in Enforcement of Campaign Contribution Rules," *Star-Ledger*, February 26, 2010.

36. David Giambusso, "Trial Begins for Former Newark Deputy Mayor Accused of Corruption," *Star-Ledger*, September 9, 2011.
37. David Giambusso, "Ex-Newark Deputy Mayor Steered City Contracts to Developer, Surveillance Tapes Show," *Star-Ledger*, September 12, 2011.
38. David Giambusso, "Key Witness Cross-Examined in Ex-Newark Deputy Mayor's Corruption Trial," *Star-Ledger*, September 15, 2011.
39. David Giambusso, "Ex-Newark Deputy Mayor Steered City Contracts to Developer, Surveillance Tapes Show," *Star-Ledger*, September 12, 2011.
40. Megan DeMarco, "Newark Corruption Trial: Cory Booker Testifies in Trial of Ex-Deputy Mayor," *Star-Ledger*, September 21, 2011. See also Morgan DeMarco, "Newark Corruption Trial: Former Deputy Mayor Testifies, Denies Steering Contracts to Local Business Owner for Kickbacks," *Star-Ledger*, September 26, 2011.
41. Morgan DeMarco, "Newark Corruption Trial: Former Deputy Mayor Testifies, Denies Steering Contracts to Local Business Owner for Kickbacks," *Star-Ledger*, September 26, 2011.
42. David Giambusso, "Former Newark Deputy Mayor Faces 20 Years in Prison Following Extortion Conspiracy Conviction," *Star-Ledger*, October 15, 2011.
43. David Giambusso, "Newark Political Group with Ties to Mayor Cory Booker Violated 'in Spirit' His Pay-to-Play Restrictions," *Star-Ledger*, April 26, 2010.
44. Joan Whitlow, "Newark Mayoral Campaign: Phony Newspapers, Bogus Banners," *Star-Ledger*, April 30, 2010.
45. Joan Whitlow, "Newark Politics and the Shirts on Kids' Backs," *Star-Ledger*, March 12, 2010.
46. Joan Whitlow, "Newark Mayoral Campaign: Phony Newspapers, Bogus Banners," *Star-Ledger*, April 30, 2010.
47. David Giambusso, "Newark Mayor Cory Booker Closes in on Second Term," *Star-Ledger*, May 7, 2010.
48. David Giambusso, "Newark Mayor Cory Booker Kicks Off Re-Election Campaign," *Star-Ledger*, April 4, 2010.
49. *Star-Ledger* editorial, "Newark's Murder-Free Month: Progress in the Fight Against Gun Violence," April 4, 2010.
50. David Giambusso, "Unbowed, Sharpe James Is Set to Return to Newark," *Star-Ledger*, April 4, 2010. See also David Giambusso, "Ex-Newark Mayor Sharpe James Is Welcomed Home By Hundreds of Supporters," *Star-Ledger*, April 6, 2010; and David Giambusso, "Former Newark Mayor Sharpe James Is Released from Virginia Prison," *Star-Ledger*, April 6, 2010.
51. *Star-Ledger* editorial, "The *Star-Ledger* Endorses Cory Booker for Re-election as Newark Mayor," May 9, 2010.
52. Associated Press, "Newark Mayor Cory Booker's National Prominence Is on the Rise," *Star-Ledger*, May 11, 2010.
53. *Wall Street Journal*, "In Newark, Cory Booker's Get Out the Vote Effort Goes High-Tech," May 11, 2010. Jersey City consultant Candice Osborne designed the software to help Jersey City Councilman Steven Fulop win his election.
54. Joan Whitlow, "After Re-Election, Newark Mayor Cory Booker's Fortunes Are Looking Up," *Star-Ledger*, May 14, 2010.
55. James Queally, "Newark Anti-Violence Group Holds 1-Year Anniversary March," *Star-Ledger*, August 2, 2010.

56. Victoria St. Martin, "Cory Booker Is Re-Elected as Newark Mayor for Second Term," *Star-Ledger*, May 12, 2010.

57. Joan Whitlow, "In Newark: Layoffs, Schools, and Minor Difficulties," *Star-Ledger*, October 1, 2010.

58. Richard Perez-Peña, "In New Jersey, Ex-Prosecutor Pleads Guilty in Bribery Case," *New York Times*, April 5, 2011.

59. David Giambusso, "Newark's $100M Budget Deficit Forces Doubling of Employee Furloughs," *Star-Ledger*, June 3, 2010.

60. Ibid. and Joan Whitlow, "Newark Council Deserves a Say in Budget Decisions," *Star-Ledger*, June 11, 2010.

61. Meredith Galante, "Hundreds of Newark Residents Attend Booker Municipal Authorities Hearing," *Star-Ledger*, July 26, 2010.

62. Joan Whitlow, "Will Water Deal Leave Newark Flush, or Soaking Wet?" *Star-Ledger*, June 18, 2010; and David Giambusso, "Newark City Council Is Increasingly Defiant Against Mayor Cory Booker's Municipal Authority Proposal," *Star-Ledger*, July 25, 2010.

63. David Giambusso, "Newark Mayor Cory Booker Proposes Budget to City Council," *Star-Ledger*, June 30, 2010.

64. David Giambusso, "Newark's Budget Woes, MUA Failure Cause Swift Deterioration of Relationship Between Booker, Council," *Star-Ledger*, August 8, 2010.

65. Mildred Crump interview, January 28, 2013, with author.

66. David Giambusso, "Newark Inauguration Speeches Signal Tense Relationship Between Booker, Council," *Star-Ledger*, July 1, 2010.

67. Joan Whitlow, "Newark's Water Fight May Leave Kids Without Pools," *Star-Ledger*, July 23, 2010.

68. Mildred Crump interview, January 28, 2013, with author.

69. Richard Cammarieri interview, December 3, 2012 with, author.

70. Kate Zernike, "Promise vs. Reality in Newark on Mayor's Watch," *New York Times*, December 13, 2012.

71. Mildred Crump interview, January 28, 2013, with author.

72. Barry Cater, "Newark Community Is Up in Arms About Local Library Closures Due to City Budget Cuts," *Star-Ledger*, July 7, 2010.

73. James Queally and David Giambusso, "More than 200 Newark Police Officers May Face Layoffs Due to $16.7M Budget Shortfall," *Star-Ledger*, July 16, 2010.

74. *Star-Ledger* editorial, "Crisis Looms for Newark Cops Unless Union Gives Back," July 26, 2010.

75. Philip Read, "Newark Council Slams Mayor Booker for 'Savage' Proposed Budget Cuts," *Star-Ledger*, July 22, 2010.

76. Ibid.

77. Joan Whitlow, "Newark's Water Fight May Leave Kids Without Pools," *Star-Ledger*, July 23, 2010.

78. David Giambusso, "Newark Swimming Pools to Be Kept Open with Help of Elizabeth Firm," *Star-Ledger*, July 29, 2010.

79. Meredith Galante, "N.J. Toilet Paper Companies to Donate Rolls to Newark After Mayor Booker's Budget Cuts," *Star-Ledger*, July 28, 2010; and *Star-Ledger* editorial, "Call Oprah, Stat! Newark City Hall Needs Toilet Paper!" July 24, 2010.

80. Meredith Galante, "Hundreds of Newark Residents Attend Booker Municipal Authorities Hearing," *Star-Ledger*, July 26, 2010.

81. David Giambusso, "Newark's Budget Woes, MUA Failure Cause Swift Deterioration of Relationship Between Booker, Council," *Star-Ledger*, August 8, 2010.

82. *Star-Ledger* editorial, "Troubled Waters Could Sink Newark Budget," July 30, 2010.

83. David Giambusso, "Newark City Council May Again Defer Vote on Mayor Booker's Municipal Utilities Authority," *Star-Ledger*, August 3, 2010.

84. David Giambusso, "Newark City Council, Mayor Booker Scramble to Fill Budget Hole After MUA Plan Is Defeated," *Star-Ledger*, August 5, 2010.

85. Cory Booker, "Solve Water, Sewer Problems," *Star-Ledger*, September 30, 2012.

86. Dan O'Flaherty, "Newark Mayor Cory Booker's Water Plan Would Lead to Worse System," *Star-Ledger*, March 13, 2012.

87. David Giambusso, "Newark City Council Approves Municipal Utilities Authority Application," *Star-Ledger*, August 11, 2012; and James Queally, "Booker Calls on Newark Council Members to Approve MUA Measure at Wednesday Meeting," *Star-Ledger*, July 1, 2012.

88. David Giambusso, "Newark City Council Grants Residents Vote Over MUA Issue," *Star-Ledger*, September 11, 2012.

89. Cory Booker interview, April 5, 2013, with author.

90. David Giambusso, "Newark's Budget Woes, MUA Failure Cause Swift Deterioration of Relationship Between Booker, Council," *Star-Ledger*, August 8, 2010.

91. Richard Cammarieri interview, December 3, 2012, with author.

92. David Giambusso, "Newark's Budget Woes, MUA Failure Cause Swift Deterioration of Relationship Between Booker, Council," *Star-Ledger*, August 8, 2010.

93. Tom Moran, "Newark Mayor Booker Faces Worst Crisis of His Career After Council Dismisses MUA Proposal," *Star-Ledger*, August 8, 2010.

94. Anibal Ramos Jr. interview, February 28, 2013, with author

95. Joan Whitlow, "A City for Sale," *Star-Ledger*, August 27, 2010.

96. Joan Whitlow, "Off-the-Cuff Remark Weakened Newark Mayor Cory Booker's Hand," *Star-Ledger*, August 13, 2010.

97. Anibal Ramos Jr. interview, February 28, 2013, with author

98. David Giambusso, "Newark Council Proposes Selling City Properties to Close Budget Gap," *Star-Ledger*, August 24, 2010.

99. Joan Whitlow, "A City for Sale," *Star-Ledger*, August 27, 2010.

100. David Giambusso, "Newark Is Entering 'New Frontier' with Idea to Sell Municipal Buildings in Time to Close Budget Gap," *Star-Ledger*, August 26, 2010.

101. David Giambusso, "Newark City Council Approves Final Changes to City's Budget," *Star-Ledger*, October 7, 2010; and David Giambusso, "After Selling Buildings to Close Budget Gap, Newark Now Faces $125M Bill from Bondholders," *Star-Ledger*, January 20, 2011.

102. *Star-Ledger* editorial, "Givebacks Needed from Newark Police, Fire Unions to Reduce Layoffs," October 4, 2010.

103. David Giambusso and James Queally, "Newark Sends Out Notifications to 2,200 Employees of Likely Job Eliminations," *Star-Ledger*, September 28, 2010; and Joan Whitlow, "In Newark: Layoffs, Schools, and Minor Difficulties," *Star-Ledger*, October 1, 2010.

104. Joan Whitlow, "In Newark, It's Six Degrees of Sanitation," *Star-Ledger*, January 14, 2011.
105. David Giambusso and James Queally, "Newark Sends Out Notifications to 2,200 Employees of Likely Job Eliminations," *Star-Ledger*, September 28, 2010.
106. Joan Whitlow, "Long Hot Summer for Murder in Newark," *Star-Ledger*, September 3, 2010. See also James Queally, "Newark Sees Spike in Shooting, Homicide Rates Over Summer," *Star-Ledger*, September 14, 2010.
107. David Giambusso and James Queally, "Newark Submits to Eliminate Nearly 1,000 City Jobs," *Star-Ledger*, August 26, 2010.
108. Sean Gardiner, "Newark's Top Cop Faces Hurdles," *Wall Street Journal*, October 11, 2010.
109. Chris Megerian and James Queally, "ACLU Accuses Newark Police of False Arrests, Excessive Force," *Star-Ledger*, September 9, 2010.
110. Deborah Jacobs, "Newark Police Department Needs an Intervention; the ACLU-NJ Turns to the Federal Government," *Star-Ledger*, September 6, 2010.
111. Chris Megerian, "Reports Show 1 in 10 Complaints Against Newark Police Officers Are Not Fully Reported to NJ," *Star-Ledger*, September 12, 2010. See also *Star-Ledger*'s scathing editorial, "Checking Newark Cops: Bring in the Feds to Probe ACLU Charges," September 17, 2010; and Joan Whitlow, "Police Discipline Is Key to Fighting Crime," *Star-Ledger*, September 17, 2010.
112. Chris Megerian, "Attorney General, Essex County Prosecutor to Review Newark Police Internal Affairs," *Star-Ledger*, September 15, 2010.
113. Joshua Chanin, "The Best Hope for Police Reform in Newark," *Star-Ledger*, January 17, 2011.
114. James Queally, "Newark Police Union Vote 'No Confidence' in City's Police Director After ACLU Petition," *Star-Ledger*, September 17, 2010. See also Mark Di Ionno, "Business as Usual for Reconfirmed Newark Police Director Garry McCarthy," *Star-Ledger*, October 7, 2010.
115. Chris Megerian and David Giambusso, "Newark Police Director Defends Department, Personal Record," *Star-Ledger*, September 16, 2010.
116. James Queally, "Newark Police Introduces Revised Community Relations Strategy," *Star-Ledger*, September 28, 2010.
117. James Queally, "Newark Police May Be First In Country to Reveal Monthly Stop-and-Frisk, Internal Affairs Data," *Star-Ledger*, July 10, 2013.
118. David Giambusso, "Newark Council Members Defy Booker, Call for Federal Probe into Police Misconduct," *Star-Ledger*, November 5, 2010.
119. James Queally, "Justice Department Investigates ACLU's Call for Federal Oversight of Newark Police," *Star-Ledger*, January 20, 2011.
120. James Queally, "Newark Police Recruits to Be Laid Off as Part of Budget Crisis," *Star-Ledger*, October 13, 2010.
121. Mark Di Ionno, "Losing Newark Police Horses Due to Budget Woes Is Philadelphia's Gain," *Star-Ledger*, January 11, 2011.
122. Alexi Friedman, "Judge Says She Is Powerless to Prevent Newark Police, Fire Department Layoffs," *Star-Ledger*, November 10, 2012. See also Joan Whitlow, "Though Newark Is Tapped out, Layoffs Are Still a Question," *Star-Ledger*, November 12, 2010.

123. David Giambusso, "Judge Delays Scheduled Layoffs for Newark Police," *Star-Ledger*, November 12, 2010.
124. James Queally and Philip Read, "Newark Police Unions, Booker Administration Continue Battle Over Proposed Layoffs," *Star-Ledger*, November 18, 2010.
125. James Queally and Alexi Friedman, "Newark Finalizes 167 Police Layoffs After Union Refuses Booker's Plea to Return to Negotiating Table," *Star-Ledger*, November 30, 2010. See also Kareem Fahim, "Fears of Regression as Newark Police Force Is Cut," *New York Times*, December 1, 2010.
126. David Giambusso and Alexi Friedman, "Laid off Newark Police Officers Cope with Unemployment," *Star-Ledger*, November 30, 2010.
127. *Star-Ledger* editorial, "Newark Union Wrong Not to Negotiate," December 1, 2010. See also Joan Whitlow, "Big Questions as Newark Braces for Cop Layoffs," *Star-Ledger*, December 3, 2010.
128. David Giambusso, "Police Departments Across the U.S. Recruit Recently Laid-off Newark Officers," *Star-Ledger*, February 12, 2011; and David Giambusso and Alexi Friedman, "Laid off Newark Police Officers Cope with Unemployment," *Star-Ledger*, November 30, 2010.
129. James Queally, "Three People Are Killed, Four Wounded in Two Newark Shootings," *Star-Ledger*, December 23, 2010. See also David Queally and David Giambusso, "Newark Shootings Leave Four Dead, Six Wounded Since Thursday," *Star-Ledger*, December 24, 2010; James Queally, "Newark Carjackings Increase by 60 Percent Past Year," *Star-Ledger*, January 10, 2011; and James Queally and Alexi Friedman, "Task Force Nets 12 Arrests in String of Essex County Carjackings," *Star-Ledger*, January 11, 2011.
130. The Associated Press, "After Dozens of Arrests, Newark Carjackings Decline Sharply," *New York Times*, March 21, 2011.
131. James Queally, "Newark Officials, Leaders to Meet with Violent Groups to Offer Them Jobs in Effort to Reduce Crime," *Star-Ledger*, March 11, 2011.
132. Cory Booker interview, April 5, 2013, with author.
133. James Queally, "Newark Officials, Leaders to Meet with Violent Groups to Offer Them Jobs in Effort to Reduce Crime," *Star-Ledger*, March 11, 2011.
134. David Giambusso, "Newark Police Director McCarthy Appears to Be Front-Runner for Top Chicago Job," *Star-Ledger*, April 29, 2011.
135. James Queally, "Newark Police Director McCarthy Accepts Job as Chicago's Top Cop," *Star-Ledger*, May 3, 2011.
136. *Star-Ledger* editorial, "As McCarthy Leaves for Chicago, Police Director Can Take a Bow," May 6, 2011.
137. James Queally, "Deputy Chief Samuel DeMaio Is Named Newark's Acting Police Director," *Star-Ledger*, May 3, 2011.
138. David Giambusso, "Newark Pastors, Council Members Ask New Police Director to Release Disciplinary Record," *Star-Ledger*, May 6, 2011. See also Joan Whitlow, "DeMaio Gets the Nod," *Star-Ledger*, May 6, 2011.
139. Deborah Jacobs, "Release Newark Police Director's Disciplinary Records," *Star-Ledger*, May 10, 2011.
140. James Queally, "Acting Newark Police Director Samuel DeMaio Vows Changes, Shrugs Off Controversy," *Star-Ledger*, May 18, 2011.

141. Jason Grant and James Queally, "Federal Investigation of Newark Police Dept. Launched; Mayor Booker Welcomes Probe," *Star-Ledger*, May 10, 2011. See also David Giambusso, "U.S. Justice Department to Launch Formal Investigation into Newark Police," *Star-Ledger*, May 8, 2011; and Richard Perez-Nuñez, "Police Department in Newark Is Facing U.S. Inquiry," *New York Times*, May 9, 2011.

142. *Star-Ledger* editorial, "Newark Should Welcome Fed Probe of Police Department," May 10, 2011.

143. James Queally and David Giambusso, "Newark Mayor Cory Booker Adviser Claims Intimidation from Police Following Critical 'Blast' Flier," *Star-Ledger*, September 30, 2011. See also Joan Whitlow, "Newark Police Fax Finding: Much Ado about Nothing?" *Star-Ledger*, September 30, 2011.

144. Tom Moran, "Gov. Chris Christie's Pension and Health Care Reform a Gift to Liberals," *Star-Ledger*, July 17, 2011.

145. David Giambusso and James Queally, "Newark Seeks Public's Help in Stemming Bloodshed, Forms 'Safe City Task Force,'" *Star-Ledger*, June 1, 2011.

146. David Giambusso, "Newark Mayor Cory Booker's Calls for Residents' Support to Reduce Violence," *Star-Ledger*, June 3, 2011.

147. James Queally, "City Gets $2M Grant to Discourage Crime," *Star-Ledger*, September 20, 2011.

148. Joan Whitlow, "Backing Away from the Streets," *Star-Ledger*, June 24, 2011.

149. Joan Whitlow, "Toy Guns Are No Longer Child's Play," *Star-Ledger*, August 26, 2011.

150. Lisa Fleisher, "Violent Nights Put Newark on Offense," *Wall Street Journal*, July 13, 2011.

151. *Star-Ledger* editorial, "Police Strategies Turn Down Heat in Newark," June 3, 2013; and James Queally, "Baraka Slams Booker Over Lack of Cops, Recent Violence in Newark's South Ward, *Star-Ledger*, June, 3103.

152. James Queally and David Giambusso, "Newark's Acting Police Chief Makes First Public Appearance," *Star-Ledger*, August 9, 2011. See also James Queally, "Newark's First Female Police Chief Brings No-Nonsense Approach to City Police Force," *Star-Ledger*, September 2, 2011.

153. David Giambusso, "Newark Mayor Booker Says He Would Have Never Allowed NYPD to Spy on City's Muslims," *Star-Ledger*, February 22, 2012.

154. Christopher Baxter, "Secret NYPD Surveillance in NJ Was Not So Secret, Former Officials Say," *Star-Ledger*, March 6, 2012.

155. Associated Press, "Report: Newark Police Allowed NYPD to Spy on Muslims, Build Secret Files," *Star-Ledger*, February 22, 2012. See also David Giambusso, "Religious Leaders, Students Rally Against NYPD Surveillance Over Newark Muslims," *Star-Ledger*, February 25, 2012; Eugene Paik, "Meeting with NJ Muslim Leaders, Booker Can't Guarantee NYPD's Newark Surveillance Has Ceased," *Star-Ledger*, February 26, 2012; and Heather Haddon and Jessica Firger, "Police Spying Fans Feud," *Wall Street Journal*, March 4, 2012.

156. David Giambusso, "Religious Leaders, Students Rally Against NYPD Surveillance Over Newark Muslims," *Star-Ledger*, February 25, 2012.

157. Heather Haddon and Jessica Firger, "Police Spying Fans Feud," *Wall Street Journal*, March 4, 2012.

158. Christopher Baxter, "Secret NYPD Surveillance in NJ Was Not So Secret, Former Officials Say," *Star-Ledger*, March 6, 2012.

159. James Queally, "Newark Police Were with NYPD Investigators During Muslim Probe 'At All Times,'" *Star-Ledger*, March 9, 2012.

160. Associated Press, "NJ Clears NYPD's Surveillance of Muslims," *Wall Street Journal*, May 24, 2012.

161. James Queally, "Group of NJ Muslims to File Lawsuits Against NYPD Over Surveillance Operation," *Star-Ledger*, June 6, 2012.

162. Cory Booker interview, April 5, 2013, with author.

163. Victoria St. Martin, "Newark High School Students Walk Out in Protest of Filthy, Unsafe School Environment," *Star-Ledger*, October 7, 2010.

164. Joan Whitlow, "Here's an Idea for Fixing Schools: Listen to the Students," *Star-Ledger*, May 7, 2010.

165. Mildred Crump interview, January 28, 2013, with author.

166. Joan Whitlow, "Can Money Buy Transformation in Newark Schools?" *Star-Ledger*, June 25, 2010.

167. Barbara Martinez, "Back to School for Newark's Booker," *Wall Street Journal*, May 7, 2010.

168. Linda Ocasio, "Clifford Janey: Q&A with Newark Schools Chief on His First Year on the Job," *Star-Ledger*, August 9, 2009.

169. Joan Whitlow, "Earning a High School Diploma Begins in Early Grades," *Star-Ledger*, June 19, 2009.

170. Winnie Hu, "Newark Starts a Summer School Aimed at Advanced Placement," *Star-Ledger*, July 8, 2009.

171. Jeanette M. Runduist, "Superintendant Clifford Janey Releases Plan to Improve Newark Schools," *Star-Ledger*, January 14, 2010.

172. Winnie Hu, "Ambitious New Model for 7 Newark Schools," *New York Times*, July 25, 2010; and Victoria St. Martin, "Newark Educators Release Plan to Turn Around Low-Performing Schools," *Star-Ledger*, September 3, 2010.

173. Jessica Calefati and David Giambusso, "Newark Superintendant Clifford Janey's Contract Is Not Renewed," *Star-Ledger*, September 1, 2010.

174. Jody Pittman, "Newark Parents Must Become Leaders on School Reform," *Star-Ledger*, April 27, 2012.

175. David Giambusso, "Newark Superintendant Replacement Will Have a Tough Task Ahead, Experts Say," *Star-Ledger*, September 2, 2010.

176. *Star-Ledger* editorial, "Hoping for a Star to Run the City Schools," September 2, 2010.

177. Josh Margolin, "Newark's $100M Grant Is a Result of Collaboration, Preparation and Fate," *Star-Ledger*, September 26, 2010.

178. Richard Perez-Peña, "Facebook Founder to Donate $100 Million to Help Remake Newark's Schools," *New York Times*, September 22, 2010. See also Josh Margolin and David Giambusso, "Facebook CEO Zuckerberg to Donate $100M to Newark Schools on Oprah Winfrey Show," *Star-Ledger*, September 23, 2010.

179. Ibid., and David Giambusso, "Newark Mayor Booker Likely to Seek Third Term on Heels of $100M Schools Grant," *Star-Ledger*, September 26, 2010.

180. Josh Margolin, "Facebook CEO Pledges $100M to Newark Schools, Announces Campaign to Raise $100M More," *Star-Ledger*, September 24, 2010. See also Barbara

Martinez, "Newark's Mayor Woos School Backers," *Wall Street Journal*, September 28, 2010.

181. Barbara Martinez and Geoffrey Fowler, "Friended for $100 Million," *Wall Street Journal*, September 23, 2010. See also *New York Times* editorial, "Facebook and Newark," September 23, 2010; Richard Perez-Peña, "Schools Run by Newark May Yet Reflect Christie's Vision," *New York Times*, September 23, 2010; and Joan Whitlow, "Not Waiting for Superman," *Star-Ledger*, October 15, 2010.

182. Josh Margolin, "Facebook CEO Pledges $100M to Newark Schools, Announces Campaign to Raise $100M More," *Star-Ledger*, September 24, 2010.

183. Richard Perez-Peña, "Schools Run by Newark May Yet Reflect Christie's Vision," *New York Times*, September 23, 2010; and Josh Margolin and David Giambusso, "Facebook CEO Zuckerberg to Donate $100M to Newark Schools on Oprah Winfrey Show," *Star-Ledger*, September 23, 2010.

184. Bob Braun, "Gov. Christie, Newark Mayor Cory Booker Attempt to Lesson Race to the Top Error with Oprah Show," *Star-Ledger*, September 24, 2010.

185. Tom Moran, "Public Support Is Integral to Newark Schools Reform," *Star-Ledger*, September 26, 2010.

186. Ibid.

187. David Giambusso, "Newark Mayor Booker Likely to Seek Third Term on Heels of $100M Schools Grant," *Star-Ledger*, September 26, 2010.

188. Josh Margolin, "Newark's $100M Grant Is a Result of Collaboration, Preparation and Fate," *Star-Ledger*, September 26, 2010.

189. Jessica Calefati, "N.J. Law May Bar Gov. Christie, Mayor Booker from Taking Active Role in $100M Newark Schools Grant," *Star-Ledger*, December 5, 2010.

190. Jessica Calefati, "Newark Mayor Cory Booker's School May Not Improve Student Performance, Study Says" *Star-Ledger*, October 12, 2010.

191. Jessica Calefati, "Former Washington DC Schools Chancellor Hesitates in Accepting Offer to Become NJ Education Chief," *Star-Ledger*, October 20, 2010. See also Michelle Rhee and Adrian Fenty, "The Education Manifesto," *Wall Street Journal*, October 30, 2010.

192. Jessica Calefati, "Christie Praises DC Schools Chief, Shows Support for Education Reform Plan," *Star-Ledger*, January 12, 2011.

193. Ginger Gibson, "Christie to Announce $584M Plan for Construction, Renovation of 10 N.J. Schools," *Star-Ledger*, February 15, 2011.

194. Jeanette Rundquist, "Newark to Launch $100M School Makeover with 'Relentless Outreach' Campaign, to Ask Residents for Ideas," *Star-Ledger*, November 2, 2010.

195. David Giambusso and Jessica Calefati, "Newark Residents Request More Parental Involvement, Better Teachers During Door-to-Door Campaign," *Star-Ledger*, November 7, 2010.

196. Jessica Calefati and Kelly Heyboer, "$100M Grant from Mark Zuckerberg Begins to Have Effect on Newark Schools," *Star-Ledger*, September 25, 2011.

197. David Giambusso and Jessica Calefati, "PENewark Outreach to Reform Newark Schools Is a Waste of Time, Money, Critics Say," *Star-Ledger*, November 12, 2010.

198. *Star-Ledger* editorial, "Newark's Extravagant Outreach Campaign Returned Little Information," January 3, 2011.

199. Joan Whitlow, "So Many New High School Choices, So Much Confusion," *Star-Ledger*, May 13, 2011; and David Giambusso, "PENewark to Launch Second Education Reform Survey," *Star-Ledger*, January 23, 2011.

200. Rohan Mascarenhas, "Newark Schools Take Step Toward Ending More Than a Decade of State Control," *Star-Ledger*, December 5, 2010.

201. David Giambusso, "N.J. Education Chief Chris Cerf, Mayor Cory Booker Present Findings on Newark Schools Reform," *Star-Ledger*, February 5, 2011; and Jessica Calefati and David Giambusso, "Acting N.J. Education Chief Cerf Revises Account of Ties to Consulting Firm," *Star-Ledger*, February 24, 2011.

202. Ibid.

203. Ginger Gibson, "N.J. Senators Stall Approval of Acting Education Chief Christopher Cerf," *Star-Ledger*, March 2, 2011.

204. Megan DeMarco, Chris Megerian, and Alexi Friedman, "Gov. Christie Blasts Ron Rice for Blocking Education Commissioner," *Star-Ledger*, December 8, 2011.

205. Richard Khavkine, "NJ Sen. Rice Calls for Feds to Look into State Control of Newark, Jersey City and Paterson Schools," *Star-Ledger*, December 6, 2012.

206. Kelly Heyboer, "Newark School Plan Would Clear Space for Charters, Shift Scores of Students," *Star-Ledger*, February 22, 2011.

207. Barbara Martinez, "Furor in N.J. Over Charter School Space," *Wall Street Journal*, March 22, 2011.

208. David Giambusso, "Mayor Cory Booker to Call for Policy of Greater Transparency in Newark Schools," *Star-Ledger*, March 1, 2011.

209. Ibid., and Kelly Heyboer, "Newark School Plan Would Clear Space for Charters, Shift Scores of Students," *Star-Ledger*, February 22, 2011.

210. Ibid.

211. David Giambusso, "Newark Mayor Cory Booker Promises to Use 'Bully Pulpit,' $200M in Funds to Reform," *Star-Ledger*, March 2, 2011.

212. Bob Braun, "School Reform Effort Between Christie, Booker Is Against the Law," *Star-Ledger*, March 7, 2011.

213. Jessica Calefati, "N.J. Report Recommends Evaluating Teachers by Classroom Performance, Student Scores," *Star-Ledger*, March 4, 2011.

214. Jessica Calefati, "Newark Needs More Money to Meet Facebook Founder Mark Zuckerberg's $100 Million Challenge," *Star-Ledger*, June 17, 2012.

215. Jessica Calefati, "Gov. Christie Announces Plan to Select Next Newark Superintendant by May," *Star-Ledger*, March 18, 2011.

216. Chris Cerf, "Doing What's Best for Newark's Students," *Star-Ledger*, March 20, 2011.

217. Barbara Martinez, "Furor in N.J. Over Charter School Space," *Wall Street Journal*, March 22, 2011.

218. David Giambusso, "More Than 1,000 Cram into Newark School to Debate Plan to Expand Charters into Newark School Campuses," *Star-Ledger*, March 23, 2011.

219. Tom Moran, "Steve Adubato Sr. Tarnishes Legacy with Cheating, Ethics, Scandals," *Star-Ledger*, November 18, 2012.

220. Luis Quintana interview, February 6, 2013, with author.

221. David Giambusso, "Newark School Board Chair Accuses Others of Being Manipulated to Vote Against 6 New High Schools," *Star-Ledger*, April 10, 2011.

222. *Star-Ledger* editorial, "In Newark, Politics over Kids," April 10, 2011.

223. David Giambusso, "Reorganization of Newark School Advisory Board Shows North Ward Power Broker's Influence," *Star-Ledger*, May 3, 2011.

224. David Giambusso, "Newark School Board Chair Accuses Others of Being Manipulated to Vote Against 6 New High Schools," *Star-Ledger*, April 10, 2011.

225. David Giambusso, "Five New Newark Schools to Get Nearly $1M from Facebook CEO Donation," *Star-Ledger*, April 13, 2011.

226. Joan Whitlow, "It's Facebook Money and Newark's Future," *Star-Ledger*, October 7, 2011.

227. Victoria St. Martin, "Youth Advocate Chosen to Administer $100M Facebook Grant to Newark Schools," *Star-Ledger*, May 17, 2011.

228. Jessica Calefati and Kelly Heyboer, "$100M Grant from Mark Zuckerberg Begins to Have Effect on Newark Schools," *Star-Ledger*, September 25, 2011.

229. Joan Whitlow, "Newark Parents Want to Be Involved—Don't Ignore Them," *Star-Ledger*, April 23, 2011.

230. Joan Whitlow, "As September Approaches, Plenty of Answers Still Sought," *Star-Ledger*, April 15, 2011. See also Joan Whitlow, "So Many New High School Choices, So Much Confusion," *Star-Ledger*, May 13, 2011.

231. David Giambusso and Jessica Calefati, "U.S. Education Secretary Says Newark Schools Reform Could Become a National Model," *Star-Ledger*, April 21, 2011.

232. Barbara Martinez, "Teacher Bonuses Emerge in Newark," *Wall Street Journal*, April 21, 2011.

233. Jessica Calefati and David Giambusso, "Newark Schools Superintendent Search Narrowed to 2 Candidates, Sources Say," *Star-Ledger*, April 22, 2011.

234. Ibid. See also Lisa Fleisher, "Newark School Pick," *Wall Street Journal*, April 23, 2011.

235. Lisa Fleisher and Barbara Martinez, "Christie Picks Newark Schools Chief," *Wall Street Journal*, May 4, 2011.

236. Winne Hu and Nate Schweber, "For Next Chief of Newark Schools, Hard Choices," *New York Times*, May 4, 2011.

237. Sheila Oliver, "Gov. Chris Christie Wrong on Newark Schools," *Star-Ledger*, May 10, 2011.

238. Winne Hu and Nate Schweber, "For Next Chief of Newark Schools, Hard Choices," *New York Times*, May 4, 2011.

239. Lisa Fleisher, "Quick Lessons in Newark," *Wall Street Journal*, May 5, 2011; and *Star-Ledger* editorial, "Meet Newark's New School Chief: A Conversation with Cami Anderson," May 8, 2011.

240. Winne Hu and Nate Schweber, "For Next Chief of Newark Schools, Hard Choices," *New York Times*, May 4, 2011.

241. Robert Curvin, "Cami Anderson Is the White Girl From Harlem," *Star-Ledger*, May 8, 2011.

242. Jessica Calefati and Jeanette Rundquist, "New Newark Schools Superintendent Says Her Family Background Prepared Her for Role," *Star-Ledger*, May 5, 2011.

243. *Star-Ledger* editorial, "Newark's New Superintendent, Cami Anderson: A Capable Woman Who Will Need a Lot of Help," May 5, 2011.

244. Jessica Calefati, "Newark Schools to Remain in State Hands, Gov. Christie Says," *Star-Ledger*, May 5, 2011.

245. David Giambusso, "Adubato Sr. Will Not Manage Newark School Advisory Board Candidates," *Star-Ledger*, January 24, 2012; and Tom Moran, "Newark Boss Steve Adubato's Moment of Truth on School Reform," *Star-Ledger*, April 22, 2012.

246. Jessica Calefati, "Board of Education Appoints New Newark Public Schools Superintendent," *Star-Ledger*, June 2, 2011; and Jessica Calefati, "Newark, Paterson and Jersey City Want School Independence from N.J. Board of Ed," *Star-Ledger*, June 13, 2012.

247. Joan Whitlow, "Newark Schools Boss Should Be Sure Cash Is Spent Wisely," *Star-Ledger*, May 27, 2011. See also Jessica Calefati, "Newark Schools Chief, Teachers Union Clash Over Seniority," *Star-Ledger*, July 26, 2012.

248. Jessica Calefati and David Giambusso, "Newark Superintendent to Announce Closing of 7 Failing Schools, New Charter School Rules," *Star-Ledger*, February 3, 2012; and Tom Moran, "Superintendent Cami Anderson Needs Support to Make Change in Newark Schools," *Star-Ledger*, March 11, 2012.

249. *Star-Ledger* editorial, "Smart Start to Change in Newark Schools," June 25, 2011.

250. Winnie Hu, "Newark Is Betting on a Wave of New Principals," *Star-Ledger*, September 15, 2011.

251. Lisa Fleisher, "Newark Mulls Teacher Buyouts," *Wall Street Journal*, May 18, 2012.

252. *Star-Ledger* editorial, "Sharing Space in Newark," June 14, 2011.

253. *Star-Ledger* editorial, "Newark School Board's Dysfunction Might Endanger Reform," August 15, 2011.

254. *Star-Ledger* editorial, "Pragmatic Superintendent Cami Anderson May Succeed in Newark," February 5, 2012.

255. Jessica Calefati, "Newark Schools Boss Cami Anderson Named to Time's 100 Most Influential People List," *Star-Ledger*, April 18, 2012.

256. David Giambusso, "Newark Mayor Cory Booker Angered by ACLU's Lawsuit Over Facebook Founder's $100M Donation to City Schools," *Star-Ledger*, August 24, 2011.

257. *Star-Ledger* editorial, "Q&A: ACLU's N.J. Leader on Suing Newark for Transparency Over Facebook Founder's Schools Donation," August 30, 2011.

258. David Giambusso, "Newark Mayor Cory Booker Angered by ACLU's Lawsuit Over Facebook Founder's $100M Donation to City Schools," *Star-Ledger*, August 24, 2011. See also Joan Whitlow, "Seeking Details of the $100 Million Deal," *Star-Ledger*, September 4, 2011.

259. Lisa Fleisher, "Newark Schools Won't Get Rich on Facebook IPO," *Wall Street Journal*, February 2, 2012.

260. David Giambusso, "Newark Must Turn Over List of E-mails Regarding Facebook Donations," *Star-Ledger*, January 27, 2012.

261. Lisa Fleisher, "Booker, Facebook Emails About $100 Million Schools Gift Released," *Wall Street Journal*, December 25, 2012; and Jenna Portnoy, "Cory Booker Releases Secret Emails on $100M Facebook Gift to Newark Schools," *Star-Ledger*, December 25, 2012.

262. Jodi Rudoren, "Putting Zuckerberg's Millions to Work for Schools," *New York Times*, November 1, 2011.

263. Jessica Calefati and Kelly Heyboer, "$100M Grant from Mark Zuckerberg Begins to Have Effect on Newark Schools," *Star-Ledger*, September 25, 2011.

264. Jessica Calefati, "25 Teams of Newark Teachers to Receive More Than $200K from Facebook Grant," February 23, 2012. See also Greg Taylor, "Newark's Facebook Money Earning Dividends," *Star-Ledger*, June 22, 2012.

265. Kate Zernike, "Contract with Merit Pay, Backed by Union Chiefs, Is Tough Sell for Newark Teachers," *New York Times*, October 28, 2012

266. Lisa Fleisher, "Newark Eyes Merit Pay for Teachers," *Wall Street Journal*, September 16, 2012; and Peggy McGlone, "Newark Teachers Would Earn Merit Pay Under Possible Program," *Star-Ledger*, September 18, 2012. See also Jessica Calefati, "If Newark Teachers Ratify Pact, District Will Be Model for Others in NJ," *Star-Ledger*, October 28, 2012; and Kate Zernike, "Contract with Merit Pay, Backed by Union Chiefs, Is Tough Sell for Newark Teachers," *New York Times*, October 28, 2012.

267. *Star-Ledger* editorial, "Newark Teacher Contract a Turning Point Teachers, Students," November 12, 2012.

268. Jeanette Rundquist, "Newark Teachers Union Approves Landmark Contract Offering Merit Pay Bonuses," *Star-Ledger*, November 14, 2012; and Lisa Fleisher, "Teachers Clear Newark Pact," *Wall Street Journal*, November 14, 2012.

269. Kelly Heyboer, "Newark Teachers Strike Historic Deal Including for Top Educators," *Star-Ledger*, October 17, 2012; and *New York Times* editorial, "School Reform in Newark," November 16, 2012. See also *Star-Ledger* editorial, "Groundbreaking Newark Teacher Contract Good for Teachers, Kids," October 28, 2012.

270. *Star-Ledger* editorial, "Lies in Newark Over Teacher Contracts," October 27, 2012.

271. Cory Booker, "Newark Can Lead in Fair Teacher Compensation," *Star-Ledger*, October 27, 2012.

272. Salvador Rizzo, "Christie Calls Booker an 'Indispensable Partner' in Newark Teachers Contract," *Star-Ledger*, November 16, 2012.

273. *Star-Ledger* editorial, "Newark Teacher Contract Puts City at Forefront of Education Reform," November 18, 2012.

274. Jessica Calefati, "N.J. High School Graduation Rates Climb 3 Percentage Points to 86 Percent," *Star-Ledger*, December 5, 2012.

275. *Star-Ledger* editorial, "Too Soon to Tell on Newark Graduation Rates," December 10, 2012.

276. Jessica Calefati, "Report: Nearly All of Newark's Most Disadvantaged Students Attend Failing Schools," *Star-Ledger*, December 12, 2012.

277. *Star-Ledger* editorial, "Newark Charter School Deserved to Close," June 18, 2013; and Eugene Paik, "Adelaide L. Sanford Charter School Appeals State-Ordered Closure," *Star-Ledger*, June 19, 2013.

278. Tom Moran, "Support Slipping for Cami Anderson, Newark's Schools Chief," *Star-Ledger*, May 12, 2013.

Chapter 6

1. Andrew Rosenthal, "Was Cory Booker Right About the Attacks on Private Equity?" *New York Times*, May 21, 2012. See also Dan Goldberg, "Cory Booker's Comments on Obama's 'Nauseating' Campaign: Gaffe or Calculated Tactic?" *Star-Ledger*, May 22, 2012.

2. www.GOP.com—Stand with Cory; and *Star-Ledger* editorial, "Cory Booker Was Right to Speak the Truth," May 22, 2012. See also Dan Goldberg, "Cory Booker's Comments on Obama's 'Nauseating' Campaign: Gaffe or Calculated Tactic?" *Star-Ledger*, May 22, 2012.

3. David Giambusso, "Cory Booker's Defense of Wall Street May Hurt His Status with Liberals, But It Won't Hurt His Bank Account," *Star-Ledger*, May 23, 2012.

4. Earl Morgan, "Morgan's Corner: Cory Booker—Secret Republican," *Jersey Journal*, May 23, 2012.

5. Josh Margolin, "Booker's Big Mouth Ruins Relationship with Obama, Cabinet Hopes," *New York Post*, June 8, 2012.

6. David Giambusso, "Cory Booker Douses Flames Surrounding Democratic Platform," *Star-Ledger*, December 7, 2012; and David Giambusso, "Cory Booker Administration Denies He's on the Outs with Obama," *Star-Ledger*, June 8, 2012.

7. David Giambusso, "Cory Booker Shouts at Democratic Convention: 'We Choose Growing Together,'" *Star Ledger*, September 5, 2012.

8. *Star-Ledger* editorial, "Booker's Been Front, Center and Maybe Looking Up," September 5, 2012.

9. David Giambusso, "Why Sen. Frank Lautenberg Will Not Attend His Own Bash at DNC," *Star-Ledger*, September 8, 2012.

10. Jenna Portney, "Christie: NJ Will Help Newark with Budget Dilemma after City Cuts Spending," *Star-Ledger*, October 2, 2012.

11. David Giambusso, "Gov. Christie Keeps Promise to Cut Newark Aid; City Will Receive $10M," *Star-Ledger*, October 4, 2012.

12. Salvador Rizzo, "Cory Booker Nipping at Chris Christie's Heels," *Star-Ledger*, October 18, 2012.

13. Jarrett Renshaw, "Cory Booker to Decide Soon Whether He'll Challenge Christie for Gov. Seat," *Star-Ledger*, November 8, 2012.

14. Jarrett Renshaw, "Gov. Christie's Re-Election Bid Would Likely Trigger Flood of Campaign Dollars in NJ," *Star-Ledger*, November 18, 2012.

15. Tom Moran, "Newark Council's High Salaries Should Be Source of Shame," *Star-Ledger*, February 26, 2012; David Giambusso, "Newark City Council Defends Its High Salaries and Staffing Levels," *Star-Ledger*, February 24, 2012; and *Star-Ledger* editorial, "Newark Council Should Cut Own Pay, Approve Mayor Cory Booker's Water Plan," March 5, 2012.

16. Joan Whitlow, "Booker, Newark City Council Acting as Foes, Not Teammates," *Star-Ledger*, March 9, 2012. See also Robert Curvin and Dan O'Flaherty, "Fixing Newark: What to Cut and What to Tax," *Star-Ledger*, June 15, 2012.

17. Bob Braun, "Congressman Donald Payne Deserved More," *Star-Ledger*, March 7, 2012, as quoted by Fred Hillman, a political writer for the *Star-Ledger* in the 1970s; *Star-Ledger* editorial, "US Rep. Donald Payne's Death a Blow to New Jersey," March 6, 2012; and Joan Whitlow, "Remembering the Man Whose Roots Grew from Newark," *Star-Ledger*, March 16, 2012.

18. David Giambusso, "As Talk Grows Over Payne Successor, Son Stands Out," *Star-Ledger*, March 11, 2012.

19. David Giambusso, "John Sharpe James to Seek Newark Council Seat," *Star-Ledger*, March 17, 2012.

20. Kate Zernike, "Melee at Newark Council Meeting Shows Rift in Mayor's Support," *New York Times*, November 21, 2012.

21. David Giambusso, "Local Leaders Fear Uproar at Newark Council Meeting Will Generate Political Aftershocks," *Star-Ledger*, November 22, 2012.

22. David Giambusso and James Queally, "Citizens Rush Council Members as Chaos Erupts at Newark City Hall Meeting," *Star-Ledger*, November 21, 2012.

23. *Star-Ledger* editorial, "No Justification for Turning Newark Council's Public Business into a Brawl," November 22, 2012.

24. Cory Booker interview, April 5, 2013, with author.

25. David Giambusso, "Cory Booker's Vote that Sparked Chaos Now Sparks Debate," *Star-Ledger*, November 24, 2012. Both Julian Zelizer and political scientist Brigid Harrison said that Booker's move could demonstrate that the mayor "could hold his own" against the governor.

26. Modia Butler interview, November 26, 2012, with author; and David Giambusso, "Cory Booker's Vote that Sparked Chaos Now Sparks Debate," *Star-Ledger*, November 24, 2012.

27. David Giambusso, "Heated Newark Council Battle Has Been Building for Months," *Star-Ledger*, December 6, 2012. Also Luis Quintana follow-up discussion, April 5, 2013, with author. He stated that many had lobbied for Ramos to be council president so Ramos could gain leadership experience to run for mayor.

28. David Giambusso, "Judge Rules Cory Booker Did Not Have Authority to Vote for Open Newark Council Seat," *Star-Ledger*, December 12, 2012.

29. New Jersey National Public Radio, WBGO 88.3 FM News, December 11, 2012. Also Mildred Crump interview, January 28, 2013, with author. See also David Giambusso, "Appellate Court Ruling Curbs Mayoral Power in Newark and Hoboken," *Star-Ledger*, July 6, 2013.

30. Jarrett Renshaw, "Governor or Senator? Cory Booker's Decision Will Set Off a Chain Reaction Among Dems," *Star-Ledger*, December 9, 2012.

31. Jason L. Riley, "Cory Booker's Options," *Wall Street Journal*, December 11, 2012. See also Heather Haddon, "Booker Leaning Toward Senate Run," *Wall Street Journal*, December 17, 2012.

32. Matt Friedman, "NJ Residents Favor Cory Booker for US Senate Seat, Poll Finds," *Star-Ledger*, November 29, 2012; and Matt Friedman, "Poll: Booker Leads Lautenberg, Other Democrats in Potential 2014 Senate Primary," *Star-Ledger*, January 24, 2013.

33. Heather Haddon, "Booker's Senate Advice," *Wall Street Journal*, December 20, 2012.

34. David Giambusso, "Cory Booker, Once Firm on Firearms, Now Gun-Shy About Weapons Ban," *Star-Ledger*, January 28, 2013; and Cory Booker, "It's Time to Emphasize Pragmatic and Achievable Gun Law Reform," *Huffington Post*, December 21, 2012.

35. Janelle Griffith, "Sheila Oliver to Cory Booker: Don't Expect Your Celebrity to Land You the Senate Nomination," *Star-Ledger*, January 21, 2013.

36. Mildred Crump interview, January 28, 2013, with author.

37. *Star-Ledger* editorial, "Lautenberg's Legacy, and Who Is Next," February 17, 2013; and David Giambusso, "Lautenberg Retirement Opens Up Fight in 2014," *Star-Ledger*, February 25, 2013.

38. Matt Friedman, "Sen. Frank Lautenberg Keeps Quiet About Re-Election Run Until Next Year," *Star-Ledger*, December 20, 2012.

39. *Star-Ledger* editorial, "Frank Lautenberg Might Deserve a Spanking—not Cory Booker," January 24, 2013.

40. Ginger Gibson, "Frank Lautenberg: Where's Cory Booker?" *Politico*, January 31, 2013.

41. Kate Zernike and Raymond Hernandez, "Challenged for His Seat at 89, a Senator Does Go Gentle," *New York Times*, February 12, 2013.

42. Matt Friedman and Brent Johnson, "Lautenberg's Family Endorses Pallone for U.S. Senate," *Star-Ledger*, July 8, 2013.

43. Matt Friedman, "Lautenberg and Booker's Tortured Hisotry Shows Up in Campaign," Star-Ledger, July 29, 2013.

44. Matt Friedman, "Court Sides with Christie, Rejects Challenge to October Special Election," *Star-Ledger*, June 13, 2013.

45. Star-Ledger editorial, "Christie's Self-Serving Stunt," June 3, 2013; and Matt Friedman and Jarrett Renshaw, "Lautenberg's Death Turns NJ Political Scene Upside Down," *Star-Ledger*, June 9, 2013. See also Kate Zernike, "Against All Odds, and Ignoring Advice, Buono Fights to Lead New Jersey," *New York Times*, June 26, 2013.

46. David Giambusso, "Booker Raises $4.6 Million in Second Quarter for Senate Run," Star-Ledger, July 11, 2013; and Matt Friedman, "Poll: Booker's Celebrity Propels Him to Nearly Insurmountable Lead," *Star-Ledger*, July 16, 2013. See also Heather Haddon, "New York Money Flows to Booker," *Wall Street Journal*, July 19, 2013.

47. David Giambusso, "Pallone, Holt and Oliver Go after Booker in Senate Debate," Star-Ledger, July 28, 2013; and David Giambusso, "Cory Booker's Celebrity Status Could Cut both Ways in US Senate," *Star-Ledger*, July 28, 2013. See also Matt Friedman and David Giambusso, "Booker Wins Democratic U.S. Senate Primary Election," *Star-Ledger*, August 14, 2013.

48. Tom Moran, "Cory Booker Ducks Fight with Governor Christie," *Star-Ledger*, December 21, 2012.

49. David Giambusso, "Booker's Big Decision on U.S. Senate Bid Ends Year of Speculation," *Star-Ledger*, December 21, 2012.

50. Modia Butler interview, November 26, 2012, with author.

51. Anibal Ramos Jr. interview, February 28, 2013, with author.

52. Cory Booker, "I'll Explore U.S. Senate Run," *Star-Ledger*, December 21, 2012.

53. *Star-Ledger* editorial, "Booker for U.S. Senate," July 28, 2013.

54. Cory Booker interview, April 5, 2013, with author. See also David Giambusso, "Booker Administration Introduces $588 Million City Budget with Significant Tax Cut," *Star-Ledger*, July 11, 2013.

55. Tom Moran, "Cory Booker Ducks Fight with Gov. Christie," *Star-Ledger*, December 21, 2012.

56. Cory Booker interview, April 5, 2013, with author.

57. Paul Mulshine, "Next on Cory Booker's Menu: Beans and Frank?" *Star-Ledger*, December 11, 2012.

58. David Chmiel, "Here's What Cory Booker Bought for $29. What Would You Buy?" *Star-Ledger*, December 5, 2012.

59. David Giambusso, "Cory Booker's Week on Food Stamps Shines Latest Light onto Statewide Struggle," *Star-Ledger*, December 14, 2012.

60. James Queally, "Cory Booker Food Stamp Challenge Days 5 & 6: Burnt Yams," *Star-Ledger*, December 10, 2012.

61. Michael Luciano, "Cory Booker and the Politics of Egomania," www.policymic.com.

62. Kate Zernike, "Promise vs. Reality in Newark on Mayor's Watch," *New York Times*, December 13, 2012.

63. Cory Booker interview, April 5, 2013, with author.

64. Ibid. "What is this [image] dynamic that—it's really interesting to me. I had a guy walk up to me at NJPAC the other day and say, 'You're the greatest mayor of Newark has ever had. I don't care what they say about you.' And I stopped him and said, 'who says that.' And he says, 'well I watch the council meetings, and I see how hated you are.' It's this weird reality—so that's interesting to me, and I'm fascinated by it as an armchair social scientist."

65. Associated Press, "NJ Mayor Carries Woman Out of Her Burning Home," *Star-Ledger*, April 13, 2012; James Barron, "After Rescuing Woman from Fire, a Mayor Recalls His Fear and Focus," *New York Times*, April 13, 2012; Seth Augenstein, "Fire Rescue Victim: I Feel Blessed to Live Next Door to Cory Booker, He Was There to Save My Life," *Star-Ledger*, April 18, 2012; and David Giambusso, "Cory Booker Recounts Risking His Life in Dramatic Fire Rescue of Newark Neighbor," *Star-Ledger*, April 14, 2012.

66. Michael Luciano, "Cory Booker and the Politics of Egomania," www.policymic.com.

67. Kate Zernike, "Promise vs. Reality in Newark on Mayor's Watch," *New York Times*, December 13, 2012.

68. Amy Kuperinsky, "Twitter Superhero: And You Thought Cory Booker Was Hot Before the Newark Fire Rescue," *Star-Ledger*, April 14, 2012; and Michael Barbaro, "Now Revealed by Stripper: Booker's Twitter Messages," *New York Times*, September 25, 2013.

69. *Star-Ledger* editorial, "Mayor Batman," April 14, 2012.

70. Cory Booker interview, April 5, 2013, with author.

71. David Giambusso, "Newark Mayor Cory Booker Plans to Go #waywire with Launch of Social Media Site," *Star-Ledger*, July 1, 2012. See also David Giambusso, "Cory Booker Helps Launch Social Media News Site," *Star-Ledger*, June 30, 2012.

72. "Chris Christie, Cory Booker Channel Seinfeld–Newman Rivalry in New Web Video," www.foxdc.com, May 15, 2012.

73. Oprah Winfrey, "Cory Booker: Saving Newark with a Smile," *Time*, May 2, 2011.

74. Michael Kruse, "The Mayor Will Save You Now," *Men's Health*, January 2013.

75. Jacob Weisberg, "Local Hero: Cory Booker," *Vogue*, January 2013.

76. Andrew Jacobs, "A Fierce Race Leaves Deep Bruises in Newark," *New York Times*, May 20, 2002.

77. S. Craig Watkins, *Hip Hop Matters: Politics, Pop Culture, and the Struggle for the Soul of a Movement* (Boston: Beacon Press, 2005), 195.

78. Kevin Mumford, *Newark: A History of Race, Rights, and Riots in America* (New York: New York University Press, 2007), 222.

79. Richard Lezin Jones, "Race, Writ Large," *New York Times*, May 5, 2002.

80. Kate Zernike, "Promise vs. Reality in Newark on Mayor's Watch," *New York Times*, December 13, 2012.

81. David Giambusso, "Local Leaders Fear Uproar at Newark Council Meeting Will Generate Political Aftershocks," *Star-Ledger*, November 22, 2012.

82. Paul Mulshine, "What Makes Sheila Run? Trouble in Cory's Back Yard," *Star-Ledger*, July 25, 2013.

83. Elahe Izadi, "The Passive-Aggressive Zen Tweets of Cory Booker," *National Journal,* February 1, 2013.

84. Maggie Haberman, "Cory Booker's Rough Primetime Debut," *Politico,* February 2, 2013.

85. David Giambusso, "Lautenberg's Death Changes Senate Race for Booker," *Star-Ledger,* June 4, 2013; and David Giambusso, "Cory Booker Keeps Quiet on US Senate Run in Special Election," *Star-Ledger,* June 5, 2013. See also David Giambusso, "With Newark Council President Vote, Ras Baraka Could Win Latino Support," *Star-Ledger,* September 22, 2013.

86. David Giambusso, "John Sharpe James to Seek Newark Council Seat," *Star-Ledger,* March 17, 2012.

87. Heather Haddon, "Newark Race Is Dynastic Showdown," *Wall Street Journal,* June 4, 2012.

88. Mildred Crump interview, January 28, 2013, with author.

89. David Giambusso, "Race Tightens to Succeed Cory Booker as Newark Mayor," *Star-Ledger,* January 20, 2013; and David Giambusso, "Newark Councilman Forms Exploratory Committee to Run for Mayor in 2014," *Star-Ledger,* March 7, 2012.

90. Tom Moran, "Support Slipping for Cami Anderson, Newark's Schools Chief," *Star-Ledger,* May 12, 2013.

91. David Giambusso, "Race Tightens to Succeed Cory Booker as Newark Mayor," *Star-Ledger,* January 20, 2013; and David Giambusso, "Newark Councilman Ramos Kicks Off Run for Mayor," *Star-Ledger,* May 31, 2013.

92. David Giambusso, "As Cory Booker Eyes Senate Run, Newark Looks to a Future without Him," *Star-Ledger,* December 21, 2012.

93. Ras Baraka interview, February 11, 2014, with author.

94. Luis Quintana interview, February 6, 2013, with author.

95. Anibal Ramos Jr. interview, February 28, 2013, with author

96. Ras Baraka interview, February 11, 2014, with author.

97. Richard Cammarieri interview, December 3, 2012, with author.

98. Modia Butler interview, November 26, 2012, with author.

99. Luis Quintana interview, February 6, 2013, with author.

100. Modia Butler interview, November 26, 2012, with author.

101. Cory Booker interview, April 5, 2013, with author.

102. David Giambusso, "Booker Made $1.3 Million on Speech Circuit '08 to '13, Disclosures Say," *Star-Ledger,* May 17, 2013; and Kate Zernike, "Newark mayor Discloses $1.3 Million in Speaking Fees," *New York Times,* May 17, 2013.

103. Anibal Ramos Jr. interview, February 28, 2013, with author

104. Cory Booker interview, April 5, 2013, with author.

105. Ibid.

106. Mildred Crump interview, January 28, 2013, with author.

107. Cory Booker interview, April 5, 2013, with author.

108. Ras Baraka interview, February 11, 2014, with author.

109. Ibid.

110. Luis Quintana interview, February 6, 2013, with author.

Index